Quicken
6·in·1

by Stephen O'Brien

A Division of Macmillan Computer Publishing
201 West 103rd Street, Indianapolis, Indiana 46290 USA

International Standard Book Number: 0-7897-1353-5

Library of Congress Catalog Card Number: 97-68708

99 98 97   8 7 6 5 4 3 2 1

Interpretation of the printing code: the rightmost double-digit number is the
year of the book's first printing; the rightmost single-digit number is the number
of the book's printing. For example, a printing code of 97-1 shows that this copy
of the book was printed during the first printing of the book in 1997.

Screen reproductions in this book were created by means of the program
Collage Complete from Inner Media, Inc, Hollis, NH.

Printed in the United States of America

President
Roland Elgey

Senior Vice President/Publishing
Don Fowley

Publisher
Joseph B. Wikert

General Manager
Joe Muldoon

Manager of Publishing Operations
Linda H. Buehler

Publishing Director
Karen Reinisch

Editorial Services Director
Carla Hall

Managing Editor
Thomas F. Hayes

Acquisitions Manager
Cheryl D. Willoughby

Acquisitions Editor
Don Essig

Product Director
Rick Kughen

Production Editor
Katie Purdum

Copy Editor
San Dee Phillips

Coordinator of Editorial Services
Maureen A. McDaniel

Webmaster
Thomas H. Bennett

Product Marketing Manager
Kourtnaye Sturgeon

Assistant Product Marketing Manager
Gretchen Schlesinger

Technical Editors
Gabrielle Nemes
Dennis Triplett
Kyle Bryant
Darralyn McCall
Nadeem Muhammed

Software Specialist
David Garratt

Acquisitions Coordinator
Michelle R. Newcomb

Software Relations Coordinator
Susan D. Gallagher

Editorial Assistant
Jennifer L. Chisholm

Book Designers
Kim Scott
Glenn Larsen

Cover Designer
Jay Corpus

Production Team
DiMonique Ford
Julie Geeting
Laura A. Knox
Heather Stephenson

Indexer
Ginny Bess
Chris Wilcox
Cheryl Jackson

Dedication

To Olwyn Mary Kerr, for far more than words can do justice.

Acknowledgments

The effort put in by the writer is nothing compared to that expended behind the scenes. At Que, there are a team of dedicated professionals who work extraordinary hours to massage, edit, cut, copy and occasionally pummel a book into shape.

This one would be far poorer if it weren't for the likes of Rick Kughen, Development editor, who has my special thanks for his pivotal suggestions, skillful steerage, constant encouragement and boundless good humor. Another huge tribute firmly belongs to Kathryn Purdum, Production Editor, for juggling a million things at once without dropping one. It's a remarkable ability, especially when dealing with an author who lives 15 time-zones and several worlds away.

I am also greatly indebted to Gabrielle Nemes, Kyle Bryant, Darralyn McCall, Dennis Triplett and Nadeem Muhammed; five highly accomplished editors who place technical and stylistic veracity above all.

Finally, big thanks are also due the Publishing Director, Karen Reinisch, and Acquisitions Editor, Don Essig. I have felt extremely privileged and not a little lucky to work with such a talented group, and the results undoubtedly speak for themselves.

Trademark Acknowledgments

All terms mentioned in this book that are known to be or are suspected of being trademarks or service marks have been appropriately capitalized. Que Corporation cannot attest to the accuracy of this information. Use of a term in this book should not be regarded as affecting the validity of any trademark or service mark.

We'd Like to Hear from You!

Que Corporation has a long-standing reputation for high-quality books and products. To ensure your continued satisfaction, we also understand the importance of customer service and support.

Tech Support

If you need assistance with the information in this book or with a CD/disk accompanying the book, please access Macmillan Computer Publishing's online Knowledge Base at **http://www.superlibrary.com/general/support**. If you do not find the answer to your questions on our Web site, you may contact Macmillan Technical Support by phone at **317/581-3833** or via e-mail at **support@mcp.com**.

Also be sure to visit Que's Web resource center for all the latest information, enhancements, errata, downloads, and more. It's located at **http://www.quecorp.com/**.

Orders, Catalogs, and Customer Service

To order other Que or Macmillan Computer Publishing books, catalogs, or products, please contact our Customer Service Department at **800/428-5331** or fax us at **800/835-3202** (International Fax: 317/228-4400). Or visit our online bookstore at **http://www.mcp.com/**.

Comments and Suggestions

We want you to let us know what you like or dislike most about this book or other Que products. Your comments will help us to continue publishing the best books available on computer topics in today's market.

Rick Kughen
Product Director
Que Corporation
201 West 103rd Street, 4B
Indianapolis, Indiana 46290 USA
Fax: 317/581-4663 E-mail: **rkughen@que.mcp.com**

Please be sure to include the book's title and author as well as your name and phone or fax number. We will carefully review your comments and share them with the author. Please note that due to the high volume of mail we receive, we may not be able to reply to every message.

Thank you for choosing Que!

Contents

Part 4: Small Business

Part 5: Investing

Part 6: Advanced Tips & Tricks

Introduction

Congratulations on your decision to use Quicken 98 for Windows. Quicken is the most powerful personal finance package available today, yet it is also one of the easiest to use.

In just a few minutes each day, Quicken will help you to take control of your finances, plan your taxes, manage your investments and more successfully run a small business. The Quicken product family is developed by Intuit Inc., the world leaders in personal and small business financial software.

While the Quicken package has previously been released for computers running MS-DOS, Microsoft Windows 3.1, the Apple Macintosh OS and Microsoft Windows 95/NT, this book concentrates on the most recent release available for Windows 95 and Windows NT, as well as Microsoft's upcoming operating system, Windows 98. It is this version of the software that leads the rest in features, ease-of-use and Internet connectivity.

If you have never used Quicken before, you can rightly feel a little stunned and confused at its sheer breadth of features. Where, amongst all this exhilarating power, should one begin? This book will help you find your way through the maze with a task-oriented approach. If you have never used Quicken before, start from the top in Part 1. However, if you need immediate help with your taxes, online services, small business or investments, feel free to jump straight to the most appropriate section.

This book is divided into the following parts:

- **Essentials** A guide to Quicken's most used and useful features. If you've never used Quicken before, make sure you start here.
- **Taxes** If you have to scramble each year to meet the filing deadline, you need Quicken's help. The software is ideal for planning and tracking your taxes, and this section will help you to do just that. You also learn how to use your Quicken data in TurboTax.
- **Online Services** Intuit has packed Quicken with Internet-savvy features, from automatic updates to the software itself through to access to a wealth of financial news and information through the bundled Microsoft Internet Explorer World Wide Web browser. This section will help you to connect

to the Internet and also help you to make the most of the time you spend online. You also learn how to pay your bills, receive electronic statements, do your banking from home and more.

- **Small Business** If you run a small business, you can use Quicken to manage your debtors, creditors, payroll tax and even your inventory. While Quicken isn't quite so adept at this as a dedicated small business package, the features are there, and this section will help you learn to use them. This section also covers the additional small business features built into Quicken Home and Business 98.

- **Investing** For most people, a financially secure retirement independent of social security handouts is well within grasp, but only if it is planned. Quicken is the perfect tool for not only planning your future financial needs, but also for making smart investments and managing them on a daily basis. This section is filled with information on using Quicken's personal investment facilities to secure your future.

- **Tips and Tricks** No software package would be complete without its share of hidden features, great tips and advanced techniques. This section will help you turn them to a distinct advantage.

Using This Book

Quicken 6-in1 is designed to help you quickly and easily learn these six aspects to Quicken. You can learn most lessons in 10 minutes or less, although some must necessarily go into a little more detail.

Each of the six parts is arranged as a complete A-to-Z tutorial, and each lesson is devoted to a single task. In you have never used Quicken before, you should start at the beginning and work you way through. However, if you are familiar with Quicken's operation, just jump to the section that either interests you most or is currently at the top of your agenda.

Conventions Used in This Book

Each lesson includes a brief introduction and then a series of simple, step-by-step instructions. As you work through these steps, you will come across small icons containing explanatory or ancillary information. These icons fall into the following categories:

Tip icons mark shortcuts and hints for saving time and using Internet Explorer more efficiently. If you like to take shortcuts, watch for this icon. In some cases, Tips also provide real world solutions to help you get the most from Quicken.

 Term icons point out easy-to-follow definitions that you'll need to know in order to understand Internet Explorer and how it fits into the scheme of the Internet. No need to pull out a dictionary when a tough term comes along. Just look for this icon and everything should be explained.

 Caution icons mark information that's intended to help you avoid making mistakes.

As you work through each lesson, you will also see text highlighted using a bold typeface.

Bold text is used to denote:

On-screen text   This highlighted word or phrase corresponds to a particular button, menu choice or other feature that you should select on your screen. Multi-step choices are separated by commas. For instance, the command to open the **File** menu and select the **Open** menu choice is shown as **File, Open.**

Okay. Are you ready? Then turn to Lesson 1 and let's begin.

Essentials

Welcome to Quicken

In this lesson, you will learn how Quicken can help you manage your finances.

Quicken at a Glance

At its simplest level, Quicken is a personal accounting system that will help you to track your income and expenses. Quicken does this by helping you take note of every sum of money that flows into or out of your checking, savings or other accounts. These transactions are recorded in an account which, just like the register used in any manual accounting system, is cross-referenced according to certain income and expense categories. By assigning every transaction to a particular category, Quicken can generate graphs and reports that total your sources of income and show you how that income was distributed.

This type of functionality is the genesis of Quicken. It is where the program began—essentially as a checkbook balancing product—and that same method of operation remains central to the Quicken software of today. However, as you probably already know, there is a lot more to this product than the juggling of a checkbook or two. The Quicken package is a powerful collection of extended capabilities, useful utilities, online reference and particularly refined interface. While the register system can track any number of checking, savings, liability, asset and investment accounts, this is only a small part of the Quicken product.

With Quicken 98 for Windows, you will be able to easily perform each of the following tasks.

Manage Your Accounts

Quicken's accounts are the most-used part of the program. You will use accounts to record your income and expenses. You can also transfer funds between accounts, and set up accounts to track your credit cards, assets, or investment account balances. Each entry placed into an account is known as a *transaction*. You will use your accounts by accessing them through a register. Figure 1.1 shows a typical Quicken register.

Almost every transaction you make is assigned to a particular category. The standard Quicken categories record and subtotal the amount spent on utilities, automobiles, educational fees, household maintenance, and the like. Categories can also record tax-related income and expenses, simplifying the preparation of your tax return.

This book will help you learn how to use registers and categories to record a large variety of general and specialized financial transactions. Part 1 deals with the general details while Parts 3, 4 and 5 turn to more specialized matters such as taxes, online services, investments and managing a small business.

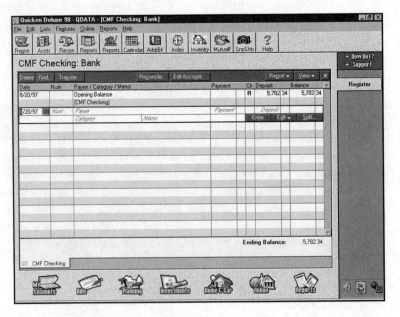

Figure 1.1   The Quicken Checking Account.

Track Your Investments

While the Investment register is similar to Quicken's other accounts, it has several special characteristics that make it perfect for maintaining a record of your holdings in fluctuating brokerage accounts.

These include the capability to:

- Easily record buy, sell, and other security investment transactions
- Automatically receive the latest stock prices across the Internet
- Access your Internet brokerage account, downloading the latest transactions

Figure 1.2 shows a single stock within an investment portfolio.

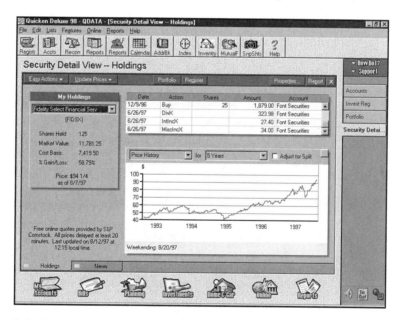

Figure 1.2 Investment accounts track transactions and stock price history.

Create Useful Reports and Graphs

Quicken boasts an extensive range of viewable and printable reports and graphs.

These will help you to:

- Easily ascertain your net worth or current cash flow
- Create permanent records of your most important data
- Print a tax schedule or summary report, providing your taxation advisor with everything he or she needs to complete your return
- Generate a wide range of business reports including profit and loss and accounts receivable
- Establish your budget variance, visually comparing your spending in certain areas

Reports are handy for onscreen viewing and for printing in an easily digestible format. Graphs provide fast, on-screen visual analysis of your data. They are a powerful means of comparing different income, expense, or investment streams and can prove more informative than the fullest of printed reports (see Figure 1.3). There are numerous reports and graphs built into Quicken and you can customize many more.

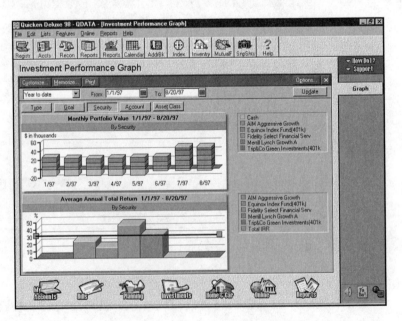

Figure 1.3   Graphs are great for developing a good sense of the big picture.

Plan Your Taxes

The Quicken Tax Planner will help you to forecast your tax due. You can also use the planner to calculate an appropriate level of extra withholding, helping you avoid penalties for late or incorrect payment of estimated tax.

The planner looks at the amounts stored under each of your "tax-related" categories. The more information you record about your income and spending, the better the job Tax Planner will do. You will learn about using the existing and setting up additional tax-related categories in Part 2.

Use Online Services

Quicken is particularly Internet-aware. In fact, with Internet access, you can download product news, updates and market quotes, as well as view hints and tips, Website reviews, and more. Even better, in this latest version, the online banking and bill paying has been updated. You can not only pay your bills through your computer but receive them as well. Figure 1.4 shows the entry point for setting up Quicken's online bill paying.

The Internet has become central to Quicken, adding timely information and functionality that goes far beyond that which could be included on CD-ROM or floppy disk. To this end, Intuit—Quicken's developer and publisher—has replaced some parts of the product with links to sites on the World Wide Web. The Marketplace used to order personalized checks and other Quicken-compatible stationery is one such example, but there are several more. This allows Intuit to provide more up-to-date information.

You can access this and the other Quicken sites on the World Wide Web using either Microsoft Internet Explorer or Netscape Navigator.

The CD-ROM version of Quicken installs Microsoft Internet Explorer 3.02.

However, if you are using Microsoft Internet Explorer 4.0, you may also view the Quicken Financial Network as a premier Microsoft Active Channel. For more information on Quicken's online capabilities, see Part 3.

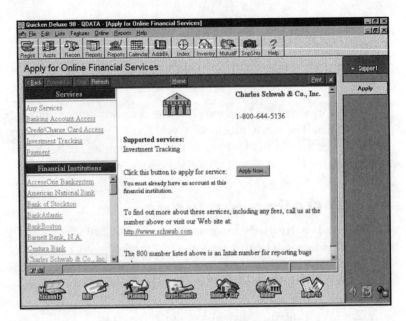

Figure 1.4 Online Services can be obtained through Quicken.

Plan Your Bill Payments

Quicken provides several features which will help you plan your bill payments and other repeating transactions:

- **Memorized Transactions** Every time you record a new transaction, it is copied to the memorized transaction list. The next time you need to use that transaction, just type in the first few letters of the payee. The rest appears automatically.

- **Scheduled transactions** These are transactions set to take place at some future date. They are stored in the scheduled transactions list but also appear in the financial calendar. Scheduled transactions can be paid automatically or after confirmation by yourself. Quicken's scheduled transactions are flexible enough to support almost any type of recurring payment from the monthly rent to annual subscriptions.

- **Alerts** These warn you when a balance, price, or other factor has gone above or below a preset level.

- **Financial Calendar** Use the calendar to plan your bill payments. It will show you when money has come in or gone out, and when it is due to do so in the future.

You will learn about these features through Part 1.

Calculate Various Financial Outcomes

Quicken's financial calculators are second to none. They will quickly tell you how much you need to save to reach a certain goal, how you can best fund your retirement, or how much you can afford to borrow given an affordable level of repayments.

Quicken supports these calculators:

- Loan
- Refinance
- Savings
- College
- Retirement

You will learn about these in Part 5.

Figure 1.5 shows the Quicken Loan Planner at work.

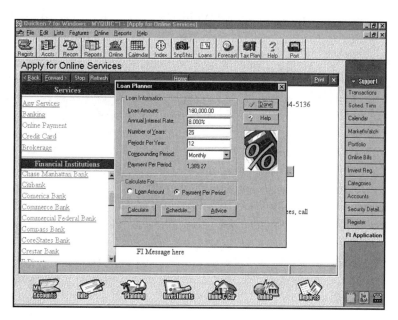

Figure 1.5 Can you afford that mortgage? Quicken will tell you in seconds.

Budget and Forecast

By setting savings goals and creating budgets, you can give yourself added incentive to keep on track with your savings and spending. Forecasting is great for gazing in to the crystal ball. You can plan ahead by extrapolating information from your current pattern of income and expenditure. You will learn about these in Part 1.

Managing a Small Business

While small business management isn't Quicken's forte, the software is still perfectly capable of handling the transactions, accounts payable and receivable, and even the payroll of almost any small business. You can read about this in Part 4.

Perform Useful Financial Research

The Quicken Mutual Fund, Mortgage Rate, and Insurance Market helpers will quickly let you sift through thousands of offerings from different companies, targeting the fund, mortgage, or insurance plan that's right for you. When combined with the wealth of information contained in the Quicken Financial Network site on the World Wide Web, you will be able to use these capabilities to make the most of your available funds, no matter how large or small they may be. Figure 1.6 shows the InsureMarket site accessible through the Quicken Financial Network.

Figure 1.6 The InsureMarket is just one of the online tools available through Quicken or across the Internet.

In this lesson, you learned that Quicken is a multitalented product; one that goes far beyond the notion of a simple personal finance system. In the next lesson, you will learn how to start and exit Quicken and backup and restore your Quicken data.

Starting and Exiting Quicken

In this lesson, you will learn how to start and exit Quicken, back up and restore your data, and use Quicken's password protection.

Before You Begin

Before you can start using Quicken, you should ensure the software is installed on your computer.

Installing the software copies the files required to run Quicken onto your computer's hard drive. The procedure also performs a certain amount of configuring, telling your operating system where it can find the main Quicken program file.

TIP **Operating System** The software that controls your computer's hardware, providing the framework through which other applications respond to your commands. Quicken can run under several operating systems, including Microsoft's Windows 95 (or the most current version), Windows NT, and Apple's MacOS.

If Quicken isn't already installed on your computer, you should install it now. For instructions, jump to Appendix A, "Installing Quicken."

What If I Use Another Operating System? While this book has been written for users of Windows 95 and eventual users of the newest Windows operating system expected to be released in 1998, Quicken 98 will also run on computers running Windows NT and Apple Macintosh software. If you use Windows NT, you can follow the instructions given in almost all of the lessons in this book with no change whatsoever. If you use a Macintosh, the changes will be more significant, but the great majority of this book will still apply.

CAUTION

Starting Quicken

To start Quicken 98, follow these steps:

1. Click the **Start** button in the Windows toolbar.

2. Select **Programs**.

3. From the Programs menu, select **Quicken** and click **Quicken 98 for Windows**, as shown in Figure 2.1.

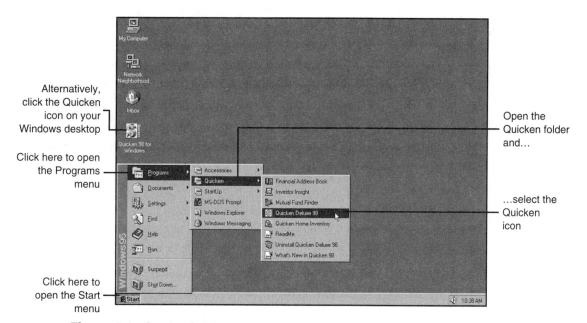

Alternatively, click the Quicken icon on your Windows desktop

Open the Quicken folder and...

Click here to open the Programs menu

...select the Quicken icon

Click here to open the Start menu

Figure 2.1 Starting Quicken.

TIP **Shorter Menu Procedures** As you have seen, spelling out individual menu procedures can take quite a lot of space. In the interests of the environment and sanity, menu procedures like those detailed above will use a shortened format similar to the following: "Click **Start, Programs, Quicken, Quicken 98 for Windows**".

The first time you start Quicken, you will be given the opportunity to electronically register the product. Registration places your details on Intuit's list of users, making you eligible for product support, software updates, and special offers. Registration also gives you optional upgrades to future versions at a reduced price. To register, simply select the Quicken menu, **Online, Update Quicken 98**. To complete this task, you need to set up Quicken to access the Internet. You will learn about this in Part 3, "Online Services."

As soon as you have completed or bypassed the registration, you will arrive at the new account setup. If you want to start using Quicken now, jump to Lesson 3 to learn how to create your first Quicken account.

Exiting Quicken

You can exit Quicken at any time. Unlike many other applications, you do not need to specifically save your data. This is because Quicken saves "on-the-fly." Every time you enter a new transaction, update share prices, record a new budget, or whatever, Quicken writes that information to your data file.

This can prove both a blessing and a curse. If you accidentally delete an account or series of transactions, there is no easy way to reverse those actions. You cannot simply revert to the previously saved file. Instead, the best you can hope is to jump back to the most recent backup. You can learn about backing up below.

Anyway, pushing these issues aside, to exit Quicken, follow these steps:

1. Select **File, Exit**.
2. If you have made any changes to your Quicken data, you will be offered the opportunity to back up your data. If you don't want to do this, click **Exit**.

Backing Up Your Data

Regular backups are important because they safeguard your data. You can lose your data for all sorts of reasons including accidentally deleting an important account, losing your computer to fire, theft, or some other catastrophe, or simply through your hard disk drive suffering a major or minor crash. No hard disk drive is expected to last more than about five years, and some are lucky to even last three. You should always back up your important files to an external source.

Fortunately, backing up your Quicken data is easy, and there's no excuse to not do so at least once each month—more if you use Quicken frequently. Just follow these steps:

1. If you want to back up your data when you exit Quicken, select the menu **File, Exit**. Click **Backup** in the dialog box shown in Figure 2.2. To initiate your own backup session, select **File, Backup**. Both actions take you to the next step.

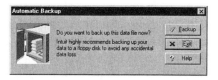

Figure 2.2 Exiting Quicken: You can choose to back up your data on the spot or simply Exit.

2. You can back up to any compatible storage medium including your hard disk drive, Zip disks, or floppy disks. To continue, click **Yes**.

 Zip Disks Similar in size to a floppy disk but store up to 70 times as much (100MB as compared to 1.4MB). Some new computers include a Zip drive as standard equipment. Other more expensive alternatives to 100MB removable cartridges do exist, giving you capacity choices of up to one or more gigabytes (one gigabyte is more than 1,000 megabytes).

3. Select the **Backup Drive** to which you want to write the backed up files, as shown in Figure 2.3. To back up to a network drive, you must first map that network connection to another drive letter. Consult your operating system manual or online help for more information on this procedure.

Figure 2.3   You can back up your Quicken files to a floppy drive, hard disk drive, or any other Windows-compatible storage device.

4. Select **Current File** and click **OK** to back up the Quicken file you were just using. To back up another Quicken file, click **Select from List** and click **OK**. You will need to choose the file using the standard file selection dialog box.

5. Quicken will proceed with the backup. If the backup file is too large for the disk, it will ask you to replace the disk with a freshly formatted disk.

CAUTION

Formatting Disks During the Backup   In nearly all cases, one or two 1.4MB floppy disks should prove sufficient. However, if you should run out of formatted disks, just wait for Quicken to prompt you for another. Then use the Windows taskbar to open Windows Explorer. Slide the blank disk into the floppy drive, find its icon in the right-hand pane, and right-click the icon using your mouse. Select **Format**, **Start**. When the formatting is complete, use the taskbar to return to Quicken and continue backing up.

6. When Quicken has completed backing up, it will exit normally.

7. Don't leave those backups lying around. Label them clearly by file and date and store them in a safe place, preferably a different building. Otherwise, a fire-proof safe is a good, but not guaranteed, storage facility. A bank's safety-deposit box is better, but you might also like to take them into the office or, if you are using Quicken in an office, take them home. You can optionally password-protect your data before backing up. You will learn about this below.

Restoring Your Data

If you ever need to use the data previously backed up, you will need to restore that data to your hard drive. Restoring is easy. Here's how:

1. From within Quicken, select **File, Restore**.

2. If you backed up to a floppy or Zip drive, insert the disk and select the appropriate drive letter using the Select Restore Drive dialog box. If you backed up to a hard disk drive or mapped network drive, just select the drive letter using the same dialog box.

3. Select the correct backup using the Restore Quicken File dialog shown in Figure 2.4.

4. Quicken will try to restore the file to its original location. If that file is a version of the one you are currently using, Quicken will ask permission to overwrite your current data. Provide approval to automatically close your file and open up the restored data. If that file is different than the file you are currently using, Quicken saves it in its original location.

Figure 2.4 Quicken can restore data files from any location accessible from your computer.

Password Protection

Quicken can password-protect an entire file or just those transactions recorded before a certain date. The former is useful for protecting your data from prying eyes while the latter is best for locking off the previous year's transactions, protecting that information from an inadvertent change. You can apply both to a single Quicken file.

Password protection does not prevent someone copying or deleting the entire Quicken file. However, even if they copy that file to another computer, they will still not be able to view its contents.

To password-protect your entire Quicken file, select **File, Passwords, File...**. Type in and confirm your chosen password. Click **OK**.

In the future, you will need to supply this password before working with the file.

To password protect transactions before a certain date, select **File, Passwords, Transactions…**. Type in and confirm the chosen password and record the date up to which you want your transactions protected. You will not be able to delete or edit transactions on or before that date without supplying the correct password. Click **OK**.

To remove the password protection, select the same menu as you did previously. Type in the previous password but leave the New Password and Confirm Password fields blank.

CAUTION

Don't Forget Your Password   If you forget your password, you will need to send your entire Quicken file back to Quicken's Technical Support department. The easiest way to do this is to create a backup on floppy disk. Just send them the disks and they will send you back the unprotected file.

In this lesson, you learned how to start and exit Quicken as well as to back up and restore and password-protect your Quicken data. In the next lesson, you will learn how to complete the new user setup and record your first Quicken transaction.

Completing the New User Setup

In this lesson, you learn how to create your first Quicken checking account and record your first Quicken transaction.

New User Setup

The first time you start Quicken, you are immediately taken to Quicken's New User Setup. This is a friendly, question-driven system that will have you up and running in just a few minutes.

 TIP   **How Does Quicken Know I Am a New User?**   The first time Quicken runs, it looks for any Quicken data file. If it doesn't find one, it assumes you are a new user and initiates the New User Setup guide.

The guide will help you get started quickly. If you are using the CD-ROM version of Quicken, insert your Quicken CD-ROM into your CD-ROM drive. This will let you listen to an explanation of each step.

Figure 3.1 shows the first step in the New User Setup. Follow these steps to complete the task:

1. Click **Next** to start.

2. Quicken needs to know a little about your private life before it can begin. Just answer these questions regarding your personal circumstances. For instance, if you are married, click **Yes** beside **Are You Married?** Quicken uses your answers to customize its income and expense categories. For example, if you answer **Yes** to **Do You Have Children?**, Quicken will add a tax-related expense category called Childcare. Indicate that you own a small business and Quicken will add a host of categories including those for Business Tax on Federal, Local, Property, and State levels.

Figure 3.1   Step this way to create your first Quicken file.

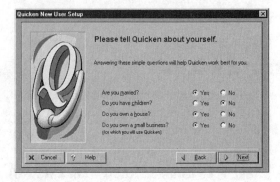

Figure 3.2   Answer these questions to help Quicken set up the right categories.

Categories   With Categories, you can see at a glance how much you are making or spending in certain areas. For example, a payment at the grocery store and another for chlorine from the pool shop would both fall under the category known as "household expenses."

3. Click **Next** to move to the Checking Account Setup.

4. The Checking Account is your first basic bank account. You can always add more accounts later on, but Quicken needs at least one to begin with. Simply type in the name that is normally associated with that account.

5. Click **Next** to answer some simple questions regarding your checking account. These questions are necessary because Quicken takes over your finances from a specific date. From that point on, you should use the program to record every transaction you make. The easiest way to coordinate the switch from manual to computerized accounting is to use the information shown on your most recent bank statement.

If you have your bank statement and want to start using Quicken right away, select **Yes** and click **Next**. The next screen (asks you to enter the statement ending date as well as an ending balance (see Figure 3.3). Enter these precisely as shown on the bank statement and click **Next**.

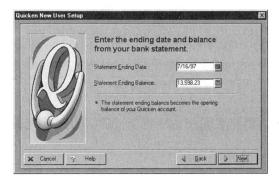

Figure 3.3   Use your most recent bank statement to coordinate the launch point for your Quicken account.

If you don't have a bank statement, just select **No** and click **Next**. Quicken will confirm that it will set up a $0.00 account for today's date. You can update your account details later by performing an account reconciliation. For more information, see Lesson 6. Click **Next** once more.

6. Use the final screen to confirm your settings. When you finish, either wander through the Quicken Overview to see a few of the product's best features, or click **Done** to jump to your checking account's register.

Congratulations! You've just set up your first Quicken account. Now you're ready to start using Quicken's registers.

Recording Your First Transaction

If you created your checking account using the balance shown on your bank statement, one of your first jobs is to enter any transactions that have already occurred but for one reason or another do not yet appear on your bank statement. These should include any checks you have written that haven't yet shown up as well as any withdrawals made from an ATM.

While you can easily wait for these to appear on your next statement before entering them into Quicken, making sure Quicken knows about them now will provide you with a more accurate account balance. It will also make your first account reconciliation a little easier.

Figure 3.4 shows the opening register screen. You should see the name of your checking account at the top of the screen as well as any opening balance entered during the New User Setup.

Lesson 7 will teach you how to record a range of transactions, however, the following steps will get you started.

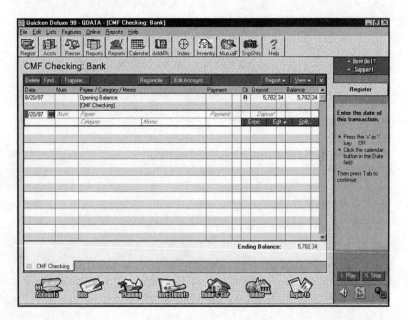

Figure 3.4 This is the first screen you will see after completing the New User Setup.

To record your first transaction, enter each of these steps. Press your **Tab** key to move between each step.

1. Type in the **Date** of that transaction or select it using the calendar icon.

2. Type in a reference number (**Num**). If you are recording a check, use the la three digits of that check's number.

3. Type in a **Payee**. Quicken stores all payees in a list so you can quickly recall that payee in the future. For now, though, you should enter the full name or, if you prefer, a convenient abbreviation.

4. Enter the **Payment** or click the calculator icon to use Quicken's built-in calculator.

5. Select a **Category**. If you have written a check, you will most likely want to store it under an expense category. However, if you are transferring between two accounts (for instance, paying off a credit card debt), you will need to create a credit card account and record the payment as a transfer. To learn more about creating different types of accounts, see Lesson 6. If you don't know the category, don't worry; you can always enter it later. After you tab to the next field, just answer **No** to Quicken's suggestions that you select a category from the list. You will learn about categories in Lesson 8.

6. Type in a **Memo**. The memo is just a note to yourself which can contain extra information about this transaction, such as the transaction's purpose.

7. You should see a completed entry looking something like that shown in Figure 3.5. Click **Enter** to record this transaction and move to the next register pair.

8. Repeat steps 1–7 for any further transactions.

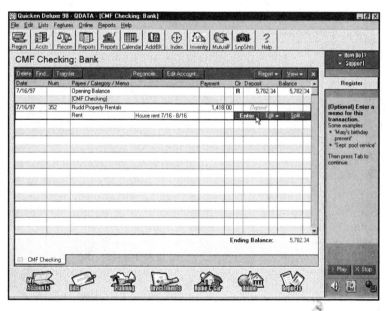

Figure 3.5 Click **Enter** to record your first complete transaction.

You've just created your first Quicken transaction. In future lessons, you will learn several shortcuts that will greatly speed the process up.

In this lesson, you learned how to complete the New User Setup and to record your first transaction. In the next lesson, you will learn about the rest of the Quicken interface.

Quicken Overview

*In this lesson, you learn to find your way around the
Quicken screen.*

Quicken is a powerful product with numerous features, yet while it can be used
on many different levels, the basics are easy.

Understanding the Quicken Screen

The first time you start Quicken, it will almost certainly seem a little daunting.
Unlike the blank piece of paper that faces you when you start a word processor,
Quicken 98 drops you straight into your checking account register but with the
entire screen surrounded by icons, menus, and buttons.

There are six parts to the highly functional border that runs around the standard
Quicken window, as shown in Figure 4.1.

Each part performs a certain task, and while there is some overlap between each
part's broader functionality (for example, many of the commands available
under the Activity bar relate directly to commands available under the menu
bar), you will find it useful being familiar with them all.

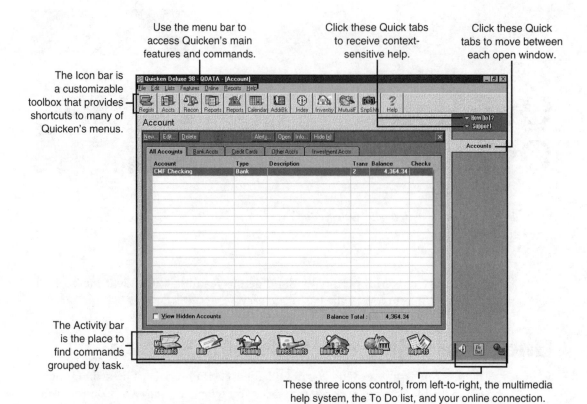

Use the menu bar to access Quicken's main features and commands.

Click these Quick tabs to receive context-sensitive help.

Click these Quick tabs to move between each open window.

The Icon bar is a customizable toolbox that provides shortcuts to many of Quicken's menus.

The Activity bar is the place to find commands grouped by task.

These three icons control, from left-to-right, the multimedia help system, the To Do list, and your online connection.

Figure 4.1 This figure shows the Quicken Screen.

Touring the Menu Bar

The menu bar is common to nearly all Windows programs. Quicken's is divided into the following major areas:

- **File** Includes major program and file operations such as opening files, changing printer settings, setting passwords, and backing up or restoring your data files.

- **Edit** Offers Windows' standard Cut, Copy, and Paste operations as well as items in context with the current window. You can also use it to search and replace certain data, use the Quicken calculator, and change the way Quicken looks and behaves.

- **Lists** Shows categories, scheduled transactions, accounts, investments, and more.

- **Features** Includes every major feature and function as well as links to external utilities or Quicken-compatible applications installed on your computer. These include TurboTax, Investor Insight, and Quicken Home Inventory.

- **Online** Provides access to Quicken-specific Web sites and financial information. You can also use this menu to setup Quicken to access the Internet. However, the first time you use an online feature, Quicken will automatically launch the Internet initialization routine. You'll learn more about this in Part 3.

- **Reports** Accesses Quicken's reports and graphs.

- **Help** Includes the Quicken Overview and a complete online electronic manual. You'll learn about Quicken's Help system in the next lesson.

Quicken's keyboard shortcuts are known as Quick Keys. You'll see them listed to the right of their menu item. For instance, beside **Features**, **Banking**, **Use Register**, you see the **Ctrl+R** Quick Key, as shown in Figure 4.2. To activate this shortcut, hold down the Control key and press the indicated letter on your keyboard.

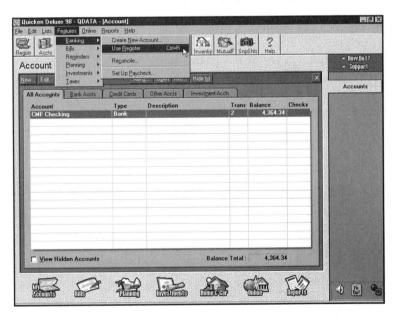

Figure 4.2 Quick Keys provide fast access to Quicken's major functions.

Just as the menu changes according to the currently active window, so too does the function of some of the Quick Keys. For instance, with a register window open, Ctrl+N will create a new transaction. However, with the accounts list open, Ctrl+N creates a new account.

As you become more familiar with Quicken, you will become equally familiar with the function of these keys, and find yourself zapping from one part of Quicken to the next without once resorting to the mouse.

 TIP **Changing Quicken's QuickKeys** Some of the QuickKeys behave a little differently in Quicken than they do in other Windows applications. You can change their behavior by selecting the menu **Edit**, **Options**, **Quicken Program**, **Settings**. Just choose between **Quicken Standard** or **Undo/Cut/Copy/Paste**. You learn about this in Part 6.

Using the Quick Tabs

The Quick Tabs bar runs down the right-side of the screen. It is divided into three areas: help, window ordering, and status icons.

Here's a quick guide to each section:

- **How Do I?** This pull-down menu acts as a context-sensitive answer wizard. In other words, it will provide answers to questions it thinks you need to ask right now. If you're stuck, this is the first place you should turn for a little assistance.

- **Support** This menu takes you to the Product Support dialog box where you access Quicken's troubleshooting system or find out how to contact technical support.

- **Other Tabs** The remaining buttons are known as Window Tabs. They display the name of every currently open window. If you have just started using Quicken, you will probably only see the Register tab. However, if you have opened other windows, you will see them listed below.

  To change windows, click the appropriate tab. To completely close a window, click the **X** in that window's upper-right corner or press your **Escape** (ESC) key. Alternatively, click the tab with the right mouse button and choose **Close: Window Name** from the list.

  Quicken remembers the tabs that were open when you exit the program and restores them once you resume. You can change this behavior using the menu **Edit, Options, Desktop. Save Desktop on Exit** is the default system. Select **Save Current Desktop** to save the windows as they are right now and restore that pattern no matter the changes you make to the window layout between now and subsequently exiting the software.

 TIP **Quick Tabs to Order** Are you unhappy with your current QuickTabs ordering? To reorder the tabs, just click them with the left mouse button and drag them up and down the list.

- **Speaker Icon** Used to turn off Quicken's multimedia help. This is the same as selecting the menu **Help, Show QCards**.
- **To Do!** Opens Quicken's Reminders window. The Reminders window stores upcoming transactions, bills that will need to be paid, checks that need to be printed, and online payments that need to be enacted.

 CAUTION **My QuickTabs Have Disappeared!** QuickTabs can be turned on and off through **Edit, Options, Quicken Program**. Under the **QuickTabs** tab in the **General Options** dialog box, simply click **Show QuickTabs** to change their status. Alternatively, click with the right mouse button anywhere within the Quicken Program background and choose between **QuickTabs On** and **QuickTabs Off**.

With the Quick Tabs bar displayed, Quicken sizes each window (register, accounts, and so on) so that it completely fills the center area of the screen. You can change the width of the Quick Tabs bar by moving the mouse over its border.

When the mouse changes to a double I-beam, click with the mouse and drag it to the left or right.

With the Quick Tabs bar switched off, each window shrinks to a preset minimum size, becoming in essence an independent entity. (This is known in Windows parlance as a Multi-Document Interface, but it really just means you can work with more than one window at a time.) In addition, the Quick Tabs bar and Activity bar disappear from the screen. With Quick Tabs turned off, you can jump between windows using the Window menu, as shown in Figure 4.3. However, you can also use the standard Windows expand and shrink buttons in the upper-right corner of each window to maximize or minimize those windows. Alternatively, drag the window border to individually resize each window.

The easiest way to turn off Quick Tabs is to click with the right mouse button somewhere within the Quick Tabs column. Select **Quick Tabs Off** from the drop-down menu.

To return your Quick Tabs to their previous state, select the menu **Edit**, **Options**, **Quicken Program** and click **Show Quick Tabs**. You will notice that you can also use this dialog box to shift the position of the Quick Tabs column from the right side of the screen to the left. There is also an option to turn the Activity bar on or off. We'll look at the Activity bar next.

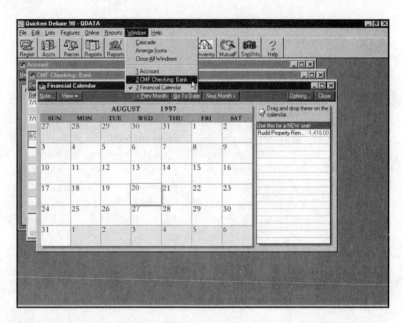

Figure 4.3   With Quick Tabs turned off, Quicken inserts a new Window menu. Use this menu to move between each window.

Using the Activity Bar

Assuming you haven't switched off the Activity bar, you should see it running along the lower edge of the Quicken screen.

The Activity bar acts a little like the Features menu in that it gives you fast access to Quicken's most popular features and procedures. However, unlike the entries under Features, these are written in plain English.

Let's take a look at the function of each. You can follow along by moving your mouse pointer over each icon:

- **My Accounts**   These activities deal with the most common register events including working with, reconciling, and viewing the accounts list and recording paychecks.
- **Bills**   Use this icon to write checks, schedule future payments, make online payments, and create alerts.
- **Planning**   You can use these activities to pay your taxes, create a savings goal, build a budget, access Quicken's financial calculators, obtain a personal credit report, and organize your emergency records.
- **Investments**   Investments are special accounts that track the value of stocks, bonds, and mutual funds. Use this menu to view and edit your entire portfolio or specific securities and to download online quotes.
- **Home & Car**   Use this activity item to access your asset and major liability accounts. You can use it to store the value of your home and car as well as to track mortgages and personal loans.
- **Online**   Quicken's online features are stronger than ever. Use this item to setup Online Banking and Bill Paying, download stock quotes, automatically update your Quicken software, and collect the latest financial news and information.
- **Reports**   Reports are incredibly useful, not only summarizing your financial data but helping you to look at it in unusual ways. Unfortunately, it won't do you much good until you've built up a little financial history, but we'll get to that in a moment.

While the Activity bar is useful, it merely replicates functionality available elsewhere. If you would like to increase the workable area of the main Quicken window, turn off the Activity bar by choosing **Edit**, **Options**, **Quicken Program…**. Under the **Quick Tabs** tab in the **General Options** dialog box, click **Show Activity Bar**. If you find the Activity Bar descriptions too wordy, you can also cut them down to size by clicking **Use Short Commands in Activity Bar Menus**.

Icon Bar

Quicken doesn't display the Icon bar by default because a lot of the icon bar functionality is replicated in the Activity bar. However, if you customize the Icon bar as explained in Part 6, you can make much better use of it.

Quicken's icon bar is switched off by default. To switch it on, click **Edit, Options, Iconbar**. This opens the Customize Iconbar window shown in Figure 4.4. Click **Show Icons**. If you want to see some descriptive text underneath each icon, also leave **Show Text** selected. When you finish, click **Done**.

Setting a Display Size   If your computer is set to a display size of 640x480 pixels (the lowest supported by Windows 95 and later), you cannot display the activity and icon bars simultaneously.

CAUTION

Figure 4.4   To display your Icon bar, select the option as shown.

The Icon bar runs along the top of the screen, just under the menu bar, providing fast access to the most common commands. This saves you traversing multiple levels of menus. Basically, click an icon and you're there.

The default Quicken icons perform the tasks shown in Table 4.1. These icons will change depending on the version of Quicken installed and the various support applications that have been bundled with it. However, the table shows the most common.

Table 4.1   The Quicken Iconbar

Icon Picture	Icon Text	Function
Registr	Registr	Brings up the Account Register
Accts	Accts	Accesses the Accounts List
Recon	Recon	Performs Account Reconciliation
Reports	Reports	Creates a Report

Icon Picture	Icon Text	Function
Online	Online	Quicken's Online services
Calendar	Calendar	Shows your Financial Calendar
AddrBk	AddBk	Opens the Financial Address Book
Index	Index	Displays the Help Index
Inventry	Inventry	Opens Quicken Home Inventory
MutualF	MutualF	Opens the Quicken Mutual Fund Finder
SnpShts	SnpShts	Shows your Financial Snapshot
Help	Help	Accesses Quicken's context-sensitive help.

The Icon bar is useful but also somewhat old fashioned. Chances are you will find the Activity bar more useful. However, if you do decide to use it, make sure you read about the customization procedure. Also, keep in mind that you can change the order of the icons simply by clicking and dragging them from one icon position to the next.

In this lesson, you learned about the parts of the Quicken screen. In the next lesson, you will learn how to access the Quicken help system.

Getting Help

In this chapter, you will learn how to use Quicken's extensive online Help.

Quicken has the Answers

While 90 percent of the work you do in Quicken will be on more than familiar territory, there are times when you will need a little help. For instance, once you know how to use one register, you know how to use them all (well, perhaps not the investment register), but what about the more complex features? What about loan forecasting? What about budgeting or creating scheduled transactions? Maybe you just feel a little frightened of bank reconciliations. Naturally this book answers those questions and more, but what if you need help when you don't have this book handy? The solution comes in the form of online Help.

How Do I?

Quicken's **How Do I?** feature is the first place you should look for help. How Do I? is context-sensitive. That means it brings up help relating precisely to the issue at hand. (It also means that if there is no context-sensitive help available, it won't prove very useful, but that is rarely the case.) For instance, click **How Do I?** with a standard account register open and you will see the Help topics shown in Figure 5.1. Just select any topic to learn more about that procedure. Click **More** to move to a more detailed list.

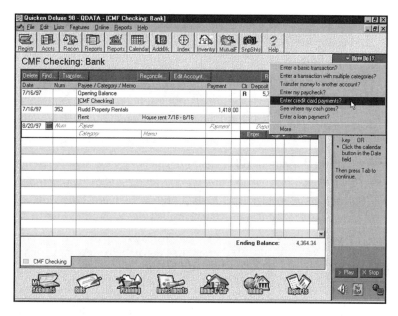

Figure 5.1 How Do I? turns complex problems into plain-English answers.

Technical Support

Use the second Quick Tabs Help option to call up more support. The Support menu offers the following choices:

- **Troubleshooting**   Help you to solve problems rather than find answers to questions or learn about certain procedures.
- **Go to Web...**   Takes you to Intuit's site on the Web where you can read list of the most common questions asked their technical support team. Fortunately, they also provide the answers.
- **Learn More by Fax...**   Receive faxes relating to your problem.
- **Call for Support...**   If all else fails, this option will help you to get in touch with the human side of Quicken's technical support.

Navigating the Help Menu

Quicken ships with a powerful bevy of helpful features suitable for almost any occasion, no matter how stumped or stymied you feel. But while that's very reassuring, you still need to know how to ask the right questions.

You will find Quicken's help scattered throughout the program. However, the major items are gathered under the Help menu, summarized in Table 5.1.

Table 5.1 Quicken's Online Help

Menu Heading	Purpose
Index	Accesses the main Help index. This is the same as selecting the Index button in the Icon bar.
Current Window... (F1)	Calls up Quicken's context-sensitive help. This is identical to the Help button in the icon bar.
Product Support	Accesses the same dialog box displayed by the Support tab described above.
Tips...	Quicken displays a tip every time you launch the program. Use this item to view more tips. Click **Contents** to see them all at once.
Overviews	View the full list of Quicken Overviews.
Show QCards	Quicken's multimedia Help system can display a spoken or written introduction whenever you enter a previously unexplored section of the Quicken software. This is only valid for the CD-ROM version, and only works with the CD inserted.
About Quicken	Displays a small information window about Quicken. This is most useful for its version number. However, to see how much memory Quicken consumes, select this menu item while holding down the **Shift** key. To summarize the number of transactions, accounts and other data in your Quicken file, select it holding down the **Ctrl** key.

TIP **Instant Help** To get help fast, press the **F1** button on your keyboard. This opens Quicken's context-sensitive Help, giving you solutions highly applicable to your current situation.

For more extensive help, select **Help, Index, Contents** and wander through the electronic books contained therein. Consult Appendix A or your Windows documentation for more information on using the Windows Help system.

In this lesson, you learned how to use the Quicken Help system. In the next lesson, you will learn how to set up and work with Quicken's many different types of accounts.

Setting Up and Reconciling Your Accounts

In this lesson, you will learn about the differences between Quicken's nine accounts. You will also learn how to set them up and how to perform a bank reconciliation.

Understanding Quicken Accounts

Even if you are new to Quicken, you already will have had some experience with Quicken's accounts. If your needs are simple, that first checking account created during the New User Setup may prove to be the only account you need. After all, it can record all of the transactions that push the balance of your bank account up or down, and it can also assign those transactions to any number of income and expense categories. However, if you maintain more than one bank account, use a credit card, invest in property, securities, or the money market, maintain an inventory, or do any of numerous other things, you will probably need to set up further accounts.

Quicken's accounts play several important roles.

- By setting up an account for each of your bank accounts, you can follow the rise and fall of each account's balance. Furthermore, balancing those accounts according to the last statement obtained will prove much easier than if all of your transactions were thrown into the one basket. Obviously, this makes a huge difference when dealing with accounts that are of a fundamentally different nature: asset and liability accounts, for instance.

- Quicken's system for customizing reports makes it easy to turn off, and thus negate the effect of certain accounts. If you run a business so small its finances are combined with your own (perhaps you run it from a studio in your home), you can still watch its net worth by turning off any

contribution made by your own personal assets or liabilities. However, to
see the much bigger picture, just restore the contribution of all accounts.

- Even though your bank savings account and your stock market investment
account are both asset accounts, your investment account is valued very
differently to your savings account. Its worth fluctuates on a daily basis
even if left undisturbed by frequent transactions. This is in sharp contrast
to your savings account, which most likely grows at a steady rate. It makes
sense to keep those accounts and the transactions that are recorded in
those accounts separate. Quicken makes it easy to do so.

Accounts are an important, if not indispensable, part of Quicken. If you just
want to balance your checkbook, you probably won't need more than one
account. But if you want Quicken and the rest of this book to give you the power
to control your financial future, you need more than just one.

Selecting the Right Account

Quicken supports nine types of accounts. While there are plenty to choose from,
all are classified as asset or liability accounts. In fact, seven of those accounts are
asset accounts while only two are liability accounts.

 Asset and Liability An **asset** is something you own: a house, car, cash in
the bank, securities investments, or money that you are owed. A **liability** is
something you owe: credit card debt, personal loans, bills that need to be paid,
a mortgage or any other funds due.

Quicken gives each type of account different capabilities. Some of the changes
are subtle, while others are more dramatic. To help you create the ones you
need, here's a quick guide to the different types:

- **Checking Account** Asset account, which supports Quicken's check-
writing and printing capability. This is a great way to save time. Rather
than writing your checks by hand, order checks from Intuit compatible
with your printer. To save more time, take advantage of the online bill
payments capability to send your payments electronically. Online payments are transmitted across the Internet to Intuit Services Corporation
(ISC). If the recipient is registered with ISC, the payment takes place
electronically. Otherwise ISC prints and mails the payment shortly before
it falls due. You can learn more about online payments in Part 3. If you also
use online banking, you'll find that online payments makes a great match.

- **Savings Account**   Asset account useful if you regularly transfer money out of your checking account (or from some other source) into a more permanent account or investment. Savings accounts typically pay higher interest rates than checking accounts and incur fewer bank fees. This type of account is great for tracking both long- and short-term deposits.

- **Credit Card Accounts**   The credit card account is, of course, a liability account ideal for managing your credit card. However, this form of account also contains a few bonus features such as the capability to specify a credit card limit (Quicken will keep you constantly appraised of available funds), and the capability to generate a reminder when you exceed your own set limit. Remember, though, that credit cards are one of the most expensive ways to borrow money. You should always try to pay your credit card off before interest is charged.

CAUTION

Debit Cards   If you use a debit card, set it up as an ordinary checking account, not a credit card account. If your debit card is attached to your checking account, don't set up a separate account. Instead, record your debit card transactions in the checking account, just as you would any other form of payment.

- **Money Market Accounts**   Asset account similar to a checking account. You can speculate on the money market on a very short-term basis (overnight is not uncommon) yet earn huge interest rates. However, it takes significant funds to do so. If you don't have funds sufficient to obtain the higher interest rates, you might consider founding or joining an investment club.

- **Cash Accounts**   Simply an asset account with slightly different register column headings: Spend and Receive rather than Increase and Decrease. In a small business situation, a cash account is ideal for tracking the level of funds in the petty cash tin or the same in one or more cash registers. In a home situation, it is a little less useful but can prove handy if you have some form of emergency or slush fund.

- **Asset Accounts**   Tracks assets large and small, such as home inventory, property equity, funds owed to you, vehicles, expensive toys such as boats and aircraft, and so on. If you lend money to someone and receive regular repayments, you can link this type of account to an amortized loan. See Part 6, Lesson 8 for more information.

TIP **Real Estate Investments**   Use Quicken to track the relative worth of your commercial investments in one account and the worth of your residential investments in another, by creating Commercial Property and Residential Property asset accounts.

You can look at the figures relating to a specific property; enter every transaction using a class especially set up to target that property. You can quickly create profit and loss expense reports that show precisely how each property performs. In addition, you can see your commercial and residential equity by looking at each asset register's balance.

- **Liability Accounts**   Great for storing short- and long-term liabilities to track personal loans, mortgages, bills to be paid, and so on. You can attach these accounts to amortized loans.
- **Investment Accounts**   Turn to Part 5, Lesson 4 to read about setting one up. Part 5 will also teach you how to use this account's register.
- **401(k) Accounts**   Track your retirement funds. When you create this type of account, Quicken automatically sets it up as tax-deferred. The software also treats this type of account as an investment account, following the fluctuating value of one or more funds. You can also read about this type of account in Part 5. This account can be used for any tax-deferred retirement account used to track investment funds. It is only available in Quicken Deluxe 98 and Quicken Home and Business 98.

Invoices/Receivables   Quicken Home and Business 98 supports a further account type known as Invoices/Receivables. You will learn how to replicate the functionality of these specialized accounts in Part 4.

CAUTION

Accounts help you track transactions that have originated through different financial avenues, just as income and expense accounts help you to track transactions that apply to different things.

By setting up a series of accounts to track as many of your assets and liabilities as possible, Quicken can tell you precisely how much you are worth. This places you in a financial feedback loop that can only prove beneficial. If you see your net worth starting to fall, you are immediately goaded into doing something about it. On the other hand, if you see it on the rise, you are given an immediate reward for your achievement. Of course, if a lot of your asset base is tied to the stock market, your net worth will rise and fall more frequently. However, even this might prove beneficial, persuading you to consider investing in areas not dependent on the vagaries of the share market.

Net Worth   Your net worth or equity is calculated by subtracting your liabilities from your assets. If all of your assets were sold up right now at their current market value (at least, according to Quicken) and all of your liabilities paid out in full, you are worth whatever is left over.

Creating a New Account

Before you create a new account, take the time to open up your list of accounts. Select **Lists, Account** (Ctrl+A). You see the window shown in Figure 6.1. Use this window to create, edit, or delete your accounts, as well as to access each account's register and adjust that account's optional information.

The figure shows just one account, the checking account created during the New User Setup. The columns show the account name, its type, an optional description, the number of transactions currently entered in that account's register, its balance and, finally, the number of checks waiting to be printed.

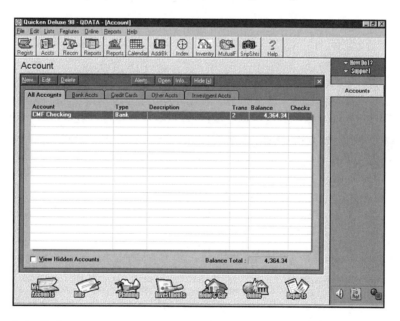

Figure 6.1   Before you create a new account, check your list of accounts.

Creating a new account is easy, but the steps required will differ according to the type of account you create. While Quicken's dialog boxes can guide you through, there is a shortcut that works for every type of account except the 401(k).

41

For the remaining accounts, start by following these simple steps:

1. With the list of accounts open, click **New** in the upper left corner, or select **Edit, Account, New** (Ctrl+N) to launch the Create New Account interview shown in Figure 6.2. As you can see, the example screen shots in this section show the creation of a credit card account.

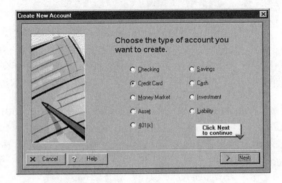

Figure 6.2 Quicken supports nine forms of accounts, based on three distinct varieties.

2. Select the account type and click **Next**.

3. Now, rather than working through Quicken's step-by-step instructions—the steps differ for each account type—just click the **Summary** tab.

4. Fill in the fields in the Summary window using the following and Figure 6.4 as a guide. If you don't see one of the fields mentioned, don't panic. It just means it isn't supported by that type of account. Skip that field and move on to the next:

   Account Name Appears on the account tab in the register window. You can use any combination of letters, spaces, and numbers, with the exception of the following characters: [ ] / : | ^.

   Description Used in various Quicken reports.

   Balance If you receive statements for this account, enter the ending balance shown on the last statement as well as the date it was issued. If you don't receive statements, and if you only want to track the value of a single asset or liability with this account, use **Opening Balance** and **Date** to record the cost (or value) and date you purchased or received that asset or incurred that liability (see Figure 6.3). To track a mix of assets or liabilities, leave the opening balance and date at zero, and enter the date and amounts of each asset or liability as individual transactions.

TIP **Downloading Statements** If you have set up your account with one of the financial institutions that supports Quicken's online services, you can simply download your latest statement. While the transactions that contributed to it will not automatically appear in your register (although copying them across is very easy), this is by far the best way to obtain the latest statement information. Check Part 3 for specific instructions.

Enable Online Banking If your account is supported by a compatible financial institution, use this option to set up the account so that you can download statements and transfer funds between accounts. With an online credit card, you can automatically download every transaction relating to that card, saving on significant typing.

Enable Online Payments This is the easiest way to pay your bills. Simply create the payment as you normally would and send it via the Internet to Intuit Services Corporation. ISC pays the payee electronically if they are registered on their system, or mails them a check if they aren't. It's that easy.

If you select any online option, clicking **Next** takes you to the online financial institution setup system where you need to create or choose an already created online financial institution. You can find out more about online banking and payments in Part 3.

TIP **Paying the Bills** While a liability account is the easiest way to track bills that need to be paid at some future date, you can achieve the same result by dating checks forward. Create the transaction in your checking account for the date the bill is due to be paid. When the day comes, print the check and mail it. If you use ISC, they will store the payment and only process it once it is due.

Credit Limit, if Applicable If you set your credit card limit in this field, Quicken can provide you with a constant reminder of the credit remaining. Quicken can also use the limit in the Alerts feature to log a reminder when you approach a preset limit. This doesn't have to be the credit card's limit but any amount you determine.

Additional Information (Optional) Click **Info** to record any extra information that you want to associate with this asset account. For example, you can record your financial institution's contact details and the account's interest rate. Quicken doesn't use this information for any of its reports or calculations, but it's good to have it on hand.

Tax Info   Click **Tax** if this account is a tax-deferred account such as an IRA or any other tax-deferred investment. If you do, make sure you also associate **Transfers In** with **W-2:Salary or wages, self**. This will decrease your reported income (and thus income tax) by however much you transfer to that account. If you have retired and are drawing on the value in this tax-deferred account, you should also associate **Transfers Out** with **W-2:Salary or wages, self**.

5. Click **Done** to save the account. If you are creating a liability account, Quicken will offer to set up an amortized loan, attached to this account. This procedure will take you between 10–20 minutes to complete. You can do so now or click **No** to create the loan later.

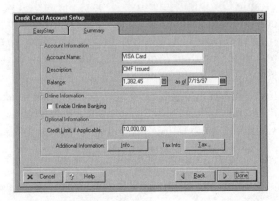

Figure 6.3   You may see more options in this summary screen if you are creating an account other than for a credit card.

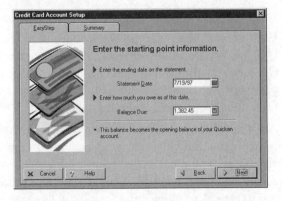

Figure 6.4   Provide a statement date and ending balance to keep your account coordinated.

Performing a Reconciliation

When you reconcile an account, you compare Quicken's records with your bank records. You should perform a reconciliation every time you receive a statement from your bank. Doing so will help you with the following items:

- Keep Quicken's accounts' data accurate.
- Update you Quicken accounts with bank charges and other fees.
- Help to deduce when the bank has made a mistake with your account.
- Keep track of which checks have been presented and those that are still outstanding.
- Accurately determine your net worth.

It is important when first setting up or subsequently reconciling an account that you establish a common starting point between your bank records and your Quicken records. It is for this reason you should always try to find the statement date and account balance when you create a new account.

If this is not possible, there is no need to worry. You can always adjust your opening balance later.

CAUTION

Don't Reconcile to the Last Cent? While it is advisable your Quicken accounts and your bank account balance, you don't have to reconcile to the very last cent. Instead, you might prefer to perform an opening balance adjustment. Alternatively, enter an adjustment transaction without assigning it to a payee or income or expense category. Simply click **Finished** on an unbalanced reconciliation and Quicken will offer to record that adjustment for you.

There are two methods of reconciliation. You should use one or the other depending on whether you are using paper-based statements or performing the reconciliation through an online account.

You will learn about performing a paper-based reconciliation below. To reconcile an online account, see Part 3.

To perform a paper-based account reconciliation, follow these steps:

1. If you are not already there, open one of your registers by selecting **Features, Banking, Use Register** (Ctrl+R), or select **My Accounts, Use My Register** from the Activity bar.

2. Use the register tabs running along the bottom of the screen to move to the appropriate register.

3. If this is the first time you have reconciled this account, take the time now to check the following (this may save you from a lot of detective work later on):

- Find the last statement you received before you started to use Quicken. This is the statement you should have used when you created that Quicken account. Make sure the opening balance in your register matches the closing balance shown on that statement. If it doesn't, you need to adjust the opening balance. Scroll to the top of the register and edit the amount shown in the second column. This is the deposit amount. You will need to confirm that you are recording a transfer back to the same account and that you are adjusting the opening balance. That's all that's required.

- Record every transaction shown on all statements received since the statement you used, to determine the account's opening balance. Ideally, that will involve nothing more than entering any bank charges and tax that have appeared in your account. If you need to record your paycheck deposits, see Lesson 7.

 TIP **Help! I'm Too Many Transactions Behind!** If you need to enter too many transactions, you can skip the intervening statements and record a subsequent balance adjustment. Perform the account reconciliation as detailed next and use the out of balance amount as your new opening balance. Of course, you will end up with an incomplete record in your Quicken accounts, but sometimes there is no other choice.

4. Click **Reconcile** to open the window shown in Figure 6.5. Use this window to give Quicken the information it needs to help you through the main reconciliation.

5. Consult your most recent bank statement and enter the opening and ending balance.

6. Run down the statement and total any service charges and interest earned. Quicken uses its default Bank Charge and Interest Inc categories, but you may change these if you want. However, it is important that Interest Inc continues to point to the correct tax-related item. You will learn about tax-related categories in Lesson 8.

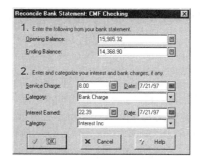

Figure 6.5 Enter your bank statement summary information. Quicken will use this as the basis for the reconciliation.

7. Click **OK** when you finish. You should see a window similar to that shown in Figure 6.6.

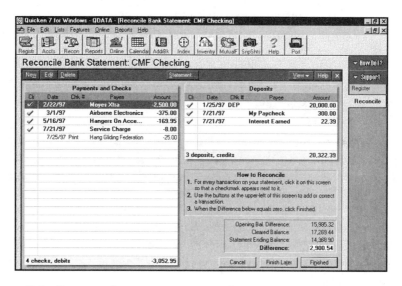

Figure 6.6 To reconcile your account, tick off those transactions already cleared.

8. Use the transaction lists shown in this window to complete the reconciliation. Mark off every transaction that appears on your statement. Your goal is not to mark off every transaction that appears in Quicken.

Use the left-hand side of the window to mark withdrawals from the account and the right-hand side to mark deposits. Bear in mind that your statement may not show the transactions in the same order they occurred in your register, as your checks probably didn't clear through your bank in the same order you wrote them.

TIP   Taking a Break   Reconciliation can take a long time...especially if you have many transactions flowing in and out of the account. So, how do you take a break and get on with something else for a while? Simply click **Finish Later**. Quicken places a **c** in the Clr column of all transactions marked to be reconciled but not quite there. When you're ready to complete the job, open the register, click **Reconcile**, **OK** past the opening dialog box and complete the reconciliation in the main window. Click **Finished** when you're done.

9. If your transactions don't match, use the New, Edit, and Delete buttons in the upper left corner of the Reconcile Bank Statement window to adjust them. Clicking **New** or **Edit** will take you to the account register. Enter or edit the transaction and click **Return to Reconcile** to jump back.

10. Once you have marked (or added and marked) every transaction that appears on your bank statement, check the difference in the lower right corner of the Reconcile window. If it equals zero, you're done. Click **Finished** to complete the job. Before returning you to your register, Quicken will offer to create a reconciliation report. Fill out the dialog box, and click **Print** to produce the report. Otherwise, click **Cancel** to return to your register.

If you can't get your account to balance, look through your past transactions. If your account has previously balanced, the problem must be occurring in this latest batch. You may need to check your deposit slips rather than your bank statement. For instance, even though you may have deposited 20 different checks, your bank may summarize these as a single figure. Try looking for duplicate entries, misplaced decimal points, and so on. The good news is that as long as you reconcile often, you limit the detective work involved in tracking down an error when an account doesn't balance.

TIP   I Can't Get This to Balance!   Don't worry if you can't get your accounts to balance. Click **Finished** and Quicken will offer to create an adjustment transaction for the out-of-balance amount. Type in the date of the adjustment, click **Adjust,** and you'll be done.

Online reconciliations are by far the easiest way to balance your account. If you haven't looked into online banking, do so today. You may find you never need to work through the headaches of reconciling your accounts again.

In this lesson, you learned about Quicken's different accounts. You also learned how to create each type of account—with the exception of the 401(k)—and also how to perform a reconciliation once it was done. In the next lesson, you will learn how to record transactions in each account's register.

Using Quicken's Registers

7

In this lesson, you will learn how to use Quicken's registers to record almost any kind of transaction. You will also learn how memorized transactions can save you time.

Three Basic Transactions

Quicken's registers can record three basic transactions:

- **Inflows** Amounts credited to an account.
- **Outflows** Amounts debited from an account.
- **Transfers** Amounts moved from one account to another.

That seems fairly simple, but these transactions can take on many guises. For instance, while an inflow is usually generated through some form of income or deposit, an inflow into a liability account such as a credit card indicates that you are paying off that credit card. Conversely, outflows usually show expenses, but not always.

TIP **Debits and Credits** While Quicken does not usually concern you with debits and credits, you may find it useful to remember that a debit does not always decrease an account balance and a credit does not always increase an account balance. Rather, a credit shows where the funds or value involved in a transaction originated, hence the term *creditor*. A debit shows where the funds or value went, if you should sell something on credit, the value of those goods goes to a *debtor*.

In theory, it would be possible for Quicken to manage your books with just two types of account: asset and liability. However, as you have already learned, that is impractical. Creating more specific forms of accounts helps to organize your finances, but the different debit and credit columns in each account help you to recognize in which column you should assign that payment or deposit. See Table 7.1 for a listing of the debit and credit column names for each account type.

TIP **401(k)** You will only have access to this type of account if your use either Quicken Deluxe 98 or Quicken Home & Business 98. You will learn about this account in Part 4.

Table 7.1 Debit and Credit Columns

Account Type	Debit Column	Credit Column
Checking (see Figure 7.1)	Payment	Deposit
Savings	Payment	Deposit
Credit Card (see Figure 7.2)	Charge	Payment
Cash	Spend	Receive
Money Market	Payment	Deposit
Investment (see Figure 7.3)	N/A	N/A
Asset	Decrease	Increase
Liability	Increase	Decrease
401(k)	N/A	N/A

TIP **Invoices/Receivables** If you use Quicken Home & Business 98, you have access to a further account type called Invoice/Receivables. This account will help you record invoices and track your debtors. You will learn more about this account in Part 5.

There are several ways to record transactions. For example, you can record payments using the Write Checks dialog box or by entering those payments directly into the register. (You learn about making payments in Lesson 9.) Quicken can also enter transactions with almost no prompting from you. You may have seen this occur when completing an account reconciliation. If the account doesn't balance, Quicken offers to automatically record an adjustment transaction. If you use Quicken's online banking features, your credit card transactions can also occur automatically.

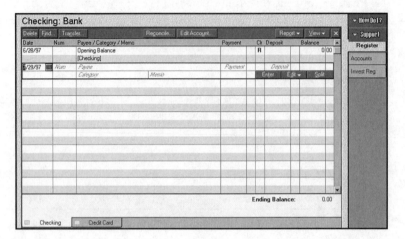

Figure 7.1 Checking accounts use Payment and Deposit columns.

Figure 7.2 Credit Card accounts use Charge and Payment columns.

Still, no matter how a transaction is entered, it will eventually make its way to one or more of your registers. This lesson, therefore, is about understanding what happens to a transaction once it gets there. You can use what you learn here to record almost any transaction by typing it straight into the appropriate register. Chances are, this is precisely what you will do 90 percent of the time.

The remaining 10 percent of your transactions occur automatically or are generated by a Quicken dialog box or other routine.

Investment: Investment								
Easy Actions ▾		Detail View	Portfolio					✕
Date	Action Memo	Security		Price	Shares	Amount Comm/Fee	Clr	Cash Bal
6/29/97 ▦	Action Memo	Security		Price	Shares	Amount Comm/Fee		
Enter	Edit ▾	Form						

Market Value: 0.00   Ending Cash Bal: 0.00

☐ Investment

Figure 7.3   Investment and 401(k) accounts are a special case with columns designed for securities.

Recording a Transaction

If you have followed this book from Lesson 1, you have already created one or more transactions. If you haven't, it's really easy. Just follow these steps:

1. If you are not already there, open one of your registers by selecting **Features, Banking, Use Register** (Ctrl+R) or **My Accounts, Use My Register** on the Activity bar. The first method takes you to the last register used, be it a banking or investment register. The second method always takes you to the last banking register used.

CAUTION

Assumptions About This Lesson   This lesson assumes you are recording transactions in a banking register. For information on recording transactions in an investment register, see Part 5.

2. Use the register tabs running along the bottom of the screen to move to the appropriate register.

TIP **Register Reordering** You may reorder your registers by clicking and holding on each register tab, dragging it left or right to its new position. Here's another tip: If you want a new register window to open for each register you select; select **Edit**, **Options**, **Register**; and turn off **Use One Check Register Window**.

3. Now you're ready to start a new transaction. Type in the **Date** of the transaction, or select it using the calendar icon. You may forward or backdate your transactions. You can also select an old transaction and simply change its date. (In fact, you can edit any aspect of any already-recorded transaction, or simply delete it altogether.)

TIP **Using the Calendar Tool** Click the calendar icon to open the calendar tool. You can do this in Quicken any time you need to enter a date, both within and outside of Quicken's registers. Use the left and right-facing arrows to move backwards or forwards one month at a time. Click on a date within the current month to enter that date in the current date field.

4. Enter the reference or check number. If you use the checking register, don't forget that you can use the pull-down menu to select **Next Check Num** to automatically enter the next check number. If you record a check that needs to be printed, select **Print** from that menu. If you are recording a check that you will place in a Quicken-compatible window envelope, discard this transaction and create the check using the check-writing capability described in Lesson 9. This will also let you place the address on that check.

5. Type in a **Payee**. Quicken stores all payees in a list of memorized transactions, helping you quickly recall that payee in the future. This is particularly handy for payments that you make regularly. Click the down arrow to see the list, as shown in Figure 7.4.

6. If you record an outgoing sum, enter the **Payment/Spend/Charge/Decrease** or click the Calculator icon to use Quicken's built-in calculator. If you record an incoming sum, enter the **Deposit/Receive/Payment/Increase** or click the Calculator icon.

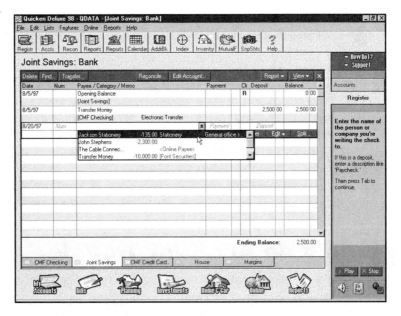

Figure 7.4 The list of past payees links directly to the list of memorized transactions.

TIP **Using the Calculator Tool** The easiest way to access the calculator tool is to click the calculator icon to the left of any numeric field. However, you can also access the calculator by selecting **Edit**, **Use Calculator…**. (If you do, click **Paste** to copy the results into the current field.) Use the calculator as you would any other, clicking **Enter** when you finish. Any amount already in the current field is used as the basis for further calculations. For example, to calculate 20 percent of the amount already recorded in the selected field, click the calculator icon, type **20** and click **%**. You can use your mouse or your keyboard for all operations.

7. Select a **Category**. Most outgoing sums are assigned to an expense category. Most incoming sums are recorded using income categories. You can select a category by entering just the first few letters of its name. Otherwise, click the down arrow and select it from the pull-down list. To record a transfer to another account, follow the steps for account transfers provided next. If you need to split this transaction across more than one category, follow the steps for recording split transactions also provided.

TIP   **What If You Don't Know Your Categories?**   Print a list. Select **Lists**, **Category/Transfer** (Ctrl+C). Click the **Income Categories** tab and select **File**, **Print List** (Ctrl+P). Make sure your printer is online and click **OK**.

8. Type in a **Memo**. The memo is a note to yourself that can contain any extra information about this transaction. Memos are most often used to note a transaction's purpose.

9. Click **Enter** to record this transaction.

Recording a simple transaction is easy. However, there are at least two ways a simple transaction can become more complex: transfers and splits.

Recording an Account Transfer

An account transfer is simply the act of moving funds between accounts. When would you need to do this? Here are some examples:

- **Paying off a credit card**   In most cases, you pay off your credit card by sending a check to VISA, MasterCard, or whomever. Assuming you maintain a credit card liability account, you should indicate this payment in Quicken by recording a transfer from your checking account to your credit card account. If your credit card and checking account are with financial institutions supported by Quicken, you can record this payment electronically online.

- **Transferring funds to a debit card**   If you use a debit rather than credit card that isn't linked to your checking account, you may need to transfer funds on a regular basis to top it up. Again, it's easiest with online payments, but it is also a simple matter to tell Quicken to either record a regular transaction or print a suitable check.

- **Regular mortgage or loan repayments**   If you have set up your mortgage or personal loan as an amortized loan linked to your liability account, you can create a scheduled transaction in Quicken that matches the frequency and amount of funds regularly drawn by your lending institution to pay off your mortgage or loan. (See Part 6 for more information on setting up amortized loans.)

- **Shifting funds to an investment account**   If you maintain an investment account with a broker, you will probably add money to it every so often as you accrue funds in your savings account. (Or you may arrange for a certain amount of your paycheck to go straight into that account.) When you write out a check to your broker, you should record it as a transfer to that account. Conversely, when you withdraw funds from your investment account, you should record that as a transfer from the investment account to the account where you deposit those funds.

Performing an account transfer is easy:

1. Fill out the transaction as normal, stopping at the category field.

2. Transfers are recorded as the destination account name surrounded by square brackets. For example, a transfer might appear as **[Credit Card]** as shown in Figure 7.5. Once you reach the category field, type a left square bracket and the first few letters of the account name to which you are transferring those funds. Quicken automatically completes the remainder of the name. For instance, to record a transfer to an account called **Investment**, you would probably only need to type **[Inv**. Quicken will complete this, recording the transfer as **[Investment]**.

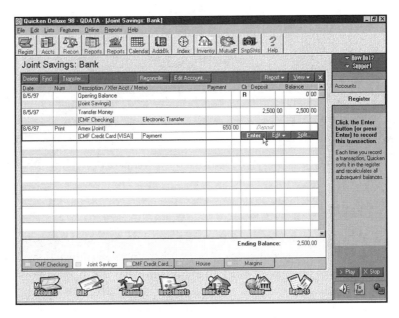

Figure 7.5   Recording a transfer to pay off a credit card.

If you transfer to more than one account or you want to apply some of the funds to a category and the remainder to a transfer, just fill out a split as described next.

When Quicken records a transfer, it replicates that transaction in the destination account, inserting the memo you used in the original transaction. To move from one to the next, use the right mouse button to click one of the pair. Select **Go To Transfer** from the pull-down list to jump to the matched transaction in the destination register, as shown in Figure 7.6.

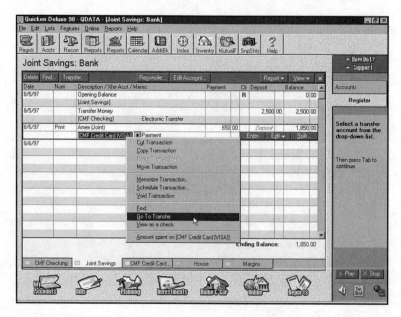

Figure 7.6   This is the other side of the credit card transfer shown in Figure 7.5.

Incidentally, if you delete one of those transactions, the other is deleted as well.

Creating Splits

A split transaction is one that uses more than one category. Typical uses include when recording paychecks and when recording transactions where the payment applies to more than one person or thing. For example, if you work at home, you can pay your utility bill using a single check, even though you can flag that payment in two different ways, part for home and part for work (See Figure 7.7). You can recognize a split transaction because Quicken places —**Split**— in the category field.

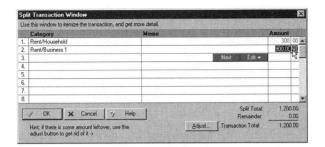

Figure 7.7 Using a split transaction to divide the one payment between household and business expenses.

To record a split transaction, fill out the transaction as normal, making sure you also enter the total amount into the appropriate register field. However, once you reach the category field, click the down arrow and follow these steps:

TIP **Setting Splits** To open the splits window, you can also click **Split** (Alt+S) in the small register menu that appears in the lower right corner of that register entry.

1. Click **Split**. This takes you to the window shown in Figure 7.5.

2. You can split a transaction up to 30 different ways, although only the first 16 will print on the check stub. Select the category as you would a nonsplit transaction, either typing in the first few letters or selecting it from the pull-down list. You can also mix transfers and categories in the one split. If you are recording a transfer, just type in the account name surrounded by square brackets. For example: **[My Savings]**.

3. Press tab and type in a memo. The memo prints on the check stub; the category doesn't.

4. Press tab once more and type in the amount. This is the component of the transaction applicable to this line of the split. You can also use the calculator to work out a percentage amount, rather than a straight dollar figure. Just leave the total as it is and click the Calculator icon. Type in the percentage and press %. Quicken will insert the total into the split's amount.

5. Click **Next** or press **Enter** to move to the next line and repeat the process for all further splits. Check the Remainder to make sure you have allocated the original total in full. Otherwise, click **Adjust** to balance the split.

6. When you finish, click **OK** to record the split and return to the register.

7. Type in a memo and press **Enter** to record the split transaction.

Splits are easy to set up, and you will find them useful in all kinds of otherwise tricky situations.

Memorizing Transactions

The more you use Quicken, the more you will repeat transactions you have performed before. By default, Quicken memorizes every transaction, storing them by payee. The list can contain up to 2,000 entries. Quicken will not memorize any transactions beyond that amount, although they will still appear in your register as usual.

TIP **Retiring Memorized Transactions** While Quicken cannot maintain a list of more than 2,000 transactions, you can keep that list down to manageable levels by automatically retiring transactions you haven't used in a specified number of months. Select **Edit**, **Options**, **Program**, **General** and click **Remove Memorized Transactions Not Used in Last ... Months**. Type in the number of months. Automatically retiring transactions after three or four months will keep your list down to manageable levels.

You can view those transactions by selecting **Lists**, **Memorized Transactions** (Ctrl+T). You should see something similar to the window shown in Figure 7.8. Any transactions you have already entered appear in this list. This is because Quicken automatically memorizes the first transaction assigned to a payee. If you are recording a Split transaction, it will assume you want to memorize the split's dollar amounts.

You can also use this list to create a new transaction. Just click **New** and follow the guide shown in Figure 7.9. Creating a new memorized transaction doesn't enter a transaction in any of your registers. However, it's a great way to set up your books to regularly record checks, online payments, deposits, and so on. While most of the columns in the memorized transaction list take their information from the columns used in the register, the two at the end are a little unusual.

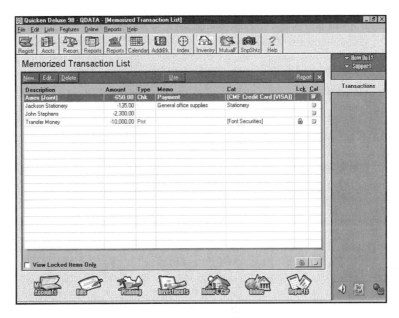

Figure 7.8 Use the Memorized Transaction List to create new, delete old, or edit existing transactions.

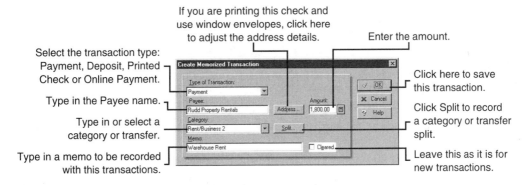

Figure 7.9 Creating a new memorized transaction.

Locked Transactions

Memorized transactions change if you re-use them in a register, adjusting either the amount, category, or memo. Quicken automatically updates the stored transaction, inserting a replica of the most recent transaction the next time you recall it.

61

A locked memorized transaction is protected from change. No matter how often you use that transaction in the future, it will not change the memorized transaction.

To change the status of a locked transaction, click in the **Lck** column.

There are two ways to change a previously memorized transaction.

The first is to use the transaction once more and adjust it as required. However, before recording it, select **Edit**, **Transaction**, **Memorize** (Ctrl+M). Quicken will ask if you want to Replace or Add the existing transaction. Select **Replace** to update the stored transaction or **Add** to create a second memorized transaction under that payee's name.

TIP   **Memorizing with the Mouse**   Another way to memorize your current or any previous transaction is to click it using the right mouse button. Select **Memorize Transaction** from the list. Alternatively, just click within the transaction and press **Ctrl+M**.

The second is to edit the transaction using the memorized transaction list. Follow these steps:

1. Select **Lists**, **Memorized Transactions** (Ctrl+T).

2. Find the transaction and click **Edit**.

3. You may edit any aspect of the transaction including the Payee. You can also use this function to convert a memorized transaction to an online payment. This is perfect if you have been using Quicken for a while but have only just started to access its online services. Click **OK** when you finish.

Calendar Transactions

Have you ever visited the Calendar view? Try going there now. Select **Features**, **Reminders**, **Financial Calendar**.

To the right of the calendar is a list of drag-and-drop transactions. This list only shows previously memorized transactions. If you haven't recorded any, it will be empty. To schedule a future transaction, select the transaction you want to use, and drag it to the appropriate date. Use the dialog box to specify when you want that transaction to occur. (You can learn more scheduled transactions in Lesson 9.)

Every transaction with the Cal column set appears in this list. To prevent a transaction from appearing in this list, jump back to the memorized transaction list and turn off the Cal icon for those you don't want to appear.

Editing, Deleting, and Voiding Transactions

Many accounting systems treat recorded transactions as if they were carved in stone. Once they have been entered…that's it. There is quite literally no way for an operator to delete a transaction once it appears on the system.

Quicken isn't quite such a stickler for accounting integrity. In fact, you can edit, delete, or void any transaction and watch the results flow through your books.

To edit any transaction, find the transaction and click the field you need to edit. Make the change as required, and click **Enter** in the small Register menu at the end of the transaction to save the changes.

To delete a transaction, click anywhere within that transaction and click the **Delete** button in the upper left corner of the register window. Quicken will ask you to confirm the action before it goes ahead.

CAUTION

Deleting Transactions Be careful for there is no way to resurrect a transaction once it has been deleted. If you want to maintain at least a partial record of that transaction, void it instead. See next.

The alternative to deleting transactions is to void them instead. Voiding effectively deletes the transaction but leaves a copy sitting in the register. This is handy if you want to retain a permanent record of that register entry. Unfortunately, voiding doesn't retain the amount of the original transaction, so make sure you copy this to the Memo field before doing the deed.

You can spot voided transactions because Quicken adds the word **Void** before the Payee's name and deletes the transaction amount.

Using the Register Edit Menu

Use the middle button of the transaction-level Register menu for common Edit functions. This button replicates the contents of Quicken's **Edit**, **Transaction** menu. You can click the menu at any time and choose from the following functions:

- **Restore**   If you have been editing a transaction, this returns it to its original form. Restore does not recreate a voided transaction.
- **New**   Jump to the bottom of the register and start a new transaction.
- **Insert**   Inserts a new transaction before the selected transaction. This starts the transaction using the same date as the current.
- **Delete**   Deletes the selected transaction.
- **Void**   Marks the selected transaction as **Void**.
- **Memorize**   Adds this transaction to the Memorized Transactions list.
- **Copy**   Copies the transaction to the Clipboard.
- **Paste**   Pastes a copied transaction into the register.
- **Go to Transfer**   Go to this transfer's origination or destination. This will move you between registers.
- **Go to a Specific Date**   Takes you to any transaction recorded on the date you specify.

Advanced Features

At the core of the register beats the heart of a simple database, but externally Quicken's registers have a range of useful and advanced features.

From here on, you're going to learn about some of the best.

Using the Right Mouse Button

In many Windows programs, the right mouse button takes on a context-sensitive role, displaying menu features particularly pertinent to the task at hand. Quicken is no exception.

The most common right button functions include:

- **Cut**, **Copy**, **Paste**, and **Move Transaction**. Moving a transaction shifts it to another register.
- **Memorize**, **Schedule**, and **Void Transaction**. You should know about memorizing transactions and you'll soon learn about scheduling transactions.

- **Find**. A great tool for searching through any register. (You can learn about it in Part 6, Lesson 9.)

The right mouse button menu can also use the object beneath it as the basis for an instant report. The report is specific only to that register. Its nature changes depending on where you click, but it can be summarized as follows:

- After you click **Payee**   For amounts outgoing, this generates a report showing payments made to that payee over the year to date. For amounts incoming, the report shows income received from that payee over the year.

- After you click **Category**   An income category generates a report for all income received into that category throughout the year. An expense category generates a report showing all amount spent on that expense through the year. A transfer totals the transfers in or out to that account.

These options are also available under the register's **Report** button.

In this lesson, you learned how to record and work with your most common transactions. In the next lesson, you will learn about Quicken's categories, classes, subcategories, and more.

Organizing Your Finances Using Categories

In this lesson, you will learn about Quicken's categories, subcategories, supercategories, and classes.

Understanding Categories and Classes

Without categories and classes, Quicken would be little more than a system for recording a long list of transactions—something you can achieve with an exercise book, a few vertical ruled lines, and a pen.

With categories and classes, you can:

- Tag your income and expense transactions. This will help you see where your income originated and how it was spent. Quicken provides numerous graphs and reports to dissect that information in a number of very useful ways.

- Automate your taxes. Categories will help you assign your income and expenses to specific deductible and nondeductible line items on the Form 1040 and its accompanying Schedules.

- Stick to a budget. By comparing your income and expenses against budgeted amounts, you can see precisely how well you are doing.

- Plan for the future. Categories help you project your spending.

- Track income and expenses across multiple categories so you can see how a series of transactions applied on a project or job basis.

Table 8.1 provides a brief summary of each transaction category and class. You will learn about them further below.

Table 8.1 Transaction Qualifiers

Type	Purpose
Category	To assign a transaction to a group of related income or expense transactions.
Subcategory	To provide further differentiation of related transactions. The subtotals are recorded in each subcategory while the total remains with the parent category.
Class	To classify transactions across many different categories. This is a filtering tool which will help you to view only those transactions applying to that class.
Subclass	To assign a transaction to more that one class.

Using Categories in Your Transactions

You may already have used categories in several of your transactions. If not, here's how it works:

1. You can record a category in any category field simply by typing in the first few letters of its name. Quicken uses the QuickFill feature to complete the category with the closest match from its list.

2. If Quicken gets the QuickFill wrong, just keep on typing. So long as that category actually exists, you will eventually have typed enough letters to arrive at a match.

3. If you try to use a category that doesn't exist in a transaction, you can create it "on-the-fly." Type in the full category name and press Tab, as if to move to the next field. Quicken will stop you with the dialog box shown in Figure 8.1. Click **Yes** to move to the Set Up Category dialog box explained in "Creating a New Category."

Figure 8.1 Creating a category without stopping by the Category & Transfer List.

Using the Category/Transfer List

Quicken includes several preset category lists that will help you categorize most of your transactions. For instance, if you have purchased your first home, you will probably require the standard set of categories used by most homeowners. If you have set up your own small business, you will also need to add a new group of small business-oriented categories to your existing set.

Quicken has six standard sets of categories built in. These are:

- Standard
- Married
- Homeowner
- Business
- Children
- Investment

You have already met four of these during the New User Setup. Remember when Quicken asked you several questions regarding your personal circumstances? For instance: Are you married? Do you have children? Do you own a house? Do you own a small business? It used your answers to build your own default category list, customized to your needs.

The category list is created on the foundation of the Standard set of categories with Quicken adding extra sets for married folk, parents, homeowners, and small business operators. If you create an investment account, Quicken automatically adds the full set of Investment categories.

However, if your circumstances change, you can still access every set of categories, no matter what you answered in the New User Setup. It all happens via the Category & Transfer List.

The Category & Transfer List shows every category included in your Quicken file. To open it, select **Lists, Category/Transfer (Ctrl+C)**. You see the screen shown in Figure 8.2. You can use the tabs across the top to view all categories, income categories, expense categories, or account transfers.

Account Transfers? While account transfers aren't categories as such, they can be used in place of categories to transfer money from one account to another. To add, edit, or delete your accounts, open the Account list. Select

CAUTION **Lists, Account (Ctrl+A)**.

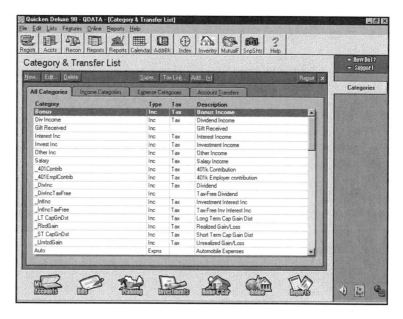

Figure 8.2 This figure shows the Category & Transfer List.

The four columns in the Category & Transfer List show the category name, its type (there are only two possibilities: Income and Expense), whether or not it has been marked as tax-related (if you see the Tax indicator in the Tax column, it has been marked), and the category's description.

Use the six buttons across the top of the window to perform the following functions:

- **New** Adds a new category to the list.
- **Edit** Edits the selected category.
- **Delete** Deletes the selected category.
- **Super** Creates a supercategory (explained later in this chapter).
- **Tax Link** Opens the Tax Link Assistant.
- **Add(+)** Adds new categories from Quicken's list of all preset categories.
- **Report** Creates a category report showing all transactions that have been flagged to that category. If that category hasn't been used, you will be told **No Matching Transactions Found**.

Creating New Categories

You can create categories for almost anything from tracking the money you spent on a holiday to noting how much you "invested" in classical CDs, dog-walkers, babysitting—the list can go on and on.

To create a new category (see Figure 8.3), follow these steps:

1. If it isn't already open, open your Category & Transfer List.

2. Click **New** to open the Set Up Category dialog box.

3. Enter a **Name** for this category. You can use up to 32 characters.

4. (Optional) Enter a **Description**. The description appears in report headings. If you don't enter a description, Quicken will use the name for the report headings.

5. Select the category type. Nearly all your categories are Income or Expense categories. However, if this is a subcategory, select the parent category from the list. You will learn about subcategories next.

6. To include this category in a Tax Summary report, click **Tax-Related**. To also include it in your Tax Schedule report, select the appropriate tax form line item from the list. If you are not sure which to apply, speak to your taxation professional. You learn more about tax-related categories in Part 2.

 TIP **Tax Deduction Finder** If you are using Quicken Deluxe 98 of Quicken Home and Business 98, you can use the Tax Deduction Finder to search out categories that should be but are not already marked as tax-related. This may save you from a trip to your taxation professional, but the results aren't guaranteed. You learn about the Tax Deduction Finder in Part 2, Lesson 10.

7. When you finish, click **OK** to save the new category or **Cancel** to quit.

 TERM **Tax Summary and Tax Schedule** The *Tax Summary* report creates a list of all your tax-related income and expenses. The *Tax Schedule* report arranges your income and expenses by tax form line items. If you prepare your own tax, this is perfect for simply transcribing each item into your return. If you use tax preparation software other than TurboTax, the tax schedule can also create a disk file to a standard format, which is importable by almost all tax preparation products. (TurboTax links directly to Quicken.) You can read more about the tax summary and tax schedule reports in Part 2.

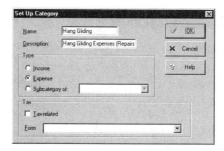

Figure 8.3 Creating a new category requires minimal information.

Adding Categories from the Quicken List

If your circumstances have changed since you first started to use Quicken, you may want to add extra categories from Quicken's master category list.

Doing this is easy and takes just a few steps:

1. Open the Category & Transfer List and click **Add (+)**. You will see the Add Categories dialog box shown in Figure 8.4.

2. Use **Available Categories** to select the appropriate superset of categories. These are listed in the bulleted list at the start of this lesson.

3. You will see available categories listed down the left. Click the categories you want to copy across (or **Mark All**) and click **Add >>** to shift them to your own category list.

4. Click **OK** when you're done.

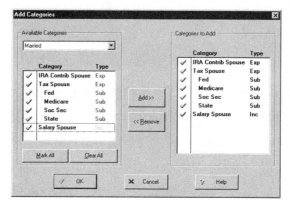

Figure 8.4 You can access the master list of Quicken categories even if you didn't answer "yes" to the category questions in the New User Setup.

Editing a Category

To edit a category, select it in the Category & Transfer List and click **Edit**. The Edit Category dialog box takes the same form as the Set Up Category dialog box, and you can use the details given previously as a guide.

You may change any aspect of a category including its name or description and its tax status. Categories can also change from income to expense or vice versa. This will not have any effect on your existing transactions, although it will change the results of any profit-and-loss reports.

Deleting and Merging Categories

To delete a category, select it from the list and click **Delete**. Confirm the deletion; any transactions assigned to that category are retained with their category field blanked.

Merging categories is almost as easy:

1. Edit the original category, changing its type so that it becomes a subcategory of the destination category.

2. Delete the original category. When you delete a subcategory, Quicken shifts all of the transactions contained in that category to the parent category, so deleting the original category transfers those transactions to the destination category.

CAUTION

Merging Some But Not All Transactions   If you need to merge some of the transactions into another category, use the recategorize utility described next. This makes it easy to separate those that need merging from those that don't.

Recategorizing Transactions

There are two ways to recategorize your transactions. The hard way is to search for and edit them by hand. The easy way is to use Quicken's Recategorization tool.

To use this tool, follow these steps:

1. Select **Edit, Find & Replace, Recategorize**.

2. Use **Search Category:** to specify the old category, or use the down-arrow to select it from the category list. You can search categories or transfers.

3. Click **Find All** to search for all transactions flagged to that category. You should see them displayed in the list below the search box. If you don't want to see transactions that are part of a category split, remove the check mark from **Show Matches in Split**.

4. To mark all the transactions in the list, click **Mark All**. Otherwise, choose individual transactions by clicking in the column to the left of Date, as shown in Figure 8.5.

5. Use **Replace With:** to select the destination category or transfer.

6. Click **Replace** to convert every marked transaction or **X** to cancel.

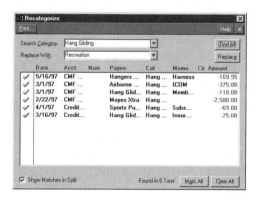

Figure 8.5   The recategorization feature is a handy housekeeping utility.

Creating and Using Subcategories

Subcategories are an ideal way to extend the concept of categories. In general, use subcategories when you need to extract more detail from a category. For example, Quicken's default categories provide just one set of bank charges. But what if you have two bank accounts? How can you differentiate between the charges applied to each?

One solution is to simply delete the original bank charges category, replacing it with two new categories called: Bank A Charges and Bank B Charges. However, this won't help you to automatically total all bank charges in Quicken's reports.

Instead, retain the original category and create two new categories called Bank A and Bank B. Obviously, you should replace these with your banks' names.

You can still assign transactions to the parent category, but you can also assign them individually to each of the subcategories. Even better, you get to determine which version you see in Quicken's reports and graphs.

To create a subcategory, follow the instructions for "Creating a New Category". However, instead of specifying an income or expense type, click **Subcategory of:** and choose the parent category from the list. The subcategory inherits the parent category's income or expense type.

You can use subcategories as easily as you do standard categories. For example, to assign any transaction to a subcategory, enter the parent category followed by a colon (:) and then the subcategory. To use the subcategory Bank A in a transaction, you would record it as **Bank Charges:Bank A**.

When you delete a subcategory, all of its transactions are automatically assigned to the parent category.

Creating and Using Supercategories

Supercategories group categories and subcategories into larger groups yet again. You can use supercategories to summarize the data contained in various categories and subcategories, providing you with a simplified view of your finances.

Once you have created your supercategories, you can use them in budgets and reports. The standard Quicken categories include four supercategories. These are:

- **Discretionary**   Includes expense categories that are not absolutely essential. For instance, one common discretionary supercategory would be entertainment.
- **Non-Discretionary**   Includes expense items that must be met. For example, taxes, medical expenses, and rent are common nondiscretionary supercategories.
- **Other Income**   Income categories such as investment and interest.
- **Salary Income**   Wages, tips, bonuses, and so on.

To view these and the categories that contribute to them, open your Category & Transfer List and click **Super**. Figure 8.6 shows the Manage Supercategories dialog box.

The left-hand list shows every Quicken category and its assigned supercategory, if any. The right-hand list shows all available supercategories.

You can create, edit, or delete supercategories by using the buttons under the right-hand list.

If you are a small business operator, pay special attention to supercategories for they can prove very useful indeed. For instance, most small business accounts try to divide the business's income and expenses into:

- **Income**   Income derived from your primary business.
- **Other Income**   Income derived from secondary sources such as that earned on investments.
- **Cost of Goods Sold**   Expenses relating directly to the manufacture of your goods. These are usually unavoidable expenses such as the cost of raw materials.
- **Expenses**   Expenses that are necessary but not directly related to the manufacture; for instance, marketing costs, office space, computers, word processing software, and telephone bills.
- **Other Expenses**   These expenses include travel and accommodation, entertainment, and anything else that tends to lie on the periphery of the business.

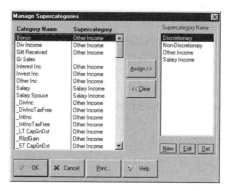

Figure 8.6 Supercategories are useful for bundling your finances up into key areas of income and spending.

Supercategories are great for organizing these rather broad areas. However, they do behave differently to subcategories. For example, there is no way to assign a transaction to a supercategory. Instead, that transaction is assigned to a category that just happens to be part of the destination supercategory. It appears under that supercategory in reports and budgets, but is never directly linked to that supercategory. Also, deleting a supercategory has no effect on the transactions assigned beneath it.

To assign new categories to a supercategory, follow these steps:

1. Create and name the new supercategory.

2. Use the left-hand list to select the categories you want to assign to the new supercategory. You can select multiple categories using Windows' standard **Shift+Click** and **Ctrl+Click** keys. For instance, to select a contiguous set of categories, click the first and **Shift-Click** the last. This will include those two categories plus all those bracketed by the selection. To select a category outside the group without losing your prior selection, hold down the **Ctrl** key and click the new category.

3. Click **Assign >>** to assign those categories to the supercategory. To remove the supercategory designation on a previous assigned category, click **<< Clear**.

 TIP   **Printing the Supercategory List**   Can't remember which category has been included in which supercategory? Never mind. Just open the Manage Supercategory dialog box and click **Print**. This prints the contents of the left-hand side of the list.

Supercategories are most useful in two situations. First, they are listed in the Budget window. You learn how to work with these in Lesson 13.

Second, should you want to collate the figures in a report according to their supercategory, select the report, click **Customize,** and look for a field called **Organization**. You will often—not always—find an option for Supercategories at the end of the list attached to this field, as shown in Figure 8.7.

Creating and Using Classes

Just when you must be thinking Quicken surely has every conceivable category option all sewn up, along comes classe. Classes are used to group transactions, no matter in which sub or normal categories they occur.

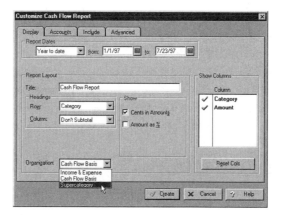

Figure 8.7 Select the Organization field in almost any report customization dialog box to arrange your report by supercategory.

For instance, let's assume you own two homes. You live in one and rent the other. The second home is mortgaged but the rent just covers that mortgage. It's a nice balance but also a very fine one. For tax reasons, you need to know if one climbs higher than the other.

There are many forms of expense incurred in the routine maintenance of any home. These are normally assigned to many different categories. However, to maintain a separate set of categories for every property would prove very unwieldy.

With classes, you only need the one set of categories. Instead, create one class for each house, ensuring you include the appropriate class with the category when recording any transactions relating to one property or the other.

Here's how classes work:

- A class is not a category or subcategory; it is a means of tagging transactions to a certain "class" of item, no matter to which category those transactions are assigned.
- By printing a report that sorts on class rather than category, you can compare the "bottom line" of different classes.
- The capability to filter all of your Quicken data through one class or another makes this feature ideal for creating individual profit-and-loss centers. Using the housing problem, it would be possible to print a profit-and-loss report filtered through the class designated to the rental property. This would immediately reveal only those income and cost transactions

directly associated with that house, telling you immediately how much profit or loss you had made. You can use this information to fine-tune your mortgage repayments.

- Classes are also ideal if you work more than one job, helping you keep your work-related income and expenses separate. By using the Copy Number system described below, you can automatically prepare tax returns for both jobs.

Creating Classes

To create a class, follow these steps:

1. Open your class list using **Lists, Class** (**Ctrl+L**).
2. This list shows all of your existing classes. It is probably empty because Quicken does not set up any classes for you. Click **New** to open the Set Up Class dialog box.
3. Enter a name for the class.
4. (Optional) Enter a description. As with categories, the description is used for report headings, if available. Otherwise Quicken just uses the class name.
5. (Optional) Type in a copy number. The copy number is used by Quicken and TurboTax when preparing your tax return reports. This is useful if you run two or more businesses and need to report on multiple Schedule Cs, or work two or more jobs and receive more than one Form W-2.

Using Classes

You can use a class with or without an associated category. The rules are as follows:

1. The class must be preceded by a forward slash (/), for instance: **/Bus 1**.
2. When used with categories, classes are recorded like this: **Category/Class**.
3. You can also mix classes with subcategories. The order goes like this: **Category:Subcategory/Class**.
4. If that isn't enough, you can treat any class as a subclass, even though subclasses aren't explicitly supported the way subcategories are. To use a class as a subclass, type in the first class followed by a colon, followed by the subclass, therefore: **Class:Subclass**. The full notation looks something like this: **Category:Subcategory/Class:Subclass**.

5. Almost anywhere Quicken calls for a category, you can use a class instead. However, make sure you check for specific class support first. For example, many reports support classes. Just check the Customize area. Chances are you can choose to group the transactions by class instead of category (or supercategory).

Reclassifying Classes

From time to time, you may find that you have entered transactions using one class and now want to assign it to another. Quicken doesn't provide a Reclassify tool for classes the way it does a Recategorize tool for categories. However, its Find & Replace easily emulates Recategorize's functionality.

 TIP **Renaming Classes** If you can get away with renaming your class rather than reclassifying all of the transactions underneath it, you'll save some time. Go to the Class List, select the Class, and click **Edit**. Type in the new name or description and click **OK**. Renaming a class updates the transactions that refer to that class, so you won't lose any information.

To reclassify your classes, follow these steps:

1. Select **Edit, Find & Replace, Find/Replace**.

2. Enter the class name into **Find:**, preceded by a forward slash (/), set **Search:** to **Category/Class**, and **Match if:** to **Contains**. Then click **Find All**.

3. The list shows all transactions that have used that class.

4. Click those transactions you want to convert, or click **Mark All** to tag them all.

5. Set **Replace:** to **Category/Class** and type the new class into **With:**, again preceded by a forward slash. In the example shown in Figure 8.8, all transactions that have used **/Business 1** as all or part of their category designation will be changed to read **/Business 2**. This works whether or not there have been categories and subcategories designated before those class names.

6. Click **Replace** to reclassify those transactions.

 TIP **Deleting Classes** If you want to delete a class rather than reclassify it, feel free to do so. Quicken won't discard those transactions. Instead, it just removes any mention of that class from your registers.

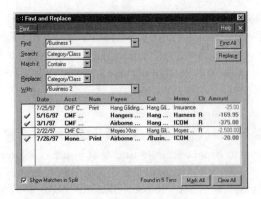

Figure 8.8 Quicken's Find and Replace tool is great for reclassifying transactions.

In this lesson, you learned about the many ways Quicken can store, flag, and categorize your transactions. In the next lesson, you will learn how to use Quicken to pay your bills, write checks, schedule future transactions, and more.

Paying the Bills

In this lesson, you will learn about writing and printing checks. You should already know how to manually record payments made either via your checkbook (hand-written checks) or your credit card. You will learn about online banking and bill paying (electronic checks) in Part 3.

Using Quicken to Pay Your Bills

Just as Quicken offers numerous ways to record and classify transactions, there at least four ways you can settle a bill:

- Write out a check and record the payment manually in your checking register
- Create and print the check entirely from within Quicken
- Pay the bill by credit card, recording the payment manually or through your credit card's online banking service
- Use Quicken's online facility to pay the bill electronically: no check, no envelope, no stamp, and no trip to the post box.

However, to use Quicken's check writing and printing facilities, read on.

It feels great to get your bills organized, and Quicken's one of the easiest ways to do so.

Getting Started

While Quicken's online payments facility is superb, it won't suit everyone. After all, you must pay a fee every time you make a payment. Also, you may prefer the satisfaction and feel of a printed check, don't have the time to wait for an electronic payment to occur, or you might not want to mess with Internet connections or the like.

In that case, feel free to leave the electronic stuff to the wonder kids. Quicken is perfectly adept at recording checks you have written manually or, even better, printed using Quicken-compatible blank checks.

In fact, for a truly professional payments system, you can't beat laser-printed checks. They can have your address and logo, a fully itemized list of the items being paid, the payee's address and more. They look good, they're professional, and their printing and postage is completely in your control.

Are you convinced? You should be. These checks look great and they take mere moments to generate. However, before you can use them, here's what you will need to do:

1. Order your checks through the Intuit Marketplace.
2. Write out each check in Quicken.
3. When you have completed the batch, print them, stick 'em in an envelope and send them on their way.

Ordering Checks with Intuit Marketplace

To access the Intuit Marketplace, either telephone Intuit direct or call up the marketplace across the Internet by selecting the Quicken menu **Online, Quicken on the Web, Intuit Marketplace**.

If you haven't yet used Quicken's Internet features, you will need to set up your Internet connection. You can read about this in Part 3.

Otherwise, assuming you have already set up your Internet connection, you will need to register with the Intuit Marketplace before you can place your first order. Fill in the form requesting information on your delivery and e-mail addresses and password.

TIP   **Changing Your Registration Details**   To change any or all of your registration details, look for your name at the bottom of any page on the marketplace site. Click your name to move to the Shopper Update page. Make the necessary changes and click Submit to store them on Intuit's system.

Once you complete the registration, use the marketplace as you would any World Wide Web site. Follow these steps:

1. Select the products you require. Onscreen prompts will help you choose options specific to that product. See next for a description of the types of checks available. Once you complete your selection, Marketplace adds that product to your shopping basket.

2. The contents of your shopping basket are retained between online sessions. Indeed, the shopping basket is only emptied when you manually remove items (click **Basket**) or finalize the order.

3. When you finish adding items to the shopping basket, click **Pay** to move to the marketplace's payments system. Select the shipment and payment method. You can use the information shown in the on-screen receipt to find out the status of your order at any time.

Check Styles

Quicken is compatible with three styles of checks. They are all available through the Intuit Marketplace:

- **Standard Checks**   These are the standard business checks without a stub. Even though there are three checks per sheet, you should be able to print them one at a time.

- **Wallet Checks**   These checks provide a perforated stub which you can tear off after printing. They're useful for paying most personal bills because the voucher gives you a permanent, printed record. Like standard checks, wallet checks have three checks per sheet.

- **Voucher Checks**   These checks are the creme de la creme of checks. With one check and two tear off stubs, the single sheet of paper gives you and the payee a generous permanent record. These checks are the most convenient for accounts payable and payroll, but they are also the most expensive.

Printing Logos

It costs a once-only fee for Intuit to prepare the artwork needed to place your logo on your printed checks.

However, if you use Standard or Voucher style checks, you can print your logo yourself. Create the logo using any drawing package and save it as Bitmap (.bmp) format. The file must be less than 64K in size. Select the menu **File, Printer Setup, For Printing Checks**. Click **Logo**, click **File** and select the bitmap. **OK** your way back out and you'll be done. Every time you print a check, Quicken will also print your logo, and it won't cost you a cent.

This shortcut works best when using a laser or good quality inkjet printer. It is not a good idea to use this system with a dot-matrix printer.

Writing Checks

If you write your checks by hand, you should enter them directly into your checking register. Use the Num/Ref field to note the last three digits in the check number and complete the payee, category and memo sections normally. You don't need to worry about recording an address as Quicken assumes you will also hand address the envelope.

TIP   **Automatic Check Numbering**   So long as you keep your checkbook and checking register synchronized, you can use the Num/Ref option **Next Check Num** instead of typing in the check number each time.

CAUTION   **Mixing Handwritten and Printed Checks**   If you use Quicken to print checks for one checking account but also write checks to that account by hand, make sure you always verify the number recorded with the Next Check Num option. Otherwise, as soon as you switch from one to the other, it will jump out of sequence. This could lead to significant confusion the next time you work through a bank reconciliation.

However, if you print your checks, you should use Quicken's check writing facility. Just follow these steps:

1. To open the check writing window, select the menu **Features, Bills, Write Checks** (Ctrl+W), or open the Activity Bar **Bills, Write a Check to Print**.
2. Check the tabs running along the bottom of the window. These show every account with check writing facilities. The list may include checking accounts, savings accounts, money market accounts, investment accounts and more. Click the one corresponding to the account you need to use.

TIP   **Reordering the Tabs**   You may already know this from using the register window. If the ordering of the checkbook tabs doesn't suit, just click them and drag them back and forth along the row using your mouse. Quicken remembers the new order and restores it the next time you open the check window.

3. The check writing window shown in Figure 9.1 is divided into two sections. Use the upper to fill out the check. The lower section lists the checks
   waiting to be printed. This list includes checks created directly in the
   checking register when the Num/Ref field was set to **Print**. Sandwiched
   between the two is the category field and the **Record Check** button. Use
   the following as a guide to filling in the check's fields:

   - **Date**   While the default entry is today's date, you can also forward
     or back date this check. Use the icon to select a date using Quicken's
     calendar tool.

   - **Pay to the Order of**   This is the standard payee list. If you have
     written a check to the payee previously, type in the first few letters of
     the payee name to recall the memorized transaction. Otherwise, click
     the down arrow to scan the list of all memorized transactions, or
     simply type in a new payee.

   - **Address**   (Optional) Use this field to record the address (if any) that
     should be printed on the check along with the payee. If you are using
     a past payee, the address is entered automatically. The address is
     only necessary if you are also using Quicken's windowed envelopes.
     This will save you from hand addressing your envelopes.

   - **Memo**   This memo field prints on the outgoing check. If you use
     Quicken's windowed envelopes, it may even be visible through the
     envelope's window so it is best to avoid using this for sensitive
     information. You might like to use the memo to show the payee's
     invoice number to you. After you have recorded this check, you can
     search for it on that invoice number as well as the payee name and
     your own check number.

TIP   **Printing Hidden Messages on Checks**   While the memo field is handy
for most messages, you should use the message line facility to include sensitive information that is hidden from view through the envelope's window. To do
this, switch on the extra message. Select the menu **Edit, Options, Write
Checks...** and click in the box for **Allow Entry of Extra Message on Check**.

- **Category** Use this line as you have any other category window. You can record categories, classes, splits (click **Split**), transfers, or just leave it blank.

4. (Optional) Click **Online Payment** to pay this check through the Online Center. If you haven't made an online payment to this payee before, you will be asked to provide an address and specify their account and telephone number. You can read about this in Part 3.

5. When you've finished, click **Record Check** to store this transaction and open a new, blank check window. If you have set Quicken to immediately print your checks, it will do just that. Otherwise, it will add that check to the "To be printed" list. To find out more about printing checks, see below.

TIP **Regular Payments** If you regularly send checks for the same amount to the same payee, see Lesson 10 to learn about scheduled payments. To learn about the online version of these payments, see Part 3.

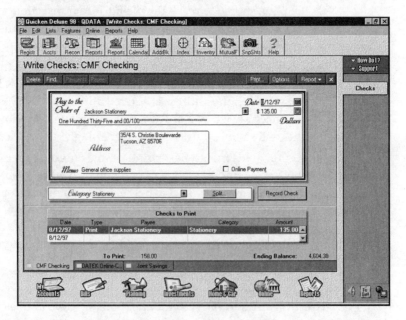

Figure 9.1 Quicken simulates a printed check, providing a blank into which you can enter the necessary details.

Printing Checks

You may print checks as a batch or individually.

When you print checks as a batch, they are stored in a special list as they are created. At the end of the day, you just need to load the blank checks into your printer and select **Print**, churning them out at once.

You may be surprised to learn that the procedure for printing individual checks is identical to printing a batch. In fact, the only difference between the two is that when you print single checks, you in effect print your checks in batches of one.

The first time you print your checks, you will need to set up Quicken to use your printer and your particular style of Quicken checks. See "Setting Up for Check Printing" below.

To print your checks, either open the Write Checks window and click the **Print** button in the upper right corner, or select **File, Print Checks** from the menu bar. The first only works when you have the check window open. The second works whenever you have a register with check-writing capabilities open.

Batch printing is most useful if you use the standard or wallet style of blank checks. This is because each sheet of paper contains three checks. While it isn't very difficult starting Quicken's printing part of the way through a sheet of checks, it is certainly more convenient to do so once every print run rather than once every check. Also, if you use your printer for other purposes besides printing checks—something applicable to almost every Quicken user—it is more convenient to load the check paper once at the start of a batch printing run than every time you need to print a check.

TIP　**Add a Second Printer**　If you do find yourself printing numerous checks each day, as well as using that printer for other purposes, considering purchasing a dual-tray printer or even purchasing a second printer that is dedicated to check runs. Cheap laser printers only cost three or four hundred dollars and inkjet printers even less. You will also find a second printer useful if both trays of your current laser are tied up with letterhead and standard paper.

Setting Up for Check Printing

Before you can print your first batch of checks, you need to tell Quicken about the checks you want to use and how you intend to print them. Just follow these steps:

1. Select the menu **File, Printer Setup, For Printing Checks**. This will open the dialog shown in Figure 9.2.

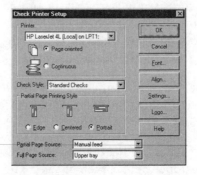

Figure 9.2   You will use this dialog to set up your printer and decide how your checks should be printed.

2. Use the **Printer** pull-down list to select your printer.

3. Choose between **Page-oriented** or **Continuous** paper. Page-oriented is most often used for laser printers whereas continuous or fan-fold paper is only suitable for impact printers.

4. Select a **Check Style**. This is the style you chose when you first ordered your checks from Quicken.

5. (Optional) Select the Partial Page Printing Style. This setting depends on your printer. If your printer prints envelopes (and therefore partial checks) hard against the left-hand edge of the paper feed, select **Edge**. (Most Hewlett-Packard printers are built like this.) If your printer prints envelopes with the envelope centered within the paper feed, select **Centered**. Most postscript printers behave like this. If your printer prints envelopes with the long edge against the printer paper feed, select **Portrait**.

6. (Optional) Select the paper sources. If your printer will always contain blank checks, leave this at automatic. However, you might prefer to specify the Partial Page Source as **Manual**. This will let you hand feed partial pages. If you want to be reminded to insert each sheet of blank checks, leave Partial Page Source and Full Page Source at **Upper Tray**.

7. (Optional) The default font is Arial, 9pt. To change this, click **Font**. Arial is an economical and easy to read typeface, so you should probably leave it as is unless you have a very specific purpose.

8. (Optional) Click **Align** to open the Align Checks dialog box. You should use this box if your full or partial pages aren't printing correctly. Click each button shown in Figure 9.3 to change the position of the printed information. You will see a new dialog that lets you adjust the fine alignment and also print a sample page. You may need to adjust each type of page several times to obtain an optimum result. However, to save yourself from burning up a lot of blank checks, simply print the samples on paper cut to the same size of the Quicken printed checks. Hold them over a blank check and up to the light to check the alignment.

9. (Optional) Click **Settings** to adjust your own printer's settings.

10. (Optional) Click **Logo** to specify a logo to include on your checks. You must import the logo from a Windows Bitmap (.bmp) file. It is limited to 64K in size. You can create the logo using almost any Windows drawing or paint packages, including the version of Windows Paint that ships with Windows 95. However, make sure you perform a test print to make sure it's okay before placing it on your checks.

Figure 9.3 The printed information on each check can be nudged horizontally and vertically.

Running Your Check Through the Printer

Once you've recorded your checks and setup up your printer, you're ready to start printing! This is the easy part—just follow these steps:

1. Open the register that corresponds to the checks you need to print.

2. Select the menu **File, Print Checks**. You will see the dialog shown in Figure 9.4.

3. This dialog looks complex, but it's really quite easy. Just type the first check number you wish to print. This is the check number shown on the page inserted in your printer. It is important that you match this up—don't just rely on Quicken's guess.

4. In the Print group select the checks you wish to print. The options are:

- **All Checks**   Print every check not previously printed.
- **Checks Dated Through:**   Print all checks recorded before or on a certain date.
- **Selected Checks**   Click **Choose** to print only those checks you mark in the list.

5. Select the Check Style. This must match the style of the blank checks inserted in your printer.

6. Indicate how many checks are on the first page. This isn't valid for Voucher Checks, but is for the other two.

7. (Optional) Use the Options group to choose whether or not to print a logo. Also, if you are using Voucher Checks, you can indicate how many additional copies you would like of each.

8. (Optional) Click **Alert** to open the Alerts window. From here you can set a warning for when this account approaches a minimum balance.

Figure 9.4   Use this dialog box to start printing Checks.

Now you're ready to print. To print just the first check in the list, click **Print First**. To print the entire batch, click **OK**. Print First is a handy way to quickly generate your oldest check. However, to print a specific check, click **Selected Checks**, then **Choose**. This will open the Select Check to Print dialog. Click **Clear All** to remove all previous checkmarks and click in the Print column of the check you need to print. Click **Done** and then **OK** to churn that check out of your printer. As soon as Quicken has finished printing, it opens the dialog shown in Figure 9.5. Don't just click **OK**. Carefully look over the checks you have printed. If you spot any mistakes, type in the number of the first check to show a mistake. Quicken will keep that and all remaining checks on the to-be-printed list, letting you have another shot at automated check printing once you've solved the problem.

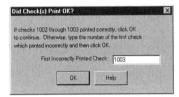

Figure 9.5 After your checks have printed, use this dialog to indicate the first of those that require reprinting.

In this lesson, you learned everything you need to know about printing checks. In the next lesson, you will learn how to set scheduled payments, reminders and alerts.

The Financial Calendar, Scheduled Payments, and Alerts

In this lesson, you will learn how to set reminders, schedule upcoming and repeated payments, and set automatic alerts.

Quicken makes bill payments easy, but if you're the type to either forget when a payment is due or you have a calendar hanging on your wall blackened with handwritten notes, you'll appreciate Quicken's reminder facilities.

The software can help in you three different ways:

1. Notes placed in Quicken's financial calendar can nudge your memory on almost any matter from when payments are due to when you should take your cat for its annual checkup.

2. Scheduled payments automatically create the payment transaction, adding it to your list of checks to be printed.

3. Alerts warn when an account balance falls below a certain level, when a stock hits a certain price, and when tax payments are due. There are many more alerts besides these. They'll help you to avoid situations that could prove costly or embarrassing to ignore.

Using the Financial Calendar

Think of the financial calendar as Memory Central. It is here you can note previous transactions, schedule future transactions, and set reminders.

To open the calendar, select the menu **Features, Reminders, Financial Calendar**.

The window shown in Figure 10.1 is made up of a monthly calendar display, a memorized transaction list, and a graph that shows selected account balances through the month. The graph isn't displayed by default, but you can turn it on by using the View pull-down menu in the upper left corner of the calendar window. You can also use this menu to turn off the memorized transaction list. The calendar always expands to fill all available space.

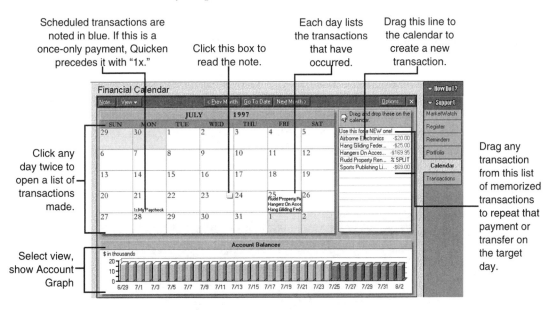

Scheduled transactions are noted in blue. If this is a once-only payment, Quicken precedes it with "1x."

Click this box to read the note.

Each day lists the transactions that have occurred.

Drag this line to the calendar to create a new transaction.

Click any day twice to open a list of transactions made.

Drag any transaction from this list of memorized transactions to repeat that payment or transfer on the target day.

Select view, show Account Graph

Figure 10.1 This figure illustrates using the Financial Calendar.

Setting Notes

The easiest way to create a reminder is to add a note to the day that reminder falls due. Quicken is limited to one note per calendar day and that note is limited to a maximum of 500 characters. However, feel free to squeeze in as many subjects as you can.

While the notes system is fairly rudimentary—you wouldn't use it for scheduling appointments, for instance—if you just want to give yourself a mental prod to call the stockbroker, send your mother a birthday card, renew your club membership, or something similar, it should prove all you require.

To set a note, select the target calendar day and click **Note** in the upper left corner of the calendar window. Alternatively, use the right mouse button to click the target day and select **Note** from the pull-down menu.

Use the Note dialog to record the message, as shown in Figure 10.2. Select a color for the note and click **Save** to inscribe it on your calendar.

CAUTION

Advance Reminders Quicken's default reminder system shows notes for the current week only. You can change this to show notes for the entire coming month using the menu **Edit, Options, Reminders…**. Set the notice under **Show notes for:**. Quicken brings all other reminders to your attention seven days in advance. If this doesn't provide you with enough notice, you can change it to provide up to 30 business days' notice. Adjust the entry for **Days in Advance** as necessary.

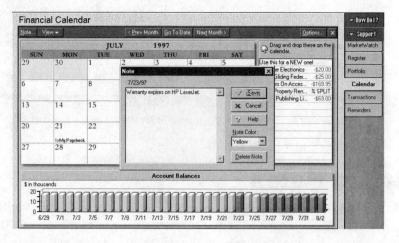

Figure 10.2 Quicken's notes are an easy way to attach short reminders to calendar days.

Scheduling Transactions

A scheduled transaction is one created and flagged for a future date. The simplest form of scheduled transaction is a forward-dated payment transaction entered into any register. Quicken recognizes forward dating and changes the register so that it displays two totals: Current Balance (the balance before taking the forward-dated transaction into account), and an all-up Ending Balance.

TIP **Forward Dating** This method works well for transactions that occur only once; however, those transactions don't integrate at all with Quicken's calendar system, and Quicken will try to print any forward-dated checks, even if they don't fall due for years.

Scheduled transactions solve problems inherent in forward dating. Not only can you set a transaction date any length of time ahead, Quicken will remind you before it falls due and also take that transaction into account in any forward-looking reports; for instance, a projected account balance.

Even better, a scheduled transaction can occur once, a limited number of times, or forever at predetermined intervals. You manage your scheduled transactions by using the scheduled transaction list. Select the menu **Lists, Scheduled Transaction** (Ctrl+J). You will see the window shown in Figure 10.3.

Scheduled Online Payments If you have already set up online payments, the window shown in Figure 10.3 will look somewhat different. You should see two tabs. One displays your standard scheduled transactions and **CAUTION** the other your scheduled online payments. You can learn more about scheduling online payments in Part 3.

Use this window to create new scheduled transactions, edit or delete transactions, bundle transactions into groups, and force early payments of transactions (select them and click **Pay**). If you have a very long list, use the pull-down menu **Sort by:** to change their order.

While you can create a new scheduled transaction by dragging one of your existing transactions from the memorized list onto the financial calendar (or by dragging the entry "Use this for a NEW one!"), you will find it easier to do so from the Scheduled Transaction List.

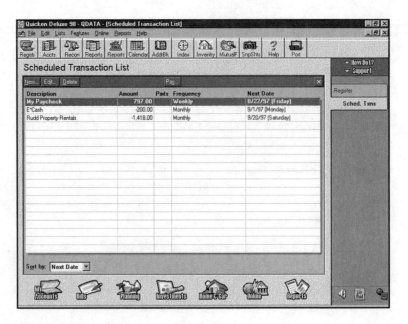

Figure 10.3 The Scheduled Transaction List.

 TIP **Scheduling a Once-Only Transaction** You don't need to create a scheduled transaction for a single future transaction. Instead, open your Financial Calendar and drag the previously memorized transaction (or the line "Use this for a NEW one!") to the target date. In the lower third of the dialog box, click **Register Transaction** and select one of the options available under the **Number** pull-down list, as shown in Figure 10.5. This is the Num/Ref field that should be familiar to you from entering transactions directly into any register. The same options apply here as they do in the register. Click **OK** to save the transaction.

You can also use this list to group related transactions so that they occur all at once. You'll learn about grouping in Part 4 where the feature is used to process a business's payroll. Meanwhile, just follow these steps to create a new scheduled transaction (see Figure 10.4). These steps assume you are creating an ordinary scheduled payment. If you need to create a scheduled online payment, see Part 3.

1. Make sure your scheduled transaction list is open. If not, select the menu **Lists, Scheduled Transaction (Ctrl+J)**.

2. Click **New...** to create a new transaction and click **OK**. If you are creating an online scheduled payment, choose **Repeating Online Payments** and click **OK**. See Part 3 for further instructions on completing this transaction.

TIP **A Real World Example**   Carol uses Quicken for all her personal finances. She has set up four scheduled transactions: One pays her rent each month; the second records a weekly deduction from her salary to her retirement account; the third transfers $200 to an investment fund every two weeks; and the fourth pays her mortgage on time, every time. As each scheduled transaction rolls by, Carol approves the payments and transfers, and relaxes while Quicken handles the paperwork.

3. Fill out the top of the dialog box as follows:

Account to use: This is the account or register you will use to record this transaction.

Type of transaction: Choose between **Payment, Deposit, Print Check,** or **Online Pmt**.

Payee   Type in a new payee or select a memorized transaction from the pull-down list.

Address   (Optional) If you are using preprinted checks and windowed envelopes, type in an address. This will save you from hand-addressing the envelope.

Date   When do you want this transaction entered into the calendar and register? Type the date or select it by using the calendar icon.

Category   This field replicates the category field from any register transaction. You may record categories or account transfers. Click **Split** to divide this transaction between two or more categories or transfers.

Amount   Enter the total of this transaction.

Memo   Whatever you enter here will be copied to the memo field in the register transaction.

4. Fill in the lower part of the dialog box by using these additional scheduling options:

How Often   The default is **Only Once**. However, you may specify a range of common frequencies from weekly to yearly.

Record in Register   If you want this to be a hands-off transaction, select **Automatically Enter**. Select **Prompt before enter** for Quicken to ask you to confirm this transaction before it goes ahead.

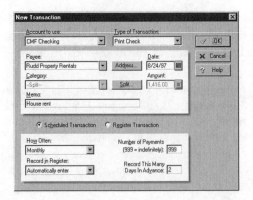

Figure 10.4 This figure illustrates recording a Scheduled Transaction.

Number of Payments Use this field to specify how many times you want this payment to occur. For instance, if you have 36 payments to make on a personal loan, enter 36 here. Use 999 for an infinite number of payments. You cannot edit this field if Only Once is selected under How Often.

Record This Many Days in Advance Use this field to specify the days in advance of the due date that you want this transaction recorded in the register. The transaction is recorded on that date as a postdated transaction. For example, a payment set to record 5 days in advance and due on January 20 would be recorded in the register on January 15. If the payment is to be made by check, the check will be printed with the date payable set to January 20. This field will help you allow for postal delays and the like if something absolutely must be paid by a certain date.

CAUTION

Billminder Users If you use Billminder (described as follows), you should know that Quicken will notify you of the payment by Billminder's own advance notice added to the notice you specify when recording the scheduled transaction. Therefore, if Billminder is set to give you 7 days' notice on all your scheduled transactions and you have selected an additional 5 days under the transaction's field **Record This Many Days in Advance**, you will receive a total of 12 days' notice (7 days + 5 days) before the transaction falls due.

5. Once you have finished, click **OK** to save this transaction.

Scheduled transactions are easy to create and a great way to see how your cash flow will appear in a month, week, or even a full year's time. The more scheduled transactions you create, the more automated your bookkeeping becomes. They are also the perfect way to never miss another important loan repayment.

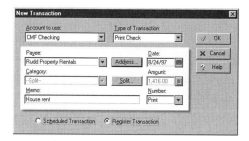

Figure 10.5   Use the financial calendar with rh4ister w?ansactions to schedule once-only payments.

Marking Scheduled Transactions as Paid

Unless you have specifically told Quicken to automatically record your scheduled transactions, you will still need to record them when they fall due.

Each of the following methods takes you to the Record Scheduled Transaction dialog box. Use this dialog box to edit the transaction, type in a memo, and specify a check number or similar. When you finish, click **Record**.

You will find your scheduled transactions within the following areas:

- **Financial Calendar**   From within the calendar, click once on the day the transaction falls due and again to open the transaction list. Select the transactions and click **Pay Now**. Record the payment as described previously.

- **Reminders List**   Open the reminders list by using the menu **Planning, Reminders**. You will also see the list if you accessed Quicken from the Billminder. Select the transaction and click **Enter in Register**. Record the payment as described previously.

- **Scheduled Transaction List**   From within the list, select the transaction and click **Pay**. Record the payment as described previously.

While it is easy to set up scheduled transactions so that they are recorded without any interference from you, keeping this step in place gives you the opportunity to verify the payment and also to make any last-minute edits. For example, if you are recording a regular rental payment, you can use the Record Scheduled Transaction dialog box to also record a memo giving the period over which that payment is valid.

Alerts

Alerts are as useful as scheduled transactions. Indeed, they are the closest Quicken comes to doing your worrying for you—and anything that can do that must be pretty good! To open the list of Alerts, select the menu **Features, Reminders, Alerts**. You will see the dialog box shown in Figure 10.6.

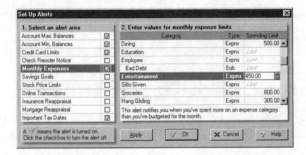

Figure 10.6   Alerts are one of Quicken's handiest features. You can set them to flag you after certain events have occurred.

Alerts perform numerous functions. Here are just a few examples:

- **Credit Cards**   If you are in the habit of bending the plastic rather more than is good for it, you can easily set an alert that will remind you when it's getting close to that snapping point.

- **Dining**   A similar problem. It's fun dining out but it's also easy to fall into the trap of doing so twice, thrice, or even more times per week. You can set an alert for this and any other expense or income category calculated on the amount you have spent so far in the current calendar month. This is not the same as Quicken's budgeting system, but it is quicker and easier.

- **Stock Prices**   Whether you dabble or invest heavily in the stock market, you'll find stock price alerts particularly useful. Simply set the upper and lower limits. If the stock price exceeds either, you'll be immediately notified.

CAUTION

Stock Splits   The stock price limits do not take stock splits into account. If the stock splits and you don't know about it, you may find the true value of your stock soaring or plummeting without triggering an alert.

- **Account Balances**   The Alerts system supports both account minimum and maximum balances. While the minimum balance on a checking account is useful for obvious reasons, the minimum and maximum balances used together are a great way to maintain a healthy balance in your various asset accounts. For instance, it is good practice to maintain a generous working minimum in your checking account but to quickly shift any surplus to short or long-term investments. You can use the surplus to pay a little extra on your mortgage (leading to high long-term benefits), or to deposit into other forms of investment. The Alerts system gives you the opportunity to establish a system for managing your finances and the encouragement to stick to it.

To create and maintain your Alerts, follow these steps:

1. Open the Alerts window (see Figure 10.6) by using the menu **Features, Reminders, Alerts**.

2. Select the target of your interest in the Alert Area list. For example, click **Important Tax Dates** to look at alerts that will help you to remember when you should pay your quarterly estimated tax.

3. The uppermost text area on the right side explains each alert and the options available. The lower right window changes according to the currently selected alert. In general, you can choose from among the following options:

   - **Numerical Limits**   These are used for the Account Balances, Credit Card Limits, and Stock Price Limits alerts. In some cases, you can set a pre-limit where you will be warned you are approaching the final limit.

- **Check Boxes** Check boxes are used in the Important Tax Dates, Online Banking, and many other alerts. Simply click the option you need to set the alert on and Quicken will do the rest.

- **Dates** Dates are used in the Insurance Reappraisal and Mortgage Reappraisal alerts. Enter a policy or lender name and set the date. You can set as many of these alerts as you require.

CAUTION

Alert Options   If you can't see any alert options, it probably means you aren't using an account or other feature appropriate for that alert. If you haven't set any stocks, you won't be able to specify upper and lower limits. Similarly, if you haven't specified any savings goals, none will appear under that alert.

4. When you have finished, click **OK** to save your changes.

Quicken displays its alerts through pop-up dialog boxes and in the Billminder utility. An alert doesn't prevent a transaction from taking place or some other event from occurring, and you can ignore it with the click of an **OK** button. Alerts exist simply to save you from tying knots around your fingers.

Using the Billminder

The Billminder is a useful helper application. When you install Quicken, the installation routine tells Windows to run Billminder every time Windows starts.

You cannot access Billminder through your Quicken menus or even via the Quicken program group attached to the Windows start menu. You can also never run Billminder alongside Quicken. However, you can use it to jump to Quicken right after you start your computer.

TIP **Running Billminder Without Rebooting Your Computer**   If you ever need to recheck your reminders without loading Quicken, you can do so quickly and efficiently with the Billminder utility. To start Billminder, click the Windows **Start** button, then **Programs, Startup, Billminder**.

Figure 10.7 shows Billminder in action. Click any folder to expand it to show the full detail of the transactions underneath, or to collapse it to view a single total. Click **Run Quicken** to jump straight to Quicken.

Billminder shows the details contained in all your Quicken files. However, if any of those files are password protected, it will hide sensitive information such as the sums involved in those transactions.

If you don't want to use Billminder, select the box **Turn Off Billminder**. To turn it back on or to adjust Billminder's other options, use the Quicken menu **Edit, Options, Reminders…**. Click the **Billminder** tab and select **Turn On Billminder** to reverse your earlier choice.

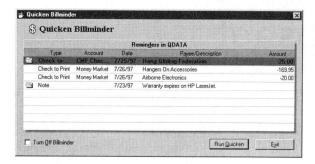

Figure 10.7   Billminder will help you start each day knowing precisely what's coming up.

In this lesson, you learned about the financial calendar, scheduling payments, setting alerts, and the Billminder. In the next lesson, you will learn how to create and customize a financial snapshot.

Creating a Financial Snapshot

In this lesson, you learn how to use the Financial Snapshots window to help you view your most important financial statistics at one time.

The Big Picture

Quicken is great at managing the particulars of your finances but what's Quicken like at delivering the big picture? As you might have guessed, extremely good. In fact, Quicken is excellent at turning a mass of information into a series of highly informative reports and graphs. The big picture is important because it helps you concentrate on the general drift of your finances. Just as worrying over every small rise and fall in a stock's price is bad news for any investor's portfolio, so, too, you should try to avoid following individual account balances. Rather, look at your real or net worth. Your equity in your home may have improved over the past few months, but perhaps at the expense of your savings or investment accounts. With Quicken, you can see how they balance.

Quicken offers two primary tools for obtaining this financial overview: charts and reports. These come together in a Financial Snapshot window, easily one of Quicken's most powerful and useful features.

Generating a Financial Snapshot

The Financial Snapshot window displays between two and six panes. Each pane contains a graph, report, or calendar notes.

While a graph or report displayed in an area one-sixth of the standard Quicken size may seem rather crowded, the graphs work admirably, well and you shouldn't experience too much trouble reading the reports. Just double-click any pane (or click **Enlarge**), and you will immediately zoom into a full-screen view. Alternatively, click **Print** to generate a printed report. Your printer probably has a much finer resolution than your computer's monitor, so a printed version of the six-pane report is significantly clearer than the same report seen on-screen.

Figure 11.1 shows a typical snapshot window. To create it, select **Reports**, **Snapshots** or click the **SnpShts** icon.

CAUTION

Why Do I Only See Four Snapshot Panes? If you are running Windows in a resolution less than 800x600 pixels—for instance, 640x480 pixels; the Windows default—Quicken can only display two or four snapshot windows at a time. To view snapshot panes in combinations of three or six, you must change to a higher resolution.

To view the base figures and percentages behind any bar in any graph, simply pause the mouse pointer over that bar for a second or two.

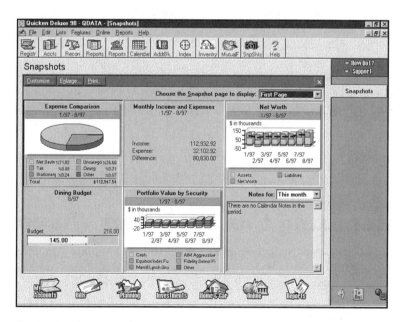

Figure 11.1 The Financial Snapshot window.

The default snapshot settings show the following windows:

- Expense Comparison
- Monthly Income and Expenses
- Net Worth
- Dining Budget
- Portfolio Value by Security
- Notes

You can change the contents of any pane to display one of many reports or graphs. Furthermore, you can display many specific reports in either text or graph form. Use the former if you prefer the accuracy of hard figures and the latter if you find the visual view more useful.

While it isn't possible to display more than six panes at one time, if you look in the upper right corner of the Snapshot window, you will see a pull-down list called **Choose the Snapshot page to display:**. As this suggests, there is no limit to the number of snapshot pages you can create. You may, for instance, adjust this First Page so that it concentrates on your net worth. A second page could concentrate on your home accounts and budgets while a third might deal almost exclusively with your investments. A fourth and final page can target your small business dealings.

Snapshots are only limited by your imagination. With the capability to not only change each page and pane but also to select the accounts, categories, securities, or other data used to generate that graph or report, it is possible to turn Quicken's financial snapshots into the single most important barometer of your financial well-being.

All you need to know is how to customize those snapshots.

Customizing the Snapshot Window

The standard snapshots are useful, but they may not prove ideal. For example, the Dining Budget snapshot is helpful, but what if you are more interested in how well you have stuck to some other budget?

To customize the Snapshot window, follow these steps:

1. With the Snapshot window open, click **Customize**. You see the window shown in Figure 11.2.

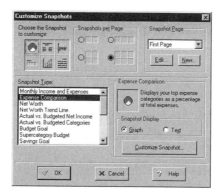

Figure 11.2 Use this dialog box to customize the Snapshot window until it shows precisely what you need to know.

2. This display is divided into several areas. Clockwise from upper left, they are:

- **Choose the Snapshot to Customize:** Click one of the boxes here to select the snapshot pane you want to adjust.

- **Snapshots Per Page** Select the number of snapshot panes you want to display at one time. Obviously, the fewer the number of panes, the more room you will have to examine the detail of each.

- **Snapshot Page** Name of the current page. Use the pull-down list to move from one page to the next.

- **(Name of Report or Graph)** This small area provides you with a quick description of the current report or graph. Where supported, it will also let you change that snapshot from a graph to a report or vice versa.

- **Customize Snapshot** Opens Quicken's standard report or graph customization window. You can customize any snapshot with as much finesse as you can any full-screen graph or report. Just select the accounts, categories, or classes to include.

- **Snapshot Type** Use this scrolling list to select the graph or report that will appear; there are 18 to choose from. At the end of the list, you will find a snapshot called <None>. Use this if you would rather display a blank pane than additional information.

TIP   **Snapshot Types**   If you are puzzled about which snapshot to choose, scroll through the list of snapshot types, reading about each in the descriptive area to its immediate left.

3. The small representation in the upper left corner is a very close approximation of each of the snapshots in the main display. Click the snapshot you want to modify. You will see its title appear below **Snapshot Type:**.

4. To change the type, just select another from the list. To switch from a report to a graph, click **Graph** or **Text**, where available.

5. To create another snapshot page, click **New** and type in the page's name. You can create subsequent pages with any number and combination of snapshots.

6. When you finish, click **OK** to save the changes and return to the Snapshots window.

The snapshot display is one of Quicken's most impressive tools. While the default layout does a great job, you will reap even greater benefit from one or more customized panes.

In this lesson, you learned how to create, use, and customize the financial snapshots window. In the next lesson, you will learn how to use Quicken's reports to answer your most important financial questions.

Getting Answers with Reports and Graphs

In this lesson, you will learn how to create, customize, and work with Quicken's reports and graphs. You will also learn about the EasyAnswers feature.

An Overview of Quicken's Reports and Graphs

Quicken's reports and graphs form a formidable team.

All of the reports and graphs are accessible through the Reports menu. Besides **EasyAnswer Reports**, **Snapshots** and, if you have created any, an entry for **Memorized Reports**, you can see the following groups:

- **Home Reports**   See Table 12.1.
- **Investment Reports**   Table 12.2.
- **Business Reports**   Table 12.3.
- **Other Reports**   Table 12.4.
- **Graphs**   Table 12.5.

To generate a report or graph, select it from the menu. This opens a Create Report dialog box similar to that shown in Figure 12.1 or a Create Graph dialog box similar to Figure 12.2.

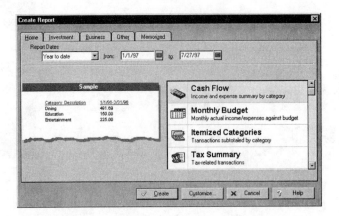

Figure 12.1   Every report begins with a dialog box similar to this.

Figure 12.2   Click **Create** to jump straight to the graph or **Customize** to change its parameters.

Each report or graph performs a different function, but many are based on similar principles. In fact, you can often spot the different methods used to build those reports just by looking in the Customization window.

Between the built-in reports, graphs, and the EasyAnswers system, it is very easy to extract the information you need, when you need it. However, if you are to make the most of Quicken, you will probably need to create your own customized versions of some of Quicken's most popular reports.

There is enormous similarity between the customization dialog boxes, so if you can use one, feel confident you can use them all.

Reports are customized four ways. These are controlled by the tabs you see in any customization dialog box (see Figure 12.3). They are:

- **Display** Adjusts the included dates, the grouping of lines, ordering of columns, and other aspects of the overall layout, such as the title and detail displayed in each line.

- **Accounts** Choose which account types should be included in this report. Even if you select every account, not all will be included. For an account to make a showing, that account must contain transactions of the type required by the report.

- **Include** Select the categories, classes, or transactions that will be searched for the data to complete your report. If the report targets an investment account or your investment portfolio, use this tab to select specific securities.

- **Advanced** Useful for specifying tax-related categories, the types of transactions to be included (deposits, payments, unprinted checks, or all), the status of checks (blank, newly cleared, or reconciled), and the inclusion of transfers and subcategories.

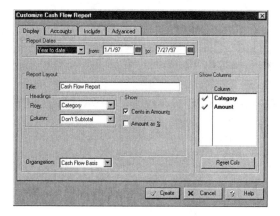

Figure 12.3 The Display tab is a great place to customize the reports presentation.

You can customize graphs in three different ways, using a dialog box quite different but also simpler than the reports. Depending on the type of graph you customize, you will tabs named Accounts, Categories and Classes, or Accounts and Include. Despite their differing titles, each of the tabs works the same way. All you need to do is place a check mark beside those items under each tab that you want included in your graph (see Figure 12.4).

TIP **Memorizing Customized Reports and Graphs** Quicken provides a simple method for memorizing your customized reports and graphs. While they appear on-screen, click the **Memorize** button, assign a title, select the report dates, enter an optional description, select an item, and click **OK**. Once you create your first memorized report, a new Memorized Reports menu item appears in the Reports menu. You will also see a new tab in the Create Report dialog box. Memorized graphs appear in their own Quicken window. You can access them by selecting **Reports, Graphs, Memorized Graphs**.

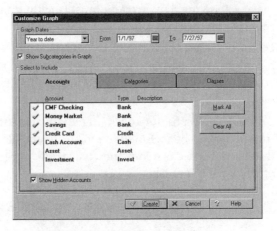

Figure 12.4 Each of the customization tabs in the graph work the same way. Place a check mark beside those items you want to include.

While customizing a report is guaranteed to get you the results you need, until you are used to the procedure, you will probably find it easiest to turn to the EasyAnswer Reports.

Getting Answers Fast

To open the EasyAnswers dialog box shown in Figure 12.5, select **Reports, EasyAnswer Reports**.

The EasyAnswers system doesn't create new forms of reports or graphs. However, it does simplify the customization of many of those described in this lesson's tables. Instead of wading through the customization dialog box, you can get the answers you need in a friendly, self-prompting format.

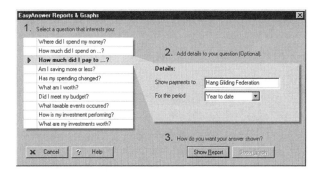

Figure 12.5 Looking for the easy answers? Look no further than the EasyAnswers dialog box.

For example, assume you want to quickly tally up how much you have paid to someone in the past year. You can follow these steps:

1. Select **Reports, EasyAnswer Reports**.

2. In the left-hand list, select the question **How Much Did I Pay To?**.

3. Use **Show Payment To** to supply the name of the payee. Quicken's QuickFill feature completes the name for you.

4. Select the period you are interested in.

5. Click **Show Report**. You should see a result similar to that shown in Figure 12.6.

Working with Reports and Graphs

Quicken's reports and graphs are anything but static displays. The buttons or fields that run across the top of the window let you change how that report or graph appears, as well as the information it conveys. Furthermore, move your mouse pointer over almost any detail line in any report (see Figure 12.6) and double-click to zoom through to the transaction or transactions that contributed to it.

The same applies to graphs. Click one of the bars in a graph showing your investment performance based on the year to date, and Quicken will give you the performance of that security over the year. Alternatively, you may arrive at a financial breakdown based on the contents of that particular bar in the bar graph.

While the specific buttons change from report to report or graph to graph, a comparatively static set runs across the very top of each report or graph window. Figure 12.6 provides a general guide.

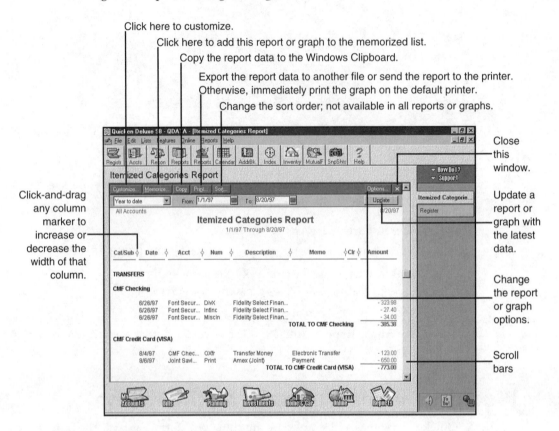

Click here to customize.

Click here to add this report or graph to the memorized list.

Copy the report data to the Windows Clipboard.

Export the report data to another file or send the report to the printer. Otherwise, immediately print the graph on the default printer.

Change the sort order; not available in all reports or graphs.

Close this window.

Click-and-drag any column marker to increase or decrease the width of that column.

Update a report or graph with the latest data.

Change the report or graph options.

Scroll bars

Figure 12.6 Working with reports and graphs.

Quicken's reporting and graphing features are some of the product's strongest features. With very little effort, you can create reports and graphs that are superbly tailored to your own needs, turning Quicken and your books into the ultimate financial analysis tool.

TIP **A Real World Example** Sharon is self-employed as a freelance makeup artist. Her business and personal books are combined in the one Quicken data file, however she keeps them in separate registers. Using the report customization features, she has been able to create two sets of memorized reports and graphs using Quicken's default reports as templates. One set targets her home and investment accounts while the other targets her business accounts. This lets her view one or the other side of her finances even while being able to take it all in as a whole.

The Quicken Reports

Quicken provides a veritable wealth of reports and graphs. These are shown in Tables 12.1 to 12.5. You can use these reports as they are or customize them to provide precisely the results you require. Each Table is split up according to the way those reports are stored under Quicken's Reports menu.

Unavailability of Some Reports   Not all of these reports are available in the standard version of Quicken. However, with the exception of the two noted as specific to Quicken Home and Business 98, they are all available in Quicken CAUTION   Deluxe 98.

Home Reports

The Home Reports shown in Table 12.1 are more useful for reporting on you and your spouse's personal finances. You will find reports under this menu ideal for calculating your net worth, searching out missing checks, preparing your tax return or managing your budget.

Table 12.1   Home Reports

Title	Description
Cash Flow	Shows your income and expenses by category for transactions included in your checking, cash, and credit card accounts.
Monthly Budget	Shows how well you stick to your budget.
Itemized Categories	Groups your transactions by category. Within each group it displays income transactions first, then expense transactions.
Tax Summary	Shows and subtotals the transactions contained in every tax-related category. This report does not include transactions made in tax-deferred accounts.
Net Worth	What you are worth.

continues

Table 12.1   Continued

Title	Description
Tax Schedule	Totals transactions flagged to tax-related categories, according to the specific tax form line items indicated during each category's setup.
Missing Checks	Lists your checks in sequence, highlighting duplicated numbers.
Comparison	Compares your cash flow across two time periods.

Investment Reports

If you use Quicken's investment accounts, you will find the reports listed in Table 12.2 particularly handy. Just one word of warning: the Capital Gains report does not take "wash sales" into account. Wash sales apply to securities sold at a loss less than 30 days after they were purchased.

Table 12.2   Investment Reports

Title	Description
Portfolio Value	Shows the value of each security and your portfolio as a whole as of a certain date. Columns include cost basis, current price and gain/loss.
Investment Performance	Shows the average annual rate of return for your investments, calculating an annual percent gain.
Capital Gains	Summarizes your long- and short-term capital gains; only accurate if you have correctly recorded your initial purchase of each of your investments.
Investment Income	Summarizes your investments, totaling capital gains, dividends received, and realized gains.
Investment Transactions	Lists all the investment transactions that have occurred over a particular time period.

Business Reports

Quicken's business reports turn the personal finance package into a powerful small business reporting facility. You can use these reports to track down debtors, prepare for tax-time, produce a balance sheet, report on the payroll and more. Table 12.3 provides a guide.

Table 12.3 Business Reports

Title	Description
P&L Statement	Creates a profit-and-loss report, totaling your business income and expenses, resulting in your net gain/loss.
P&L Comparison	Compares the profit and loss across two time periods.
Cashflow	Identical to the Home Cashflow report.
A/P by Vendor	Summarizes your accounts payable by vendor. The vendor information is extracted from unprinted checks in your checking account.
A/R by Customer	Summarizes your accounts receivable by customer. This information is extracted by searching for transactions that haven't cleared through your asset accounts.
Job/Project	A profit-and-loss report filtered by class.
Payroll	Shows the income and expenses incurred under any category containing the word -**Payroll**-.
Balance Sheet	Summarizes your assets and liabilities; similar to the Home Net Worth report.
Missing Checks	This is identical to the Home Missing Checks report.
Comparison	This is identical to the Home Comparison report.
Tax Schedule	Creates a list of transactions assigned to tax-related business categories. (Only available in Quicken Home and Business 98.)
Schedule C	List Schedule C transactions taken from your tax-related business categories. (Only available in Quicken Home and Business 98.)

Other Reports

The reports shown in Table 12.4 are less specialized than the rest, but are equally useful in a personal finance or small business situation. They tend to target broad swathes of transactions, but are also useful when used as the basis for highly customized reports.

Table 12.4 Other Reports

Title	Description
Transaction	Shows a listing of all transactions from one or more registers, along with a running balance.
Summary	Subtotals by account, category, or class.
Comparison	Compares the income and expenses incurred in a single account over two time periods.
Budget	Compares your actual income and expense supercategories to your budgeted supercategories. If you don't use supercategories, it looks at your actual categories instead.
Account Balances	Summarizes the balances in all your accounts.
Reconciliation	Creates a reconciliation report for the current account; handy if you want to store a paper record of the opening and closing balances and transactions that haven't cleared. You can only select this report option from within a register.

Graphs

Quicken's graphs shown in Table 12.4 are bundled together under one menu. While many of these share titles similar to the reports listed in the previous tables, they display that data in a very different way. Their interactive nature makes them perfect for playing with your data, viewing them from a multitude of directions.

Table 12.5 Graphs

Title	Description
Income and Expense	Shows your income and expenses across categories and through the year.
Budget Variance	Compares your income and expenses by supercategories according to your budget.
Net Worth	Displays your net worth over the year to date. The graph shows the changing relationships between your assets, liabilities, and equity.
Investment Performance	Displays the value of your portfolio as well as its average annual rate of return You can view this graph by type, goal, security, account, or asset class.

Title	Description
Investment Asset Allocation	Displays a pie chart showing the mix of your investments by asset type. As your needs change, so should the assets. This chart will help you adjust the balance.

In this lesson, you learned about Quicken reports. You should now know how to create and memorize reports and graphs using the EasyAnswer system, the standard menu options, and through the customization capabilities. In the next lesson, you will learn how to use Quicken's budget planning facilities.

Budgeting and Forecasting

In this lesson, you will learn how to create and maintain a realistic budget, keep track of your achievement using a progress bar, and use Quicken's forecasting feature.

Banking On a Budget

Budgeting is not an exercise in frugality. It is about planning and balance. No matter how big or small your income, a budget will not only help you decide how you can distribute that income, but also help you to stick to the plan.

While the Alerts tool's Monthly Expenses reminder is the quickest and easiest way to rein in your expenditure—you learned about this in Lesson 10—you will gain far more benefit through learning about Quicken's specialized budgeting system.

With Quicken's built-in budgeting, you can:

- Create a realistic budget based on the previous year's figures.
- Use supercategories to look at broader tracts of your income and expense categories.
- Develop as many budgets as you require, taking into account best and worst scenarios, and more.
- Create reports and graphs that show you precisely how well you are sticking to that budget.
- Keep a constant tab on the budget using Quicken's Progress Bar.

A budget is a powerful financial organizer, yet creating one is easy. Furthermore, you shouldn't think of your budget as constraining. Actually, a budget is quite the opposite. Budgets give people a sense of freedom, helping them know when they can make that next purchase, whether large or small.

For example, imagine you have created a budget of your most important items. These might include groceries, mortgage repayments or rent, education, medical, utilities, tax, basic clothing, and automotive. These are your *nondiscretionary* items because you cannot avoid spending money on them. When you budget for these items, you budget for your basic essentials. Now, add any other items you consider vital to your lifestyle. These might include your holidays, entertainment, Internet and cable connections, theatre tickets, eating out in style once or twice a week, and so on. These are items that you enjoy but can probably do without. They are known as *discretionary* items.

A budget such as this establishes how much income you need to set aside for your basic essentials. You have also established a buffer zone for those things that are nice, but you don't necessarily need.

Budgets don't limit your spending. However, they help you establish solid working minimums. Any income that exceeds that minimum can be spent any way you want. If you can afford it, eat out every day of the week, even if you have only budgeted for one night a month. Alternatively, you might decide to put the surplus into an investment account, buy a new TV, restock the wardrobe, or whatever.

Using the Budget Window

You can create a budget in several easy steps. Here's the general plan:

1. Open the Budgeting tool.
2. Adjust the budgeting parameters.
3. Record the budget amounts in applicable categories.
4. Save and track the budget.

To open the budgeting tool, select **Features, Planning, Budgets**. Figure 13.1 provides a general guide to using the Budget window.

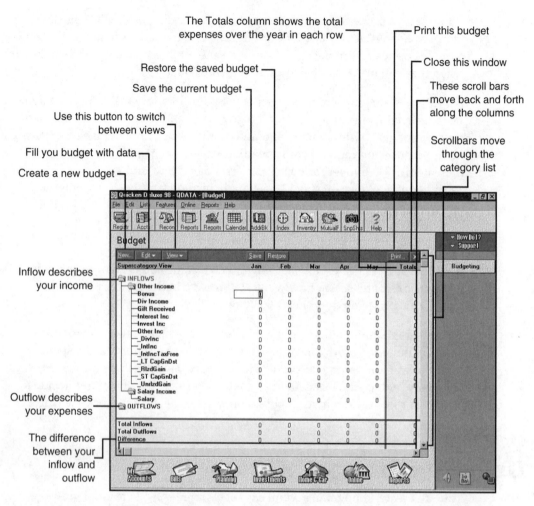

The Totals column shows the total
expenses over the year in each row

Print this budget

Restore the saved budget

Close this window

Save the current budget

These scroll bars
move back and forth
along the columns

Use this button to switch
between views

Scrollbars move
through the
category list

Fill you budget with data

Create a new budget

Inflow describes
your income

Outflow describes
your expenses

The difference
between your
inflow and
outflow

Figure 13.1   Using the Budget window.

Adjusting Your Budget's Parameters

Before you start creating your budget, decide how particular you want to be.
The Budget window supports a budget defined on a monthly, quarterly, or
yearly basis. To move from one to the other, select **View, Months, Quarters,** or
Years.

TIP **Switching Between Months, Quarters, and Years** Even if you change from months to quarters and quarters to years, Quicken retains your original data. If you don't change the figures in one of the other views, as soon as you get back to the original entry point, Quicken will restore the data contained in your original columns. If you start entering information in a coarser view such as quarters or years and then switch to months, Quicken averages the budgeted information to fill the new columns.

Before you start recording your budget, you need to choose between using standard categories and supercategories.

Limiting the budget list to supercategories is useful because the hard work has already been done for you in determining your discretionary and nondiscretionary items. If you need to add a category to a supercategory or think you can safely remove a category from a supercategory—remembering that you don't have to record a budget amount next to every category—select **Edit, Supercategories**. This will take you to the Manage Supercategories dialog box described in Lesson 8.

You may prefer to work with your standard categories in their standard list format. If that's the case, leave of the supercategories view. Use **View, Supercategories** to cycle between the two. Quicken will continue to divide the categories by income and expense (or inflow and outflow) but will ignore all other divisions, except those between categories and subcategories.

TIP **Budgeting on Transfers to Other Accounts** If you record regular transfers to other accounts to manage, perhaps, retirement or investment funds, you can budget for these along with other income or expense items. Select **View, Transfers** to place a check mark beside that menu item. Transfer budget items begin with **FROM** (for income items) or **TO** (for expense items) and are followed by the transfer account. To budget for regular transfers to a retirement account, search for the category **TO IRA** or **TO 401(k)**, or similar.

Recording Your Budgeted Amounts

Once you decide how to construct this budget, it's time to start recording the budget amounts.

If you are new to Quicken, you can do this by entering the amounts into each cell in the Budget window. Amounts typed into Income or Inflow categories appear in black, indicating these are positive amounts. Amounts typed into Expense or Outflow categories appear in red. While it is possible to record a negative income, it isn't possible to reverse the sign of an expense category.

For a detailed budget, this will take quite a while. Fortunately, Quicken provides several shortcuts that will help you to fill in the amounts automatically. Open the Edit menu and you'll see these commands:

- **2-Week** Helps you to budget for items you receive every second week (see Figure 13.2). For example, if you receive a paycheck on a biweekly basis, your pay dates will not follow the calendar months. Quicken doesn't calculate the portion of pay earned in any month. Rather, it applies the amount entered by the number of paychecks you will receive in that month. On most months, that's two, but on several calendar months of the year you may receive three paychecks. Make sure you have an income category such as Salary selected before choosing this menu item.

Figure 13.2 The two-week calculator will help you to budget for items that don't cycle by calendar month.

- **Copy All** Copies the budget data to the Windows Clipboard. This is only useful if you want to export your budget to another program such as a spreadsheet—in which case you can easily paste it in.
- **Clear Row** Clears any budget amounts entered into the current row. This is a useful way to quickly reduce the current budget category to zero.
- **Clear All** Erases the entire budget, returning every cell to a zero amount.
- **Autocreate** Use this item to base your current budget on previous Quicken data. You'll learn about this in a moment.
- **Fill Row Right** Copies the contents of the current cell in the current row to all cells to its right. For example, if you face a monthly rental bill of

$1,200, enter it once in the January column and select this menu item to copy that amount right through every remaining column, all the way to December.

- **Fill Columns** An extension to the Fill Row Right command. Instead of copying the contents of the current cell along the current row, this option copies every cell in the current column to its immediate right, and continues to do so until it has filled every column.

- **Supercategories** Use this item to access the Manage Supercategories dialog box.

As you can see, the easiest way to create a budget if you have never used Quicken before is to enter a single line of figures. Just fill those rows you want to budget, ignoring the rest. Then select **Edit, Fill Columns** to copy those values to the right.

TIP **Cleaning Up the Budget Display** Once you have filled in your budget, you can get rid of all of the rows displaying zero amounts. Select **View, Zero Budget Categories** to remove the check mark. That's all there is to it. Don't forget: If you want to add a new category later, select this menu once more to redisplay those zero amount rows.

If you have been using Quicken for some time, you can use your existing data to complete the budget. Once you've done that, edit those values as required and save the budget.

Save Your Budget! Quicken doesn't automatically save your budget each time you update a cell. You must click the **Save** button or close the Budget window for Quicken to update your budget data.

CAUTION

To create a budget using your existing data, select **Edit, Autocreate**. You will see the dialog shown in Figure 13.3. Follow these steps:

1. Use the **From:** and **To:** dates to bracket those transactions you want included in the Autocreate calculation. For example, if you started a new job three months ago, you would probably want to use the first of the month after that new job began so as to base the calculation on your most recent circumstances. However, if your finances haven't changed too much, you may prefer to base your autocreate on the entire past year. And even if you have started a new job, you can still base autocreate on the past year, manually editing your income account to show the new salary.

2. Select the rounded amount using the **Round Values to Nearest** pull-down list. You can round to the nearest $1, $10, or $100.

3. Choose the basis for the calculation. Select **Use Monthly Detail** to replicate the amounts month-by-month for the bracketed period into this budget. Select **Use Average for Period** to calculate the average inflow or outflow for each category through the bracketed period. For example, if you do select only three months out of the entire year, you should apply the average for each period instead of copying the monthly data. This will fill your new budget with the closest approximation to your current circumstances.

4. (Optional) Click **Categories** to select the categories and accounts you want to include in this autocreate. Adjust the check marks beside each or use **Mark All** or **Clear All** to hit the lot in one swoop. Click **OK** when you're done.

5. Click **OK** to create the budget and Quicken will go to work.

6. Adjust any entries as required and click **Save** to store the budget.

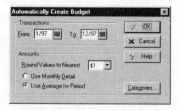

Figure 13.3 Autocreate will help you to build a new budget based on your previous Quicken values. To create a budget for the '98 financial year, you could use your '97 values as shown here.

Creating Multiple Budgets

Okay, so you've created a budget. What if you want to make another? Just click **New** at the top of the Budget window and fill out the options as follows (see also Figure 13.4):

Name   Appears on all reports; edit the name Quicken provides as required.

Description   Only used in the Manage Budgets window.

Create Budget Options   You have three choices:

- **Autocreate Budget**   To go straight to the Autocreate dialog box.
- **Zero-Filled Budget**   To build a budget from the ground up with zeros throughout.
- **Copy Current Budget**   Copy the details from your current budget to the new budget.

Figure 13.4   Naming and creating a new budget.

Click **OK** to create the new budget. To switch between them, select **View, Other Budgets**. This opens the Manage Budgets window shown in Figure 13.5.

Click **Create** to create a new budget as previously described. Select a budget and click **Open** to make it the default. Otherwise, you can also **Rename** and **Delete** budgets as required. Click **Done** when you finish.

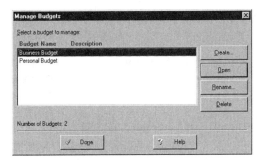

Figure 13.5   It's easy managing more than one budget.

Tracking the Budget

While creating a budget or even managing multiple budgets is quite easy, there's little point if you don't also track how well you are sticking to that budget.

Quicken provides three ways to do this. They are:

- Generate a Budget report.
- Create a Budget Variance graph.
- View a Progress bar.

Generating a Budget Report

Creating a Budget report is easy; simply select **Reports, Other, Budget**. Quicken compares your income and your expenses against the budgeted amounts. This report works on the year-to-date and provides simple, totaled figures. Use the first pull-down menu at the top of the report window to change the period, or type the first and last dates directly into the next two fields. Click **Update** to make these changes in the report.

To compare your income and spending to your budget on a monthly basis, select **Reports, Home, Monthly Budget**.

Creating a Budget Variance Graph

A Budget Variance graph is useful for showing how closely you managed to stick to your budget. The graph calculates the totals accrued by each budgeted category and shows you first how favorably or unfavorably those totals compare to your budget and second, which categories were the worst offenders.

This graph provides information that is more useful than a report—after all, you can easily extract the data provided in the graph simply by reading your Budget report. And like all of Quicken's graphs, it does a great job of presenting that information in a clean, easy-to-understand format.

Creating this graph is easy: select **Reports, Graphs, Budget Variance**. You will see a graph similar to that shown in Figure 13.6.

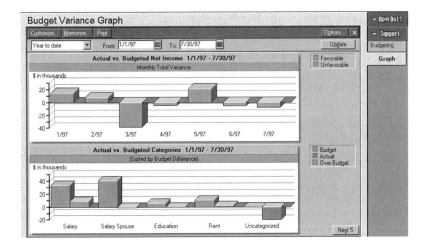

Figure 13.6 This budget is literally all over the place, although a lot of it can be put down to the purchase of a new car in March.

The upper half of the graph shows your budget variance in dollars, month by month. Quicken displays each month as a favorable or unfavorable amount. The more favorable the amount, the higher your net income.

 Net Income (or Variance) Your income minus your expenses. You can achieve a positive net income by either spending less than you accounted for, by generating more income than you had estimated, or both.

While the upper columns tend to bundle all of your categories together, you can view the breakdown for any month by double-clicking that column.

The lower graph shows the budget variance for your individual categories calculated across that entire period. The categories are arranged by their budget difference. This time, double-clicking any column will show the performance of that category across the entire period.

If you have more than five budgeted categories, click **Next 5** in the lower right corner of the graph window to scroll to the next five. Keep clicking and you will eventually end up back at the first five.

Viewing a Progress Bar

If creating a report or graph seems a little tedious every time you want to check on your budget, consider using the Progress bar.

The Progress bar is a nifty graphical display of two gauges that slide into place at the bottom of the Quicken screen. You can toggle it on or off by selecting **Features, Planning, Progress Bars**. Alternatively, click **Close** at the far left side of the Progress bar.

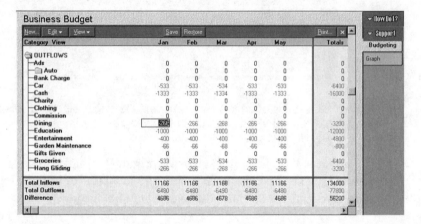

Figure 13.7 Keep a close tab on your budget or savings goal with the Progress bar.

The standard Progress bar displays your nondiscretionary expenses on the left and your dining budget on the right. Your spending this month in the nondiscretionary supercategory and the dining category appears as a bar that creeps up each gauge. To jump to those items within your current budget, double-click the appropriate gauge.

To change the gauges or the way they appear, click **Cust,** which is located at the far right side of the screen. You will see the dialog box shown in Figure 13.8.

You can change each gauge independently, selecting **Savings Goal**, **Budget Goal,** or **Supercategory Budget**. Click the button immediately underneath the drop-down list to specify the savings goal, category, supercategory, and the date range that applies. Click **OK** when you finish.

Figure 13.8 By customizing the Progress bar, you can visually track almost anything from single categories to supercategories to savings goals.

Forecasting

Forecasting shows how your accounts are expected to develop over time.

It can do this using an existing budget as the base, or by summarizing the flow of funds using a combination of past history and future scheduled transactions. It also provides the facility to enter additional once-only or repeating transactions.

None of the information you record in the forecasting tool is used elsewhere in Quicken. In other words, you cannot convert a forecast transaction to an actual transaction. However, you can build a budget based on amounts estimated through the forecasting tool. The forecaster works over a period from one month to two years, starting at any time.

You can use the forecaster to search for times when an important account approaches dangerously close to zero; to ask questions such as: "What if I moved to that new apartment and paid twice my current rent?"; or simply to see how much you can expect to save (and what you can therefore afford) if you stick to your current expenditure pattern.

To create your own forecast, follow these steps:

1. Select Features, Planning, Forecasting.
2. By default, you will see a base scenario calculated on your scheduled income and expense transactions. The four buttons along the top of the window perform these functions:
   - **Scenario** Save the existing forecast graph to a new scenario. Use this button to compare two scenarios at the one time.
   - **Accounts** Mark the accounts included in the current forecast.

- **Create** Creates a new forecast taking in the date range you specify. Click Advanced to choose the basis for the new scenario. For example, do you want to use scheduled payments, estimated payments, or both, or build this forecast using your saved budgeting information.

- **Track** Assigns existing categories to forecast items you create. This is only required if you will use this forecast as the basis for a budget.

3. Select the period over which the graph applies using the pull-down menu in the lower-left corner of the display. Click << **Prev** and **Next** >> to move the starting date of that period backwards or forwards.

4. Click **Income Items** to change existing or add new forecast income transactions. Click **Expense Items** to do the same for forecast expense transactions. Amounts shown under Known items refer to those in your scheduled transaction list. Estimated items are taken from the accounts with previous history. Click **New** to add an item or **Edit** to change an existing item. The options available under the New/Edit dialog box are identical to those used to record a scheduled transaction. However, you will need to click **More** to specify the number of repeating payments and a suitable income or expense category.

5. When you finish, select File, Print Forecast to print a permanent copy.

In this lesson, you learned how to create a budget, keep tabs on your progress, and peer into your financial future. In the next lesson, you will learn how the Debt Reduction Planner can help you get out of debt sooner and how the Savings Goal will help you once you are in credit.

How to Reduce Your Debt and Start Saving

In this lesson, you learn how to use the Debt Reduction Planner to reduce your debt and save on interest payments. You will also learn how to set financial challenges for yourself using Quicken's Savings Goals.

Reducing Your Debt

Quicken's budgeting, financial planning, and transaction recording features all help you keep a tight rein on your expenses. But what should you do if your debt has already spiraled out of control?

There are many ways to reduce your debt. One of the best is to convert high interest debt, such as small personal loans and credit cards, into a low interest mortgage or home equity debt. By combining all those small debts into one large debt, you will find your finances easier to manage and easier to budget for, and you will probably qualify for a lower interest rate.

Quicken can't help you with loan aggregation, but if you are using the Deluxe or Home and Business versions of Quicken, it can certainly help you reduce your debt. This capability is built into a great utility called the Debt Reduction Planner. You can find it by selecting **Features**, **Planning**, **Debt Reduction Planner**.

It takes a little while to work through the plan, but once you finish, you'll have everything you need to save yourself time, interest payments, and money. You'll also have a fancy graph (see Figure 14.1).

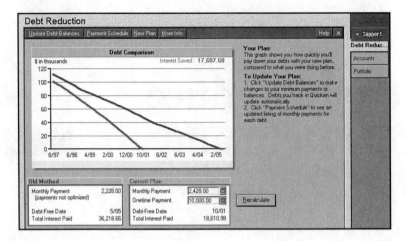

Figure 14.1 The Debt Reduction Planner.

The planner isn't just for those whose debt appears insurmountable. It can be used by anyone, no matter the level of indebtedness (from a $50 credit card bill to a $500,000 housing bill).

The Debt Reduction Planner works on some simple principals:

- Pay off your debts in order from the highest interest rate to the lowest. Pay the minimum only on the lower interest rate debts until it is their turn to be paid off. Ignore the actual amounts, it's the interest rate that counts. This may seem counter intuitive, but it works.

TIP　**A Real World Example**　Jodie has $5,000 in credit card debt that costs her 20% per year in interest. She has a $20,000 car loan costing her 10% per year in interest. She can afford to pay off $5,000 over the course of one year. Which should she reduce first? (We'll ignore the complexities of compounding interest.)

Let's work it out, ignoring the complexities of compounding interest: 10% of $20,000 = $2,000 in Year 1. 20% of $5,000 = $1,000. By paying off the $5,000 credit card debt first, her interest for the second year comes to $20,000 at 10%, or $2,000. However, if she paid $5,000 off the $20,000 debt, her interest for the second year would equal $15,000 at 10% PLUS $5,000 at 20%, or $2,500 all up, making her $500 worse off by not reducing the debt with the highest interest first.

- Apply a lump sum to your debt. For example, if your savings are only earning 4% in the bank, use them to cut back the credit card debt that is probably costing you four times as much.

- Review your budget. Cut back your spending where you can and apply those savings to reduce your debt faster.

- Once you have paid off the first debt, keep the same level of repayments going. Apply them to the second debt. Once its has been paid off, apply the same level of repayments used for the first and second debts to the third, and so on. The more you pay off, the faster your debt will shrink, the more you'll save in interest and the sooner you'll be out of debt.

The Debt Reduction Planner will take you through these steps, showing you the level of interest you have saved and how much quicker you will be completely debt free.

 TIP **Need Financial Help?** If you cannot meet your current repayments and want help, contact the Consumer Credit Counseling Service (CCCS) on 1-800-388-2227. You can read about this service in your Debt Reduction Action Plan.

Creating a Debt Reduction Plan

Before you start creating your plan, make sure your liability accounts are up to date. Ideally, perform a reconciliation for each account using your most recent statements. If you use online banking, download your most recent transactions.

To create your plan, follow these steps:

1. Open the planner by selecting **Features**, **Planning**, **Debt Reduction Planner**. You will see an introductory window. Click **Next**.

2. Insert your Quicken CD-ROM when prompted and make sure your computer's speakers are switched on. The planner is packed with multimedia movies, as shown in Figure 14.2. If you don't have your CD-ROM handy, click **Cancel** when prompted; then click **Next** to move to each new stage.

3. (Optional) Take the CD-ROM tours for some good advice on deciding if you are in too much debt and why you should start this plan today.

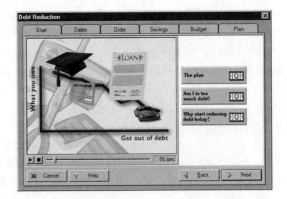

Figure 14.2 Step 1 in your debt reduction.

4. Click **Next** once more. This will take you to the **How Much Do I Owe?** dialog box, as shown in Figure 14.3.

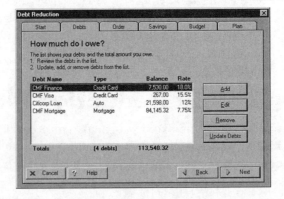

Figure 14.3 Stage 1: Use this dialog box to edit listed debts or to add other debts.

5. Use this dialog box to edit your existing debts and to add new ones. Make sure you enter the correct balance, interest rate, and type of debt. You must also provide your current level of monthly repayments and the minimum level of repayment acceptable to the lender. Quicken will reduce your repayments on the lower interest debts to that minimum until your high interest debts are paid off. If you change your Quicken liability data, click **Update Debts** to reimport those details. When you finish, click **Next**.

6. The next screen summarizes your existing debt situation. Pay special attention to the figures in the Results window. These tell you how long it will be before you pay out your existing debt as well as the interest you will have to pay along the way. Your goal is to reduce these figures. Click **Next**, read the information screen, and click **Next** once more.

7. Use the screen shown in Figure 14.4 to check over the recommended payment order for your debts. If you would like to change it, click **Change Payment Order?** and click **Next**. Use the next screen to adjust the position of each repayment up or down. Watch the Results window; your interest saved will reduce. If you don't want to change the order, click **Next**.

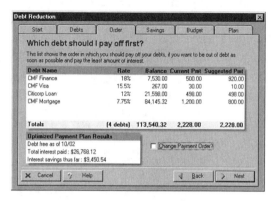

Figure 14.4   Stage 2: You can adjust the payment order, but you will end up paying more interest if you do.

8. The next screen summarizes your savings and investments. Use this to set an optional once-only payment to reduce your debt by a lump sum. Remember that the money in your savings account is probably earning less interest than the liability is costing you. Therefore, applying your savings to your liabilities will always work in your favor. If you decide to apply a onetime payment, enter it here. You will also need to record the payment in Quicken's books. The figure here is only used for hypothetical purposes. Click **Next** to continue.

9. You have now worked your way to the final stage. Use the **Where Can I Cut My Expenses?** screen to decide how you can trim your budget. Quicken calls up the largest categories from your discretionary budget items and provides a handy calculation of the average monthly spending. Record the amount you intend to trim from each in the **Amount to Cut Back** fields. For example, if you spent an average of $249 each month on dining and intended to cut this back to $149, enter $100 into **Amount to Cut Back**. Click **Recalculate** to see the effect this has on your interest payments. Click **Next** when you finish to view the debt reduction plan.

10. You should now have an effective debt reduction plan similar to that shown in Figure 14.5. Click **Print This Action Plan** for a hard copy. The Payment Coupons tell you how much you should pay through to the remainder of the year.

11. Click **Next** and then **Done** to return to the main Debt Reduction window shown at the start of this lesson. You can use this window to adjust your monthly or one-time payments (don't forget to click **Recalculate**), to **Update Debt Balances** using the latest Quicken data, or to obtain **More Info** on reducing your debt using Quicken's online services.

Figure 14.5 The Action Plan provides the results of your hard work.

Setting Savings Goals

If your debt is down to manageable levels, you can start setting savings goals. Quicken's savings goals show your incremental progress. They're easy to set, easy to update, and best of all, they "hide" your money from you so you won't be tempted to spend it.

Here's how savings goals work:

1. You specify a name, the total amount you are striving to accrue, and the date you want to meet it.

2. Quicken creates a new asset account using the name of that savings goal.

3. You use the buttons at the top of the Savings Goal window to contribute funds to or withdraw funds from the savings goal account.

4. When you look at the balance of the account used to contribute that money to the savings goal, you will see a balance minus those funds already contributed. Therefore, if you really have $10,000 in your bank account but you have contributed $4,000 to a savings goal, you will see a balance of just $6,000, even though you still have $10,000 in the account. However, each savings goal is an asset account, so your Net Worth reports show your true equity.

5. When you perform a reconciliation, Quicken negates any transfers made to your savings goal accounts. Therefore, your bank statements and the information you see on-screen will always correlate.

Figure 14.6 shows a savings goal in progress.

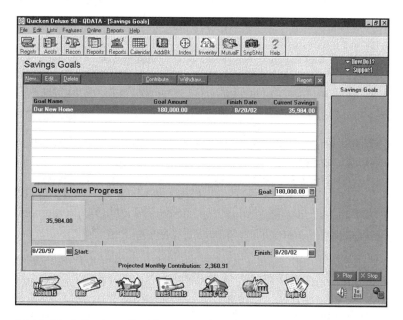

Figure 14.6 Each Savings Goal features a handy progress indicator. You can also display this indicator using Quicken's Progress bar.

Creating a New Goal

To create a new savings goal, follow these steps:

1. Open the Savings Goal window by selecting **Features**, **Planning**, **Savings Goals**.

2. Click **New** to open the Create New Savings Goal window. Enter a name, amount, and completion date. The name must not be used by an existing Quicken asset account or category. Click **OK**.

3. When you need to contribute funds to the account, click **Contribute**. Specify the account you are contributing from, the amount (Quicken calculates an amount for you based on the number of months left to run) and the date it was contributed. This transaction is recorded as an account transfer, removing the funds from the original account (and thus changing the available balance), and depositing them in the savings goal account.

4. To withdraw funds, click **Withdraw**, specify the account you are transferring those funds to, as well as the transfer date. Unless you transfer to a completely different account, withdrawing funds restores your original account's balance by the amount of that withdrawal.

 TIP   **Scheduling Savings Goal Payments**   You don't have to use the Contribute and Withdraw commands to adjust the balance in the savings goal. Instead, if you want to regularly contribute to your savings goal, set up a scheduled payment that transfers those funds as required.

After you contribute funds to your savings goal, you can still see how much money you have in your real-world account. Go to that register and select **View**; toggle **Hide Savings Goals** on and off. When Hide Savings Goals is selected, Quicken temporarily hides all of the transfer transactions. This adjusts the balance of that account to its real-world status. However, select that menu once more and the transfers pop back and the balance goes down.

Completing a Goal

When you complete your goal, you don't have to do anything special. Quicken will continue as usual. However, if you complete the goal and can't wait to spend those funds, you should delete the savings goal by selecting it in the Savings Goal list and clicking **Delete**.

When you delete a savings goal, you need to tell Quicken what to do with the savings goal account. The software offers you the choice of keeping the transactions and the savings account. If you decide to keep them by clicking **Yes**, you can still view your register with savings goal contributions hidden or displayed. In fact, all that happens is that Quicken removes the savings goal graph.

However, you will probably want to delete the account so that you can transfer the funds back to your real account. Once they've been returned, you can spend the funds using Quicken's expense categories to track those payments.

In this lesson, you learned how to reduce your debt and set savings goals. In Part 2, you will learn how Quicken can help with your Federal Tax.

Taxes

Understanding Your Income Tax

*In this lesson, you will learn the basics of Federal income tax,
how Quicken can make preparing and filing your tax returns a
little less daunting, and how you should choose the right tax form.*

Two Things in Life

Benjamin Franklin believed there were only two things certain in life: death and taxes. While Quicken can't do much about the first, it can certainly help out on the second.

Filing the 1040 is one of the most onerous duties a taxpayer must face. It's not so much that the forms are particularly complex. You could, for instance, opt for the 1040EZ, a piece of cake compared to the rigorous Form 1040. Rather, it's the dread that if you make a mistake, you might well end up dealing with a rather irate IRS. It is here that software such as Quicken works best. Not only will it decrease your opportunity for error, it will also ensure that every transaction conducted throughout the financial year remains fully annotated and categorized.

As you already know, Quicken maintains a record of all of your income and expenses. Furthermore, amounts paid to particular categories are automatically targeted at certain items on the Form 1040. This makes tax preparation practically instantaneous. In fact, at the click of a button you can immediately see just how much tax you will owe or be owed. Printed reports will give you all of the information you require, ready for transposition into your income tax return.

Quicken will help you to complete your tax in the following ways:

- Electronically track all of your income and expenses
- Categorize items so that they are automatically targeted at certain parts of the Form 1040 and its related Schedules
- Calculate in advance your withholding and estimated tax
- Generate reports that will help you to fill in your tax forms or give a tax professional everything he or she needs to know to quickly appraise your income and expenses
- Ensure your calculations are always accurate and up-to-date
- Enable electronic filing, reducing your waiting time for a refund from 40 to 21 days
- Track down valid deductions
- Interface with various editions of TurboTax, giving you one of the most powerful software combinations for personal, business, and corporate Federal and State tax preparation

Helping Yourself

However, before Quicken can do any of this, it needs a little help from you. You should use Quicken throughout the year to record every financial transaction you make, whether or not those transactions appear to have any direct taxation relevance. The following list shows just some of the transactions you should be tracking through Quicken:

- Income from every source, be it through wages, self-employment profits, investment income, unemployment benefits, or gifts.
- All of your expenses, especially those used for professional purposes, but also those incurred on a personal basis.
- All your investment funds. (Quicken's investment system is perfect not only for staying on top of your investment, but also for calculating your long- and short-term capital gains.) This should include all transactions associated with maintaining an investment portfolio—such as purchases and sales—as well as monies channeled into retirement funds and tax shelters.

By the end of the financial year, you will be ready to unleash Quicken on your tax forms. Just follow these steps:

- Ensure Quicken is up-to-date at least through the end of December. Tally its data with that shown on the information returns you have received throughout and at the end of the year. These returns should include all Form W-2s, Form 1099s, and so on. Be very accurate; copies of these forms also go to the IRS where they are stored and checked by computer against your own return.

 TIP **Form W-2s For Other Fiscal Years** In general, employees work to a calendar fiscal year. If you work to a different year such as July 1 to June 30, you should apply your Form W-2s to the fiscal year in which they were issued.

- Give your tax professional your Quicken data. If they are Quicken-savvy, create a copy of last year's transactions and hand this across on a disk. (You may even be able to e-mail it across the Internet, but only do so with a password-protected file. Don't e-mail the password; telephone it through.) Otherwise, just print out the Tax Summary, Investment Income, and Capital Gains Reports. (Some of the information contained therein will be common to more than one report, but it provides a useful breakdown of your financial information from several points of view.)

- If you are preparing your own tax return, print a Tax Schedule report, decide which tax form you should use, and copy that information across.

- Close off last year's books, creating a copy using the menu **File, Year-End Copy**, storing it in a safe place, preferably well away from your existing copy of the data.

 TIP **Closing Off** Quicken can record thousands of transactions during the course of a single year. If you think you need to slim down Quicken's data files, you should select the menu **File, Year-End Copy..., Start New Year**. This will archive last year's transactions and delete them from the current data file.

- Print a Transaction report, customizing it to include all of Quicken's registers. Print this on paper and store it with the electronic copy of last year's books created in the previous step.

 TIP **How do I prepare my state returns?** State return preparation isn't one of Quicken's strong points, but the software does interface very well with another of Intuit's products, TurboTax State. This software is customized for almost every state. For more information on this or other Intuit tax products such as Tax Planner, contact Intuit Direct Sales on 800-4-INTUIT (800-446-8848) or visit their Web site at **http://www.intuit.com**.

Using the Right 1040

There are three primary taxation forms. These are the Form 1040EZ, the Form 1040A and the Form 1040. No matter how many sources of income or jobs you had throughout the year, you should still only file one form. The question is, which?

 TIP **Obtaining IRS Forms** You can obtain all IRS forms and publications by calling 1-800-TAX-FORM. In numerals, that's 1-800-829-3676. You can also dial 703-487-4160 from your fax machine to transmit copies to your own fax. Alternatively, you can get the forms and publications at the IRS site on the World Wide Web. You'll find them at **http://www.irs.ustreas.gov/forms_pubs/ top-forms.html**. The easiest way to view these is using the PDF (Portable Document Format) files supported by Adobe Acrobat. The viewer is available from the Adobe Systems site at http://www.adobe.com.

Quicken's Tax Schedule report has been optimized for the full Form 1040, even though you can copy that information into any type of form. However, if you also use TurboTax, you can choose between the three main forms. To determine your eligibility for each, either work through the requirements below or speak to your tax professional.

Form 1040EZ

The 1040EZ is the simplest of the taxation forms. You can use it if all of the following are true:

- You are single or married (and filing jointly).
- You (and your spouse, if this is a joint filing) were under the age of 65 at the start of the new year, and neither of you was blind at the end of January 1997.

- You do not claim any dependents.
- Your taxable income (combined income, if filing jointly) is less than $50,000.
- Your income was generated through wages, salaries, tips, unemployment compensation, interest (limited to $400), Alaska Pemanent Fund dividends, taxable scholarship and fellowship grants.
- You did not receive an advance earned income credit.
- You do not owe employment taxes on wages paid to a domestic employee.

The 1040EZ is a single page form accompanied by a 29-page information booklet. It provides for wages, interest, unemployment compensation and dependents, along with income tax withheld and the earned income credit. You use the tax table printed in the booklet to calculate your dues or rebate. Sign it, pay it, and you're done.

If you aren't eligible to file the 1040EZ, you might be able to file the Form 1040A instead.

Form 1040A

The 1040A is the next step up in complexity, although at just two pages, it isn't much of a leap. The form's main points include support for dependents, IRA deductions and household employment taxes. This form allows for dependents, estimated tax payments, household employee taxes, separate filings, exemptions and other forms of income.

You can use it if:

- Your wages are from those specified in the 1040EZ as well as dividends, pension-annuity and IRA distributions
- Your taxable income is less than $50,000
- The only income adjustment comes through claiming your contribution to an IRA
- The only credits are those for a child or care for a dependent, the elderly or totally disabled and/or an earned income credit

Table 1.1 Form 1040A Schedules

Schedule	Description
Schedule 1	Interest and Dividend Income
Schedule 2	Child and Dependent Care Expenses
Schedule 3	Credit for the Elderly or the Disabled
Schedule EIC	Earned Income Credit
Schedule H	Household Employment Taxes

While the 1040A gives single people and couples a little more opportunity to explain their income and expenses, making the most of all possible deductions takes a Form 1040. Fortunately, Quicken makes this particularly easy. Furthermore, there is no penalty for filing a Form 1040 when you would have been eligible to file, say, a 1040EZ or 1040A.

Form 1040

The Form 1040 gives you the full range of reporting options. In its paper-based format, it can prove a little scary, but with a little bit of electronic wizardry by your side, it's a cinch.

We're not going to go through all of the situations in which you would need to file a Form 1040, but here are a few of the more common (or interesting):

- You earned $20 or more in tips in any month and did not report these to your employer.
- You need to pay self-employment tax.
- You earned $50,000 or more in taxable income.
- You have itemized your deductions (a Quicken special).
- You have an interest in or signature authority over a foreign bank account.
- You sold or exchanged capital assets or business property.
- You received a lump sum distribution.
- You earned foreign income.

Like the 1040A, the 1040 only uses up two pages; however, its numerous related schedules provide lots of room for further information. See Table 1.2.

Table 1.2 Form 1040 Schedules

Schedule	Description
Schedules A & B	Itemized Deductions
Schedule C	Profit or Loss From Business
Schedule C-EZ	Net Profit From Business
Schedule SE	Self-Employment Tax
Schedule D	Capital Gains and Losses
Schedule E	Supplemental Income and Loss
Schedule EIC	Earned Income Credit
Schedule F	Profit or Loss From Farming
Schedule H	Household Employment Taxes
Schedule R	Credit for the Elderly or the Disabled

The remaining lessons in this section will help you to make Quicken a very tax-effective product. You'll also learn how to calculate your estimated tax, adjust your withholding tax to suit, and prepare your tax return. Just bear in mind that Quicken does not replace a tax professional. While the Deluxe version in particular is packed with all kinds of taxation advice, you should always keep the number of your tax professional or accountant handy for those times when you need an answer fast.

This leads to a word of warning: From time to time this book quotes certain tax regulations and provides general advice on how you should manage your Quicken data so as to simplify your end-of-year preparation. The accuracy of the quotes or recommendations cannot be guaranteed as the tax system is subject to constant change. This book is not a tax guide and it won't provide all of the information you need to create an ideal or even adequate tax return. It makes no attempt to replace the services or knowledge of a tax adviser. The only advice that can be given with 100% certainty is that if you ever have a question regarding a taxation issue, ask the IRS or your taxation professional.

In this lesson, you learned how Quicken can simplify your tax preparation. In the next lesson, you will learn how to set up and use Quicken's tax-related categories.

Setting up Tax-Related Categories

2

In this lesson, you learn how Quicken's tax-related categories and the Tax Link Assistant can automatically organize your taxes.

Tax Preparation

Quicken doesn't replace the advisory services of a tax professional, but it will greatly simplify your tax preparation through its powerful report generation and figure collation. In other words, while Quicken isn't very good at structuring your portfolio to minimize taxation liability; come the end of the financial year, it will certainly make filing the 1040 about as easy as can be. However, before Quicken can help you with your 1040, you need to do the following:

1. Set up your tax-related categories.
2. Link the tax-related categories to tax form line items.
3. At filing time, print out the tax-related reports or transfer Quicken's data to tax preparation software such as TurboTax.

Categories group transactions that were used for a similar purpose. The transactions that contribute to these categories retain their original information, including any memos. They also add to the totals stored under certain income and expense categories. In this way, transactions provide a very fine granularity of information. Categories are coarser but have the advantage of collecting (or categorizing) many related transactions. Tax-related categories are a subset of Quicken's other categories; they deal purely with tax-related items. For example, while Quicken might track your household expenses in certain expense categories, this probably has no bearing on your tax return. However, other expenses do, and these need to be bundled up into tax-related categories and assigned to specific lines within the 1040.

You have two options when setting up tax-related categories: You can define a category as tax-related and have it appear on Quicken's Tax Summary report; or you can define a category as tax-related but also link it to the Form 1040. This creates a Tax Schedule report.

A Tax Summary lists all of the transactions that have taken place in tax-related categories. Tax summaries are a midway point between the detail of, say, a complete profit and loss report and the less specific information required to fill in the 1040. If you have any doubts about which categories are suitable for certain areas of the 1040, take the Tax Summary and give it to your tax adviser. Alternatively, the Tax Deduction Finder can help you determine those that should become tax-related.

The Tax Summary is handy if your taxes aren't too complicated. In this sense, it's perfect for the 1040EZ. However, if you aren't eligible for the simplified form, you should set up Quicken to handle tax schedules.

The Tax Schedule also itemizes each transaction, but it does so in the context of the 1040 and its attendant Schedules. The data contained in the Tax Schedule is arranged as it will need to appear on the filing. This information can be exported to taxation preparation software, electronically lodged or simply printed and copied across by hand.

However, before any of this can happen, you need to set up your tax related categories.

Specifying Tax-Related Categories

The default Quicken installation includes a large number of categories that are both tax-related and linked to tax form line items. These categories should cover most people's needs, but you might also need to set up an additional category that isn't already included in Quicken.

 TIP **A Real World Example** Marianne is a keen private pilot who enjoys flying herself to business appointments and conventions. Quicken doesn't have an "AvGas (Aviation Fuel)" category in its default installation. However, the gasoline is a legitimate and deductible business expense, so Marianne can ensure any transactions assigned to that account appear on her taxation reports via an AvGas category. This keeps those expenses separate from her usual automotive expenses.

A category can be marked as tax-related either when you first set it up or any time thereafter. Marking a category as tax-related does not affect any of the transactions that have or will pass through that category. The tax-related information is only used when producing the Tax Summary and Tax Schedule reports.

To set up and designate a new category as tax related, follow these steps:

1. From the menu, select **Lists**, **Category/Transfer** (Ctrl+C). See Figure 2.1.

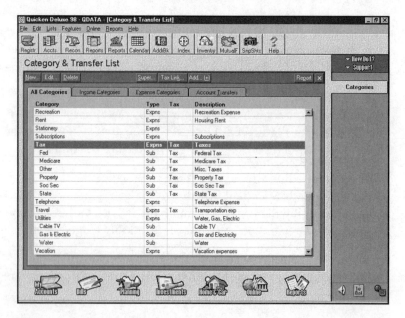

Figure 2.1 Use the Category and Transfer List to quickly see the standard and tax-related categories.

2. Click **New**.

3. Type in a name, optional description and select the type: **Income**, **Expense** or **Subcategory**.

4. Click **Tax-related** to mark the category, as shown in Figure 2.2.

5. Click **OK** to save the category or **Cancel** to quit.

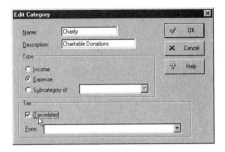

Figure 2.2   Marking categories as tax-related will make them appear on the Tax Summary report.

You should now see the word "Tax" in the Tax column of that category. This means that category will be included in all Tax Summary reports.

To change an existing category so that it becomes tax-related, follow these steps:

1. From the menu bar, select **Lists**, **Category/Transfer** (Ctrl+C).

2. Highlight the category within the list and click **Edit...** to open the Edit Category dialog box.

3. Click **Tax-related** and click **OK** to save the changes.

The Tax indicator will appear in that category's tax column.

Specifying Tax Schedule Categories

A Tax Schedule category must be related to a specific line within either the Form 1040 or its Schedules. Before you can do this, you should check that Quicken is set up for this type of category.

From the menu bar, select **Edit**, **Options**, **Quicken Program**. Click the **General** tab and place a check mark beside **Use Tax Schedules with Categories**. If it is already selected, just leave it as is.

To specify a new or existing category as a tax schedule item, follow these steps:

1. Open up the Category List by selecting the menu **Lists**, **Category/Transfer** (Ctrl+C).

2. Choose an existing category and click **Edit** or, if you want to create a new category, click **New** type in the name and description and specify the type.

3. Place a check mark beside **Tax-related**. If Tax-related is already selected, leave it as is.

4. Click in the **Form** drop-down list and select the form or schedule as shown in Figure 2.3. If you don't see the Form drop-down list, check Quicken's Options as detailed above.

5. Click **OK** to save the changes or **Cancel** to exit.

Figure 2.3 Select the Form 1040 or Schedule line item for tax schedule categories from this drop-down list.

TIP **Canceling a Tax Schedule Category** Scroll up to the top of the Form's list where you will see a blank line. Select this to cancel a category's tax schedule relationship and click **OK** to save.

Assigning a Form or Schedule Item isn't for the faint of heart. After all, there are several hundred choices available, and choosing the incorrect one could have dire consequences for your income tax liability. If you find the process a little daunting (and there's no particular reason why you shouldn't), try using the Quicken Tax Link Assistant instead.

Using the Tax Link Assistant

Quicken's Tax Link Assistant is a handy little device designed especially to help you to assign Form 1040 and Schedule items to particular categories within your accounts.

The Tax Link shown in Figure 2.4 won't do your work for you, but it will make it easier to work out which categories are most applicable to certain 1040 and Schedule items.

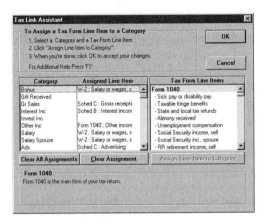

Figure 2.4   Use the Tax Link Assistant to assign categories to line items on the Form 1040 and its Schedules.

The upper section displays general instructions while the lower is used to show the specific characteristics of the currently selected Form 1040 or Schedule category.

To use the Tax Link Assistant to set up your tax schedule categories, follow these steps:

1. From the menu bar, select **Features**, **Taxes**, **Set up for Taxes**.

2. Use the list box headed **Category** to select the Quicken category you want to adjust. The list box headed **Assigned Line Item** shows the currently assigned Form 1040 or Schedule item.

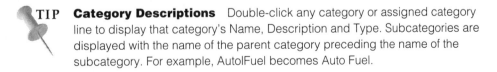

TIP **Category Descriptions**   Double-click any category or assigned category line to display that category's Name, Description and Type. Subcategories are displayed with the name of the parent category preceding the name of the subcategory. For example, Auto|Fuel becomes Auto Fuel.

3. To change the assigned tax-related category, select from the list box headed **Tax Form Line Items**. Read the description provided in the lower panel and, when you're ready, click **Assign Line Item to Category**.

4. To delete an Assigned Line Item, click **Clear Assignment**. To delete all Assigned Line Items, click **Clear All Assignments**.

5. Click **OK** to confirm the changes or **Cancel** to leave the Tax Link Assistant.

In this lesson, you learned about setting up tax-related categories. In the next lesson, you will learn how to use Quicken to track your income.

Quicken and Your Income

3

In this lesson, you will learn how income relates to tax, what you can get away with, what you can't, and how Quicken can help steer you through your money maze.

Your Income

The money you make (income) can come from any number of sources. If you're lucky enough to have a stable, full-time job, then the majority of your income will arrive in the form of compensation for your time. This might include a salary or wage, tips, commissions, and bonuses. However, income isn't limited to those items.

For some, the primary source of income will be generated by a range of investments. For others, income might come in the form of alimony, unemployment benefits, compensation settlements, and more. Certain forms of income are tax-exempt while other types of income can be offset against expenses, thus reducing the taxable component. It is important to keep these different forms of income separate. This will help you not only when it comes tax time, but also to track your return on investment and to plan for the future.

How Quicken Registers Income

Like all accounting or financial packages, Quicken is built around a series of registers. Each register is used to store the transactions flowing into and out of a particular facet of your financial affairs. These avenues include asset and liability accounts such as your credit card, checking account, or, for small business users, accounts receivable.

Asset An asset is anything you own that has value. Examples include real estate, automobiles, furniture, company shareholdings, and amounts that you are owed. **Liability** A liability is anything that you owe. Examples include bills that will need to be paid, mortgages and personal loans, and credit card accounts that are in debit.

Every account has amounts flowing in and amounts flowing out. Some of these amounts come from outside the Quicken books whereas others are simply indicative of the transfer of money between different Quicken registers. For example, enter a deposit into your credit card account and you will probably do so by transferring those funds from your checking account. Quicken removes that amount from the checking account and posts it to the credit card account. Incidentally, this is carried out internally by crediting the checking account and debiting the credit card account. While this may seem counter-intuitive, credits are always used to show where money comes from. They have nothing to do with increasing the value of an account. For instance, if you borrow money, it comes from a creditor. Similarly, debits are used to show where the money has gone. Again, lend money to someone and they become a debtor. You don't actually need to know this to use Quicken, but it's always helpful to understand what goes on behind the scenes.

Reporting Standard Income to the IRS

Income equals profit. That's a straightforward but occasionally misunderstood point. If income was defined as incoming funds, then whenever you sold your business or house, you would suffer a capital gains tax. Instead, personal income is more like gross profit. Fortunately, the IRS is more interested in taxing you on your net profit. You may go out and earn a wage, but there are certain unavoidable costs associated with doing that. If you have to buy a uniform to perform your job, you can claim that against your taxable income.

Tax free This is a term used, abused, and often confused. Being able to claim a purchase against tax does not make it free. If John pays for a magazine subscription directly related to his profession, the subscription amount isn't removed from John's tax bill. Rather, he won't have to pay tax on the money he had to earn to purchase that item. If he pays around 27 percent tax on his earnings, then he will have saved himself 27 percent of the purchase price because he won't have to pay tax on that money. Under no circumstance can he save 100 percent of the purchase price.

The IRS is interested in receiving information about all of your income—for obvious reasons. These are reported as totals on the Form 1040 and expanded within certain schedules. However, the IRS is only interested in seeing this income split by type, so it is very important that you slot each form of income into its appropriate Quicken category. It is also a good idea to store other forms of income such as IRA distributions, alimony, pensions, and annuities in their own separate categories.

Fortunately, the standard Quicken categories include the most common forms of income. Just use your paycheck stubs as a guide to which income should go where. If you do this from day one, you'll fly through the end of year maneuverings. Quicken also includes a paycheck assistant which will help you decide the categories to which your should allocate your paycheck. You can learn about this in Part 6.

 TIP **Cross-checking Your Income**   Use your Form W-2s to cross-check the income Quicken reports at the end of each year. This is a great way to pick up on mistyped transactions, ensuring the information supplied by Quicken matches the information already in the hands of the IRS.

You will see the default income categories in Table 3.1, as well as their linked tax line items. However, take a look at your Category and Transfer list and you probably won't see every single one of these. In fact, Quicken constructs your own category list according to the answers you gave to the questions asked during the New User Setup.

 TIP **Is settlement money taxable?**   The IRS believes that only that part of a court award that replaces your present income is taxable. According to the IRS FAQ located at **http://www.irs.ustreas.gob/tax_edu/faq/faq2.htm**, this includes interest on the award, compensation for wages or profits, punitive damages, damages received for breach of contract, patent or copyright infringement or interference with business operations, or any amount received under the Age Discrimination in Employment Act.

If you need to add an income category, use this table and the Tax Link Assistant as a guide for assigning that category to a specific line in the Form 1040 or its schedules. For example, if you receive alimony, you will need to create a separate income category.

TIP **A Real World Example** Janice receives alimony from her ex-husband. Alimony appears as a separate item on the Form 1040…in fact, it doesn't even appear on the 1040EZ or 1040A—so Janice uses Quicken to create an income category, assigning it to Line 11, Alimony Received of Form 1040 through the Tax Link Assistant, as shown in Figure 3.1.

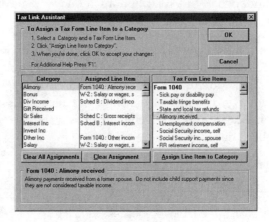

Figure 3.1 Assigning a new Alimony income category to the appropriate 1040 line item through the Tax Link Assistant.

In general, if you need to create a new income category (rather than just any old category), follow these steps:

1. Open the Category/Transfer List by selecting **Lists, Category/Transfer** (Ctrl+C).

2. Make sure the All Types tab is selected and check for that category under the current list.

3. If it's not there, click **Tax Link** and check the rightmost window Tax Form Line Items. If you find an item specifically related to the income category you need to create, you're set. Otherwise, you will need to do some research to discover the most appropriate tax line assignment. Remember: if in doubt, talk to your tax professional.

4. Click **Cancel** and create a new category as described in Lesson 5, "Introduction to the Tax Planner."

5. Click **Tax-related** and use the Form drop-down list to select the previously noted category.

If you look through the Tax Link Assistant, you will notice that Quicken approaches some of these categories from the reverse direction. Salary and wage items link back to the original Form W-2, rather than to specific lines within the Form 1040.

Table 3.1 Standard Income Categories

Category	Type	Tax-related Category	Description
Bonus	Income	W2: Salary or wages, self	Bonus Income
Div Income	Income	Schedule B: Dividend Income	Dividend Income
Gift Received	Income		Gift Received
Gr Sales	Income	Schedule C: Gross receipts or sales	Gross Sales
Interest Inc	Income	Schedule B: Interest Income	Interest Income
Invest Inc	Income	Tax-related	Investment Income
Other Inc	Income	Form 1040: Other income, misc	Other Income
Salary	Income	W2: Salary or wages, self	Salary Income
Salary Spouse	Income	W2: Salary or wages, spouse	Spouse's Salary Income

Reporting Other Income

Every employer you have worked for through the previous year must supply you with a Form W-2 before the end of January 31. The W-2 includes twenty-one numbered boxes that cover gross pay, withholdings, actual income received, reported tips, medicare and social security tax, and the like.

If you earn a salaried wage and don't have any other forms of income save a little bank interest here or there, your tax preparation should prove very simple indeed; Quicken will already have every income-related category you could possibly require. However, in any other situation, you will need to create your own income categories.

Table 3.2 summarizes the income categories as they appear on each Form or Schedule.

Table 3.2   Form and Schedule Income Items

Form	Type
1040EZ	Total wages, salaries and tips. Includes all wages, salaries, bonuses, commissions, fees, sick pay, holiday pay, severance and dismissal pay, prizes, awards and tips.
	Taxable interest income
	Unemployment compensation
1040A	Wages, salaries and tips, etc.
	Taxable interest income
	Tax-exempt interest income
	Dividends
	Total IRA distributions
	Total pensions and annuities
	Unemployment compensation
	Social Security benefits
1040	Wages, salaries and tips, etc.
	Taxable interest
	Tax-exempt interest
	Dividend income
	Taxable refunds, credits, or offsets of state and local income taxes
	Alimony received
	Business income (or loss)
	Capital gain (or loss)
	Other gains (or losses)
	Total IRA distributions
	Total pensions and annuities
	Rental real estate, royalties, partnerships, S corporations, trusts, etc.
	Farm income (or loss)
	Unemployment compensation
	Social security benefits
	Other income

Form	Type
	Total Interest/Dividends
	Total Business Income/Loss
	Total Capital Gains/Losses
	Total Other Income or Losses
Schedule B (Interest and Dividends)	
	Taxable Interest Income (Interest comes from current account investments.)
	Dividends (Dividends are generated by investing in mutual funds, stocks and shares.)
Schedule C (Business Profit/Loss)	
	Revenue
Schedule D (Capital Gain/Loss)	
	Short Term Gains/Losses
	Long Term Gains/Losses
Schedule E (Rents/Royalties)	
	Rents
	Royalties
	Partnerships
Schedule F (Farm Income)	
	Sales
	Supplemental Payments
	Other Income

Use the Tax Link Assistant to verify that the ones you'll need are already included in Quicken. If not, you need to create these categories, linking them to the appropriate line items. Just remember: Quicken tags income by the Form W-2 items, not the Form 1040 line items.

In this lesson, you learned about applying your income to Quicken. In the next lesson, you will learn about using deductions to reduce your taxable income.

Understanding
Deductions

4

In this lesson, you learn about standard and itemized deductions and how you can use the latter in Quicken.

Two Categories

Deductions let you reduce your tax liability. Some deductions exist as part of state- or Federally-initiated tax relief schemes for the disadvantaged or low income earners. Other deductions exist to encourage investment in savings or retirement plans. Still others exist because without them you would be unfairly penalized for the costs associated with doing your job or running your business.

Deductions fall into two broad categories: those that apply before your Adjusted Gross Income (AGI) are known as adjustments to income. Those that apply after are either standard deductions or itemized deductions, depending on which you choose. To arrive at your taxable income, you must apply both sets of deductions and then take into account any exemptions.

TIP **Entering Exemptions** Exemptions don't usually make an appearance until tax time. However, you will see them in the Quicken Tax Planner discussed in Lesson 5.

Publication 17 of the IRS lists the following possible adjustments to your AGI:

- Payments to an IRA (Individual Retirement Arrangement)
- Moving expenses you pay
- Alimony you pay
- Self-employment tax
- Self-employed health insurance

- Payments to a Keogh retirement plan
- Payments to a self-employed SEP
- Payments to a SIMPLE plan
- Penalty on early withdrawal of savings
- Other deductions: amortization of the costs of reforestation; contributions to Internal Revenue Code Section 501(c)(18) pension plans; expenses from the rental of personal property; expenses of certain performing artists; certain required repayments of supplemental unemployment benefits; foreign housing deduction; jury duty pay given to your employer; and, part of the cost of qualified clean-fuel vehicle property

TIP **Deducing Deductions** These deductions are limited both by the size and the conditions under which they may be claimed. The Tax Deduction Finder included with Quicken Deluxe will help you to explore those limits. If you aren't using the Deluxe version of Quicken (and possibly even if you are), you should speak to your taxation consultant about applicable deductions. You will learn about the Tax Deduction Finder in Lesson 9 of Part 6.

You are allowed two types of post-AGI deductions on your tax return: standard or itemized. The Tax Planner will help you choose between one or the other. However, you are disallowed from claiming the standard deduction if:

- You are married, filing separate returns and your spouse has itemized deductions;
- You have changed your accounting period and are filing the return on a shorter than 12-month tax year; or
- You are a nonresident or dual-status alien (unless you are married to a U.S. citizen or resident at the end of the year, in which case you may choose to be treated as a U.S. citizen).

The general principle for choosing between itemized and standard deductions is to go for whichever will provide you with the greater total deduction.

The Standard Deduction

The standard deduction is fixed each year. In 1996 it started at around $4, 000, but could climb as high $6, 700.

The Tax Planner built into all versions of Quicken 98 also contains the latest standard deductions and tax thresholds.

167

Itemized Deductions

Itemized deductions are listed on Schedule A and may only be used with Form 1040. Allowable itemized deductions fall into the following categories:

- Medical and dental expenses
- Taxes you paid
- Interest you paid
- Gifts to charity
- Casualty and theft losses
- Job expenses
- Miscellaneous deductions

These are subject to the same restrictions as other deductions, although the rules have been designed to make them very straight forward. Most of the qualifiers and limitations are built into the Quicken Tax Planner—and you can always hit the help key (F1) for further information. However, because the Tax Planner prefers to receive its data from Quicken, you should make sure Quicken has been correctly set up to handle your deductions.

Setting Up Quicken For Deductions

Quicken manages deductions by linking expense categories to line items within the Form 1040 and its Schedules. So long as you use the correct category when entering transactions into Quicken's registers, those payments will also appear in the Tax Planner and on your tax return.

Table 4.1 shows all of Quicken's default expense categories. You will only see the complete list if you chose to import every form of category in the original Quicken interview. However, you may also pick and choose between these categories by clicking the **Add (+)** button in the Category & Transfer List.

To check that Quicken can handle your deductions, just follow these steps:

1. Select the menu **Lists**, **Category/Transfer** (Ctrl+C) to open the Category & Transfer List.
2. Look through Table 4.1. If you see a category marked as "tax-related," it will only appear on the Tax Summary report. However, if you see a category that refers to a specific 1040 or Schedule line item, that category will appear on the Tax Summary and Tax Schedule reports.

3. If you see a deduction that you think you will require, check your Category & Transfer List. If it isn't there, click **Add (+)** up the top of the list and add that category.

4. Finally, double-check that those categories marked purely as Tax-Related shouldn't also be applied to a specific 1040 or Schedule line item. For example, the 1996 version of Quicken didn't link the charity expense account to Schedule A, Cash Charity Contributions. (Of course, donations to a charity are only deductible if that charity is on the approved donations list.) If you have any doubts (and even if you haven't), consult a tax professional. Show them Table 4.1 and ask them which categories you should set up and use for your own taxation purposes.

Table 4.1 Standard Expense Categories

Category	Type	Tax-Related Category	Description
Ads	Expense	Schedule C: Advertising	Advertising
Auto	Expense		Automobile Expenses
Fuel	Subcategory		Auto Fuel
Insurance	Subcategory		Auto Insurance
Service	Subcategory		Auto Service
Bank Charge	Expense		Bank Charge
Car	Expense	Schedule C: Car and truck expenses	Car & Truck
Cash	Expense		Misc. Cash
Charity	Expense	Tax-related	Charitable Donations
Childcare	Expense	Form 2441: Qualifying childcare expenses	Childcare Expense
Clothing	Expense		Clothing
Commission	Expense	Schedule C: Commissions and fees	Commissions
Dining	Expense		Dining Out
Education	Expense		Education
Entertainment	Expense		Entertainment
Gifts Given	Expense		Gift Expenses

continues

continued

Category	Type	Tax-Related Category	Description
Groceries	Expense		Groceries
Home Repair	Expense		Home Repair & Maint.
Household	Expense		Household Misc. Exp
Insurance	Expense		Insurance
Insurance, Bus	Expense	Schedule C: Insurance, other than health	Insurance (not health)
Int Paid	Expense	Schedule C: Interest expense, other	Interest Paid
Interest Exp	Expense		Interest Expense
IRA Contrib	Expense	Form 1040: IRA contribution, self	IRA Contribution
IRA Contrib Spo	Expense	Form 1040: IRA contribution, spouse	IRA Contribution Spouse
Late Fees	Expense	Schedule C: Other business expenses	Late Payment Fees
Legal-Prof Fees	Expense	Schedule C: Legal and professional fees	Legal & Prof. Fees
Meals & Entertn	Expense	Schedule C: Meal and entertainment	Meals & Entertainment
Medical	Expense	Schedule A: Medicine and drugs	Medical Expense
Doctor	Subcategory	Schedule A: Doctors, dentists, hospitals	Doctor & Dental Visits
Medicine	Subcategory	Schedule A: Medicine and drugs	Medicine & Drugs
Misc	Expense		Miscellaneous
Office	Expense	Schedule C: Office expenses	Office Expenses
Recreation	Expense		Recreation Expense
Rent	Expense		Housing Rent
Rent on Equip	Expense	Schedule C: Rent/lease vehicles, equip.	Rent-Vehicle, mach, equip

Category	Type	Tax-Related Category	Description
Rent Paid	Expense	Schedule C: Rent/lease other bus. prop.	Rent Paid
Repairs	Expense	Schedule C: Repairs and maintenance	Repairs
Returns	Expense	Schedule C: Returns and allowances	Returns & Allowances
Subscriptions	Expense		Subscriptions
Supplies, Bus	Expense	Schedule C: Supplies (not from COGS)	Supplies
Tax	Expense	Tax-related	Taxes
Fed	Subcategory	W-2: Federal tax withheld, self	Federal Tax
Medicare	Subcategory	W-2: Medicare tax withheld, self	Medicare Tax
Other	Subcategory	Tax-related	Misc. Taxes
Property	Subcategory	Schedule A: Real estate taxes	Property Tax
Soc Sec	Subcategory	W-2: Soc. Sec. Tax withheld, self	Soc Sec Tax
State	Subcategory	W-2: State tax withheld, self	State Tax
Tax Spouse	Expense	Tax-related	Spouse's Taxes
Fed	Subcategory	W-2: Federal tax withheld, spouse	Federal Tax
Medicare	Subcategory	W-2: Medicare tax withheld, spouse	Medicare Tax
Soc Sec	Subcategory	W-2: Soc. Sec. Tax withheld, spouse	Soc Sec Tax
State	Subcategory	W-2: State tax withheld, spouse	State Tax
Tax, Business	Expense	Schedule C: Taxes and licenses	Taxes & Licenses

continues

Table 4.1 Continued

Category	Type	Tax-Related Category	Description
Fed	Subcategory	Schedule C: Taxes and licenses	Federal Tax
Local	Subcategory	Schedule C: Taxes and licenses	Local Tax
Property	Subcategory	Schedule C: Taxes and licenses	Property Tax
State	Subcategory	Schedule C: Taxes and licenses	State Tax
Telephone	Expense		Telephone Expense
Telephone, Bus	Expense	Schedule C: Utilities	Telephone Expense
Travel	Expense	Schedule C: Travel	Transportation exp
Utilities	Expense		Water, Gas, Electric
Cable TV	Subcategory		Cable TV
Gas & Electric	Subcategory		Gas and Electricity
Water	Subcategory		Water
Utilities, Bus	Expense	Schedule C: Utilities	Water, Gas, Electric
Vacation	Expense		Vacation expenses
Lodging	Subcategory		Motel/Hotel Costs
Travel	Subcategory		Transportation exp
Wages	Expense	Schedule C: Wages paid	Wages & Job Credits

In this lesson, you learned how Quicken can help you to track your deductible expenses. In the next lesson, you will learn to use the Tax Planner.

Introduction to the Tax Planner

In this lesson, you will learn how to use the Tax Planner to calculate your tax bill and estimated tax payments.

The IRS collects two forms of income tax through the year: withholding and estimated tax. Withholding tax is paid as you earn it by removing an amount from salaries and wages, tips, taxable fringe benefits, sick pay, pensions and annuities, gambling winnings, unemployment compensation and some federal payments.

While this could easily account for the total income tax payable by many wage earners, it doesn't cover all possibilities. Estimated tax handles the rest. It may also be used to catch up in areas where the withholding tax rate doesn't prove sufficient.

TIP   **Tax Facts**   When Federal income tax was introduced in 1913, the highest tax rate was just 7 percent. That remains the lowest top marginal rate ever recorded. The highest marginal rate ever was 94 percent, imposed during the peak of the Second World War.

The highest tax bracket for the 1996 tax year was 39.6 percent for income over $271,663.

Should You be Paying Estimated Tax?

Estimated tax is used for both income and self-employment tax and is reported on Form 1040-ES, Estimated Tax for Individuals. It applies to all U.S. citizens and residents as well as nonresidents aliens (dependent on the terms of a tax treaty, if one exists); essentially, anyone who earns an income from the U.S. or its territories.

There are, however, several conditions which need to be met before you must pay estimated tax. To establish your liability to pay estimated tax, work through each of these steps:

1. Calculate your witholding tax, credits and estimated tax for the current financial year. Think of this as your total tax.

2. Is your estimated tax less than $500? If so, you don't need to pay estimated tax.

3. Will your withholding tax and credits form at least 90% of your total tax calculated for the next tax return? If so, you don't need to pay estimated tax.

4. Will your withholding tax and credits equal at least 100% of the total tax paid on your previous return? If so, you don't need to pay estimated tax.

5. If you can answer yes to all three of the following questions, you also do not need to pay estimated tax:

- Was your tax liability for the previous financial year zero?
- Were you a U.S. citizen or resident for the whole year?
- Did your previous return cover the full 12-months?

You can avoid paying estimated tax by increasing the amount of withholding tax that you already pay. To do this, lodge a new Form W-4 with your employer requesting the extra deduction. In the next lesson, you'll learn how to calculate that extra withholding.

TIP   **Refunds and estimated payments**   One of the easiest ways to reduce your estimated payments for the upcoming year is to apply your tax refund from the year past to the current year's estimated payments. Enter the amount of the refund that you wish applied to your estimated tax on Form 1040 or Form 1040A.

Why should you worry so much about meeting your estimated tax payments? If you fail to pay or do not pay enough, you may be charged a penalty. Furthermore, if you miss the estimated tax payment date, you may be charged a penalty even if you believe you will receive a refund when you file your return.

Introducing the Tax Planner

To open the Tax Planner, select the menu **Features**, **Taxes**, **Tax Planner**. You will see the dialog box shown in Figure 5.1.

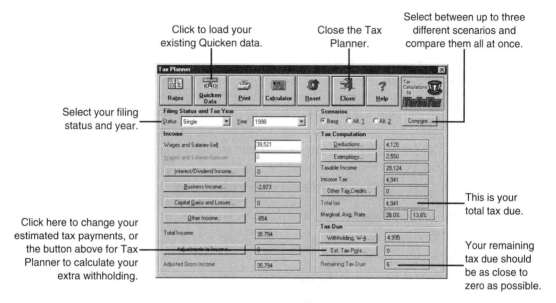

Click to load your existing Quicken data.

Close the Tax Planner.

Select between up to three different scenarios and compare them all at once.

Select your filing status and year.

Click here to change your estimated tax payments, or the button above for Tax Planner to calculate your extra withholding.

This is your total tax due.

Your remaining tax due should be as close to zero as possible.

Figure 5.1 Use Tax Planner to calculate your total tax exposure.

Quicken's Tax Planner is based in part on TurboTax. It combines the current taxation regulations with a clever system that can predict your estimated tax for the year ahead.

The Tax Planner will not only determine your eligibility for estimated tax but also show you how key financial decisions may affect those amounts.

In short, Tax Planner will help you to:

- Estimate the tax you will owe at the end of the year
- Calculate the correct withholding tax
- Provide different scenarios to establish the advantages or disadvantages of filing separately or jointly
- Show how major decisions such as buying or selling a home will affect your end of year tax bill
- Interface with Quicken to download your existing tax information

175

Tax Planner is like a smart spreadsheet: just enter the values where required and it will instantly calculate your tax due. The Tax Planner is useful for calculating your tax liability for both the current financial year and the next. As the first installment of estimated tax for the next year must be paid when you lodge your income tax return for the current year, you will almost certainly use Tax Planner in both these situations.

 TIP **Automatic Data Entry** As a starting point, you may also load last year's Quicken data or the data to date for the current year by clicking **Quicken Data** in the Tax Planner's iconbar. The Tax Planner will annualize or forward project that data to come up with totals for the new financial year.

You should take the time before you start to use the Tax Planner to gather together as much information about your financial affairs as possible. Try to find as much documentation as you can on the following:

- Bank statements
- Paycheck stubs
- Receipts for taxes paid
- Interest payment records
- Medical and dental receipts
- Child care receipts
- Receipts from charitable contributions
- Dividend and annuity records
- Records of payments to an IRA
- Last year's tax return
- If filing jointly, the same again for your spouse

In this lesson, you learned about the Tax Planner utility. In the next lesson, you will learn how to use Tax Planner to plan your taxes for the year ahead.

Using the
Tax Planner

In this lesson, you will learn how to enter your data into the Tax Planner window.

Calculating Data

Tax Planner can work with your existing Quicken data or provide an electronic blank which you can use to look at a whole new scenario. Actually, you have a choice of three scenarios, but we'll get to that later.

If you want to use the Tax Planner to calculate your liability based on existing data, follow these steps:

1. Select your filing status using the **Status** pull-down list.
2. Select the appropriate year in the **Year** pull-down list.
3. Click **Quicken Data** to import your existing financial information from Quicken. (It is at this point that the decision to meticulously assign your categories and tax-related information will really pay off. You did do that, didn't you? Fortunately, it's never too late.) Quicken imports data from the start of the current year through to the last day of the previous month. (In other words, if you use the Tax Planner mid-May, Quicken will import data from 1/1/97 to 4/30/97.)

CAUTION

No Items Found If you have no previous Quicken data or you have not told Quicken which tax-related categories connect to Form 1040 or Schedule line items, you will see the message "No items found to import. You may need to set up tax schedules for your Quicken Categories."

If you do have data you would like to use, make sure the tax-related categories are set up in Quicken by clicking **Close** and checking the categories under **Features, Taxes, Set up for Taxes.** If you don't have any existing data, simply ignore this message.

4. Use the Preview Quicken Tax Data to select the items that are to be annualized through the year. See Figure 6.1 to select those items that should be annualized and those that shouldn't. When Quicken annualizes, it forecasts a total for the year according to the average already incurred by that account. Typically, you will want to annualize your wage or salary, medical expenses and interest income. However, you probably won't want to annualize rarely occurring totals such as capital gain on the sale of your house. Double-click an item to toggle its annualization status. Alternatively, **Annualize None** and **Annualize All** apply a blanket annualization to the lot. When you're done, click **OK** to copy that data to the Tax Planner.

 TIP **A Real World Example** Jeff, a self-employed plumber, is using Tax Planner to work out his estimated tax payments through 1998. He imports his Quicken data at the end of the first three months. One of the expenses incurred during that period relates directly to the purchase of a new set of tools…something he rarely needs to do. He decides not to annualized the purchase as it was a one-off expense. However, he does annualize his income over those first three months. This provides a truer projected picture of his profit and loss, income and estimated tax.

Double-click any line to toggle its annualizing status.

Click here to switch off all annualizing…

…or here to switch it all on.

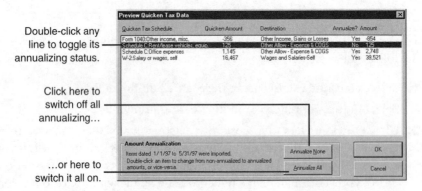

Figure 6.1 Select the items you need annualized. This will project the total to date forwards to arrive at an estimated total for the entire year.

 TIP **Using Last Year's Data** If you would like to use last year's data as the basis for the next financial year, select the previous financial year and click **Quicken Data**. Select the annualizations and click **OK**. Then change the financial year to the next financial year.

Unfortunately, the precise tax rates for the next financial year are rarely available when the Tax Planner software is finalized, so Tax Planner relies on some intelligent guesses. However, you can edit the tax rates or update them by visiting the Intuit site on the Web.

Figuring Your Adjusted Gross Income

The Tax Planner window is a little different to the rest of Quicken, although the reason can probably be chalked up to the sheer complexity of the tax regulations.

If you want to massage this data into relevant shape, you'll need to know how each of the fields and buttons works. Here, then, is a quick guide:

- **Wages and Salaries-Self**   Enter or adjust the total wages and salary you expect to earn through this or the following year. The IRS considers your income in terms of total compensation, but there's plenty of room later on to enter any other employment benefits you may receive.

- **Wages and Salaries-Spouse**   Use this field for your spouse's wage or salary.

- **Interest/Dividend Income**   Click this button to open the dialog box shown in Figure 6.2. These figures flow through to Schedule B. You'll find your taxable interest income noted on copies of the Form 1099-INT that is filed with the IRS by the organizations that pay you interest. Dividends come from banks, S-corporations, mutual funds, stocks and bonds and so on and are shown on Form 1099-DIV

Figure 6.2 Enter your interest and dividend income, rounding cents to the nearest dollar.

- **Business Income**   Click this button if you file a Schedule C with the rest of your tax return. This will open the dialog box shown in Figure 6.3.

TIP   **Quicken Home and Business 98**   This version of Quicken is targeted at small business users with a special Schedule C report. You can find it and a Tax Schedule report under the **Reports, Business** menu.

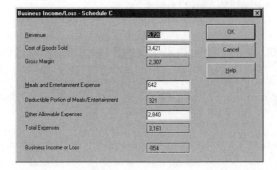

Figure 6.3   While the IRS requires that you file a Schedule C for every business you operate, this is not supported by Tax Planner. Instead, you should use this window to insert the totals as calculated across every business.

If you are uncertain how to calculate your business income and expenses, you should talk to a tax professional.

TIP   **Quicken Home and Business 98**   This version of Quicken is targeted at small business users with a special Schedule C report. You can find it and a Tax Schedule report under the **Reports, Business** menu.

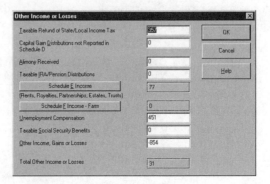

Figure 6.4   Even if your business is bleeding red like this one, you must still report your profit or loss on Schedule C.

- **Capital Gains and Losses** Click this button if you expect to fill out a Schedule D. If you held your investment for one year or more, it is a long term capital gain or loss. If you held your investment for less than one year, it is a short term capital gain or loss. While this window is used for simple capital gains and losses such as stocks and bonds, it is also used for more complex issues such as the sale of real estate or business investments. If you are unsure what counts and what doesn't, consult a tax professional. IRS Publication 17 also makes a good starting point. It is available from any IRS office or across the Internet from their Web site at **http:// www.irs.ustreas.gov**.

- **Other Income** Click this button to open the dialog shown in Figure 6.4. This dialog is a catch all for the other bits and pieces that can contribute to one's income tax. These include rents, royalties, farm income, alimony, revenue from a partnership, unemployment compensation and so on.

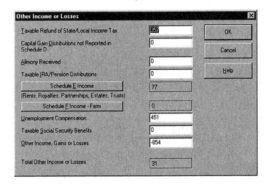

Figure 6.4 Tax Planner has numerous dialog boxes hidden under its main window. Other Income shown here is just one example among many.

- **Adjustments to Income** Adjustments to income include IRA deductions, alimony, moving expenses and other IRS-specified items. Once your total adjustments have been subtracted from Total Income, you will have your Adjusted Gross Income.

Specifying Deductions

As discussed in Lesson 4, you can choose between an itemized deduction or the standard deduction whichever turns out to be the greatest.

Click **Deductions** in the Tax Planner main window to open the dialog box shown in Figure 6.5.

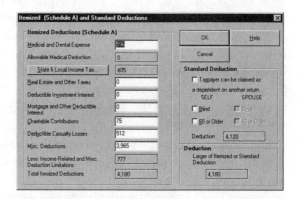

Figure 6.5 Tax Planner automatically chooses the most beneficial deduction method.

Use the left side of the Deductions window to list your Schedule A deductions including State and Local Income Tax. Many of these deductions have further conditions associated with them, but Tax Planner includes all the pertinent rules. Use the right side of the window to calculate your Scheduled Deductions.

Entering Your Itemized Deductions

Let's take a quick look at the requirements of Schedule A:

- **Medical and Dental Expense**   You are only allowed to claim those expenses for which you weren't reimbursed. You may, however, claim medical and dental expenses for yourself, your spouse (providing you were married at the time your spouse received the treatment or at the time you paid for it) and any dependents. You may not claim expenses incurred for cosmetic reasons, even if that treatment was prescribed by a doctor. For example, you cannot claim health club fees, weight loss programs or cosmetic surgery, even if undertaken on medical orders.

- **Allowable Medical Deduction**   Your allowable medical deduction is the total medical and dental expenses greater than 7.5 percent of your adjusted gross income.

- **State and Local Tax Payments**   Use this dialog box to enter your state and local estimated and withholding tax. Tax Planner projects the withholding payments forward but you'll need to work out your own estimated tax payments. (This part of the Tax Planner also lacks the annualization of the Quicken Data input.)

- **Real Estate and Other Taxes** Deductible real estate taxes cover state, local or foreign tax on real property not used for business purposes. If that property is under a mortgage, you may need to contact the lender to determine how much has already been paid on your behalf in real estate taxes.

  You may also deduct taxes on personal property, but only if the state or local tax is based on the value of the personal property, charged on that personal property and calculated on a yearly basis. This means a single up front tax payment when you purchase, say, the family car, is not tax deductible, although an annual registration fee could very well be.

- **Deductible Investment Interest** The allowable investment interest deduction should be calculated on Form 4952. Simply take the total and insert it here.

- **Charitable Contributions** You may apply a deduction equal to 100 percent of your allowable charitable contributions (including expenses incurred raising money for the charity), although the maximum in total deductions is generally limited to 50 percent of your adjusted gross income. Tax Planner will look after this limit for you. Not all contributions are deductible. For instance, you may not deduct money given to a civic league, social and sports clubs, labor unions and chambers of commerce, or amounts spent on the purchase of lottery tickets or raffles, even if the lottery or raffle was organized by a valid charity. Contributions to most foreign organizations are not allowed, with the exception of some Canadian and Mexican charities, although you may be able to contribute to a local chapter. And remember, you must have receipts for contributions over $250. The IRS maintains a list of recognized or valid charities. For more information, get in touch with your local office.

TIP **A Real World Example** Jeannie sells Michael $25 in lottery tickets for a draw run by a valid charity. However, to sell those tickets, Jeannie had to travel to Michael's farm, incurring gasoline costs of $10. Jeannie can claim that $10 as a charitable contribution, but Michael may not claim the cost of the lottery tickets.

- **Deductible Casualty Losses** These losses include those for casualty and theft. Casualty is damage, destruction or loss of property through an event which is identifiable, sudden, unexpected and unusual. IRS Publication 17 categorizes these events as earthquakes, hurricanes, tornadoes, floods, storms, volcanic eruptions, shipwrecks, mine cave-ins, sonic booms, vandalism, fires, car accidents and similar. Casualty does not include disease, gradual deterioration or drought. Theft includes any property that you have had stolen, so long as you can establish ownership, demonstrate when it was stolen and can show that it was stolen. You should calculate the deductible amount as follows:

Loss = Fair Market Value - Salvage Value - Insurance/Reimbursement Received.

The Loss is the total amount you may claim as a deduction.

- **Miscellaneous Deductions**   Use this field for everything else including the cost of preparing your tax return, employee business expenses (for example, travel expenses, entertainment expenses…50 percent is the usual deduction, and gift expenses), investment fees, union dues, uniform fees and almost any other expenses associated with earning an income for which you are not reimbursed.

- **Less: Income-Related and Miscellaneous Deduction Limitations**   Tax Planner applies the deduction limitations calculated on your adjusted gross income.

- **Total Itemized Deductions**   This field equals the total deductions allowed under Schedule A.

Calculating Your Standard Deductions

Standard deductions are far simpler. Follow these steps:

1. If you are being claimed as a dependent on another return, click in the box starting **Taxpayer can be claimed as**.

2. If you or your spouse is blind (presumably only partially), click the appropriate **Blind** box. Note that you are considered blind if you cannot see better than 20/200 in the better eye with glasses or contact lenses, and that your field of vision is not more than 20 degrees. If your (or your spouse's) vision can be corrected beyond these standards by contact lenses, but wearing them for longer than brief periods causes you pain, infection or ulcers, you may still claim the blind deduction.

3. If your (or your spouse's) 65th birthday was on or before January 1st on the year for which you are filing the return, you should click the appropriate **65 or Older** boxes.

When you're done, Tax Planner will display whichever is higher of your itemized and standard deductions and copy this figure back to the main Tax Planner window.

Calling in the Exemptions

Think of an exemption as a gift from Congress, handed down to provide tax breaks where they are needed most. Historically, exemptions were supposed to cover the total food costs for one person through the year. Today, of course, that isn't close to the case, but exemptions are still some of the most powerful tax deductions you will find.

Everyone is worth one exemption and during the 1996 tax year every exemption was worth a $2,250 tax deduction. The trick to exemptions comes in determining just who gets to claim that deduction. For example, if you are single, have no dependents and are not being claimed as a dependent, you may apply that exemption to yourself and claim the deduction.

However, if someone else claims you as a dependent, your exemption and subsequent deduction goes to them and you may not claim that deduction for yourself. (As every dependent's Social Security Number must be entered on the return of the person claiming them as a dependent, it is a trivial matter for the IRS to automatically flag multiple claims for exemptions on the one dependent.

The IRS does not look upon your spouse as a dependent. You may only claim a spousal exemption if you both file jointly (in which case there is no net gain). If you file separately, you may only claim his or her exemption if he or she has no income and that exemption is not being claimed elsewhere. The IRS applies a five part test to establish dependency. Potential dependents must satisfy each part.The test is not built into Tax Planner but is included in the Quicken Deluxe online books and is also included in the IRS Publication 17. Exemptions are phased out when your adjusted gross income exceeds a certain ceiling. Tax Planner takes this into account.

Other Tax Credits

Click **Other Tax Credits** to open the window shown in Figure 6.6.

Like the Other Income window discussed earlier, this is something of a catch all for the bits and pieces that would turn the main window into an unmanageable, non-navigable mess.

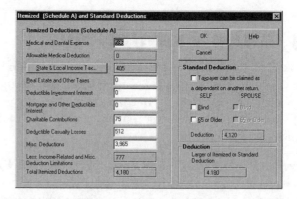

Figure 6.6 Use Other Tax Credits to catch up with all of the other odd deductions and credits that should apply to your return.

As it is, this dialog box provides a rather useful overview of your (and your spouse's) main sources of income.

To use the dialog box, follow these steps:

1. Use the upper pane, Self-Employment Income tax, to adjust your final income. The first line takes its total from the information you entered under Schedule C, Business Income and Schedule F, Farm Income.

2. Tax Planner assumes any amounts entered under Schedules C and F were earned by yourself. If they were earned by your spouse, you must enter a negative amount in **Other Income** and the identical but positive amount in your Spouse's **Other Income**. For example, if you and your spouse worked equally running a part-time market and it turned a profit of $4,000 for the year, and you are filing joint returns, you should enter $-2,000 in your **Other Income** and $2,000 in your spouse's. This will balance the $4,000 entered into your return under Schedule C, Business Income.

CAUTION

Filing Self-employment Returns The IRS regulations state that you must file Schedule SE (attached to Form 1040) if:

You were self-employed and your net earnings from self-employment were $400 or more, or

You had church employee income of $108.28 or more.

3. Add any remaining income that wasn't reported on Schedules C and F to whatever amount is already in **Other Income**.

4. Use **Other Wages** to enter any other wages from which Medicare and social security tax have been withheld but which weren't reported elsewhere in Tax Planner.

5. Use the lower pane, Alternative Minimum Tax, to calculate whether or not you are liable for this additional tax. **Tax Preference Items** increase the amount of AMT taxable income. These include claiming for accelerated depreciation of property acquired prior to 1987 and tax-exempt interest on nonessential private activity bonds. These and **Other Adjustments**, are explained on the instructions for Form 6251.

TERM

Alternative Minimum Tax (AMT) AMT is used to increase your tax if you are receiving an unusual level of tax benefit through certain itemized deductions and other exemptions. Basically, AMT works like this: calculate the actual monetary benefit from those deductions and/or exemptions. Add that amount to your taxable income and calculate your new income tax. If that income tax is greater than your usual income tax, you will have to pay a penalty. AMT is usually figured using Form 6251, but Tax Planner can also do it for you.

6. Enter any other taxes you have incurred in **Other Taxes**. These include tax on foreign income, tax attributable to early retirement plans, and tax on lump-sum distributions.

7. Tax credits directly reduce the amount of tax you must pay. This is, if you will, the most powerful form of tax deduction. Use **Tax Credits** to enter the total amount. Typical credits include the following:

Child and Dependent Care Credit (use Form 2441, Child and Dependent Care Expenses)

Credit for the Elderly or the Disabled (use Schedule R along with Form 1040)

Earned Income Credit (use Schedule EIC with Form 1040A or Form 1040)

Nonrefundable credits (credit for prior year minimum tax, mortgage interest credit, credit for electric vehicles and foreign tax credit)

Refundable credits (credit for excess social security tax or railroad retirement tax withheld, credit from a regulated investment company, and credit on diesel-powered highway vehicles).

In this lesson, you learned how to copy or enter your financial data into the Tax Planner window. In the next lesson, you will learn how to interpret the results.

Understanding the Results

In this lesson, you will learn how to interpret Tax Planner's calculations, work with multiple scenarios and edit Tax Planner's tax rates.

Tax Planner

It takes some time to complete the entry of data, but once you're done, Tax Planner delivers the results on a plate. Just take a look at the lower right corner of the Tax Planner window. You should see the following fields:

Total Tax   This is the total tax you must pay throughout the year.

Marginal, Avg. Rate   Your marginal tax rate is that rate applied to the final bracket of your income. It is shown as a percentage in the left hand box. The marginal rate is also referred to as your tax bracket. The average rate is that applied across your total income. This is the real percentage of the tax you will pay. It is shown to the right of the marginal tax rate.

Calculating Tax Due

Use tax due to work out how much withholding tax you should be removing from your paycheck or, alternatively, how much you should be paying in estimated tax.

To calculate your withholding tax, follow these steps:

1. Click **Withholding, W-4** to open the dialog shown in Figure 7.1.

2. This panel calculates the total annual withholding from the amount withheld to date, the amount removed each pay period and the number of pay periods yet to come. In **Withholdings To Date**, enter the total amount of Federal withholding tax removed from your paychecks so far. (Note: this is not the number of instances withholding tax has been withdrawn.)

3. Enter your **Next Pay Date**.

4. Select your **Pay Period**.

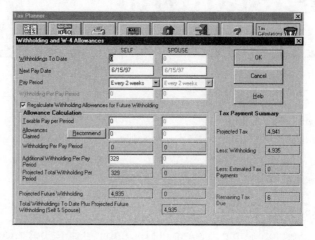

Figure 7.1 Use the Withholding dialog to calculate how much extra withholding should be removed from every paycheck.

CAUTION

Deciding Between Every 2 Weeks and Twice/Month The correct choice depends on whether you earn a salary or a wage. Wages tend to accumulate every week or two and are calculated on the number of hours you work. For continuity, you will almost certainly be paid on a specific day of the week or month. A salary runs through the year and tends to be paid on a calendar basis, for example the first and 15th day of each month, no matter which day of the week it falls upon.

5. In **Withholding per Pay Period**, enter the amount of Federal Tax that is being withheld every pay period.

6. If you would like Tax Planner to calculate the actual amount of tax that should be withheld from you wage or salary every paycheck in order to fully cover your estimated tax, select **Recalculate Withholding Allowance for Future Withholding** and continue to Step 7. Tax Planner will take into account the total already withheld and the number of pay periods remaining in the financial year.

7. In **Taxable Pay Per Period** enter your gross pay less pre-tax deductions.

8. Enter the number of allowances you are claiming in **Allowances Claimed**. Click **Recommend** for Quicken to calculate the ideal withholding. If you have also made one or more estimated payments, you should fill in that section first, as described below, and then jump back to this window and click **Recommend**.

9. To hold more than the recommended, enter the desired amount into **Additional Withholding per Pay Period**.

10. **Projected Total Withholding per Pay Period** is the amount you should enter on Form W-4 and file with your employer.

11. **Refund Due** is the total tax you will be owed from IRS at the end of the year. If this figure is negative, then you will owe that amount to IRS.

12. Click **OK** when you're done to drop back to the main Tax Planner window.

Entering Your Estimated Tax Payments

Click **Est. Tax Pmts** if:

- You have already made estimated payments
- You intend to make estimated payments
- You chose to have your previous year's refund applied to this year's estimated payments

To fill in the dialog, follow these steps:

1. In the first text field type in your estimated taxes paid so far.

2. In the second text field type in the estimated taxes you expect to pay through the end of the year. If you will be using Tax Planner to work out the shortfall and add it to your withholding tax, just leave this blank.

3. In the third field, enter the refund from last year that you chose to apply to this year's estimated payments.

4. Click **OK** when you're done.

Setting Scenarios

The Tax Planner is useful not only for working out your end of year tax liability but also for playing around with various situations to see how you can reduce that tax.

For example, what would happen to your tax situation if you and your spouse jumped from separate to joint filing? For that matter, what will happen to your taxes in the next financial year?

Tax Planner makes this sort of speculation easy. To work with different scenarios, follow these steps:

1. Enter you base data as described in the previous lesson.

2. In the Scenarios area of the main Tax Planner window, click either of the alternate scenario buttons: **Alt. 1** or **Alt. 2**.

3. If you would like to use your current data in the new scenario, click **Yes**. Otherwise, click **No**.

4. Adjust that data as necessary. Click any of the scenario buttons to jump back and forth between scenarios. Tax Planner even remembers those scenarios between Quicken sessions.

5. To reset a scenario and start over, click **Reset**. You may choose to **Reset All** scenarios or **Reset Current** scenario only.

6. To see how the scenarios stack up against each other, click **Compare**. When you're done, click **OK**.

Editing the Tax Rates

Tax Planner's tax rates for the financial year in which the product is released are always accurate. Those for the next year are another matter altogether.

Click **Rates** to open the dialog shown in Figure 7.2. Use this dialog to edit the existing and future tax rates, if known. If you receive a list of tax rates, you will be able to copy these into the fields provided. There are many other tax rates in effect, but most are linked to inflation. Tax Planner sets inflation at 3 percent and applies this to those hidden rates.

TIP **Finding the Latest Tax Rates** The easiest way to get the latest tax rates is to contact Intuit on the Internet. Intuit's Tax Table Service is provided at **http:\\www.intuit.com\tts**.

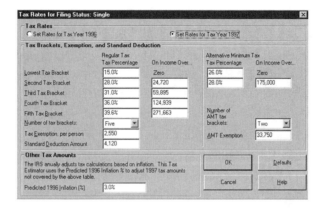

Figure 7.2 Tax Planner adjusts the tax rates for the next financial year according to the percent inflation.

In this lesson, you learned how to interpret Tax Planner's results, to jump between multiple scenarios, and to update the Tax Planner tax rates. In the next lesson, you will learn how to link Quicken to TurboTax for the ultimate in do-it-yourself tax preparation.

Linking Quicken to TurboTax

In this lesson, you learn how TurboTax and Quicken combined provide a total 1040 solution.

Quicken and TurboTax

Quicken and TurboTax make a powerful pair. With Quicken automatically categorizing all your financial data and TurboTax grabbing those details and dropping them into your Form 1040, tax-time couldn't be simpler.

Using TurboTax will bring you these benefits:

- A simple step-by-step interview makes filling in the 1040 a piece of cake.
- TaxLink will pull in your data from Quicken, saving significant retyping.
- The Tax Advisor will kick in with personalized money-saving advice.
- Tips help you to plan your taxes for the year ahead.
- Audit Alerts let you know when an item on your return falls outside the norm, helping to stave off that audit.
- The U.S. Average Comparison feature draws on previous IRS statistics to show you how the items on your return compare to others in the same income bracket.
- If you've purchased TurboTax Deluxe, the CD-ROM includes numerous onscreen publications including most of the IRS's major efforts, several income tax handbooks and video advice from taxation experts.

If that isn't enough, the TurboTax product includes every major form and worksheet required by the IRS. This includes the three versions of the Form 1040 (1040EZ, 1040A, and 1040 Standard), all of the associated schedules, and all of the forms required for specialized procedures such as filing for an extension, selling property, foreign earned income, and some eighty more! Each of the forms comes with a "Guide Me" tutor which will step you through the items and let you know when you've gone wrong.

TurboTax ships in three flavors: HeadStart Version, Final Version, and Deluxe. The HeadStart version lacks some of the features of the Final Version but is released a little earlier. If you purchased the HeadStart directly from Intuit, you are already registered and will receive the Final Version in February. However, if you purchased the HeadStart Version elsewhere, you must register to receive the update. Do not try to send in your return based on the HeadStart version.

TurboTax Deluxe is the Final Version with added extras. In addition, Intuit publish TurboTax for Business and TurboTax State. All of these products interface with Quicken.

Product Under Construction   TurboTax 97 was under early develoment at the time of writing and not available for documentation. The information contained in this lesson pertains to TurboTax 96. TurboTax 97 may contain new or changed features.

CAUTION

So, that's enough of TurboTax's features. How does it help Quicken users?

Linking to Quicken

If you haven't yet installed TurboTax, do so now. Once TurboTax is installed, you can access it through the Windows **Start** menu or within Quicken by selecting **Features**, **Taxes**, **TurboTax**.

TurboTax can work with your financial data in several ways. You can, for instance, import last year's TurboTax data and use that as the basis for the current year. Alternatively, you might import tax return data that was prepared by your taxation professional. So long as that data has been saved in the TXF format, TurboTax shouldn't have any trouble working with it. However, for our purposes, what you really want to do is work with your Quicken data.

When you copy your Quicken data to TurboTax you do so along a one-way pipe. If you need to adjust that data, it is important that you adjust it in Quicken first, then import the updated information into TurboTax.

You should also know that your Quicken data on its own probably is not sufficient to create a complete tax return. You must verify it by either working through the step-by-step interview provided in TurboTax or by editing each of the TurboTax forms on-screen.

The easiest way to import your data into TurboTax is to do so with the TaxLink Assistant. When you do, keep the following points in mind:

- TurboTax will find the file you've most recently used in Quicken—usually QDATA.QDB. To import data from a different file, open that file in Quicken first.

- Make sure you have completed recording all financial information for the year you are filing this return.

- You do not need Quicken running to perform the import. TurboTax launches Quicken if necessary while it copies the necessary data. When it has finished, it also closes Quicken down.

- If your Quicken data is password-protected, you must provide that password before the data can be imported.

- TurboTax imports data contained in Quicken categories marked as Tax Form Line Items. However, you can reassign any tax-related Quicken category from TurboTax, assigning Tax Form Line Items to any categories already marked as tax-related but not linked to a specific line or form.

- TurboTax automatically looks for tax data pertaining to its version year. That means that TurboTax 97 will only look for and read data earmarked for the 1997 tax year. You cannot use TurboTax 97 for any other tax year unless you import data saved in the TXF format. To create a TXF file, from Quicken select **Reports**, **Home**, **Tax Schedule**. Click **Create** and, once the report appears, click **Export**. Assign a name to the file and click **OK**.

Reviewing Your Imported Data

Once you have imported your Quicken data, you will have numerous opportunities to review that information. If you imported using the TaxLink facility, this includes reassigning categories to other Tax Form Line Items. Unlike changes to the data itself, you can copy changes to the categories back to Quicken, ensuring your Quicken category information and TuboTax category information remain matched.

The TaxLink can reassign individual transactions as well entire categories. Just select the transaction or transactions in the hierarchical list and link them to another Tax Form Line Item.

Completing Your Return

With your data imported, you can choose to use the EasyStep process to complete your tax return, or throw caution to the wind and fill in your return form by form. Before filing, make sure you use TurboTax's review feature to go through your return, searching for errors or omissions. Don't forget that while TurboTax is a very capable product, you should always seek the advice of a taxation professional. When you finish, you can print and post your returns or file them electronically. The latter will attract a small additional fee but has the advantage that you will receive any refund due sooner than through a printed return.

In this lesson, you learned about how TurboTax integrates with Quicken. In the next lesson, you learn how to find useful tax deductions.

The Tax Deduction Finder

In this lesson, you will learn how to use the Tax Deduction Finder to minimize the tax you will need to pay at the end of the year.

The Tax Deduction Finder

The Tax Deduction Finder is a powerful interrogative tool that will help you decide whether you are eligible for certain tax deductions.

At first glance, the Tax Deduction Finder seems rather complex, but as soon as you have completed one deduction assessment, you will know how to complete the rest. In this lesson, we have used the example of deciding if a bad debt can be claimed as tax deductible.

To use the Finder, just follow these steps:

1. Select the menu **Features, Taxes, Tax Deduction Finder**. The screen you will see is shown in Figure 9.1. This figure provides a guide to the Finder's principal commands and features.

2. As the screen suggests, you should start by choosing a deduction type.

3. Then select the actual deduction. This list changes according to the deduction type specified above.

4. To establish if you meet the basic criteria for any deduction, answer the questions shown in the third list. Just click under **Y** if the answer is Yes, and **N** if it's No.

5. If you believe you are eligible, click **More Information** to find out more about that deduction.

6. Finally, to track any future transactions that may be eligible for that deduction, click **Create a Category**. You will see a dialog similar to that shown in Figure 9.2. Use this category when you record those transactions. You may also need to adjust some of the transactions you have already entered into your registers.

Choose your major deduction category.
For example: employee, homeowner,
individual, investor and more.

Click in the Y (Yes)
or N (No) column for
each question.

Select a deduction type. Use the scroll bars to move up and down the list.

Click here to read more about the conditions associated with this deduction.

Click here to create a specific tax-related category for this deduction.

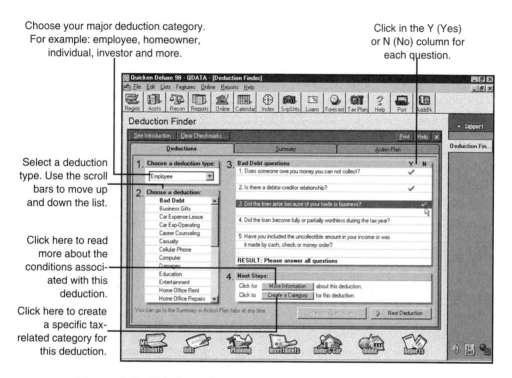

Figure 9.1 This figure illustrates the Tax Deduction Finder.

Figure 9.2 This figure shows the Creating a Bad Debt category dialog box.

CAUTION

Don't always trust the deduction finder! Quicken cannot know for certain whether you are eligible for a deduction. Always look under **More Information** if it suggests you are eligible. This will tell you a little more about the deduction. You must also speak to a tax professional. The requirements for many deductions are very, very complex, and if Quicken tried to establish the full set of circumstances, it would take you much longer to complete each question.

7. Once you've finished the current set of questions, you can move on using **Next Deduction**. However, there is no need to complete these deductions in sequence, or even to complete them at all. If you are not sure about one deduction, just leave it at whatever stage of completion and move on. Quicken will remember your answers for next time.

8. When you have finished answering all of the deductions that interest you, click the **Summary** tab. This will show you how many deductions you may be eligible for out of each category.

9. Finally, click **Action Plan** to see what you should do to support your claim for this deduction with the IRS (see Figure 9.3). You can also print yourself a copy using the **Print** button in the top-right corner of the window.

10. (Optional) If you think you've made some mistakes and would like to start over, click **Clear Checkmarks...** and confirm the action. This removes the checkmarks for every previous question, giving you a clean slate.

The Tax Deduction Finder is a great utility for helping you find ways to reduce your tax bill—or even earn yourself a refund! However, even though you have already heard this twice before, you must speak to a tax professional before claiming a deduction based on the Tax Deduction Finder's assessment. There are no guarantees that the Tax Deduction Finder will lead you to all of the deductions you are eligible for, and it may even turn out that it falsely indicates your eligibility for some. It's an easy, powerful utility, but you should always use it with caution, make sure you have paper-based backup, and speak to someone who makes finding tax deductions their business.

In this lesson you learned how to use the Tax Deduction finder—with some reservations. In the next Part, you will learn how Quicken can help you to manage your small business.

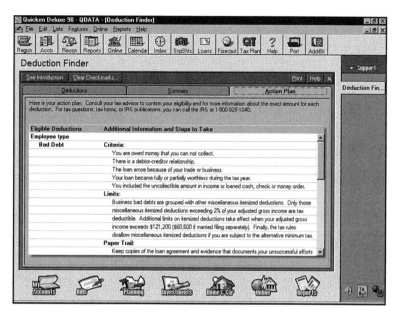

Figure 9.3   Always refer to the action plan. The plan will help you prove your deductions to the IRS.

Online
Services

Taking Quicken Online

In this lesson, you learn how to set up your system to use Quicken's online services.

Quicken's Online Features

Today, almost everyone who uses a personal computer also uses the Internet, whether through work, college, or via an Internet service provider from their home. Quicken 98 includes many robust Internet features that allow you to receive stock updates, pay bills, manage your bank accounts online, and much more.

 Internet Service Provider Usually shortened to ISP, this term refers to the person who supplies your Internet connection. You might connect through a very small, local ISP, or you might use a larger provider such as America Online, CompuServe, Microsoft Network, or your telephone utility. The ISP will bill you for the time you spend using the Internet. Keep this in mind: Although the Quicken Internet capabilities are apparently free of charge (with some conditions discussed later), you still must pay the telephone company connect fees and long-distance fees—if any—and your ISP's online fees. However, if you just want to use Quicken's own Internet facilities, Intuit can set you up a free account. For more information, read on.

When it comes to the Internet, Quicken is no slouch. In fact, its online capabilities contribute an enormous amount to the software's total functionality.

Using its Internet services, you can:

- Manage your banking and receive and pay bills.
- Pay for and order Quicken-compatible checks and windowed envelopes.
- Pay for and order other software products integrated with Quicken.
- Perform great financial research in almost no time at all.
- Update your security prices.
- Download the latest financial headlines.
- Quickly grab any improvements and bug fixes made to your existing Quicken software.

The online features crop up throughout Quicken, but you will also find nearly all of them huddled under the Online menu. Click the menu right now and we'll go for a quick tour, just to show you what's in store. After you click **Online**, you should see the following entries (see Figure 1.1):

- **Online Center**   The Online Financial Services Center. From here, you can do all of your online banking and bill paying.
- **Online Financial Services Setup**   This menu will help you to enable your online accounts through compatible financial institutions.
- **Financial Institutions**   View the list of services provided by various institutions as well as their contact details, and apply for their online services.
- **CheckFree**   An older bill-paying standard now superseded by the Open Financial Network. The Open Financial Network is limited to participating financial institutions; however, through them, you can obtain account balances and perform other transactions online. CheckFree works with any U.S. checking account but allows you only to pay your bills online. This menu will set up your software to use CheckFree. Once you select this option, you will see a wide range of menu choices.

CAUTION

CheckFree Users   If you are a CheckFree user, you may already have had experience using the service through previous versions of Quicken. The online facilities and procedures described in this part of the book are, for the most part, not applicable to CheckFree accounts, with the exception of online bill payments. This part of the book considers procedures valid only for users of the replacement online banking, payments, and billing system included in Quicken 98.

Figure 1.1   The Online menu acts as the launch point for all of Quicken's Internet features.

- **Get Bills Online**   Online billing is a new Quicken feature that you can use to receive your bills electronically rather than by mail. This is electronic commerce of the future today. Zero paperwork and zero hassle brought to you by the Open Financial Exchange standard for transferring financial data over the Internet.

Open Financial Exchange   Someone once said: Standards are wonderful; there are so many to choose from. The Open Financial Exchange is yet another standard, but one which stands an excellent chance of success. Developed by Intuit, Inc., CheckFree Corporation, and Microsoft Corporation, it specifies how electronic financial data should be exchanged across the Internet. It is a free specification and can be used by software developers and financial institutions to offer customers using Internet connections services as diverse as banking, billing, and payments, as well investing, financial planning, tax return lodgment, and more. Because the specification is free and supported by the heavy-weights of the electronic payments and software industries, it will most likely become the most widely supported standard of its type.

- **Update Quicken 98**   No software is ever completely bug free, and Intuit spend a good deal of time squashing those that managed to stow away only to resurface after the software was released. This menu will automatically update your software with the latest bug fixes and enhancements. It also downloads the latest stock prices, market news, and more. If you haven't set up any online stocks, you will be prompted to set this up the first time you choose this item.

- **Quicken on the Web**   This submenu bundles together all of the Quicken sites on the World Wide Web. While you can get to these through other bits of the program, this makes for a very handy collection.

- **Internet Connection**   This submenu will help you to set up your Internet connection and also control how it connects and when it should disconnect.
- **Disconnect**   Cancel your Internet connection.

This list doesn't define the true extent of Quicken's Internet capabilities, but it does form the core. Other capabilities include communicating via e-mail with your financial institution, funds transfer between accounts, stock quote and news downloads, electronic account statements, the automatic recording of your credit-card purchases, and access to a truly astonishing amount of financial information not just on Quicken's sites but anywhere on the entire World Wide Web.

Before You Start

When you purchased Quicken, you also purchased the right to access the Quicken Financial Network. QFN acts as the gateway through which you can use the services previously described, even though QFN does not generate all of the information used by these services. The online securities price quotes, for example, are provided by another company altogether.

However, you are allowed to use these services at no charge for a period of one year starting from the moment you register your software.

In 12 months' time, you can either upgrade to the latest Quicken version, thus garnering another year's access, or you can arrange to pay Intuit a small fee for continued access using your existing software. (Intuit will send you an e-mail about 10 months into the trial setting out the options and costs.)

Still, before you can use Quicken's Internet features, you need to ensure you have the right hardware and software. Check for the following items:

- Obviously, you need a personal computer. What you might not know is that it is difficult to surf today's graphically heavy Internet with anything less than a computer based on an Intel 486 chip running at 66MHz (or equivalent competing CPU) with at least 8M of RAM. This is the absolute minimum. Of course, today's entry-level computers are much, much faster and will help make your browsing very efficient.

- Some form of Internet provision. You may connect to the Internet free of charge through Intuit's own service, but your access is limited to the Quicken Financial Network. Even though that includes all of the features previously mentioned, it isn't possible to move beyond the Intuit site on the Web. You may find this a little limiting, but if you are not already on the Internet, the Intuit access is a great place to start.

  If you want to use the rest of the Internet, you will need to apply through Intuit to upgrade your access, or connect through another Internet Service Provider.

- Hardware to connect to the Internet. Depending on the type of service provided by your ISP, you will need either a:

  - **Modem**   These are used for dial-up ISPs. Your modem should operate at a speed of at least 9600 bits per second. If you need to purchase a new modem, don't buy one that runs at any less than 33,600 bps (often referred to as 33.6Kbps).

  - **ISDN**   This system is fast, cheap, and reliable, offering transfer speeds approximately two to four times the speed of most modem connections. Before you can use ISDN, you need to set up an ISDN line through your telephone service company, as well as a special connection with your ISP. This may cost more than a standard modem connection.

  - **Cable Modem**   Cable connections require their own style of modem. Where supported, two-way cable Internet connections are incredibly fast, but such support is a rarity. Most cable connections receive information through a cable modem but rely on a slower telephone-connected modem to send data back the other way. For further information, you should speak to your cable company or your ISP.

  - **Network Proxy**   If you will be accessing the Internet through an existing link provided by your LAN (local area network), your computer is already attached to that network. As the network is also attached to the Internet, you have all of the hardware you need. Instead, you will need to set up your computer to use the networked Internet connection. If you need any help, speak to your network administrator.

- Software to connect. All of the most recent versions of Windows can support the Internet through any of the connections previously detailed. Your Internet Service Provider will provide you with specific instructions on how to set up your version of Windows to access the Internet through their service. Alternatively, read the section on connection through Intuit later in this lesson.

- World Wide Web browser. Quicken ships with Internet Explorer 3.02. This was installed when you installed Quicken. Once you have that and the other items in this list, you have everything you need to use Quicken's Internet capabilities (see Figure 1.22).

Figure 1.2 With a Web Browser installed, you can access enormous amounts of financial information across the Net.

 TIP **Are Online Transactions Secure?** During any online session with Quicken, your data is encrypted using passwords and PINs. As you keep your PIN secret, no one else should be able to access your accounts.

But what about data in transit? Isn't the Internet full of all kinds of security holes?

Well, it was. But improvements in encryption technology ensure that the amount of time it would take someone to decrypt your financial information would cost far more than any benefit they could derive. However, if you should ever intentionally or accidentally send data across an unsecured connection, that information can be read by anyone who is snooping.

To help security, Quicken doesn't store your PIN on your computer. While you have to enter it every time you send a batch of online transactions, this ensures that should someone try to use your computer in situ or remove it from your premises altogether, they still won't be able to access your accounts.

Certain information is stored on the computers belonging to Intuit and Intuit Services Corporation. There is a possibility that hackers could gain access to those computers, just as they seem to be able to do with most bank computers.

Don't forget that you can also assign a password to your Quicken files. This will prevent anyone but you from accessing your accounts and online services. (Don't just rely on the Windows password. Even under Windows NT, it may still not prevent someone from accessing your files.)

Connecting Quicken to the Internet

After all that, connecting Quicken to the Internet will probably prove a lot easier than you might have thought.

The first time you try to access any Internet service (including the Quicken software registration), you will be presented with a dialog box called Internet Connection Setup. (You can open this at any time through the menu **Online, Internet Connection, Setup**.)

Use this dialog box to specify the method you want to use to connect to the Internet (see Figure 1.3). The options include an existing Internet connection, a network connection, or Intuit's own free Internet connection. After you've made your choice, click **Next**.

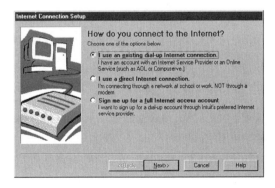

Figure 1.3   Select your chosen Internet Connection from the three provided.

Depending on your choice, Quicken may search your hard drive for any Internet service providers, displaying a list of your existing dial-up connections. Make your selection and click **Next**.

Next, you should see a Browser Preference message letting you know that Intuit recommends you use Microsoft Internet Explorer 3.0 or later. Click **Next** to continue.

Select your favorite browser from the list—if displayed—and click **Next**.

Quicken will now offer to optimize your connection through a diagnostic service. You can't lose anything by doing this, so just select **Yes, I want to send diagnostic data.** and click **Next**.

The next screen summarizes your choices so far (see Figure 1.4). Yours most likely will differ from the figure. Click **Finish** to complete the setup.

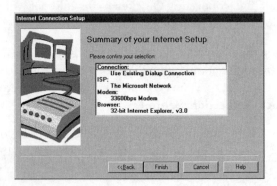

Figure 1.4   Check the summary to make sure the configuration has gone as planned.

The final dialog box presents you with your Internet Connection Options. Select them as follows:

- **Prompt me to update Quicken '98 on Startup**   Check this if you want Quicken to present the update dialog box when it starts. If so, the next time you start Quicken, a dialog box will ask if you would like to update immediately, or wait until later.

- **Prompt me to close my connection after 5 minutes of no activity**   The default value of 5 minutes will maintain your Internet connection for that period of time before automatically closing the connection. You may want to increase this period if you often have breaks of that length between Internet sessions.

- **Keep my Internet connection open after updating Quicken '98** Check this box to prevent Quicken from automatically canceling your Internet connection after it has completed updating.

Click **OK** once you have completed this dialog box. If all has gone well, your Internet connection is now ready to roll.

CAUTION

The Internet Didn't Connect! What Now? If the test fails, check that your modem is connected to your telephone line. Otherwise, you may need to reinstall your ISP's software or modem drivers. You should contact your ISP and consult your modem documentation for more information. If you are using Intuit's own Internet connection, contact Intuit technical support.

Quicken's Internet facilities are divided into two major services: financial transactions and information. The financial side requires at least one account with a participating financial institution. You will learn about obtaining and configuring these accounts in Lesson 2. The financial facilities encompass online banking, payments, and billing, and comprise the first group on the Online menu, from Online Center to Get Bills Online.

Even if you don't see the need for these services, you can still make great use of Quicken's other Internet capabilities. These are all provided by the Quicken Financial Network. They fall under the Quicken on the Web menu. So long as you have a working Internet connection and are within your first 12 months of using this version of Quicken, they are essentially free, very useful, and extremely informative. And, best of all, you can start using them right away.

In this lesson, you learned about Quicken's Internet services and how to start your own Internet connection. In the next lesson, you will learn how to set up your Online Center.

Setting Up and Using the Online Center

In this lesson, you learn how to apply for financial services, enable your accounts, and access the Online Center.

Getting Started with the Online Center

The Online Center is the heart of Quicken's online banking, online payments, online investing, and online billing.

With online banking, you can:

- Download up-to-the-minute statements and account balances
- More easily reconcile your accounts
- Transfer money between accounts
- Communicate with your financial institution using e-mail—even if you don't have an Internet e-mail address
- Save time by copying your account or credit card transactions from the electronic statement straight into Quicken

If that's not enough, with online payments you will be able to:

- Electronically pay your bills to anyone within the U.S., regardless of whether they have a computer.
- Do away with handwritten checks, envelopes, and stamps.
- Schedule your bill payments in advance so that the bills will be paid on-time, every time, even if you've taken a six-month holiday.
- Stop payments online.

Online investing will let you:

- Record the latest price movements, providing your with an up-to-date value of your investment holdings.
- Download the latest cleared transactions, balances, and positions.
- Automatically record commissions and other costs associated with your investment account.
- Update the cash balance in your investment account.
- Automatically register stock splits and other transactions that adjust the level of your holdings.

Finally, with online billing, you can receive your bills electronically, as long as the debtor has organized to transmit them via the ISC system. When you pay those bills, the transaction is automatically entered in your register. To use any of these facilities, you must first set up your Online Center. This is easy and will only take you a few minutes. To set up the center, select the menu **Online, Online Financial Services Setup**. You should see the dialog box shown in Figure 2.1.

The dialog box has five functions:

- Click **Tell Me More** to go on a tour of the Online Center's features. This button opens a Help window where you can read about Online Financial Services or take a video tour. You need to close the Help window and, optionally, video window to return to the Get Started with Online Financial Services dialog box.
- Click **Set Up** to set up your Internet connection or, if you already have done so, to specify your Internet Connection Options. You learned about these tasks in Lesson 1.

CAUTION

Registering Quicken   If you have not yet registered Quicken, the Quicken 98 User Setup dialog box will advise you to do so before you can use the product's Internet features. This occurs when you click **Apply Now**, described next. You must click **Continue** and complete the registration to gain access to those features. Once you have finished, you can go on with your Online Financial Services setup.

- Click **Apply Now** to view the list of services (banking, online payment, credit card, and brokerage) and the financial institutions that support them. Once you apply, you will receive an information pack in the mail providing your account numbers and pins. You learn about applying for an account next.

- Click **Enable Accounts** after you have received the information pack. Enter the details where prompted to complete the setup so that you can use the online accounts.

- Click **Financial Institutions** to go to the list linked through **Apply Now**.

Figure 2.1 This figure illustrates the first step in setting up your Online Center.

Applying for an Account

To use Quicken's newest online facilities, you must have an account with a participating financial institution.

Unfortunately, while the convenience of online banking and bill paying is quite wonderful, none of the services are free. Online banking costs just a few dollars per month, but online payments are a different matter. These cost around $10 per month for up to 20 payments. Extra payments thereafter cost about $0.50 each but are usually billed in groups of five or ten. The specific details depend on your financial institution, but the information isn't difficult to track down.

To start the setup process, make you are in the Online Financial Services Setup dialog box shown in Figure 2.1. Click **Apply Now**. This button will take you to the list of participating financial institutions maintained on the QFN Web site. If you are not already online, Quicken will automatically dial or make the connection for you. If it doesn't, you may need to manually connect your Dial-Up connection.

You should see a window similar to that shown in Figure 2.2.

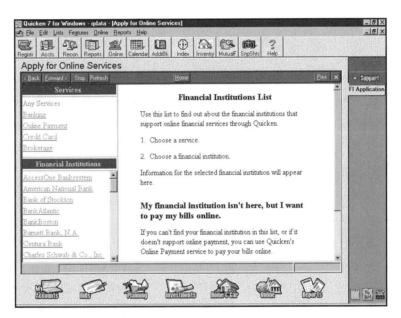

Figure 2.2 Almost every day, more financial institutions join the Open Financial Network and thus this list.

It takes very little time to apply for a service. Just follow these steps:

1. Select the service you wish to apply for using the upper left-hand pane. Quicken uses your selection to hone the lower list, showing only those institutions supporting that specific service.

2. Look for your financial institution in the list shown in the lower left pane. You must have an existing account with that institution to successfully apply for online services. If you can't find your institution, you're out of luck. You can, however, still pay your bills online by applying for an Intuit Services Corporation CheckFree account. Call CheckFree Customer Service at **1-800-462-6765** for more information. If you have your Web browser set up, download a CheckFree application form from **http://www.quicken. com/banking/enroll.html**.

3. If you do find your financial institution, click on its name and then click **Apply Now** in the right-hand pane (see Figure 2.3). Follow the directions shown on your screen. Within a few days you should receive a package in the mail providing your PIN number and an account information sheet. You will need this information to complete the Enable Accounts procedure discussed later.

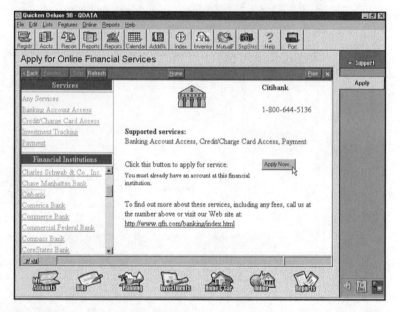

Figure 2.3   Click here to complete the online account application through your financial institution.

4. If you want to apply for other services, repeat these steps.

Enabling Your Quicken Accounts

At this point, it must be assumed that you have applied for and received your account information for each of the online services you want to use.

Your final task, then, is to provide Quicken with the information it needs to successfully conduct transfer, payments, statement downloads, and so on.

Again, this will only take a minute or two. Follow these steps:

1. From the Online Financial Services Setup dialog box, click **Enable Accounts**. This will take you to the Internet Connection Options dialog box. Click **OK** to move to the Select Financial Institution dialog box shown in Figure 2.4.

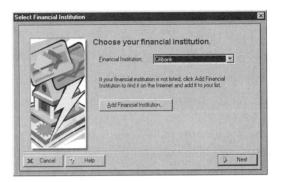

Figure 2.4 This figure illustrates selecting the online institutions.

2. If this is the first time you have set up such an account, click **Add Financial Institution** to add a new entry. Quicken will connect to the Internet and display a special Financial Institutions list. Select the institution from which you have received your online account information.

3. Now you can select the appropriate institution from the drop-down list of financial institutions. Once you have selected the institution, click **Next** to continue.

4. Figure 2.5 shows the Online Account Setup dialog box. As you can see, you can choose to create a new account as you go, or edit an existing account. If you create a new account, you will need to work through some dialog boxes not described here that step you through creating a new account. You can read about these in Part 1. To change an existing account, select it from the list. Click **Next** to move on.

5. Use the next dialog box to select the type of online service this account supports. Selecting a service that isn't supported causes connection errors and other problems. Make sure you only select those you have applied for. Click **Next** when you have finished.

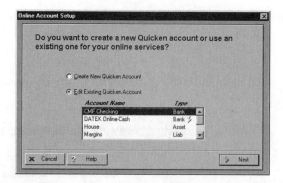

Figure 2.5 You can create a new account on the fly, or give an existing account online capabilities.

6. Turn to your information sheet and type in the routing number and click **Next**. This is used to identify your bank.

7. Type in your account's account number and select the account type. Click **Next**.

8. Type in your Customer ID. This is also shown on your online account's information sheet. Click **Next** to move on.

9. Finally, you should arrive at the first part of the account Summary Screen. Check the information shown and click **Next** to move to the second Summary Screen. Give the details a final check against your information sheet and click **Done** to save the account.

10. Read the Service Agreement Information page, click **OK** to move past this and you'll be finished.

Well done! Now you're ready to tackle the Online Center.

TIP **Canceling Online Accounts** If you ever need to cancel an account's online capabilities, select the menu **Lists, Account** (Ctrl+A), select the account in the list and click **Edit**. Remove the check marks next to those online aspects you wish to cancel. You will see the options marked as **Enable Online Banking**, **Enable Online Payment**, and **Enable Online Investment**.

Using the Online Center

Once you have set up your online accounts, the hard work is done. You will be able to enjoy all of the enormous convenience of electronic banking with almost no administrative hassle.

All of your online transactions take place through the Online Financial Services Center, also known as the Online Center. From here, you can do all of your banking, bill paying, and investing, as well as swap e-mail with your financial institution.

In the next few lessons, we'll look at the specifics of banking, bill paying, and so on. For now, though, let's take a quick look at the Online Center.

Select the menu **Online, Online Center**. You may need to **OK** your way past an Internet Connection Options dialog box and a second dialog box requesting permission to get updated information about your financial institutions. Eventually, you should see an Online Center window similar to that shown in Figure 2.6.

The tabs in this window will change according to the number and type of online accounts you have open with the selected financial institution. The contents of the lower pane also undergo more than one metamorphosis. The supported tabs are as follows. Remember, you probably won't see them all at once:

- **Transactions** This tab shows all of the downloaded transactions for each account.
- **Transfers** This tab is used to record transfers between accounts held at the same financial institution. Unfortunately, there is no way to make transfers between accounts held at different institutions.
- **Payments** Use this tab to record online payments. These can be recurring and scheduled in advance.
- **Balances** This tab shows the balance of cash held in your online investment accounts.
- **Holdings** This tab is linked to balances. It shows the value of stocks held through each investment account.
- **E-Mail** Use this tab to create and send or receive and read e-mail exchanged between you and your financial institution.
- **Marketspace** This tab is used by your financial institution to promote new or improved services and other account options.

These tabs are a little more complex than can be swallowed in one sitting, but you will learn about them in upcoming lessons.

However, the majority of the Online Center behaves the same way, no matter which tab is selected. Figure 2.6 will help you find your way around.

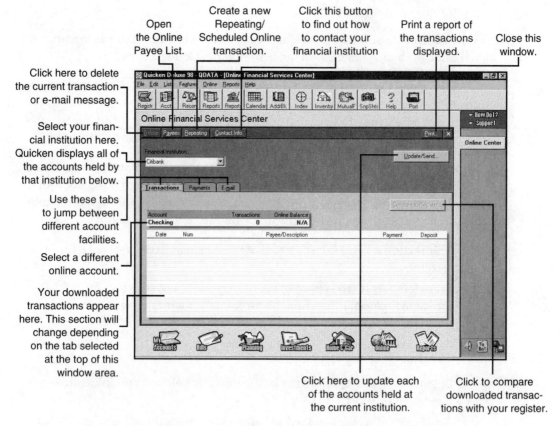

Figure 2.6 This figure shows the Online Center.

In this lesson, you learned how to select your financial institution and enable your accounts. In the next lesson, you will learn how you can do your banking from home.

Online Banking

In this lesson, you learn how to download your account's current statement, reconcile your online account, download and pay off credit card balances, and transfer funds between accounts.

Getting Ready to Bank Online

By now, you have set up your financial institutions and accounts. All that remains is to integrate those services with your Quicken registers.

When you go online, you will normally follow these steps:

1. Open the Online Center and update the accounts held under each financial institution. Each time you update, Quicken performs these tasks:

   - The online center downloads the most recent statements for every account you hold with that institution. The minimum payment and date due for credit card accounts are entered into the financial calendar.

   - Any account transfers or other instructions are communicated back to the institution.

   - Outgoing e-mail is sent and incoming e-mail received.

2. You should then compare the downloaded transactions to those already stored in the register. Quicken can automatically match certain downloaded transactions with existing transactions and you can easily copy new transactions to your register.

The first time you go online, Intuit recommends you only update your Quicken account balances. In other words, don't start your first online banking sessions with an account transfer or similar.

This mini-update ensures that your financial institutions and Quicken are starting from common ground. It is the same concept as starting any new account using the opening balance shown on your most recent statement. If you don't perform this coordinating step, you will find it more difficult to make the balances match in the future.

Once your Quicken accounts and your bank accounts have come to an agreement on the actual bank balance, you can start to play around with transferring funds between accounts and so on. We'll look at that in a moment. For now, though, let's grab that first bunch of data. Keep in mind that this is the data according to the bank. It will show any cleared checks but it won't show checks which are yet to be presented. This data may also show banking fees and taxes already deducted and other transactions that you may not know about.

Downloading Your First Transactions

The following steps are the steps you will follow whenever you update your accounts. Figure 3.1 shows an online account with transactions.

Your financial institution supplies up to 90 days of transactions the first time you connect to the online service, so you may find yourself facing an extensive list of previous transactions. If you aren't interested in retaining historical transactions or just don't want to work through such a long reconciliation, feel free to delete all those before the date you started using Quicken.

To begin your first online transaction, follow these steps:

1. Select the menu **Online, Online Center**.

2. If it isn't already selected, find your financial institution in the pull-down list. If you can't find your financial institution, you will need to go back and follow the steps in Lessons 1 and 2.

3. Click **Update/Send** to go online. Quicken will access the Internet using the connection method specified in Lesson 1.

4. You will see the Instructions to Send dialog box. Click **Send** to continue. (In the future, you will see a PIN field in this dialog. You must enter your PIN before you click **Send**.)

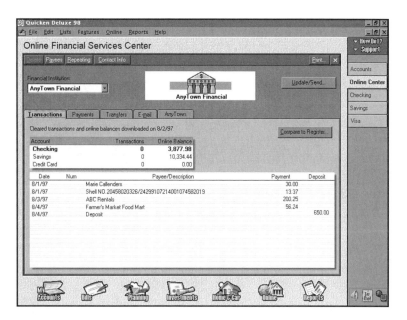

Figure 3.1 This figure shows an online account with transactions.

5. The first time you go online, you need to change your PIN to one that you create. This is a simple security measure which appears in the Change Assigned PIN dialog. Type in the Assigned PIN (the PIN you received on your Information Sheet) and enter your new PIN twice—just to make sure you haven't entered a typo the first time around. When you've finished, click **OK**.

6. Quicken will complete the download and drop you back at the Online Center, downloading up to 90 days of transactions.

CAUTION

Closing Your Internet Connection The default setting in **Online, Internet Connection, Setup** specifies that Quicken should close your connection five minutes after the cessation of activity. To close your connection sooner, select **Online, Disconnect**.

Once you have downloaded the latest transactions, you need to update your register. Follow these steps:

1. With the Online Center open and the online account selected in the window, click **Compare to Register**. This button isn't active unless there are entries in that account's transactions list. You will see a window similar to that shown in Figure 3.2.

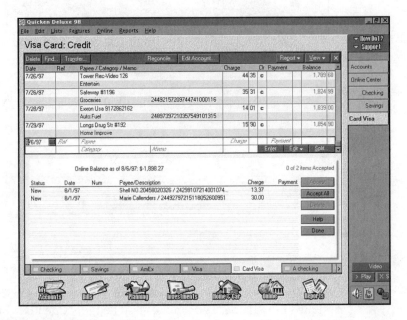

Figure 3.2 This figure shows how downloaded checking account transactions are compared to the checking register.

2. This split window shows your current Quicken register transaction in the upper section and your downloaded transactions below. The buttons to the right of the downloaded transactions are used to compare your downloaded transactions to those in the register.

3. You will see the word "Match" in the Status column to the left of any transactions that Quicken believes match those already entered into your register. Quicken attempts to match your transactions first by the order in which they occurred, looking back to transactions in your register that took place 90 days ago. It then searches for a match by amount. If there have been two transactions over the previous 90 days for the same amount, Quicken matches against the first. If the amount doesn't match, it tries to match on check numbers, comparing the digits in the downloaded transaction to the same number of digits falling at the end of any check numbers

recorded in your register. Therefore, if the downloaded transaction's check number is "101," this could be matched in your register against check numbers 53101, 1102101, or just 101.

 TIP **Matching Transactions Without Check Numbers** If a transaction doesn't have a check number, Quicken compares the amount to any non-numeric entry in the Num field recorded over the previous 30 days. For example, a downloaded transaction marked as "TXFR" for $60 could be matched to a transaction for $60 marked in the Num field as ATM.

4. Edit the details on any matched transaction by clicking the downloaded transaction. Quicken will take you to the matched transaction in the register. If it has been matched incorrectly, see step 6.

5. Quicken indicates transactions that couldn't be matched with the word "New" in the Status column. You can **Edit** these by clicking the downloaded transaction. Quicken copies the downloaded transaction to the last line in your register where you can adjust any of its details. Typically, you will need to match it to an existing payee and add a category or memo. Just record these in the register as you do for recording or editing any other Quicken transaction. However, before you accept a transaction as new, make sure it isn't a duplicate of one you previously recorded. If you suspect it is, click the **Delete** button to the right of the downloaded transaction. This deletes the downloaded transaction while retaining the original in your Quicken register.

6. If a transaction has been matched incorrectly, click it with the right mouse button and select **Unmatch Transaction** from the menu. Quicken will try to match the downloaded transaction with a more recent entry. If it doesn't succeed, it marks that transaction as New.

7. If you know that the transaction should match an existing register transaction but doesn't, select the register transaction and click **Edit**. (This assumes your original register entry is incorrect, therefore you need to edit it to match the downloaded transaction. If it is the downloaded transaction that is incorrect, you should contact your financial institution as soon as possible. Just retain the register entry as it is.) Adjust the check number, date, and amount until they all correspond. The new transaction is now marked as a match against your existing transaction.

8. If a transaction matches a transaction previously matched or marked as cleared, the transaction is a duplicate. Click **Delete** beside the downloaded transaction to remove it. This retains your original Quicken transaction.

9. To approve a transaction's match, click **Accept**. Quicken marks the register transaction as cleared, placing a "c" in the Clr column. A cleared transaction is a transaction that has been presented and passed through the bank. It is not the same as a reconciled transaction. You will learn how to reconcile your online accounts next.

10. If all of the transactions marked as Match are correct and you are also happy with those marked as New, click **Accept All** to copy all your new transactions to your register and to mark all your matched and new transactions as cleared. You will return to the Compare to Register window, but with Accepted showing in the Status column of your downloaded transactions. Click **Done** to leave the Compare to Register window. If not all of your downloaded transactions have been accepted, Quicken will display a dialog box warning that you haven't finished matching those transactions. Click **Finish Later** to return to the Online Center.

 TIP   **Duplicate Check Number Found**   If you see a dialog box with this title after clicking Accept All, you are trying to import a new transaction with a check number identical to a previous transaction. Click **Accept** to record this new transaction. You will have two transactions in your register assigned to a single check number. Click **Skip** if these transactions should match. This rejects the new transaction, retaining the one already recorded. After you have finished reviewing duplicate check numbers, you may need to correct the recorded transaction so that it matches the transaction downloaded from your account.

Now that Quicken has all of the transactions your bank believes it should have, you're ready to reconcile that account. Fortunately, while the steps are almost identical to a paper-based reconciliation, your list of transactions should be perfectly up-to-date, making online reconciling an almost automatic process. You can read about online reconciling later in this lesson.

Updating Online Credit Cards

Online credit card accounts are a slightly special issue because Quicken takes advantage of two features inherent in any credit card statement.

First, look at any paper-based credit card statement and you will see that it shows the payee for every transaction along with the date and amount.

Quicken uses this information to search for any previous credit card transaction made to that payee. If it finds a previous transaction, it takes note of the category used and applies that category to the current transaction. You may edit this as required, but more often than not, that category should turn out to be just the one you needed.

With date, payee, amount, and category all supplied for you, the new transaction is ready to be copied into your credit card register.

TIP **Copying New Credit Card Transactions** If you regularly go online and don't live close to your credit card's limit, you might as well use the credit card matching procedure instead of recording new transactions manually. All of the information you require is included in the downloaded transaction, and the category comes supplied. Just go online once or twice a week to update Quicken's credit card account in seconds.

As you have probably seen, along with your transactions, a paper-based credit card statement also shows the minimum payment due and the date that payment is due. Quicken uses this information to set a reminder in your financial calendar. Of course, if you do what all financial planning advisers recommend and pay off your credit card balance before any interest payments fall due, you will never need to rely on this facility, but it's handy nonetheless.

What's Happened to IntelliCharge? IntelliCharge is the name of Quicken's now superseded online credit card system. If you have been using a previous version of Quicken with an IntelliCharge account, that account is auto-
CAUTION matically upgraded to an Online Credit Card.

Paying Off Your Credit Card Balance

Now that you've seen the balance of your credit card and downloaded the transactions, you probably want to make a payment. While you can make this payment through an electronic transfer, this only works if your credit card and the account you will be making the payment from are held with the same financial institution and are both setup for online banking. However, as you will see, there are several other payment options. Whichever the case, just follow these steps for problem-free payments:

1. Make sure you have downloaded the latest credit card transactions. This will ensure your register is up-to-date but, more importantly at this juncture, provide Quicken with the most recent closing balances for your credit card account and the account from which you will be making the payment.

2. From the Online Center select your credit card's financial institution and click the **Transactions** tab.

3. Select your credit card account in the account list and click **Payment Information**. This button only appears when a credit card account is selected, but you won't be able to select it until you have downloaded your first monthly statement. You may not be able to do this until one month has passed since your last paper-based statement.

4. In the Credit Card Payment Information window shown in Figure 3.3, click **Make Payment**.

Figure 3.3 The Payment Information window summarizes your credit card status.

5. In the Make Credit Card Payment window, use the **Amount to Pay** pull-down list to choose from:

    • **Minimum Amount** Select this if you just want to pay the minimum required, as indicated on your most recent downloaded statement.

    • **Full Amount** Select this if you want to pay the full amount owing on the credit card account.

    • **Other** Select this to specify any other amount to pay.

6. Click **Payment Will Be** to select the payment method:

    • **Printed Check** Select this for Quicken to print the check for you. If you are using windowed envelopes, make sure you enter the payee's address.

- **Handwritten Check** Select this to record the payment in your Quicken register as a handwritten check.
- **Online Payment** Choose this option if you will be making the payment from an account setup for online payments.

7. Finally, use **Pay From** to select the account from which you want to make this payment.

TIP **My Credit Card Isn't Online But My Checking Account Is. Can I Still Pay My Credit Card Balance Online?** It depends. Ask your credit card institution (most likely through your local bank) whether or not they will accept payments without the tear-off footer of your credit card statement. If so, just use the Online Payments facility of your online account to write a check to the credit card company, just as you would when paying using a paper-based check. However, make sure you include the credit card account number in the memo—otherwise the credit card company won't know where to apply that payment. Chances are the credit card company is registered with Intuit Services Corporation. This means they will receive the payment electronically. However, even if they aren't, the check will still arrive by postal mail.

Performing an Online Account Reconciliation

Each time Quicken downloads the most recent transactions, it also takes note of the ending account balance. The next time you perform an account reconciliation, Quicken will use this as the basis for that reconciliation.

Reconciling an online account is easier than reconciling a paper-based account simply because you don't need to enter those odd account transactions made by your bank for fees, taxes, and so on. To reconcile your online account, just follow these steps:

1. Update your account as previously described and match and accept transactions as required. You must perform this step for the reconciliation to be up-to-date with the latest data. However, if you have already performed an online update once today, don't worry about doing so again.

2. Open that account's register and click **Reconcile** at the top of the register pane, rather than in the iconbar, if displayed.

3. If you have never downloaded data into this account, you will be asked to do so now. If you haven't downloaded data in the last two days, you will also be asked to do so now. However, if you have carried out Step 1, you should zip straight through.

4. The next dialog box you see will let you choose between reconciling to a Paper Statement or Online Balance. Make sure Online Balance is selected and click **OK**, as shown in Figure 3.4.

Figure 3.4   Make sure you select Online Balance when reconciling an online account.

5. Now you should see the Reconciliation pane. All of the transactions already accepted into your register through the Online Center are checked as Cleared. Look at the **Difference** in the lower right corner of the Reconciliation window. This is based on your Quicken account's cleared balance. That's really the balance of your account's cleared and reconciled transactions. The **Cleared Balance** should match your **Online Balance**, giving a **Difference** of zero.

6. If the Difference does equal zero, click **Finished** to complete the reconciliation. Otherwise, check the list for duplicated transactions or transactions mistakenly marked as cleared or reconciled. To edit any transaction, select it and click **Edit** in the upper-left corner of the Reconciliation pane. You also can add **New** transactions or **Delete** existing transactions.

And that's it! Now that you know how to download the latest transactions and perform a reconciliation, you're ready to tackle the more interesting side of online banking: electronic transactions. This is the part that saves you from making those pesky trips to the bank.

Transferring Funds Between Accounts

Quicken doesn't yet support transfers between accounts held with two difference financial institutions; however, you can easily do so between two accounts held with the same institution.

Why would you use this facility? There are quite a few possibilities. For instance:

- **Mortgage or loan repayments** You can easily set up a scheduled transaction that will handle your repayments automatically. Alternatively, you may set up a minimum repayment through your bank and use the online account transfer facility to boost those payments. Why? Any extra payments made early in a loan have a much greater effect on the total interest you will pay than those extra payments made toward the end of the loan.

- **Transfers to an investment account** There's little point leaving spare funds sitting in your checking account if they could be working twice as hard elsewhere. It is so easy to electronically transfer funds between accounts that you can easily achieve and constantly adjust the optimal balance between your checking accounts and your short or long-term investment accounts.

- **Keeping a working fund in a joint account** This is handy if you and your partner like the independence of separate income streams but live on a joint expenses account. Just specify the transfer amount as required. You might each add $200 to the joint account every week, using it for shared living expenses. Personal purchases are made from your separate accounts.

CAUTION

Transfer Timing Transfers between accounts usually don't occur until the next business day, even though your Quicken account balance changes to immediately reflect that transfer. Therefore, if you make any immediate online payments from the account you are transferring the funds to, be careful that you don't do so with insufficient funds.

Of course, there are many other times when you may need to perform regular account transfers. Doing so electronically makes it so easy that you probably will come up with some reasons that you would never tackle if you had to organize the transfers manually.

Just follow these steps:

1. To perform an account transfer, you must have two online accounts with the one financial institution. If you haven't yet set up the second online account, you can do so through the menu **Online, Online Financial Services Setup, Enable Accounts...**, or by editing the account through **Lists, Account** (Ctrl+A).

2. Select the menu **Online, Online Center**.

3. Choose the **Financial Institution** and click the **Transfers** tab. Figure 3.5 shows an account that has already had transfers.

4. Select your originating account using **Transfer Money From:**.

5. Select the destination account using **To:**.

6. Type in the **Amount:** or click the calculator icon to use Quicken's built-in calculator.

7. Click **Enter** to record the transfer. It will be added to the lower list in the Transfer tab along with a Status message showing that it has not yet been sent.

8. To send the transfer immediately, click **Update/Send**. Otherwise, feel free to record further transfers, payments, and so on as required.

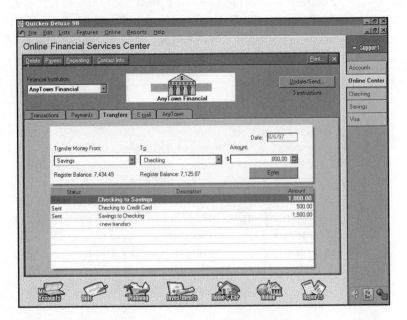

Figure 3.5 This figure illustrates an account with previous account transfers.

TIP   **Batch Transactions**   Quicken stores online instructions between sessions. If you like, you can build up quite a collection and then go online as little as once each week to send them in one batch.

CAUTION

What If the Transfer Doesn't Occur?   There are many reasons a transfer may not take place, including through having insufficient funds in the account doing the transferring, through to some error at the banking end of the transaction. If the transfer doesn't occur, you will receive notification via e-mail or the phone. So that your Quicken accounts continue to balance, you should delete the transfer from either register. (Deleting one side of a transfer automatically deletes the other.) You should also delete the transfer from the Online Centers' Transfer tab. Just select it and click **Delete** in the upper left corner of the window.

Transfers are very quick and easy; they should only take you a few seconds and you may well find you use them more often than you ever would when going through a bank. Unfortunately, it isn't possible to schedule regular transfers. However, if the account you are transferring from has an online payments facility, you can set up a regular payment to your other account. You will lean about online payments and scheduled online payments in Lesson 4.

In this lesson, you learned how to update and reconcile your banking and credit card account balances. You also learned how to transfer funds between accounts. In the next lesson, you will learn how to make once-only and regular online payments and also how to receive bills online.

Online Payments and Online Billing

In this lesson, you will learn how to make online and repeating online payments and also how to receive your bills online.

Using Quicken 98 to Pay Online

Once you have started making online payments, you may well wonder how you ever got along without them. Quicken's version of online payments is extraordinarily convenient, especially when compared to previous methods.

In Quicken 98, online payments come courtesy of the Open Financial Exchange system you learned about in Lesson 1. The system is totally integrated with your financial software, meaning that you only ever have to record those transactions in one place at one time (see Figure 4.1). Furthermore, once you send the payment it isn't totally out of your hands; you can find out its status at any time.

 TIP **What If Your Bank Doesn't Support Online Payments** You can still write payments through the Intuit Services Corporation by providing ISC with the authority to access your account. You can learn about this next.

To make an online payment, you need the following:

- An account set up for online payments.
- The payee's name, address and telephone number (you must have all three).

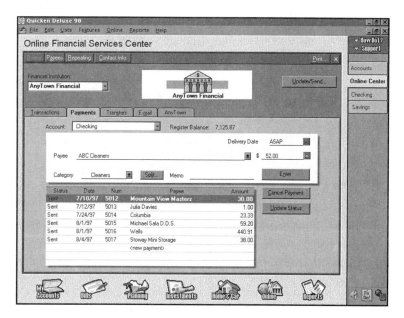

Figure 4.1   This figure shows a series of online payments already made.

If you haven't yet applied for online payments, do so now. You can set up an existing account by going through the menu **Lists, Account (Ctrl+A)**. Online payments are supported by Quicken's checking, savings, money market and credit card accounts. You can also make online payments from a checking account that is linked to an investment account. Select the account and click **Edit** at the top of the pane. (Alternatively, select the account and then choose the menu **Edit, Edit Account, Edit**.) Click **Enable Online Payments** and **Next** and follow the steps, recording the financial institution, account number and so on.

Once you've done that, you're ready to roll. Follow these steps to make your first online payment:

1. Open the Online Center.

2. Select the **Financial Institution** where your online payments account is kept.

3. Click the **Payments** tab.

4. You can fill out the online payment as you would any check. However, there are a couple of important differences. Let's go through them field by field:

Account   Select the account which you will use to make this payment. The current balance is displayed to its right.

Delivery Date   By default this payment will be delivered as soon as possible. However, you can also set this payment for a future date. The payment is delivered according to the delivery date minus that payee's lead time. Make sure you leave enough time for the payee to receive and process the payment. Otherwise you may incur late payment penalties.

Lead Time   The lead time is the time it takes for a payment to reach its destination. Most payees who support electronic funds transfer have a lead time of one or two business days. However, if the payment must be posted, the lead time grows to four days. Quicken looks after the lead time for you. For example, when you create a new payee, the lead time is set to four business days. When one you go online, Quicken establishes if this payee is supported for electronic payments. If so, that lead time is cut to the previously-mentioned one or two business days.

You can see the lead time for each of your payee's through the Online Payee List.

Payee   Unlike handwritten or printed checks, each of your online payee's must be added to a special Online Payees database. Just type in the full payee's name and press Tab. Quicken will respond with the Setup Online Payee dialog box. For further information, see the section "Creating an Online Payee."

$ Type in or calculate the total amount for this payment.

Category   Select a category or click **Split** to split the payment between multiple categories.

Memo   Record a memo if desired. This field is optional and may or may not be sent to the financial institution or your payee. Therefore, be careful what you record as the recipient may see the contents of this field when they receive the payment.

5. Click **Enter** to record the payment. You will see it added to the payments list.

6. To record another payment, just start over at Step 4.

Canceling a Payment

Canceling a payment that has already been made is quite easy. Simply follow these steps:

1. Open the Payments tab of the Online Center.
2. Select the transaction you want to remove in the transaction list.
3. If the payment hasn't been sent, click **Delete** in the upper left corner of the window to remove it from the list.
4. Otherwise, you need to chase the payment electronically. Just click **Cancel Payment**. Quicken will ask you to confirm the cancellation. Click **Yes** to create the instruction. You will now see a Stop Sign symbol displayed next to the original payment.
5. It is important that you send the cancellation instruction as quickly as possible. Click **Update/Send** to go online and forward that and any other instructions yet to be sent.

Inquiring About a Payment

Just as you can stop a payment that has already been sent, you can also inquire about its status. The response you get back depends on how your financial institution chooses to handle such inquiries. However, whether you receive an automated response or personal attention, the procedure is the same. Follow these steps:

1. Open the Payments tab of the Online Center.
2. Select the transaction you want to inquire about in the transaction list.
3. Click the button **Update Status**. You should see a dialog titled **Payment Inquiry**.
4. To send a request for an update on its status, leave Update Status selected and click **OK**. If you would like to create a longer text message, select E-mail Message, click **OK** and complete the E-mail message.
5. The next time you update that account, the payment inquiry will head off to Intuit Services Corporation, following in the footsteps of your original payment.

Creating a New Online Payee

There are two ways to create a new online payee: through the payee drop-down list in the online payments window, or by clicking the **Payees** button at the top of the Online Center window to open the list of currently defined online payees. Now click **New** to add a new entry.

Whichever way you go about it, you will end up at the Set Up Online Payee window shown in Figure 4.2. Filling it out is easy:

Name: Enter the full name of this payee as it would normally appear on a check. Use the down arrow to call up entries from Quicken's list of memorized transactions.

Street: This can be a street or postal address. If the payee doesn't support online payments, your payment will be printed and posted. Obviously this is the address to which it will be posted.

City: Record the payee's city. For postal sorting purposes, it is important that you do so here rather than in the second line of the Street.

State: Type in the abbreviation or select the state from the list.

Zip: And don't forget the ZIP Code.

Account #:   This is the number the payee uses to identify you. Do not enter the payee's account number here. Instead, use the account number or reference number that the payee has used to identify your previous payments. This might be a telephone number, customer number, loan number, and so on. If you are sure you don't have an account number, record your surname instead. However, make sure you contact your payee a few days after the payment has been made to make sure it went through the system and was correctly credited to your account.

Phone: You should record the phone number you normally use when you have a question about your billing. If there are any problems processing the online payment, Intuit Services Corporation (or CheckFree) will call that number to follow your payment through.

And that's it! When you've finished, click **OK** to save the new or edited Payee. You will see the confirmation dialog shown in Figure 4.3. From now on, that online payee will be available from the drop-down list in the Payments tab of the Online Center.

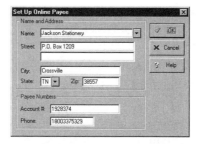

Figure 4.2 This figure shows adding a new online payee.

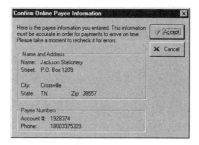

Figure 4.3 Carefully verify the account information for each newly created online payee.

Repeating Online Payments

Repeating online payments are perfect for bills you receive regularly that are always for the same amount. Examples include cable connection fees, online service subscriptions, regular deposits in an investment account, loan repayments, garden maintenance, and more.

These payments might seem identical to repeating scheduled payments, but there is one important difference.

When you create the instruction for a repeating online payment, it is sent and stored at Intuit Services Corporation. Thirty days before each scheduled payment is due, ISC sends you a special note letting you know that it has created and post-dated that payment. The payment is automatically recorded in your register.

In this way, whether you go online regularly or not, your payments will still be made. (In fact, you should be careful that if you cancel your service, you also cancel the repeating payments. Luckily, you can do this simply by deleting it from your repeating payments list. This generates another instruction which cancels the payments stored at ISC.)

To create a repeating online payment, follow these steps:

1. Select the menu **Online, Online Center** and click **Repeating**. (Alternatively, open the menu **Lists, Scheduled Transaction** (Ctrl+J), select the **Repeating Online** tab and click **New.**)

2. A completed dialog is shown in Figure 4.4. Fill out the top of the dialog box using these fields:

   First Payment: This is the date that you want the first payment made. The actual payment will be generated according to the payee's lead time but postdated so that it can't be banked until the first payment is due.

TIP **Estimating the Date Payment Is Due** Calculate the First Payment date according to the next payment due based on an unpaid statement received from the payee. Just use the date payment is due, even if that payment is overdue. Thereafter, your payment will reach the payee right on time.

   Account: Which account do you want the funds to be drawn from? If you have just one online payment account, you cannot choose an alternate account.

   Payee: Select from your list of online payees. To create a new online payee, type in the name and press **Tab**. Fill in the Set Up Online Payee dialog box as described in the previous heading "Creating a New Online Payee."

   Memo: Depending on your financial institution, this memo may or may not be visible to the institution or payee.

   Category: Type in a category or account transfer or select the category from the drop-down list. Otherwise, click **Splits** to divide the payment as required.

   Amount: Record the total amount for a single payment.

Figure 4.4   This figure shows recording a repeating online payment.

3. The Schedule group provides the following fields:

> **Frequency:**   Select how often you would like this payment to occur. For example, you would probably pay a cable subscription once a month.
>
> **Duration:**   Unlimited will keep the payment running indefinitely. However, you can also limit the payments to a certain number such as 12 monthly payments. Quicken calculates and displays the due date of the final payment.

TIP   **Temporarily Disabling Online Transactions**   To disable a repeating online transaction that you believe you may need in the future, just edit it so that the **Duration:** is set to stop after 0 payments. When you need to get it going again, either enter a figure greater than zero, or change it to **Unlimited**.

4. Finally, specify how much forewarning you want of this payment in **Prompt To Connect**… Just specify how many day's notice you need. While the payment will go ahead even if you don't go online, Quicken provides a warning that the payment will occur. As soon as you go online, it downloads the next payment transaction, keeping your register balance right up to date.

5. When you've finished, click **Authorize** to save the transaction.

CAUTION

Account Numbers So that the payee at the end of the repeating transaction knows from whom this money is coming at such regular intervals, make sure you have entered the correct **Account #** into the payee's entry in the Online Payee List. You can open the list by clicking **Payees** in the Online Center.

Once you have entered your repeating online payments, return to the Online Center and click **Update/Send**. You may see a dialog box that asks whether Quicken should enter the payment (into the register) before going online. Click **Yes** to record those transactions before the instruction is sent to your financial institution. Click **No** to only record those transactions after they have been successfully transmitted. After Quicken connects to your financial institution, you will see a dialog similar to that shown in Figure 4.5. The first time you access this online accounts, click **Send** to send the transactions and create a new PIN when prompted. If you have made payment before through this account, the figure shown will look a little different. Enter your PIN in the box provided and send the payments on their way.

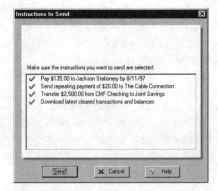

Figure 4.5 Quicken lists the online transactions before they are sent.

Receiving Bills Online

Quicken's Online Billing is a quick and easy way to receive your bills from participating creditors, pay those bills through the Quicken Online Billing Web site, and automatically record those payment transaction in the appropriate Quicken register.

This turns your bill payments into a totally electronic procedure.

Online Billing is based around a Quicken site on the Web. This site is subject to constant revision, making it impossible to provide step-by-step instructions. It isn't available in all geographic regions and is targeted chiefly at paying the utilities' bills.

Here's the general procedure:

1. To get started with Online Billing, select the menu **Online, Get Bills Online**. This will load the Web browser, connect you to the Internet (you may need to do this manually), and access the Welcome to Online Billing page at the Online Billing site.

2. To see if any of your regular payees support online billing, click **Biller List**. If you do pay bills to an online biller, click **Back** to return to the Welcome page and click **Apply Now**. (You might also be able to apply from the Biller List page.)

3. Fill out Your Personal Information form including your Tax ID and other identifying information. Click the right arrow at the bottom of the pane to move forward.

4. At the Online Biller List, select the business type, and select the online billers you want to receive electronic bills from. Click **Add** to copy them to the list **My Online Billers**.

5. Go to the Quicken Online Billing Home Page.

6. The upper left pane shows any bills you have received. The right pane displays any messages received from your online billers. Use the left pane to check those bills you want to pay.

7. Click **Enter Payments** to open the Pay Online Bills dialog box. Select the account you will use to pay the checked bills as well as the payment method. You can choose between Online Payment, Printed Check, or Hand-Written Check. When you finish, click **OK**.

8. Each of the payment transactions will appear in your Quicken register or the Online Center. You can adjust the amounts before they are paid.

In this lesson, you learned how to record single and repeating online payments and to access Online Billing. In the next lesson, you will learn how to use your Online Center to exchange e-mail with your financial institution.

E-Mailing Your Financial Institution

In this lesson, you will learn how to compose and send e-mail and receive and read the replies.

E-Mail

Electronic mail (e-mail) is wonderfully convenient. Trillions of e-mail messages flash around the world every year, courtesy not just of the Internet but also many other public and private networks. E-mail is popular because it is essentially free, blazingly fast, and wonderfully flexible.

Quicken supports e-mail, but not to the same extent as an e-mail account organized with an Internet service provider. However, you can use it to communicate with your financial institution, and you don't even need to remember a complex e-mail address.

Managing Your E-Mail

Managing your e-mail is quite easy. Go to your Online Center using the menu **Online**, **Online Center**. You may need to click **OK** to move past the Internet Connection Options dialog box. Once you reach the Online Center, select your **Financial Institution** and click the e-mail tab. You will see a window similar to that shown in Figure 5.1.

The lower part of the window lists all of your e-mail messages waiting to be sent, already sent, or already received.

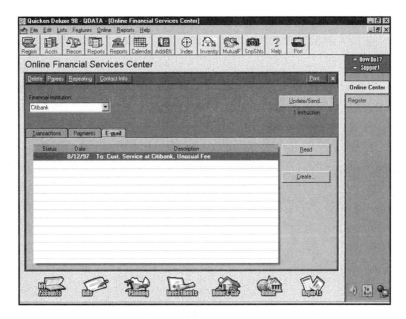

Figure 5.1   Use the E-mail tab to manage, create, and read your e-mail.

To create an e-mail message, follow these steps:

1. Click **Create**. Use the next dialog to select the type of e-mail you want to create. Is it about online banking or online payments? If it is about the latter, click **E-mail about an online payment** and select the appropriate account. (You cannot select this unless you have already sent an online payment.) This will create a list of all payments made using that account. Select the payment from the list. If you haven't made any payments, you can only create an e-mail about online banking. Click **OK** to continue.

2. Create your message in the Message to... dialog shown in Figure 5.2. The **To:** address is filled out for you by Quicken, although you can also change it if required. This isn't an address in the sense of a traditional e-mail address, so there's no need to worry about "@" symbols or domain names. However, you should enter your name in the **From:** field and type in a **Subject**. Select the account this message is about and create the message in the message pane.

CAUTION

Don't Press Your Enter Key   Do not press the Enter key to create a new line in the message pane. There is no permanent way to create blank or spacer lines in your message. (Actually, there is one way, but Quicken strips the blank lines when it sends the message, so the end result is the same.) If you do, Quicken will interpret the key-press as "Okaying" the message. You need to select the message in the message list of the Online Center and click **Delete**. Then start over. If you don't delete the first message, Quicken sends both.'

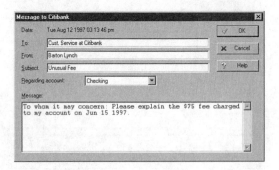

Figure 5.2   Quicken's e-mail messages are very simple.

3. Once you have finished the message, click **OK**. Quicken sends the message the next time you update your accounts with that financial institution.

To read a received e-mail message or any message you had previously created, select it within the list and click **Read**. You will see the window shown in Figure 5.3. There's little you can do at this point besides click **Print** to print this message or **Close** to return to the list. To print the entire list of e-mail messages, return to the list and click **Print...** any time the E-mail tab is open. Finally, to delete your message, select it within the list and click **Delete**.

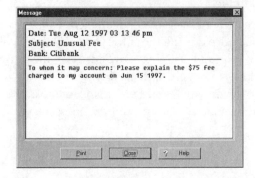

Figure 5.3   To read your e-mail, either double-click the message or select it and click **Read**.

In this lesson, you learned how to send, receive, and read your e-mail. In the next lesson, you will learn how to manage your online investment accounts.

Managing Online Investment Accounts

In this lesson, you learn how to use an online investment account with your investment register.

Understanding Online Investment Accounts

Investment accounts seem fairly straightforward: you put money in, you buy and sell shares or other securities, and you take money out.

While it may look this simple from your end of the deal, it's rather different from the other. Besides the transactions directly linked to buying and selling stocks, you may need to deal with any of the following:

- Commissions relating to a purchase or sale. These may be fixed cost or percentage-based.
- Deposits and withdrawals that change the cash balance.
- Interest income earned on your account's cash balance.
- Interest expenses accrued through purchases on margin.
- Portfolio management fees.

When you record a transaction such as share purchase or sale, Quicken records it as a single event. However, this may not be how it happens in the real world. Instead, multiple transactions have taken place including the actual transfer of shares, the payment of commission, transfers to or from a linked checking account and more.

With an online investment account, these transactions can be automatically recorded in your register. This will help you to not only resolve any misunderstandings that may arise with your broker, but also help you to follow the statements you receive. In fact, your recorded transactions will precisely match those shown on the printed transaction history of your brokerage account, keeping your online investment account in precise lock-step with your actual portfolio.

TIP **Keeping Stock of Your Net Worth** Even if you aren't a very active trader, you will still find significant benefit in using an online investment account alongside your other online accounts. After all, it only takes a few seconds for you to download the latest checking, credit card, and savings account balances and transactions. Update your investment account at the same time and you will know precisely how much is in each account, as well as the current value of your stock. If you like to keep track of your net worth week-by-week if not day-by-day, you'll find this one of the most convenient ways to do so.

Getting Ready for Online Investing

If you don't yet have an investment account, you can set one up now using the instructions provided in Part 5, Lesson 6. You need to apply for the online facility and then wait until you receive an information pack from your investment service. Within that pack is an information sheet specifying the password, account details, and other information required to set up Quicken to access your account.

Once you receive the information pack, you can proceed with the rest of this lesson. To convert an existing investment account to an online version, follow these steps:

1. Apply for online account access as described in Lesson 2. You may need to set up a new financial institution as well as enable your investment and, if you have one, a linked checking account. In a few day's time you should receive your information pack. Once you have that, you can continue with these steps.

2. Select the menu **Lists**, **Account** (Ctrl+A).

3. Select your investment account and click **Edit** at the upper left side of the window pane. Otherwise, select the menu **Edit**, **Account**, **Edit**. You will see the Edit Investment Account dialog shown in Figure 6.1.

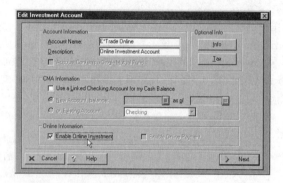

Figure 6.1 Use the Edit Investment Account dialog box to convert an existing account to an online account.

4. Check **Enable Online Investment** to set up this account for online transactions. If you have a linked checking account and also want to make online payments, check **Use a Linked Checking Account for my Cash Balance**, and then check **Enable Online Payment**. If you use a linked checking account that does not already exist in your Quicken account list, type in the balance shown on your most recent statement in the field **New Account, balance** and indicate the date shown on the statement. (If you haven't yet received a statement, record the amount you used to fund the account and the date it was set up.) If this is an existing account, select it using the pull-down list beside **or, Existing Account**.

5. Click **Next** to move into the series of "Enable Online Account" questions. Fill in the gaps using the data shown on your information sheet, clicking **Next** between each pane. When you see the Summary tab, review the data you have entered and edit if necessary. If you are sure it is correct, click **Done** and carefully read the Service Agreement Information. Click **OK** and your investment account will be ready.

Using the Online Investment Center

Open your investment center using the menu **Online**, **Online Center**. Select your investment financial institution from the pull-down list.

The Online Investment Center provides four standard tabs. These are:

- **Transactions**   This shows any downloaded transactions that have not yet been accepted into your register.

- **Balances**   These are the balances of each of your online investment accounts. This information is not used in Quicken and for various reasons may not match the balances shown in your Quicken registers. For example, your brokerage may have recorded a stock purchase and commission as two separate transactions, whereas it appears as a single transaction in Quicken. In addition, there may be certain charges incurred or interest received that you haven't yet recorded in your register. For this reason, it is easiest to use the online investment account transaction downloading as your soul method of recording investment transaction. By only relying on downloaded transactions rather than recording them yourself, you will guarantee that your own investment register always matches the register stored on your broker's computer system.

- **Holdings**   This tab shows your holdings according to your financial institution. This information does not originate from Quicken. Double-click any stocks to view more information.

- **E-mail**   You have already learned about e-mail in Lesson 5. You can use this tab to correspond with your investment institution.

If you have a linked checking account set up for online payments, you will see:

- **Payments**   You can use this tab to make online payments just as you do through an online checking account. See Lesson 4 for more information.

The Online Investment Center does not provide a separate Investments tab. Instead, you use the Transactions tab to perform all of your investment updating functions. Therefore, the rest of this lesson concentrates on how you can use this tab to keep your investment register up-to-date.

Updating Your Investment Register

To update your investment register, you need to:

1. Download the latest transactions.

2. Match downloaded securities with your existing securities.

3. Compare the downloaded transactions to your investment register.

Let's get started.

Downloading Investment Transactions

Follow these steps to download your most recent investment transactions:

1. Open your Online Center using the menu **Online**, **Online Center**.

2. Select your investment institution from the pull-down list of all financial institutions. You should see the tabs described above.

3. Click **Update/Send**. This opens the Instructions to Send dialog box. You will need to enter a PIN or change your existing PIN in the next dialog box. Click **Send** to update your account.

4. After a short time, Quicken will tell you whether or not the download succeeded.

Comparing to Your Register

Once you have downloaded the transactions, you are ready to either copy new transactions to your register or to compare the downloaded transactions with any pre-existing. This procedure will update your Quicken account with the latest investment information.

To do so, just follow these steps:

1. From the Online Center, select your investment account and click **Compare to Register**.

2. Quicken will try to match the downloaded securities against those already in your securities list, automatically matching those with the same ticker symbol. If it can't match ticker symbols, it tries to match the full security name. In some cases, you may have recorded the name in a slightly different manner to its listing on the stock exchange, for example, leaving out a word such as "Incorporated" or "Corporation" or similar. If Quicken can't make the match, you will see the Match Securities window. To complete the match, follow these extra steps:

   • Try to match the downloaded security at the top of the window to those listed in the box.

- If you succeed, click Yes and then click Next. Once you have com
pleted the matching for all securities, click Done.

- If you don't have a match for that security, just click No. Quicken will
automatically create that security for you. Click Next to move on to
the next and Done when you've finished.

Ticker Symbols   These are the codes used by securities on the world's
financial exchanges. Ticker symbols usually relate to the name of the security.
For instance, Intuit Corporation's ticker symbol is INTU. AT&T uses the symbol
T while Netscape Corporation uses NSCP. Fortunately, you don't need to know
these ticker symbols to download the prices for those stocks; Quicken can look
them up for you.

- The Compare to Register window shows your investment register up
the top and your downloaded transactions below. Select each down
loaded transaction which matches the same transaction in your
register and click Accept. If every transactions matches, click Accept
All. Transactions that are similar but don't quite match are marked as
Near Match. Check these carefully against your register and fix one
or the other.

- If you can't find a match for a particular downloaded transaction,
there are three possibilities:

    1. The transaction is new. Click Accept to copy it to your register.

    2. The transaction is part of a set which, together, correspond
    to just one transaction in your register. You should adjust just
    one of these to match your register transaction and delete the
    rest. For example, you may see two transactions, one for a stock
    purchase and the other for the commission. Delete the one for
    the commission and match the stock purchase to the stock
    purchase already recorded. Edit the transaction so that it is
    equal to the stock purchase plus commission. Alternatively,
    delete both online transaction if you are certain your register
    transaction is correct.

TIP **The Easiest Way to Keep Your Investment Register Up to Date** You can avoid worrying about matching fractured transactions simply by always accepting online investment transactions without manually recording them prior. Not only will this save you a lot of typing, it will also do away with any concern over matching downloaded transactions to those you already have recorded.

   3. The transaction is related to a marketing message, price update, or similar transaction. Just select, read, and delete it.

The online investment account isn't perfect, and there are lots of situations where you may need to sit back and carefully consider how your downloaded transactions really compare to your investment account.

However, once you develop a feel for it (and the way your investment institution records your transactions), you'll find it far more of a boon than a chore.

In this lesson, you learned how to convert an existing account to an online investment account, download the latest transactions, and compare them to you register. To learn more about investing, turn to Part 5. Coming up next: You will learn how Quicken can help you take control of your small business finances.

Small Business

Understanding Small Business Accounting

In this lesson, you learn how to set up Quicken so that it satisfies your small business accounting requirements.

Though Quicken doesn't boast the widest range of features available for a small business accounting package, it still has many features that small business owners will find useful. Quicken is ideal for tracking accounts receivable and payable, setting up individual profit centers, creating profit-and-loss and balance-sheet reports, and handling those pesky business details such as the petty cash.

Older releases of Quicken featured an invoicing module. This was dropped in later versions after Intuit developed QuickBooks, their specialized small-business software. However, invoicing and several other handy small business features have appeared once more in Quicken Home and Business 98. Intuit have also developed many other small business products. Table 1.1 shows their complete software family.

TIP **Small Business on the Web** If you are connected to the Internet, you can learn more about QuickBooks at **http://www.intuit.com/quickbooks/**.

For more small business tips and advice, go to **http://www.intuit.com/quickbooks/biz_connection/index.html**.

To purchase any of the products listed in Table 1.1, visit **http://www.intuit.com/quicken_store/**.

Table 1.1 Intuit Software

Product	Category	Platform
TurboTax	Federal Tax Preparation	Windows
TurboTax Deluxe	Federal Tax Preparation with Tax Planner and Personal Finance-Oriented Online Books	Windows
TurboTax for Business	Federal Tax Preparation with Tax Planner, Depreciation Expert and Personal Finance and Business-Oriented Online Books	Windows
TurboTax State	State Tax Preparation	Windows
MacInTax	Tax Preparation	Macintosh
Quicken Macintosh	Personal Finance	Windows/
Quicken Expensable	Expense Manager	Windows
Quicken Business Macintosh Law Partner	Pro Forma Documents and Advice	Windows/
Quicken Deluxe Macintosh	Personal Finance	Windows/
Quicken Financial Planner	Financial Planning	Windows
QuickBooks	Small Business	Windows
QuickBooks Pro	Small Business	Windows

How Quicken Will Help

Every business needs to maintain a basic set of books. By maintaining these books with Quicken, you can easily:

- Analyze the business's profit and loss
- Work out the best sources of revenue
- Prepare for tax time
- Keep on top of slow payers
- Pay the business's bills on time

- Know precisely the amount of funds in the bank
- Breakdown costs by job or project
- Prepare a balance sheet
- Maintain a full set of books, greatly enhancing resale value

If you use Quicken Home and Business 98, you will have access to these additional capabilities:

- Printable invoices
- True debtor management with a new Unpaid Invoices window
- An easy way to record credits and refunds
- Customer address lists
- Item sales, although without inventory management
- Service sales
- Staggered payments on one invoice
- Reimbursable expenses

Is Quicken Right for Your Business?

Before going any further, you should realize that Quicken isn't perfect for every business. While it will work fine for many small businesses, it might not work for yours. How can you tell? Ask yourself these questions:

- **Does my business need invoicing?** If you need to generate invoices, you likely will need a broader software package, such as QuickBooks, for example.
- **Does my business need to manage inventory?** If so, you should look to QuickBooks. Quicken does keep track of the value of your inventory using an asset account. But, if you want inventory management, QuickBooks is your best bet.
- **Do I need to manage a payroll?** Quicken can handle some payroll problems, but not all. It doesn't apply any intelligence to the multiple deductions that make up any pay check and won't prove much help when it comes to printing out Form W-4s at the end of the year. If you need payroll, consider QuickPay. This is a separate product, but one which can swap data with Quicken, updating your books every pay period. Even better, consider this: the cost of Quicken and QuickPay is close to that of

QuickBooks on its own, which includes a fully integrated payroll package, along with all its other great small business features. If you want true payroll, not just a way to keep track of the various payroll deductions, look to QuickBooks.

- **Do I need to generate quotes?** Quicken won't help you with bids and estimates. However, QuickBooks Pro can. In fact, knock out a quote and, once it has been accepted, you can convert it to a full-blown invoice at the click of a button.

- **Do I need to manage a list of contacts for marketing?** Quicken doesn't do it, but QuickBooks does.

Integrating Your Business and Personal Finances

There are two ways to use Quicken with your small business. The first is to build your business data around your personal data. This is useful for very small businesses that don't have too many transactions.

Combining your business and personal data has the following advantages:

- Easy transfer of funds between accounts.
- Simplified tax preparation.
- Apply a split to payments to differentiate the personal and business components.

TIP   **A Real World Example**   John is a painter who works from his home studio. When he pays his electrical utility bill, he splits the bill 80 percent paid by the household and 20 percent by his studio. He only has to enter the transaction once. At tax time, Quicken automatically credits the components to personal expenses and deductible business expenses.

- Fewer files to back up.
- When Quicken starts, it automatically loads the default file. With combined files, you will never need to navigate the **File, Open** dialog box.
- Corrections to mistaken allotments are easy.

The other more rigorous method is to create a second Quicken data file devoted exclusively to your business. This method has some advantages and some disadvantages:

- Your data is kept separate so you can assign different passwords to each file. This may be important for security reasons.

- You won't need to resort to quite so many classes and subclasses, saving some initial setting up and ongoing data entry.

- You can set up Quicken with customized snapshots that show the most important graphs and reports according to each set of data, instead of trying to compromise.

- If you sell your business, you can turn over the business data without also turning over your personal information.

- The primary disadvantage: you may need to double-up on some of your data.

- Also, using two data files is totally unworkable if you use a common checking account for your business and personal banking.

Setting Up Quicken for Your Business

Like any accounting package, Quicken features a chart of accounts made up of categories and registers. In its most simple incarnation, this chart can consist of nothing more than your checking register. However, it might also include liability accounts for credit cards, investment accounts (really a form of asset account) for tracking a fluctuating portfolio, and maybe even a cash account to keep track of the level of funds.

This chart of accounts is also perfectly well-suited for small business purposes. All you need to do is add accounts for the bank, payables, receivables, petty cash, payroll withholding, and, in some circumstances, inventory.

TIP   **A Real World Example**   Mad Max Car Sales is a small second-hand car yard with rarely more than twenty cars in stock. The owner/operator maintains a nice set of books and tries to reflect the value of those cars in his Quicken snapshots. By creating an asset account labeled Inventory, he can add cars to the inventory, using the license plate as the reference. The value of those cars is automatically reflected in his "How Much Are You Worth" graphs. The asset value is eventually transferred to his checking account (along with the profit component from Gross Sales) once payment has been received.

Of course, this is easy when inventory transfers are few and far between. It's certainly not advisable for anyone dealing in hundreds of inventory transactions each day.

Before adjusting your chart of accounts, you should decide whether your business uses cash or accrual-based accounting. This decision will have numerous ramifications, not the least with the IRS, which doesn't like you to change the basis after your first return.

Cash-based accounting is easier than accrual-based accounting. Expenses aren't recognized until the money actually changes hands, and income isn't taken into account until the money is in the bank.

To use cash-based accounting, you should record bills payable as checks post-dated to when they need to be paid. Quicken's Billminder will let you know when they come up. Receivables are recorded when the payment is made, not when the invoice is issued. The amount is entered directly into the checking account and credited to a gross sales income account.

TIP **Billminder** This utility is separate to the main Quicken program but can still access your data to let you know when bills and other scheduled transactions or alerts are coming up. Billminder runs whenever you start Windows. You can learn about this utility in Part 1, Lesson 10.

Accrual-based accounting tracks accounts receivable and accounts payable as they are incurred, not when they are eventually settled.

This method of accounting is more complex but gives you a more accurate financial picture. For instance, one look at the accounts receivable register will tell you precisely how much you are owed. A similar glance at accounts payable tells you how much you owe. Use this information to create a balance sheet and you'll know just how healthy your business really is. Simply apply the old accounting equation equity = assets – liabilities. Equity equals the walk away worth of your business. Of course, no one sells on equity. There might be as much unrealized value in good will, product development, client lists, franchise fees and so on.

TIP **Home and Business Users** If you use Quicken Home and Business 98, you can use the specialized register called Invoices/Receivables for your accounts receivable instead of the asset account detailed in Table 1.2. This is preferable to making a standard asset account mock up because it also enables you specify when those invoices fall due. You learn about the special facilities tied into the Home and Business edition through the rest of this Part.

Creating Small Business Accounts

If you decide to use accrual-based accounting, you need to set up asset and liability accounts. However, even if you are using cash-based accounting, you may still need to create some of these accounts to handle a cash-box, register float or the like. Whichever the case, follow these steps:

1. From the menu bar, select **Lists, Account**.

2. Click **New** to open the Create New Account dialog box.

3. Select the type of account you want to create using Table 1.2 as a guide (start with the easy ones: Receivables and Payables, adding more if and when you need them) and click **Next**. Don't forget that if you are using Home and Business edition, you should use Invoices/Receivables to track your debtors. Figure 1.1 shows a typical account list for a small business setup.

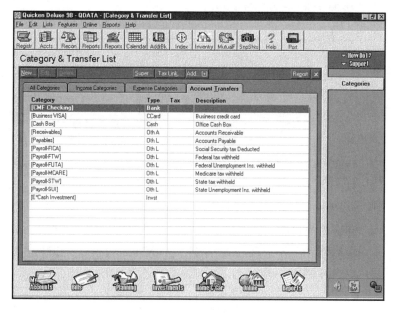

Figure 1.1 A sample list of asset and liability accounts.

4. Enter the **Account Name** and **Description**, avoiding these characters [ ] / |
: ^ and click **Next**.

5. If you know the current balance of this account, click **Yes** and **Next**. If you don't, click **No** and **Next**.

6. If you clicked **Yes**, enter the **As of Date** and **Balance.** Then click **Next** to continue to the Summary. Otherwise, just click **Next** once to jump to the final EasyStep screen, and once then go to the Summary.

7. (Optional) Click **Info** to add additional information to this account. This is most useful for bank, credit card and loan accounts, but only for your own purposes. Quicken doesn't use this information—not even the tax rate—in any of its calculations. Click **OK**.

8. (Optional) Click **Tax** to link transfers into or out of this account to Form 1030 or Schedules. For business purposes, most of the Schedule C, Profit or Loss From Business information is covered by the Income and Expense categories although you may find cause to link a tax-deferred investment account such as an IRA to the Form 1040. Click **OK**.

9. Click **Next** to complete the account and add it to the list.

Table 1.2   Account Types

Name	Type	Use For
Receivables	Asset	Storing the value of invoices awaiting payment.
Payables	Liability	Storing the value of bills that need to be paid.
Inventory	Asset	Tracking the value of your stock.
Petty Cash	Asset	Balancing the petty cash drawer.
Cash Float	Asset	Balancing the cash register.
Furn. & Fittings	Asset	Tracking the value of your office furniture and fittings.
Plant & Equip.	Asset	Tracking the value of your business equipment.
Motor Vehicles	Asset	Tracking the value of the business car fleet.
Payroll	Liability	Staying on top of withholding tax and other payroll deductions.
Sales Tax	Liability	Keeping track of any sales tax collected.
Loans	Liability	Storing the startup costs and other loans you or other people make to the business.

The Asset and Liability accounts satisfy only a small part of the requirements for a business bookkeeping system. Most business use the following additional forms of account: Income, Expenses, Cost of Goods Sold, Other Income. and Other Expenses.

So far in this book you've looked at the first two types of accounts, but what about the rest?

Using Categories for Small Business

Quicken's Income and Expense accounts are known as categories. Categories group related income and expense transactions. For instance, you might pay your telephone accounts to two or more telecommunications companies, but by noting those payments as a telephone expense, you can look over your books and see at any stage precisely how much has been spent, no matter who received the payment.

Categories are important because they help you track your income and expenses, not only by the debtor or creditor, but also by how that money was used. At tax time, categories are also the perfect way to bundle up and claim your legitimate deductibles.

If you specified that you were using Quicken for your business when you installed the software, you will find a complete set of small business categories already built into your Quicken books.

You can verify their presence by selecting **Lists, Category/Transfer**. You should see these categories mixed in with those used for your personal finances. If you don't see these categories, you can import them by doing the following:

1. Select **Lists, Category/Transfer**.
2. At the top of the new window, click **Add** (+). You will see the window shown in Figure 1.2.
3. Pull down **Available Categories** and highlight **Business**. The business categories will appear in the scrolling list on the left.
4. Click **Mark All** to flag every business category.
5. Click **Add >>** to copy those categories to the scrolling list on the right.
6. Click **OK** to complete the import or **Cancel** to exit.

CAUTION

But What If I've Already Created Some of My Own Categories?
Don't worry, Quicken won't wipe out your existing information. Any existing categories with the same name are retained and the imported category discarded.

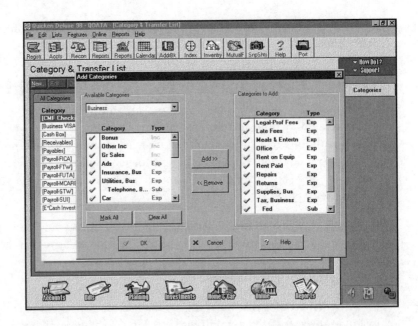

Figure 1.2 Quicken includes many sets of income and expense categories that load according to the answers given in the Setup Interview.

Double-Entry Accounting

By assigning categories, Quicken can keep track of your books using at least some of the principles of double-entry accounting.

 TERM   **Double-Entry Accounting**   This accounting method maintains the integrity of a set of accounting books by ensuring that every transaction is documented in one or more ledgers that show precisely where it came from and where it went.

Categories are good, but they are also somewhat limited. For example, how would you normally go about separating a business payment from a personal payment if your books are built around a combination of both?

The best solution is to use classes. Classes are discussed in Lesson 2, but there are also three other possibilities. You should know these procedures because you can apply them when classes aren't appropriate:

- **Use a second checkbook and bank account.** Use a second checkbook and bank account to separate your business and home banking. This will simplify your record keeping and should ease day-to-day business management.

- **Use separate categories.** For instance, your business might have paid for some of the expenses incurred by your vehicle while you personally paid for the remainder. In this situation, you can create two Auto expense accounts. Call one Auto(Home) and the other Auto(Work). That's one solution, but if you ever just want to quickly see how much you spent during the year on your car, you need to manually add those accounts.

- **Create a series of subcategories.** Subcategories solve the problem mentioned above. Under Auto, you can create two subcategories: one for home and the other for work. Now when you print an expense report you can decide whether you want to see those categories in their full detail or just their totals grouped under the Auto category header. The problem with subcategories is that you would need to create them for every income or expense account where you would like to track home and business transactions separately.

In this lesson, you learned how to prepare Quicken for your business books. In the next lesson, you will learn about a more powerful categorizing solution: Quicken's classes.

Classes for Business Transactions

In this lesson, you learn how to use classes to separate business transactions from personal transactions, and one job or project from another.

Categorizing Transactions with Classes

A class is a way of further categorizing categories and transactions. As you know, categories are already divided into income and expense variants. Whenever you record a transaction that isn't a transfer to another account, you assign it a category. In fact, Quicken will remind you if you try to do otherwise, although it can't enforce the issue.

Classes are a little like an alternative form of category. In some instances, you might use a class as if it were a subcategory. For example, you might have one account called College Tuition, but by creating one class called Sally and another called John, you can further break down any checks made to College Tuition for each child.

However, in other situations you will use the class as a superset of categories. Quicken works best for small businesses if each customer and vendor (and optionally, job or project) becomes an individual class. Transactions are assigned to the usual categories but also to the target class. Any reports and graphs can then be targeted by that class alone. Therefore, while you might normally view your spending by all checks across the entire year, you can also see precisely how much was paid to Mario's Plumbing by choosing to view checks that only applied to the Mario's Plumbing class.

Quicken's default data file doesn't set up any classes. That's because your classes should really be determined by precisely what you want to accomplish. Still, if you find classes rather confusing, here are some ideas for class names and uses:

- **Personal**   Use to mark your personal transactions.
- **Business**   Use to mark your business transactions.
- **House1...House*n***   If you have more than one house, you can create classes called House1, House2, and so on to keep track of the money spent on each.
- **Car1...Car*n***   Same principle, different targets.
- **Client Name**   Assign a unique class name to each of your clients to create a list of accounts receivable by client (in other words, a statement) in a matter of seconds. Try to keep the client's class short so as to save on typing. If you use Quicken Home and Business, you can use the automatic client classifier built into the invoicing system.

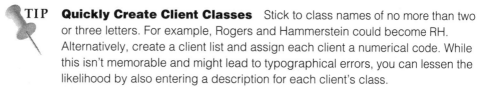

TIP   **Quickly Create Client Classes**   Stick to class names of no more than two or three letters. For example, Rogers and Hammerstein could become RH. Alternatively, create a client list and assign each client a numerical code. While this isn't memorable and might lead to typographical errors, you can lessen the likelihood by also entering a description for each client's class.

- **Vendor Name**   Useful for quickly seeing just how much you've spent on paperclips and toner cartridges with XYZ Stationery, even if those expenses are normally stored in different categories.
- **Sales Staff**   Instantly find out exactly how much income each member of your sales staff generates.
- **Jobs/Projects**   Break down your income and expenses by job or project. Perfect for creating individual profit-and-loss reports.
- **Department**   Work out how much each department is receiving and spending by marking the transactions with a department class.

As you can see, classes are more than just flexible: They can perform almost any categorizing task you can imagine.

Creating Classes

Creating classes is also very easy. Just follow these steps:

1. From the menu bar, select **Lists, Classes** to open the list.

2. Click **New** and you see the Set Up Class dialog box shown in Figure 2.1.

Figure 2.1 Use short class names and fuller descriptions.

3. Type in the **Name** as you want it to appear in Quicken's registers.

4. (Optional) Enter a **Description**. Descriptions appear in report headings.

5. (Optional) Type in a **Copy** number. Copy numbers are used by Quicken to post transactions to particular forms. For instance, if you operate two businesses, create a class for one business with one name and assign it copy number 1. Give the second business its own class and assign it copy number 2. Now Quicken will assign business one transactions to copy 1 of Schedule C of your 1040 tax return. Business two transactions will go to copy 2 of Schedule C. Without copy numbers, Quicken would assume you want the transactions lumped together on the one Schedule C. Copy numbers are also useful for tracking multiple W-2s.

6. Click **OK** to save the new class or **Cancel** to exit.

7. Click **Close** (**X**) to exit the Classes window.

 TIP **Printing a Ready Reference** To keep track of classes, print a handy list. Open the class list from the menu bar by selecting **Lists, Class**. Select **File, Print**. Click **OK**.

Creating a Subclass

Subclasses aren't like subcategories in that they don't exist within a hierarchy.

However, to treat any class as a subclass, just enter it after the parent class as described previously. To view reports or graphs using the subclass, enter it the same way. For an overview of that report or graph, use the class name on its own. For example, you could enter two office furniture transactions using these categories, classes and subclasses: **office/furniture:leon** and **office/furniture:front**. Figure 2.2 shown an example using the clients T&S and a Housing project. Now you can see at any time how much was spent on Leon and how much was spent on the reception area. To see how much was spent on all furniture, classify a report using **office/furniture**. To see how much has been spent on the office in total, look at **office** on its own.

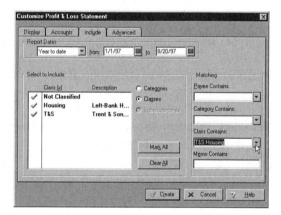

Figure 2.2 Subclasses don't exist separately from classes, but they can be specified as required using the colon (:) separator, shown here.

Using the Class

Once a class has been created, using it is easy. Just follow these basic rules:

1. You can use a class anywhere you would use a category including in the transactions register and when customizing reports.

2. A class isn't a substitute for a category. A class always follows the category name and is separated from the category by a forward slash (/), for example: **category/class**.

3. A class can be treated as a subclass by attaching it to the parent class with a colon (:), for example: **category/class:subclass**.

TIP   **Automatic Class Entry**   You've probably already noticed how Quicken automatically completes the category name for you, highlighting the additional characters in reverse type. Quicken does the same for classes. Type in enough characters to uniquely identify those classes and subclasses and move to the next field. Quicken will search for the first classes to match those sets of letters and complete their names for you. This means that "cl" would become class and "su" subclass. To make the most of this hidden feature, make sure the first two or three letters of each class name uniquely identifies that class.

Filtering Reports with Classes

Reports can provide an overview, a segment of relevant data, or a minute part, all with categories, subcategories, classes, and subclasses. To quickly and easily customize almost any Quicken report so that it displays only those transactions belonging to a certain class or subclass, follow these steps:

1. Select your report from the **Reports** menu.

2. Click **Customize** either in the upper-left corner of the report window or along the lower edge of the Report Creator dialog box.

3. In the left-hand box titled **Select to Include**, click **Classes**.

4. (Optional) To deselect all classes, click **Clear All**. To reselect them, click **Mark All**.

5. Select the classes you want to include by clicking beside each on the left-hand side of the Class list. Quicken places an arrow beside those that will be included. This works on a toggle system, so just click once more to deselect each class.

6. (Optional) You can't use the Class list to specify subclasses. Instead, select the parent class and then type the subclass into the right-hand section of the dialog box under Class Contains. Alternatively, click the down arrow and select the class from the list. Specify further subclasses using the colon (:) separator, for example: **class:subclass**.

7. Click **Create** to generate the report.

In this lesson, you learned about using classes and subclasses. In the next lesson, you will find out how you can use Quicken to track your debtors.

Managing
Your Debtors
(Cash-Based)

In this lesson, you will learn how to manage your debtors using cash-based accounting.

Debtor Management with Quicken

To succeed in business, you must manage debtors. An out-of-control receivables account can spell disaster. Every entry in the receivables account represents work already performed and money that is yours.

However, the opposite is true as well. You can have too tight a rein on the receivables—a grip that might prove equally disastrous. The question, then, is one of finding the middle path. Quicken's debtor management facilities will help you to do just that. The precise method you should implement depends on whether you have decided to use cash-based accounting or accrual-based accounting.

Cash-Based Accounting

There are at least three ways to handle receivables with cash-based accounting. These are manually, by direct depositing, and through deferred depositing.

 TIP **Quicken Home and Business** The additions to Quicken in the Home and Business edition are built around an accrual-based accounting system, the usual choice for all but the smallest of businesses. You will learn about recording invoices and receiving payments through Quicken Home and Business in Lesson 4.

Using a Manual Register

This is the easiest method. Just type your own invoices using a template built into your word processor, typewriter, or computer. (Of course, if you use Home and Business Edition, you can use it's own invoice-recording capability, as described in Lesson 4.) When you receive payment, enter the amount as a deposit transaction in your checkbook register. Follow these steps:

1. Select **Features**, **Banking**, **Use Register** and select the Checking register using the tabs at the bottom of the screen.

2. Enter the date payment was received. By default, Quicken sets this as today's date.

3. Click on the next field. Select **Deposit** from the pull-down list.

4. In the **Paid By** field, enter the customer's name. You only have to do this once. Quicken will remember and automatically complete the Paid By name on future invoices after you have typed in the first few letters of that customer's name. If you have numerous customers, you might prefer to assign a customer number. This approach can save a lot of time, at the expense of constantly referring to a printed list.

5. Click in the deposit column and enter the amount. Don't be confused by the Payment column. That's for payments coming *from* you, not going *to* you.

6. Click in the category field and select Gr Sales (Gross Sales). If this transaction attracts tax, you should split the category so that the appropriate components go where they're needed. Record the tax as a transfer to a Sales Tax liability account. This will prevent it from appearing as income, quietly accruing as a liability until it needs to be paid.

> **TIP** **A Real World Example** Margot's Fashion House runs a successful mail-order catalog. Freight represents a significant component of every sale and each invoice should reflect that cost. Margot solved the problem by creating an additional Freight expense category. Now every invoice is split between the Gross Sales component (which, in turn, is further categorized by a class showing the product that was purchased) and a Freight component. This gives Margot a far more accurate picture of her profit and loss.

7. (Optional) Follow the category with a class as shown in Figure 3.1. You should separate this from the category by typing a forward slash (/).

8. (Optional) Record a memorandum. The Memo might specify the invoice number, describe the nature of the invoice and contain other useful reminders. You will probably find it easiest to add a letter or three to the invoice number to help it stand out. For example, invoice number 356 might become Inv356.

9. Click **Enter** or press **Return** to complete the transaction.

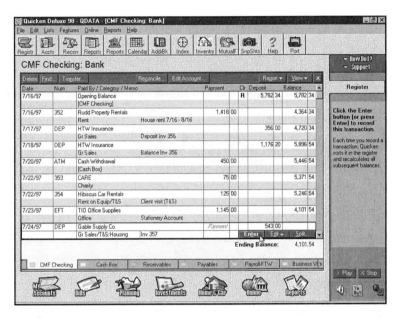

Figure 3.1 Storing transactions by category and class is a great way to build extra information into your business's books.

Direct Depositing

A slightly messier method, but one that lets you track your invoices electronically, is to record them in the checking register as soon as they are created, postdating them to show when the payment falls due.

Postdating Entering a transaction using a future date. A blue horizontal line marks the current date with future transactions below it (see Figure 3.2). The **Ending Balance** still shows the balance as if all transactions had been processed but a new total called **Current Balance** shows the balance of that account at that moment—that is, before taking the future transactions into account.

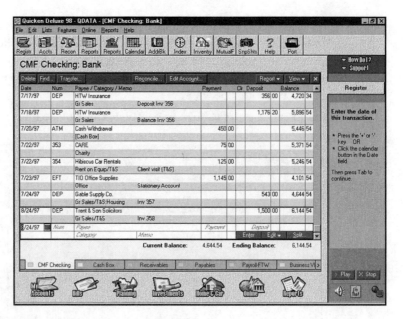

Figure 3.2 Postdating is easy in Quicken.

Entering invoices into the checking register has the following disadvantages:

- If a payment doesn't arrive, your Quicken bank balance will not be accurate.

- Storing potential transactions alongside actual transactions may be confusing.

- Quicken's debtor management functions don't behave as you might expect. For example, Quicken assumes you have received payment on the date it fell due. The accounts receivable reports will never recognize an overdue invoice.

Nevertheless, for a small business with few invoices and good clients who typically pay on time, a purely cash-based approach is efficient. To try this method, follow these steps:

1. Select **Features, Banking, Use Register**, and select the Checking register using the tabs at the bottom of the screen.

2. Enter the date the invoice is due.

TIP **Fast Dates** If your invoices always are due on the last day of the month, press **h** within the Date field to automatically jump to that date. Alternatively, the **+** (Plus) and **−** (Minus) keys push the date forward and backward one day at a time.

3. Click Num and type in the Invoice number. You will probably find it easiest to add a letter to the invoice number to separate it from check numbers.

4. Type in the Payee.

5. Click the deposit column and record the amount.

6. Under category, select Gr Sales (or any other appropriate income category), splitting to allow for sales tax, if required.

7. (Optional) Follow the category with a class. You should separate this from the category by typing a forward slash (/).

8. (Optional) Record a Memorandum. The memo might describe the nature of the invoice or contain other useful reminders.

9. Click **Enter** to complete the transaction.

Track When Invoices Have Been Paid? When you receive payments, edit the memo for that transaction, inserting PAID before the existing memo.

CAUTION

Deferred Depositing

Deferred depositing is useful if you use the cash-based method described in this lesson but need to maintain a list of invoices similar to that available under the accrual-method described in the next lesson.

Deferred depositing looks similar to the accrual method (they both use an accounts receivable asset account), but there are a couple of important differences:

- Invoices aren't credited to Gross Sales until payment is received. Until that point, those invoices remain uncategorized.

- Your profit-and-loss reports won't show sales until they've been paid, but your balance sheet will still categorize those invoices as an asset.

For deferred depositing, follow these steps:

1. Select **Features, Banking, Use Register** (Ctrl+R) and select the Receivables register using the tabs at the bottom of the screen. (If you don't see an Accounts Receivable asset account, you should create one as described in Lesson 1 of this part.)

2. Enter the date the invoice is due.

3. In the Num field, type in the Invoice number.

4. Type the Payee in the Payee field.

5. Enter the invoice amount in the Increase field.

6. (Optional) Type a note in the Memorandum field.

7. Click **Enter** to complete the transaction. You will see the dialog box shown in Figure 3.3 asking for confirmation that you don't want to use a category. If you don't want to see this message in the future, place a check mark beside **Don't Show This Message Again**. Whichever the case, click **No** to continue.

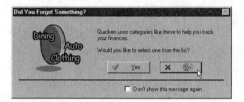

Figure 3.3 Click no if you are asked to select a category when using deferred depositing under a cash-based system.

Okay, the invoice has been entered but how do you handle payment? When payment comes in, you need to do the following:

1. Select the original invoice.

TIP **Finding an Invoice** Click **Find** at the top of the register's window to open the dialog box shown in Figure 3.4. Type the invoice number in the **Find** field. Click **Search:** and select **All Fields**. Then click **Find All**.

Figure 3.4   Quicken's Find feature is a great way to get to an invoice in a hurry.

2. Select **Gr Sales** as the category, splitting the transaction as necessary.

3. (Optional) Follow the category with a class. You should separate this from the category by typing a forward slash (/).

4. Click **Enter** to confirm the edited transaction.

5. Start a new transaction by clicking below your existing transactions.

6. Confirm today's date, and enter the same invoice number you used when recording the original invoice.

7. Type in the payee.

8. Click in the decrease column and enter the amount of the payment.

9. Click in the category field and create a transfer by selecting your checking account from the bottom of the category list.

10. Type in an appropriate memo.

11. Quicken will complete the transaction and insert a matching transaction into your bank account's register showing the deposit of funds.

In this lesson, you learned how to track your debtors using cash-based accounting. In the next lesson, you will learn to do the same using accrual-based accounting.

Managing Your Debtors (Accrual-Based)

In this lesson, you will learn how to use accrual-based accounting to manage your accounts receivable.

Accrual-based Accounting

Accrual-based accounting is more complex than cash-based accounting but has the decided advantage of providing you with a more accurate financial picture. The accrual-method also provides a cleaner and clearer documentation of the flow of funds through your accounts. For that reason, it is recommended for all but the very smallest of businesses.

CAUTION

Changing Your Accounting Method   Your accounting method is fixed according to the choice made on your first income tax return, but you may apply to change from cash to accrual or back the other way by applying to the IRS on a Form 3115, Application for Change in Accounting Method. A fee will be charged with the application, whether or not the change is approved. The form must be filed within the first 180 days of the fiscal year in which the change is requested.

In this lesson you will learn how to operate two accrual-based systems. You will need the first if you use Quicken 98 or Quicken Deluxe 98. The latter is only applicable if you use Quicken Home and Business 98.

Both accrual systems use an accounts receivable asset account to track your debtors. Why an asset account? Because those debtors owe you that money and it must be assumed they will eventually pay. Conversely, accounts payable is a liability account.

Like all Quicken accounts, accounts receivable takes the form of a register. If you use cash-based accounting, you won't have any need for this, but accrual-based accounting relies on a form of deferred depositing. The system works like this:

- A summary of every invoice is entered into the receivables register as that invoice is created. The income from that sale is categorized as necessary. This means there's no need to go back and search for that invoice when the payment comes through.

- Payments are treated as a transfer of assets, leaving the income accounts as they were, but depleting the receivables register and boosting the bank account.

- Because the invoices are kept in their own register, managing a lengthy list is significantly easier than when they are mixed in with the bank account.

Recording Invoices

The method you use to record invoices will depend on whether you are using Quicken or Quicken Deluxe, or Quicken Home and Business.

Using Quicken or Quicken Deluxe

Ensure you have set up a Receivables asset account as described in Lesson 1 of this part and then follow these steps (Figure 4.1 shows a sample first invoice):

1. Select **Features, Banking, Use Register**, and select the Receivables register using the tabs at the bottom of the screen.

   Quicken will automatically place the cursor on a new entry.

2. Enter the date the invoice was created. Normally, you would leave this as today's date.

3. Click the Num column and type in the Invoice number.

4. Enter the Payee.

5. Use the Increase column to record the amount.

6. Select an income category. If you collect sales tax, you should record the appropriate amount as a split to a Sales Tax liabilities account.

7. (Optional) Follow the category with a class. You should separate this from the category by typing a forward slash (/).

8. (Optional) Record a memo. The memo might describe the nature of the invoice or contain other useful reminders.

9. Click **Enter** to complete the entry.

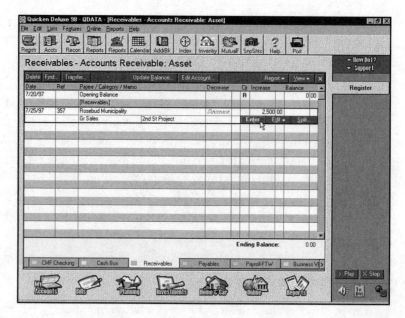

Figure 4.1 A receivables account is the ideal way to track outstanding accounts.

Using Quicken Home and Business

Ensure you have set up the Invoices/Receivables account as described in Lesson 1 of this part. Then follow these steps:

1. Select **Features, Business, Create Invoice**. You will see the Create Invoice dialog shown in Figure 4.2.

2. Record the Customer name and fill in the Bill To and Ship To addresses as required. When you create future invoices, you can select the same customer using a pull-down list which attaches via a down arrow to the Customer field. The addresses and other invoice details are stored with the customer.

3. Record the date, due date, invoice number, and customer's purchase order number, if applicable. By default, the due date is set for 30 days after the invoice date. Click **Options** to change the default setting.

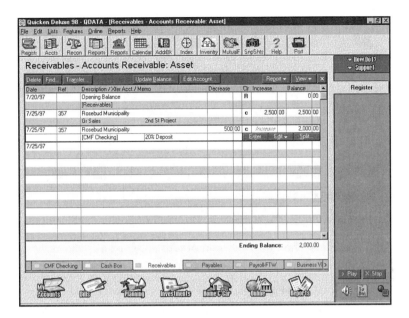

Figure 4.2 Quicken Home and Business adds a handy invoicing utility.

4. Fill in the columns for each invoice item. Use the Item column to record a product or service code. Quicken opens the Edit Item dialog box where you can record the product name or number, a description, Category/Class, the usual rate and its taxability. From then you can select the item from the Item column. The category, description and rate fill in automatically. If the item has been marked as taxable, Quicken will place a "T" in the final column.

TIP **Creating a Service Invoice** If you work in the service industry, you will probably prefer a more open invoice format. This is discussed next under Customizing Home and Business Invoices. When you reach the customization dialog box, turn off the Item check box and click **OK**. This removes the item column, leaving Category, Description, Quantity, and Rate—perfect if you charge by the hour.

5. Click **Next** to record this item and move to the next. When you finish, enter an optional customer message and memo, confirm the tax and click **Enter**.

TIP **Recording Reimbursable Expenses** A reimbursable expense is one that you incurred on behalf of your client. Reimbursable expenses are indicated as such in your checking register by clicking in the Exp column unique to Quicken Home and Business. Once you have recorded reimbursable expenses, you can bill them to your client by clicking **Expenses** in the invoicing screen. Click in the Use column beside each expense you want included on the current invoice.

Customizing Home and Business Invoices

By customizing the invoice screen, you can:

- Adjust the information that will appear on each invoice
- Select the columns used for each item entry
- Create several different invoices, each ideal for a specific task
- Add your logo and other details to the invoice so that you can print the invoices as they are created

To adjust the standard invoice, go to the invoice dialog box by creating a new invoice as described above. However, instead of filling in the fields, click Template and select **<Edit>**. This takes you to the Edit Template dialog box shown in Figure 4.3.

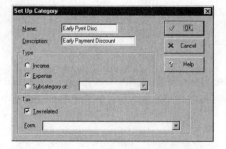

Figure 4.3 Edit your printable invoice templates from Quicken Home and Business.

To create a new invoice type, select **<New>** instead of create. Use the Template field in the main invoicing dialog box to select the invoice type required for the current entry.

The Edit Template dialog box provides five main areas:

- **Template Name**   Type in a name for this form of invoice.
- **Columns**   Select the columns you want to include in each invoice and adjust the column names as needed.
- **Company Address**   Click Print Company Address and enter your business's address details as required.
- **Fields**   Select the fields and field names to be included at the top of each invoice.
- **Print Options**   Choose your logo (it must be saved in Window Bitmap format), whether or not you want lines and shading to be used on the invoice and the number of blank lines required between each item. Why wouldn't you want to print lines and shading? This invoice format is compatible with the pre-printed business stationery available through the Intuit Marketplace. If you are using pre-printed stationery, the lines and shading are already there.

When you finish, click **OK** to save the adjusted or new invoice format.

Recording Payments

Now you've reached another decision point. There are two ways to record payments made by your customers:

- **Open Item**   This method tracks the status of each invoice. An open invoice is one that has either not been paid or only partially paid. A closed invoice is one that has been fully paid. Payments are applied to particular invoices rather than the account balance as a whole. The Open Item method is most useful when you deal with goods and products rather than specific services.
- **Balance Forward**   This method tracks the account balance rather than individual invoices. Payments are applied to the earliest open invoices. If the payment is larger than the invoice, the invoice is treated as closed and the remainder of the payment applied to the next oldest invoice and so on.

TIP   **A Real World Example**   The management of Big Frank's Fast Food has been foolhardy enough to provide the regular customers with tabs. The tabs are recorded at the end of each day but the customers only pay at the end of each month. Rather than trying to match grease-stained invoice duplicates with those in their computer, Big Frank and Co simply take whatever money is handed across and apply that to the tab, starting from the oldest component and working forwards.

287

Whichever method you use, stick to it. As always, if there is any doubt, consult your taxation professional.

Recording Payments with the Open Method

The following steps apply to users of Quicken and Quicken Deluxe 98. (See the heading "Recording Payments with Quicken Home and Business 98" if you fit that category instead.) To use the open method to record customer payments, do the following:

1. Open the Receivables register.

2. Enter a new transaction, setting the date as the date you received payment.

3. Enter the invoice number in the Ref field.

4. Type in the payee, or select the payee from the drop-down list.

5. Enter the amount of the payment in the decrease column.

6. Move to the category field. Click the down arrow and select your checking (or deposit) account from the end of the list. Confirm the date, type in the invoice number as a description and enter the amount.

7. Quicken will complete the transaction and insert a matching transaction into your bank account's register showing the deposit of funds.

8. Quicken's Accounts Receivable report only displays those transactions whose Clr field is blank. To prevent paid transactions from appearing in this report, click in the payment transaction's Clr field to mark that transaction as cleared. A small "c" appears in that column. Quicken will open a dialog box asking if you would like to use the reconciliation feature. Just click **No**.

 TIP **Cleared Transactions and Reconciliations** A cleared transaction is not yet reconciled. Instead, it exists in a temporary state. When you perform a reconciliation, previously cleared transactions will appear already marked in the reconciliation window. From that point you will find it easy to confirm them as reconciled.

9. Finally, find the original transaction (or transactions) and click in the Clr field to mark that (or them) as cleared—answering **No** as above. From now on, neither the original invoice nor the payment will appear in your Accounts Receivable reports.

Figure 4.4 shows the transaction pair with the cleared original above and the cleared payment about to be confirmed below.

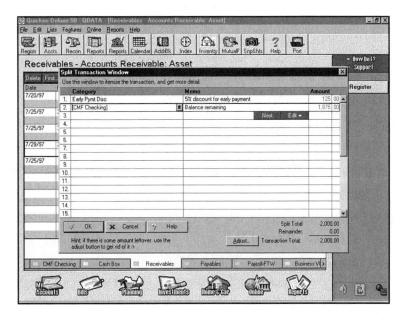

Figure 4.4 A completed payment transaction.

Recording Payments with the Balance Forward Method

If you want to use the closed method to record your customer payments, follow these steps:

1. Open the Receivables register.
2. Enter a new transaction setting the date as the date you received payment.
3. Enter the invoice number in the Ref field.
4. Type in the payee, or select the payee from the drop-down list.
5. Enter the amount of the payment in the decrease column.
6. Move to the category field. Click the down arrow and select your checking (or deposit) account from the end of the list. Confirm the date, type in the invoice number as a description and enter the amount.
7. Quicken will complete the transaction and insert a matching transaction into your bank account's register showing the deposit of funds.

8. (Optional) There is no need to mark off individual transactions as cleared—Quicken simply tracks the outstanding balance and you can see at any time how much your client has owed, how much that client has paid, and the amount those two figures are out of balance. However, to clean up your reports you may choose to mark off any original invoices that have been paid in full as cleared (click in the Clr column and answer **No**). Balance this by also marking any payment that has been fully allocated as cleared. Keep in mind, though, that the remaining payable invoices may not match the out of balance amount because some invoices may be paid in part but not in full.

Recording Payments with Quicken Home and Business 98

If you use Quicken Home and Business 98, you should follow these steps instead:

1. Select **Features, Business, Receive Customer Payment** or, if you already have the Customer Invoices register open, click **Create New, Customer Payment** directly above the register. You will see the dialog box shown in Figure 4.5.

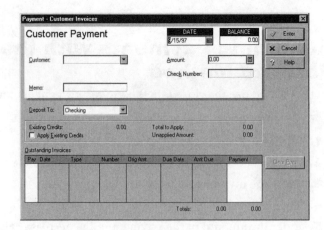

Figure 4.5 Quicken Home and Business matches outstanding invoices against payments received.

2. Select the Customer and enter the Amount received.

3. (Optional) Record a check number and memo.

4. Select the Deposit To: account (this is required to record the transfer of funds).

5. Use the Outstanding Invoices window to indicate the invoices to which this payment applies. If you are using the Open method, mark off each invoice as required. If you prefer the Balance Forward method, start with the oldest and work forwards. Quicken won't close off an invoice until it has been paid in full, however it does remember partial payments already made.

6. Click **Enter** when you finish to record the payment.

Printing a Debtor Report

If you are using Quicken or Quicken Deluxe, you can create an outstanding debtor's report, by selecting the menu **Reports, Business, A/R by Customer**. You will see the window shown in Figure 4.6. Click **Create** to view the report on-screen. To produce a hard copy, click **Print** and **OK**.

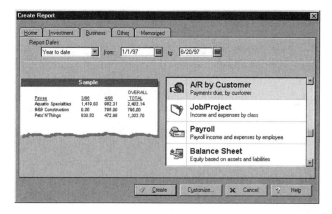

Figure 4.6 Quicken's most popular business report may be the accounts receivable by Customer report.

If you are using Quicken Home and Business, you have access to far more complete debtor management functions. To view outstanding invoices on screen, select **Features, Business, Unpaid Invoices**. Once the Unpaid Invoices window appears, use the **Sort** pull-down menu to change the list so that it displays unpaid invoices arranged by Customer, Date, Amount, or other. Use the **Options** pull-down menu to view only those invoices past due.

Either **Print** this list or create an A/R by Customer report as described previously.

TIP **Viewing Unpaid Invoices** To view any of the invoices listed in the Unpaid Invoices window, just double-click them with your mouse. Quicken moves to the Invoices register and opens the original invoice form. You can also open the form by double-clicking any invoice shown in the Invoices register.

In this lesson, you learned about managing your debtors on an accrual basis. The next lesson will show you how to handle bounced checks.

Handling
Bounced Checks

In this lesson, you earn how to enter the multiple payments required when a customer bounces a check. This will help you to recover your original fees as well as the insufficient funds charged against your account by the bank.

Dealing with Bounced Checks

In most accounting systems, bounced checks are handled by applying additional transactions to reverse the original payment, resurrect the invoice, and forwarding the insufficient funds charge to the client.

This is known as *full audit trail accounting.* It is a useful way to ensure that the transactions that took place in the checking account are also reflected in Quicken. Furthermore, when you receive an account statement, you can reconcile those transactions line by line.

To correct a bounced check in Quicken, you need to perform these tasks:

- Create an entry in your checking register for the original payment plus bank charges. The original payment is transferred back to receivables while the bank charge is marked as a "bank charges" expense item.

- Create a new entry in the receivables register for the total of the bank charge, assigning it to "Other Inc." This is marked as payable by the original debtor and will appear on that debtor's Accounts Receivable reports. If you use Quicken Home & Business, you can optionally edit the transfer transaction above in the Invoices/Receivables register, recording the bank charge transaction on a second line.

- Once you receive payment for the new total, transfer those funds back to the bank account.

This system ensures that the charge is marked as an expense. While eventual payment of the charge will be noted as income, the expense and income transactions balance each other and won't contribute to the business' taxable income.

Once final payment has been made, the funds are transferred back to the bank account. This might seem quite complex, but not once you've done it a few times. Simply follow these steps:

1. Select **Features, Banking, Use Register**, and select the Checking register using the tabs at the bottom of the screen.
2. Enter the date the check bounced.
3. Type the invoice number in the Ref. column.
4. Type in the client as the Payee.
5. Record the payment. This is the total of the original invoice plus the dishonor fee.
6. Move to the category field. Click the down arrow and click **Split**.
7. Type in **[Receivables] in the Category column** and enter the original invoice amount as shown in Figure 5.1. (If you use Home and Business, type in [Invoices/Receivables] instead.)

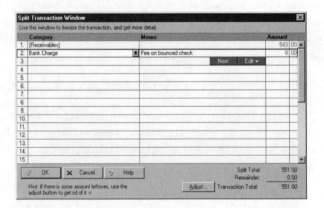

Figure 5.1 Split transactions provide a convenient way to tie bank charges to bounced check reversal transactions.

8. Click the next line and type in **Bank Charge**. (This account is imported along with the other business categories.) Enter a memo such as "Bounce fee on Q131" and type in the amount of that fee.

9. Click **Finished** to save the split.

10. Enter a memo such as **Transfer to A/R plus bounce fee**.

11. Click **Enter** to save this transaction.

12. Click the Receivables tab at the bottom of the screen to shift to the Accounts Receivable register. (If you use Home and Business, click Invoices/Receivables instead.) You will see a new transaction. This is the transfer from the checking register.

13. If you use any version of Quicken other than Home and Business, create another transaction with the following properties:

   - **Date**   The day the check bounced
   - **Ref**   The original invoice number
   - **Payee**   The debtor
   - **Increase**   The amount of the bank charge
   - **Category**   Other Inc (Other Income)
   - **Memo**   Invoice for bounce fee

   If you do use Home and Business, follow these alternative steps:

   1. Change the Type of the transfer from the checking register to "Invoice."

   2. Click **Category** and then the down arrow. Select **Form** to open the invoicing screen.

   3. Add a new line to the invoice items list marking the category as "Other Inc." The Item is optional, but you should record a Description such as "Invoice for insufficient funds charge."

   4. Type in the total, mark the Tax field in the totals area as required and click **Enter**.

Figure 5.2 shows the Checking register with the payments previously described. Due to the bank's fee, the balance is $8.00 in the red.

Figure 5.3 shows the Receivables register. Even though the original invoice was paid in full, there is now a resurrection of that transaction as well as an additional $8.00 fee to recover the costs of the bounced check.

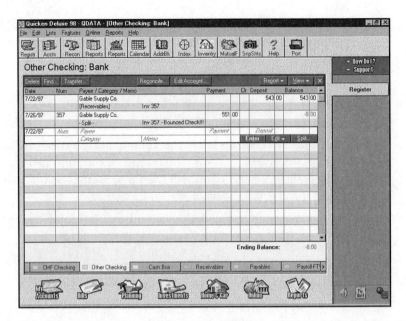

Figure 5.2 This figure shows only those transactions relating to the bounced check.

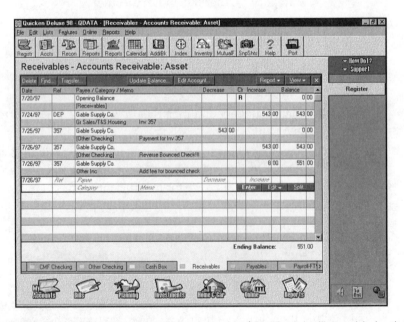

Figure 5.3 The old $53.50 charge is now equal to $61.50 and still payable by the original customer.

When you receive payment for the new total amount, process it the usual way, transferring it to the deposit account. Just don't forget that you need to look after the original invoice plus the extras incurred in the second transaction.

In this lesson, you learned how to create the transactions that handle a bounced check. In the next lesson, you will find out how to apply refunds and credits for goods or services that were canceled after you received payment.

Applying Refunds and Credits

In this lesson, you learn how to reverse invoices and write refunds or apply credits.

A Brief Caution

While Quicken seems to complicate some small business accounting functions, its handling of refunds and credits is very easy. Please note, however, that this lesson does ignore the ramifications for anyone also maintaining an inventory register. If that includes you, this lesson is valid, but you will also need to reverse the transactions that originally depleted your inventory.

Applying Refunds

Refunds apply to unpaid invoices, partially paid invoices, and fully paid invoices. The way you handle each depends on whether you use cash-based or accrual-based accounting. However, if you use Quicken Home and Business, an accrual system, you only need to learn one procedure. It's important to understand why the occasionally lengthy routines in this section are necessary.

Quicken and the term *audit trail* are totally separate. It is possible to delete or void any transaction going back to the day you first installed the package. Any changes that transaction made to the books is reversed, quickly and simply.

However, this approach is not without its risks. Being able to delete a transaction means wiping out data; a record that could one day prove crucial. It is far better to leave the record and reverse the changes that record made to the income and asset sides of the accounting equation by applying a correcting transaction.

This is especially important if it involves transactions that have passed through the bank account. This is the only way Quicken's version of your bank account will match the bank's version (minus any bank-originated credits or debits), turning account reconciliation into a clear-cut procedure that doesn't rely on guesswork.

Reversing an Unpaid Invoice

There are three ways to reverse an unpaid invoice:

- **Create a Negative Duplicate**   This corrects any contribution that invoice made to the income categories but is an unnecessary complication. You can safely ignore this method.
- **Void the Invoice**   This retains the transaction but removes the total, thus also removing that invoice's contribution to the books.
- **Delete the Invoice**   This method simply wipes out any record of the original invoice.

To void an invoice, find the original and select **Edit, Transaction, Void Transaction** (Ctrl+V).

 TIP **Voiding Transactions**   You don't have to lose your record of the total of the original transaction when you void it. Just type that total into the Memo field. This will leave you with a permanent and complete record.

To delete an invoice, find the original and click **Delete**. See Figure 6.1. If you'd rather not delete or void the original invoice, you should rectify the contribution that invoice made. The method you need to use depends on whether that invoice is fully paid, or partially-paid.

Reversing a Fully Paid Invoice

You can reverse a fully paid invoice without worrying about whether you use the cash or accrual methods. Both work the same.

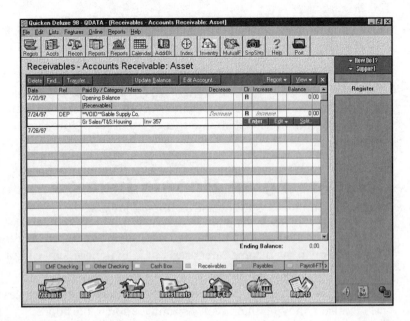

Figure 6.1 Voiding a transaction wipes out the contribution that transaction made to the books.

This procedure is identical whether you use Quicken, Quicken Deluxe or Quicken Home and Business. While the latter offers a special refund facility (it is available under **Features, Business, Issue a Refund**) it simply replicates the method described here, albeit through a different dialog box.

This procedure is simplified to avoid the accounts payable register. In strict terms, the amount of the refund should become an account payable, but under Quicken, it adds at least another two steps and your audit trail won't suffer from avoiding it. So, to reverse a fully paid invoice of any type, follow these steps:

1. Select **Features, Paying Bills, Write Checks**.
2. Fill out the check using these details:
    - **Date**   The default is today's date, but you can future- or post-date the check as necessary.
    - **Pay to the Order of**   Select the original invoice payee.
    - **$**   Enter the total refund.
    - **Address**   Type in the payee's address.

- **Memo**   Use a self-explanatory memo such as **Refund on Invoice Q1119**.
- **Category**   Specify the Returns expense category.

3. (Optional) Click **Online Payment** if your checking account is linked to the Online Center.

4. Click **Record Check** to store this check. Quicken will add the check to your "to be printed" list.

What If I Don't Print Checks or Use Online Checks?   Don't panic. Just create a new transaction in the checking register and write the check by hand.

CAUTION

This is what happened:

- You created a check that would act as the refund payment.
- The category was specified as **Returns**. This tax-related expense category will ensure the accuracy of future profit-and-loss reports and your end-of-year return.

Figure 6.2 shows a completed check on a payment in full.

Reversing a Partially Paid Invoice

The procedure for reversing a partially paid invoice adds to those for refunding a fully paid invoice.

If you use Quicken Home and Business, you should create a credit first and then pay a refund. You learn how to do this later in the lesson.

To reverse an invoice (as shown in Figure 6.3), follow these steps:

1. Select **Features, Banking, Use Register,** and select the **Receivables** register using the tabs at the bottom of the screen.

2. Create a new transaction with the following details:
   - **Date**   Set this to the date the sale was canceled.
   - **Ref**   Use the original reference number.
   - **Payee**   The payee should be the original payee.

- **Decrease** Enter the amount left outstanding on the original invoice. For instance, on an invoice of $200 where $50 has already been paid, you should decrease accounts receivable by $150.

- **Category** If you use the cash-based method, match this to the original invoice—probably Gr Sales (Gross Sales). Don't convert it to an expense account.

If you use the accrual method, match this to the Returns expense category.

- **Memo** Enter a useful description such as **Reversal of balance**.

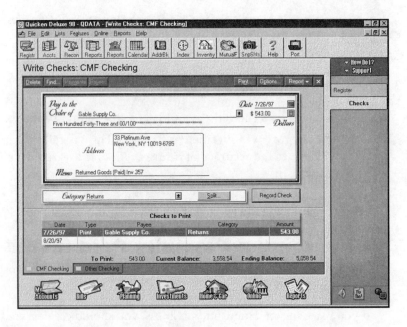

Figure 6.2 Creating a refund on an item paid in full is as simple as writing out a check and flagging it to the Returns expense account.

3. Press **Enter** to save the new transaction.

4. Click in the **Clr** column of the new and original invoices to mark them as cleared. This will prevent them from appearing on future reports.

So far, you have canceled any amount left owing on the original invoice. To take care of the amount already paid, you should write a refund check.

1. Select **Features, Paying Bills, Write Checks**.

2. Fill out the check using these details:

   - **Date**   The default is today's date, but you can future- or post-date the check as necessary.

   - **Pay to the Order of**   Select the original invoice payee.

   - **$**   Enter the total refund. This is the amount already paid on that invoice. For instance, on an invoice of $200 where $50 has already been paid, you should enter an amount of $50. If there is a cancellation fee, remove that from this amount. You don't need to assign the cancellation fee to a category because it has already appeared under Gr Sales.

   - **Address**   Type in the payee's address.

   - **Memo**   Use a self-explanatory memo such as **Refund of deposit on Invoice Q1119**.

   - **Category**   Specify Returns.

3. Click **Record Check** to store this check. Quicken will add the check to your "to be printed" list.

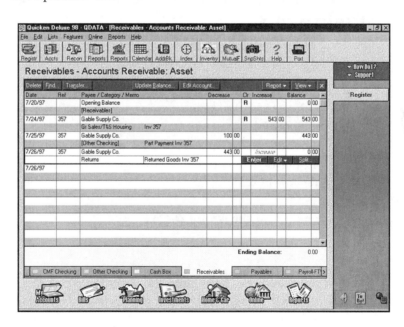

Figure 6.3   A reversal of a partially paid invoice.

If you write your own checks, create a transaction using the same details in your checking register.

Applying Credits

A credit is an alternative to a refund that is used against existing amounts outstanding or those that will be incurred in the future.

In this sense, a credit is a method of cutting down on a little paperwork. Instead of posting a refund check to your client, he or she tells you to use the money against current or future debts, saving them the effort of sending a return check back to you.

Before applying a credit, you should talk to your client to confirm that is what they want you to do. Otherwise, they might wait for a refund that never arrives. A credit only applies when an invoice has been partially or fully paid, for that is the only time you will be expected to return funds.

The procedure is identical for cash- and accrual-based accounting, but it changes according to the specific edition of Quicken you are using.

Crediting with Quicken Home and Business 98

Crediting and refunding fully or partially-paid invoices with Quicken Home and Business is easy. Follow these steps:

1.   Select **Features, Business, Record a Credit**. You will see a dialog box that looks almost identical to the Invoicing dialog box. You use it to create a credit invoice.

2.   Complete the dialog indicating those items you are providing a credit for. Record the total and optionally print the credit note. You should give this to your customer.

TIP   **Completing the Credit Dialog**   For more information on completing the credit dialog, turn to Lesson 6 in this part.

3.   The transaction has been recorded as a credit. You can now apply it to other outstanding invoices simply by choosing **Features, Business, Receive Customer Payment** and selecting **Apply Existing Credits**. If there is any amount to refund, select **Features, Business, Issue a Refund**. Provide the **Account** and **Type of Transaction**, and enter the **Customer**. If you are printing and posting this check or sending it as an online payment, make

sure you also select and then fill in **Address**. Record the **Amount** and an optional **Memo**. Select or enter a **Number** and click **Enter**.

Crediting a Fully Paid Invoice

If you use a version of Quicken other than Quicken Home and Business, you face a slightly longer journey.

For the sake of your financial book's internal documentation, not to mention the management of your own liabilities, these procedures shift the credit to the Payables register until such time as you can apply it to another invoice. This is also more convenient should your client change his mind and decide to take the money after all.

When an invoice has been paid in full, the balance from the Receivables asset account will have shifted to your Checking asset account. To create a credit on the returned goods, it is only necessary to generate a new transaction in Payables. By applying this transaction to the Returns expense account, you ensure its value is correctly reflected in your books. The procedure is easy (see Figure 6.4) and can be applied to both cash and accrual accounting systems. Simply follow these steps:

1. Select **Features, Banking, Use Register,** and select the **Payables** register using the tabs at the bottom of the screen.

No Visible Payables Tab You probably just need to create one. Check out the instructions in Lesson 1 and return here when you're done.

CAUTION

2. Create a new transaction with the following details:
   - **Date** Set this to the date the sale was canceled.
   - **Ref** Use the original reference number.
   - **Payee** The payee should be the original payee.
   - **Increase** Enter the total amount of the original invoice.
   - **Category** Type in Returns.
   - **Memo** Enter a useful description such as **Credit on invoice Q645**.

3. Press **Enter** to save the new transaction.

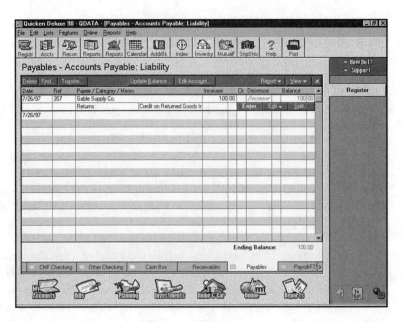

Figure 6.4 Credits on goods paid in full don't require account transfers. Instead, the credit for the credit is simply sent to the Returns expense account.

To apply this credit to a future sale, use [Payables] in place of [Checking] when recording a payment made. This prevents the payment from appearing in the Checking asset account (thus increasing your bank balance when no payments have been physically received). Instead, it comes from the Payables liability register. Do not use [Payables] when recording the invoice. You should use [Payables] only when recording the payment.

Crediting a Partially Paid Invoice

When crediting a partially paid invoice, you should wipe out the original debt and create an Payables entry for whatever was left over. This is the amount already paid. The procedure differs considerably depending on whether you are using the cash or accrual accounting methods.

If you are using the cash method, follow these steps:

1. Select **Features, Banking, Use Register,** and select the **Receivables** register using the tabs at the bottom of the screen.

2. Create a new transaction with the following details:

- **Date**   Set this to the date the sale was canceled.
- **Ref**   Use the original reference number.
- **Payee**   The payee should be the original payee.
- **Decrease**   Enter the amount left outstanding on the original invoice. For instance, on an invoice of $200 where $50 has already been paid, you should decrease accounts receivable by $150.
- **Category**   Match this to the original invoice—probably Gr Sales (Gross Sales). Don't convert it to an expense account.
- **Memo**   Enter a useful description such as **Reversal of balance**.

3. Press Enter to save the new transaction.

4. Click in the **Clr** column of the new and original invoices to mark them as cleared. This will prevent them from appearing in future reports.

At this point, the accounts receivable is balanced. However, no recompense has been made for the amount already paid. To correct that, follow these steps:

1. Select the Payables register using the tabs at the bottom of the screen.

2. Create a new transaction with the following properties:

- **Date**   Use the date the sale was canceled.
- **Ref**   Refer to the original invoice number.
- **Payee**   Type in the customer's name.
- **Increase**   Enter the total amount paid on that invoice at the time it was canceled.
- **Category**   Type in **Returns**. This will attribute the cost of this credit to your Returns expense account.
- **Memo**   Try something useful such as **Credit on cancellation of Invoice Q1912**.
- Press **Enter** to save the transaction.

Your accounts payable now shows a debt the same as any bill that might need to be paid. The difference is that you can apply this debt to any future invoice by using [Payables] in place of [Checking] when recording a payment made.

The accrual method for recording credits on partially paid invoices is similar but significantly different. Follow these steps:

1. Select **Features, Banking, Use Register,** and select the **Receivables** register using the tabs at the bottom of the screen.

2. Create a new transaction with the following details:
   - **Date**   Set this to the date the sale was canceled.
   - **Ref**   Use the original reference number.
   - **Payee**   The payee should be the original payee.
   - **Decrease**   Enter the total amount shown on the original invoice, not the amount paid or the balance owing.
   - **Category**   Send this amount to the Returns expense account.
   - **Memo**   Enter a useful description such as **Reversal of invoice Q1019**.

3. Press Enter to save the new transaction.

4. Click in the **Clr** column of the new and original invoices to mark them as cleared. This will prevent them from appearing in future reports.

Now you have an interesting situation. Your accounts receivable balance is lower by the amount already paid on the original invoice. To correct this, that amount must be transferred to accounts payable. Follow these steps:

1. Select the **Payables** register using the tabs at the bottom of the screen.

2. Create a new transaction with the following properties:
   - **Date**   Use the date the sale was canceled.
   - **Ref**   Refer to the original invoice number.
   - **Payee**   Type in the customer's name.
   - **Increase**   Enter the total amount already paid against that invoice at the time it was canceled.
   - **Category**   Type in [Receivables] to transfer the cost of this transaction from your accounts receivable.
   - **Memo**   Type in **Credit on cancellation of invoice**.

3. Press **Enter** to save the transaction.

Now the credit is sitting in accounts payable, yet your income and expense categories correctly reflect the original sale and subsequent return.

To apply this debt to any future invoice, just use [Payables] in place of [Checking] when recording a payment made, as shown in Figure 6.5.

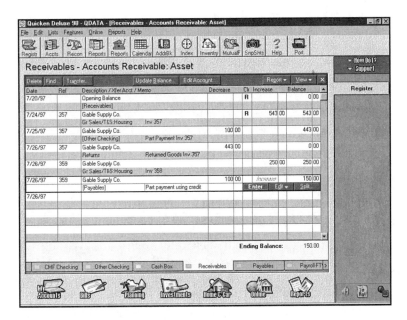

Figure 6.5 This Receivables register shows the original invoice and part payment, credit for the total invoice amount, the incurring of a new debt, and part payment on that debt through a transfer from Payables.

In this lesson, you learned how to work with refunds and credits. In the next lesson, you'll find out how to manage your creditors.

Coping with Your Creditors

In this lesson, you learn how Quicken can help manage your accounts payable with both cash-based and accrual accounting systems.

Understanding Accounts Payable

The accounts payable is diametrically opposed to accounts receivable: instead of an asset account, it represents a liability account, and instead of adding to your bank account, satisfaction of those liabilities tends to decrease your bank account. However, the accounts payable register acts like any other Quicken register, so using it isn't difficult. In fact, you'll find the procedures very, very easy.

TIP **Quicken Home and Business** The Home and Business edition makes no special allowance for Accounts Payable. Unlike Invoices/Receivables, you won't find a special Purchases/Payables register. If you require extensive support for this function, you should probably investigate QuickBooks. Otherwise, you can implement a fully-operational accounts payable system using the procedures described in this lesson as easily as can users of any other Quicken edition.

Like accounts receivable, the way you use your accounts payable will depend on whether your accounting system is cash- or accrual-based. In a cash-based system, you don't count your bills as expenses until they have actually been paid. Conversely, in an accrual-based system, a bill is considered an expense as soon as it has been incurred.

As the method can radically change the way you pay your bills, you need to look at them separately.

Handling Creditors with a Cash-Based System

As with receivables, there are at least three ways to handle creditors using a cash-based system. The easiest is to maintain a manual payables register, relying on written checks to record the transactions.

This method has the advantage of simplicity and the disadvantage of complexity. The simplicity comes through a minimal amount of computerized data entry. The complexity arises as soon as the number of creditors increase. It is far better to let Quicken's significant business bookkeeping expertise look after your creditors than to either keep a manual system or no system at all. Still, if the manual system interests, you, jump to "Making Payments," midway through this lesson. The procedure is identical to making payments using an accounts payable register save for one important difference. More on that later in this lesson.

Using Accounts Payable to Track Your Payments

While postdating checks is a great way to ensure that they don't go out too soon or too late, setting up an accounts payable liability register is good for organizing your finances when you have more than a handful of creditors.

If you don't already have this register, you should create one now using the instructions provided in Lesson 1 of this section. If you're not sure whether you have one or not, select **Lists, Account** to open the list of all registers. If you see an entry labeled Payables, as shown in Figure 7.1, that's the one you need.

The Payables register is a liability account, making it the opposite of an asset. In other words, as this register increases, your liability increases and your equity decreases. The only way to make it decrease is by satisfying some of those liabilities: possibly by writing out a check or applying that liability to an entry in the Receivables register (this is a credit payment, as discussed in Lesson 6).

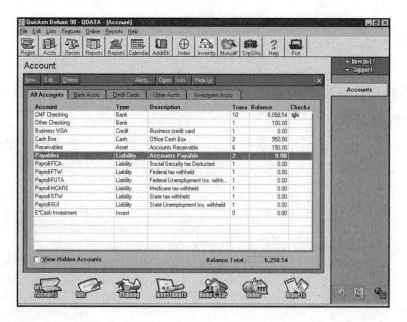

Figure 7.1 Check for the Payables register using your Account List.

By storing your payable accounts in this register, you keep them separate from the rest of the books. This makes it easier to not only see the bills that are coming up but also to apply Quicken's specialized accounts payable reporting tools.

To create a new transaction in the accounts payable register under the cash method of accounting, follow these steps (see Figure 7.2 for a sample):

1. Choose **Features, Banking, Use Register,** and select the **Payables** register using the tabs at the bottom of the screen.

2. Fill out the transaction using the following details. Click in each field to move the cursor to that position:

   - **Date** With the cash-method of accounting, enter the date the payment is due. This defers the entries that will be made in the expense categories until the date the payment should be made. If the payment is for some reason delayed, edit the date in this transaction to suit.

What If I Lose Track of Those Payments? You have two options: don't create the transaction until the bill will be paid (in which case you might as well resort to entering transactions directly into your checking account,

continues

continued

doing away with the Payables register), or make sure you check Quicken every day and mark those bills that have been paid by clearing them. This means that every time you pay a bill, click in the **Clr** column of both the original and the payment transactions. While this won't filter the register's on-screen list, it will give you an easy way of mentally doing so and does act as a filter for Quicken's Accounts Payable by Vendor report.

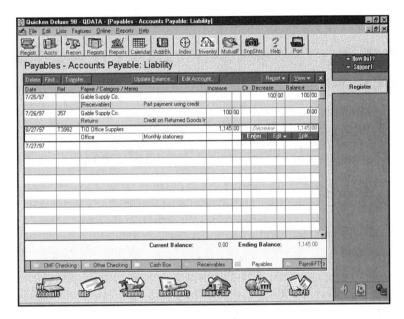

Figure 7.2 Entering a forward-dated transaction into the Payables register.

- **Ref**   A handy reference you can use to specify a purchase order number or the creditor's own invoice number and so on.
- **Payee**   Enter the creditor's name, or click the down arrow and select that name from a list of past transactions.
- **Increase**   As the liabilities account increases, so does the amount you owe. Record the total of the purchase here, including any taxes, freight, and other incidentals.
- **Category**   Select your expense category. If this payment applies to multiple expenses or expenses across different categories, click **Split** to open the Split Transaction dialog box.

- (Optional)/ Follow the category with a class, using the forward slash (/) as a divider.
- **Memo** The memo is for your purposes only. If you think this transaction requires a memory prodder, enter a useful one here.

3. Click **Enter** to save this transaction. Quicken will store the transaction and update the register. Notice that the balance of the account is now "in the red," indicating this balance is money you owe.

Handling Creditors with an Accrual-Based System

Accrual-based accounting is useful for those businesses that move from the micro to small stage and beyond. If you use accrual-based accounting, you will be penalized by the need to enter more transactions but rewarded with a far more accurate outlook on your books. This will help you to plan for the future.

The system works like this:

1. Every bill is entered into the accounts payable register as that bill is received.
2. Payments are treated as transferring your assets from the checking account into accounts payable, as shown in Figure 7.3. This wipes out the Payables debt and also decreases the checking account, ensuring your books are balanced at all times.
3. At the end of the day, you can see precisely how much you owe through the balance remaining in the Payables register. Meanwhile, your balance sheet reports will precisely reflect your equity in the business. Also, because all bills are kept together, managing your accounts payable is easy.

To store forthcoming payments under the accrual system, follow these steps:

1. Select **Features, Banking, Use Register,** and select the **Payables** register using the tabs at the bottom of the screen.
2. Fill out the transaction using the following details. Click in any field to move there immediately:
   - **Date** Enter the date you incurred the expense. You can leave that at the date you received the invoice, although there may be some ramifications at tax time.

- **Ref** Choose a handy reference number such as your own purchase order number or perhaps your supplier's invoice number.
- **Payee** Type in your supplier's name, or click the down arrow and select it from the list.
- **Increase** Enter the total amount of the debt incurred including any incidentals such as tax and freight.
- **Category** Select your expense category. If this payment applies to multiple expenses or expenses across different categories, click **Split** to open the Split Transaction dialog box.
- (Optional) Follow the category with a class, using the forward slash (/) as a divider.
- **Memo** The memo is for your own purposes only. If you think this transaction requires a memory prodder, enter a useful one here.

3. Click **Enter** to save the transaction.

At this point, your expense accounts have increased and your liability account has increased. To decrease your liability account, you need to transfer an asset, most likely by making a payment through your checking account.

Making Payments

Making payments is as easy as writing a check, and you don't need to decide between open item or balance forward methods (as is the case with your own debtors), or even if you should be using the cash- or accrual-based methods of accounting. However, it does depend on whether you use printed checks or handwritten checks.

Recording Printed Checks

If you print your checks on Quicken-compatible blank checks, follow these steps:

CAUTION

Where Can I Find Blank Checks for My Printer? You can order your checks directly from Quicken. Select **Features, Bills, Order Checks** and follow the on-screen instructions. Online ordering is also explained in Part 3.

1. Select **Features, Paying Bills, Write Checks** to open the dialog box shown in Figure 7.3.

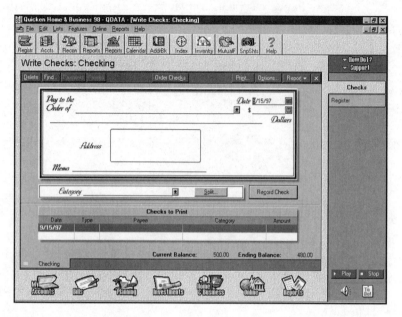

Figure 7.3   Write Checks mimics a check book's own look and style.

2. Fill out the check using the following details. Click in any field to move the cursor to that position:

- **Date**   The default is today's date. If you want to postdate this payment to the date the payment is due, type in the due date or use the Calendar icon to select it from an on-screen calendar.

- **Pay to the Order of**   Type in the creditor's name or click the down arrow to select it from the pull-down list.

- **$**   Enter the amount of the payment. Please note that Quicken does not make any sales tax or similar calculations. If you need to add anything to the payment total, click the Calculator icon to use Quicken's on-screen calculator.

- **Address**   Type in the address. If you selected a previous payee from the pull-down list, Quicken will enter this for you.

- **Memo** The memo should jog your memory so that one glance at the transaction entry tells you everything you need to know. However, it is also optional.

- **Category** Choose between the following:

  - If you are paying for an entry in the accounts payable register, type in **[Payables]** here. This will transfer the funds from the checking account to accounts payable, satisfying the liability.

  - If you are paying directly without using the accounts payable register, select an appropriate expense category. Choosing the right one makes the difference between good books, bad books, and next-to-useless books. If you have any doubts about which category you should use, speak to your accountant.

TIP **Splitting Categories** If a check covers many different expense categories (for example, a single credit card payment might apply to business and personal expenses in all sorts of categories), click **Split** to open the split transaction dialog box and enter each part of the payment on a separate line. The split transaction dialog box is explained in Part 1 of this book.

3. Click **Record Check** to store this check.

4. To print your recorded checks, see the "Printing Checks" section later in this lesson.

Recording Handwritten Checks

If you write out your checks by hand, you can bypass the Quicken Write Checks window and enter your transaction directly into the register. Payment is transferred from the checking account to the Payables register, as shown in Figure 7.4. To create the payment, follow these steps:

1. Select **Features, Banking, Use Register,** and select the **Checking** register using the tabs at the bottom of the screen.

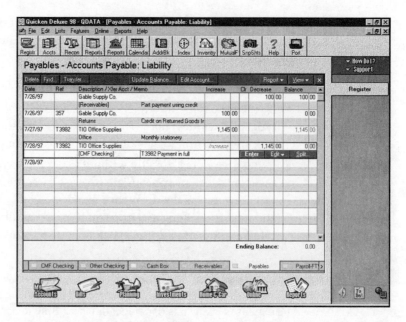

Figure 7.4   Notice the original payable plus the other back half of the payment transfer entered into the checking account. This deletes the Payables balance.

2. Fill out the transaction using the following details. Use the tab key to jump from one field to the next, or just click in that field to move the cursor immediately:

   - **Date**   The default is today's date. If you want to postdate this payment to the date the payment is due, type in the due date or use the Calendar icon to select it from an on-screen calendar.

   - **Num**   On handwritten checks, use this field to store your check numbers. If this is your first check, enter the number of that check now. You can record future checks—assuming they are serially numbered—by selecting **Next Check Num** from the drop-down list.

   - **Payee**   Type in the creditor or click the down arrow to select a previous creditor from the list.

   - **Payment**   Type in the total amount of this check. Use the calculator to work through any additional payments such as sales tax.

- **Category** Choose between the following:
  - If you are paying for an entry in the accounts payable register, type in **[Payables]** here. This will transfer the funds from the checking account to accounts payable, satisfying the liability.
  - If you are paying directly without using the Accounts Payable register, select an appropriate expense category.
- (Optional) Insert a forward slash (/) and follow the category with a class.
- **Memo** Type in an optional memorandum.

3. Click **Enter** to record this check and move onto the next.

Printing Checks

Quicken won't prompt you to print your checks every time you create a new one. Instead, it stores the checks in a list. Before printing your first batch of checks, make sure you have set all of the relevant parameters under **File, Printer Setup, For Printing Checks**. The options are described in Part 1.

 TIP **Check Lists** You can find out which checks need to be printed by either looking in the Write Checks window (select **Features, Paying Bills, Write Checks,** the checks are shown in the lower window) or by looking at the Checking register. All unprinted checks are shown with the word **Print** in their Num fields.

Once you're ready, you can print those checks either from the Write Checks window (click the **Print** button in the upper right corner) or by selecting **File, Print Checks**.

In this lesson, you learned about managing an accounts payable register and issuing payment. In the next lesson, you will find out practically all there is to know about using Quicken to manage a cash box or cash register.

Running a Cash Box or Cash Register

In this lesson, you learn how to use Quicken to manage a cash box, petty cash, or cash register float.

Managing a Cash Box or Register

While it is nice to imagine a world where all income arrives in the form of checks waiting to be banked and all outgoings take the form of checks waiting to be written, this is hardly ever the case.

People like to pay for small items by cash, and the availability of an automated check writing system such as Quicken isn't going to change anyone's mind, so most small businesses run a cash register or, at the very least, a cash box. This is used to record either some, the majority, or all of the transactions that occur throughout a business day.

The cash box (or petty cash box) acts as a temporary bank account. The *float* is the amount of cash placed in the box at the start of the day. All transactions that change the balance of the cash box must be noted and used to update Quicken's income and expense categories, as well as the cash box asset account.

The cash register—not to be confused with Quicken's own registers—is just an automated cash box. Used properly, it will record and categorize every transaction passing through it. At the end of the day, a special report provides you with the totals for each category. These can be entered into Quicken as grouped account postings, rather than as individual transactions. In other words, if you sold 20 magazines totaling $89.76, you would enter that total as a single transaction, rather than as 20 individual sales.

In Quicken, there's nothing difficult about maintaining a cash box or cash register, so long as you stay organized. When you set one up you will need to keep the following in mind:

1. Decide on a float; the float is the amount that you start with each day. There is no formula for working out how much float you need, but one half of the day's typical cash receipts is a good starting point.

2. Never start or end a day without knowing how much is in the float. This is absolutely vital for keeping a solid set of records.

3. Every transaction into or out of the cash box or register must be noted. This used to be done by writing each transaction into a book, but electronic registers handle this automatically. However, if you want to store your sales in subcategories underneath Quicken's Gr Sales, or at least under different classes, your cash register must support however many different income types you want to track.

 TIP   **Managing Petty Cash**   The petty cash box is no different from the cash box or register except that it is used for those business purchases that are too small for you to be bothered with writing out a check. Instead, withdraw the petty cash and leave a note stating precisely how much you withdrew and what it will be used for. The note will help to categorize the expense at the end of the day. Once you've purchased the goods, staple the note to the sales receipt and return it to the cash box along with any change. If the receipt isn't particularly explicit, just jot down details of the purchase on its reverse.

4. If you use a cash box and have Quicken set up next to your front counter, you can use Quicken directly to manage your transactions. It doesn't connect to an electronic till like some accounting packages, but it does save the time you would otherwise spend transposing figures from a cash book to Quicken.

5. At the end of the day, you should total the cash box, enter the transactions or totals into Quicken, remove and store the float, and bank the balance.

The procedures for setting up and using the cash box and cash register are almost identical, so we'll just use the term cash box from now on.

Setting Up a Quicken Cash Box

Quicken makes setting up a cash box easy. Follow these steps to create the account shown in Figure 8.1:

1. Select **Lists, Account**. At the very least, you will see the checking account, but you may also see Receivables and Payables, the two trading accounts.

2. Click **New** to start the Create New Account interview.

3. Specify **Cash** as the type of account. A cash account is really an asset account, except that Quicken changes the Payment and Deposit columns in the register to Spend and Receive.

4. Click **Next** to move to the next dialog box.

5. Type in the account's name. This is the name that will appear in the tabs at the bottom of the register screen. It is also the name you will need to type in every time you perform an account transfer (that is, between the left and right square brackets, as in [cash box]).

6. Type in an appropriate description.

7. Click **Next** and then **No** to specify that you don't know how much cash you have. This bypasses the opening balance question, but that is okay for now.

8. Click **Next** twice more to move to the account summary, and click **Done** to approve the account's specifications. You've created a cash box asset account.

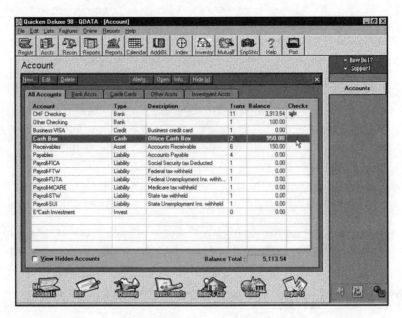

Figure 8.1 The Cash Box is another form of asset account.

Using the Cash Box

Your cash box or register is an asset, just like your bank account. This means that you can choose to transfer money from your bank account to the cash box without going near your income and expense categories.

That transfer is the same as if you were to go to your bank and withdraw a $500 float from your business's account, putting that into the cash box. At the end of the day, you might take that $500 and return it to your bank account. Throughout the day, the business's asset level has remained the same (assuming nothing else changed).

However, your cash box probably won't stay the same throughout the day. If it acts as a register, then the balance of your cash box will rise as people use your products or services and compensate you with cash payment.

If the cash box acts as a petty cash box, it probably will have gone down because you will have found cause to dip into the box to pay for office stationery or other small expenses.

 TIP   **Personal Purchases**   You should never use the petty cash box to pay for your personal purchases unless you either replace the money or note it in the books as withdrawals. Otherwise, Quicken's version of your business's income and expenses will never match reality.

Every time you take money from your bank account and put it in the cash box, you should note it in Quicken. Every time the reverse happens, you should note that as well.

Transferring Funds to the Cash Box

Let's make some assumptions: It's Monday morning and you've decided the time has come to set up a formal cash box. You head down to the bank and withdraw $300 from your business bank account. You've been reading up on this cash box business and you've set up the Cash Box account as instructed.

To specify the transfer of funds, as shown in Figure 8.2, follow these steps:

1. Select **Features, Banking, Use Register,** and select the **Cash Box** register using the tabs at the bottom of the screen.

2. You will see the transaction marking the Opening Balance. Jump to the line following that and type in a new transaction with the following details:

   - **Date** Use the default of today's date.
   - **Ref** Ignore.
   - **Payee** Cash Float.
   - **Receive** Enter the amount being transferred. In our example, that's $300.
   - **Category** Specify a transfer from your checking account, for example [checking].
   - **Memo** Ignore.

3. Click **Enter** to continue.

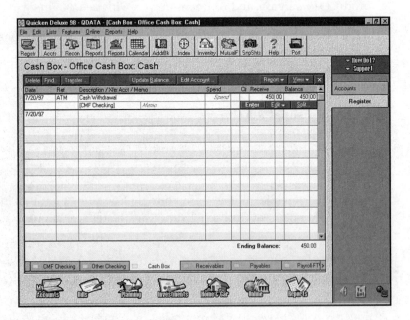

Figure 8.2 Setting up the opening cash float.

Storing Transactions as They Happen

Now that you have a cash box with money in it, you can either enter transactions as they occur, or leave them until the end of the day. Say you head down to the stationery store to pick up some copier paper. Just follow these steps to enter the transaction shown in Figure 8.3:

1. Select **Features, Banking, Use Register,** and select the **Cash Box** register using the tabs at the bottom of the screen.

2. Enter a new transaction with the following details:

   - **Date**   Use the default of today's date.
   - **Ref**   Ignore.
   - **Payee**   Type in the name of the payee. For example, you can enter **The Paper Merchant**.

 TIP   **Bypassing the Payee**   It is not necessary to record the name of the payee for all purchases unless you are interested in using that information later on—perhaps to create a report based around that customer or vendor. For insignificant items, you may prefer to create a general payee such as **Miscellaneous Office Supplies**. For over-the-counter sales, you might create a payee called **Cash Sales**. Incidentally, this means you can quickly analyze your cash sales as compared to other types in future graphs and reports.

   - **Spend/Receive**   If this is a purchase, enter the total under **Spend**. In our example, that might be $20 for several reams of copier paper. If you receive funds through a sale, enter the total sale price under **Receive**.
   - **Category**   If this is a purchase, specify an expense category; for example, **Office**. If you have sold an item or service, enter an income category such as **Gr Sales** (Gross Sales).
   - **Memo**   Type a note such as **five reams copier paper**.

3. Click **Enter** to store the transaction.

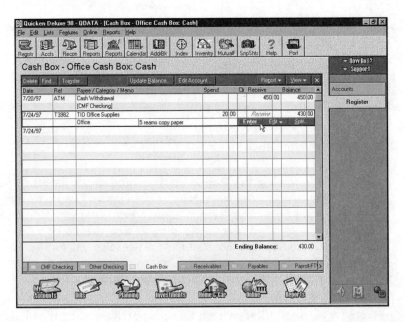

Figure 8.3   Cash transactions can come straight from the Cash Box account with minimal difficulty.

Storing Transactions in Bulk

It isn't always convenient or efficient to store individual transactions as they occur. Instead, you might find it easier to total up the sales throughout the day (or if it has been a particularly slow day, throughout the week) and enter those totals as bulk transactions.

The easiest way to total up sales in different categories is to use a cash register. By matching the classifier buttons on the register to your categories or classes within Quicken, the register can easily add up the sales of one type or another.

Rather than entering each individual transaction, take those totals and type them into Quicken, as previously described for single sales. If you want to be efficient, you enter the total for all sales as the amount received and use the Category field's **Split** button to assign each part of that sale to different categories or classes, as shown in Figure 8.4.

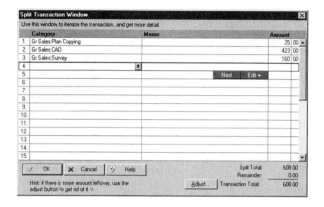

Figure 8.4   Using subcategories for sales can make more sense of split transactions.

TIP   **A Real World Example**   The Happy Hardware Store has two cash registers, around 10,000 items in stock, and routinely makes hundreds of sales each day. Rather than storing each transaction, John, the manager, takes the daily totals from each register. Each sale is categorized by its product type: for example, paint, building, electrical, and so on. These match the income subcategories previously set up under Gr Sales in Quicken. John simply applies the totals as single sales to each income category using the Splits window. This keeps the Quicken registers clean, the books up to date, and the income categories packed with useful information.

Balancing the Cash Box

At the end of the day (or week), you should balance the cash box, separating tomorrow's float from today's banking. The balance forms your gross cash income. However, it has already been applied to the various income and expense categories, so all you need to do is transfer the amount you decide to deposit back to your checking account.

Follow these steps:

1. Select **Features, Banking, Use Register**, and select the **Cash Box** register using the tabs at the bottom of the screen.
2. Type in a new transaction with the following details:
   - **Date**   Use the default of today's date.
   - **Ref**   Ignore.
   - **Payee**   Cash Float.

327

- **Spend** Enter the amount you are going to deposit in your checking account.

- **Category** Specify a transfer to your checking account, for example, **[checking]**.

- **Memo** Ignore.

3. Click **Enter** to continue.

Figure 8.5 shows a series of transactions that might take place over one day in a cash box account. The second transaction places a $300 float into the account. The next transaction shows miscellaneous income from the cash register totaling $278.98. This is attributed through the split shown in Figure 8.4. The fourth transaction shows miscellaneous office expenses of $20.

The balance of the account at this point is $558.98. The final transaction transfers $258.98 of this to the checking account. Assuming the operator would like to start tomorrow with a float of $300, that amount represents the balance of the funds above the float.

Of course, these funds need to be dropped into the bank, otherwise Quicken's idea of the checking account's balance would differ from reality. Most businesses do this by placing the funds into the bank's night deposit safe.

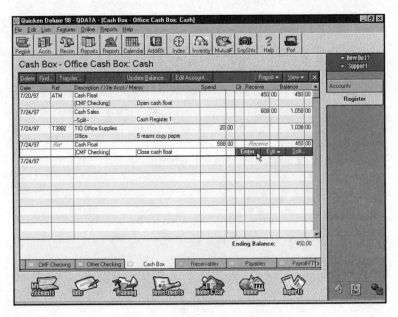

Figure 8.5 A typical day's transactions for the Cash Box account.

Useful Cash Reports

The Cash Box is useful to electronically document the incoming and outgoing flow of cash funds through your business. If you don't have an electronic cash register, you can also use Quicken as an electronic version. After all, it has all of the features of most cash registers, and many more besides.

However, Quicken excels even if you do have an electronic cash register by providing an immediate check on the balance of that register.

To see a fully documented balance, follow these steps:

1. Close off the cash register, printing the end-of-day summary.

2. Enter that summary into your Register account.

3. Enter any Spend transactions that have been stored on credit notes in the register's tray.

4. Work out how much you want to deposit in the bank and store that transaction.

5. To create a register report, click a blank transaction, and then click **Report** in the upper right corner of the window. Select **Register Report** from the pull-down list.

CAUTION

I Don't See a Register Report!   You probably still have a previous transaction selected. Make sure you're on a new transaction before pressing the **Report** button. Still, here's a useful tip: if you ever want to create a report about payments to a particular vendor, receipts from a certain client or incoming and outgoings on a particular category, select that section of any transaction, click **Report,** and choose the automatically customized report from the pull-down menu.

6. The Register Report is shown in Figure 8.6. It is a complete report of the transactions going into and out of the account and takes the form of a statement with opening and closing balances. You should get into the habit of printing these at least once a week (and more often if the account has a lot of activity). This is the perfect way to track down any mistakes that might have resulted in the bank's version of your account disagreeing with your own. It's also perfect material for proving to the IRS just how complete and professional your bookkeeping really is. Even better, it takes almost no effort at all. Just click **Print** and you'll be done.

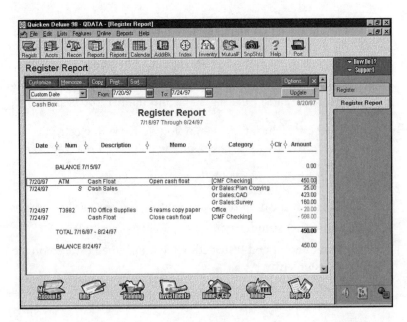

Figure 8.6   The Register Report is a great way to prove that your Cash Box or Register Float has balanced. Print it for a permanent record.

In this lesson, you learned about using Quicken to manage a cash box or cash register. In the next lesson, you will learn about using Quicken for your payroll.

Managing the Payroll

In this lesson, you learn how Quicken can help set up a payroll and create paychecks or transactions at the end of every pay period.

Payroll Responsibilities

The responsibilities involved in running a small business double if that business maintains a payroll. All of a sudden, you will find that you are not only responsible for your own tax as a sole proprietor, but everyone else's as well.

Every paycheck is made up of a complex melange of compensation, employee withholdings, and employer contributions. As a sole proprietor, you may be liable for: income tax, self-employment tax, and estimated tax. However, as an employer, you will be responsible for each of your employee's: social security tax, Medicare tax, Federal and State income tax withholding, and Federal unemployment (FUTA) tax.

You will also have to ensure that each employee fills out Form I-9, Employment Eligibility Verification, and Form W-4, Employees' Withholding Allowance Certificate; make any extra deductions requested; and deposit the relevant deductions using Form 8109 or the IRS's new EFTPS (Electronic Federal Tax Payment System).

At the end of the year, you will need to fill out Form W-2 for each employee summarizing the wages paid, pay withheld, and any contributions made by your company on behalf of the employee.

Yes, managing the payroll is an onerous job, but there's no way to escape it, and the penalties for those who try can be very harsh indeed. Quicken is not a payroll package, but it is in a good position to help you to manage this mess.

By creating a series of payroll liabilities accounts, you can use Quicken to keep track of amounts withheld and your business's contributions. At the end of every pay period, memorized transactions will automatically create the last paychecks for each employee. Quicken can also create reports that will help you to fill out the payment deposit forms.

It should be pointed out, though, that using Quicken for payroll is not as easy as using a dedicated payroll package. If you need to manage more than a small handful of staff, seriously consider purchasing QuickPay from Intuit.

With Quicken's Payroll facilities, you can:

- Print the full paycheck breakdown on voucher checks.
- Total earnings and deductions by employee or across the entire payroll.
- Calculate your own payroll tax liabilities.
- Print reports that will help you to complete your monthly or quarterly payroll tax returns.
- Print checks to cover those returns.
- Store payroll information for faster processing in the next pay period.

In this lesson, it is impossible to cover all of your obligations as an employer—that would take a book on its own! Rather, this lesson shows you how to use Quicken to manage your payroll. The distinction is important and also acts as a disclaimer. We cannot guarantee that everything you need to do is covered here. Instead, we recommend you obtain, read, and understand the IRS's Publication 15, Circular E, Employer's Tax Guide.

 TIP **Obtaining IRS Publication 15** You can obtain Publication 15 and other IRS material by calling 1-800-TAX-FORM. You can also dial 703-487-4160 from your fax machine to receive copies on your own fax. Alternatively, all the publications are available at the IRS site on the World Wide Web. You'll find them at **http://www.irs.ustreas.gov/forms_pubs/top-forms.html**. The easiest way to view these is using the PDF (Portable Document Format) files supported by Adobe Acrobat. The viewer is available from the Adobe Systems site at **http://www.adobe.com**.

Setting Up the Payroll

It takes a little bit of work to set up Quicken for payroll and you may be tempted to skip some of this. Please don't! Quicken's payroll reports rely on the existence of certain accounts, and if you don't name them precisely as suggested here, your payroll system will not work. It is a lengthy procedure, but you only need to do it once, and from then on it will work like a dream.

To use Quicken's payroll features, you must create a series of expense categories and liability accounts. The categories and accounts achieve two purposes. First, any contributions made by your business are fully tax deductible and the expense categories will track these. Second, the withholdings deducted from the employee's gross pay, along with your own business's contributions, will accrue in those liability accounts until such time as you pay them. This means that your balance sheet and profit-and-loss reports will always present an accurate picture.

Creating the Payroll Categories

Before using Quicken to manage your payroll, you must create a category called Payroll with subcategories under it to track each kind of payroll tax contribution your business makes (see Figure 9.1).

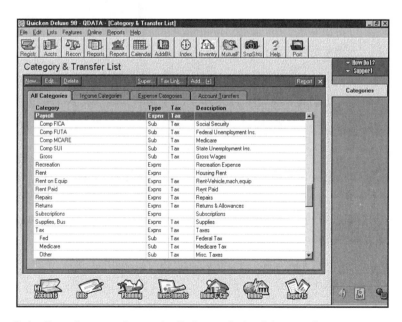

Figure 9.1 Payroll categories track all of your deductible payroll expenses.

CAUTION

Don't Use the Tax, Business Category   This is used for taxes that originate from your business's income, not those collected on behalf of its employees. Also, when Quicken creates the payroll report, it looks for a category beginning with Payroll.

To create the main category, follow these steps:

1. Select **Lists, Category/Transfer (Ctrl+A)**.

2. Click **New** and create the category using the following details:

- **Name**   Payroll
- **Description**   (Ignore)
- **Type**   Expense
- **Tax**   (Ignore)

3. Click **OK** to save.

Now you need to create each of the subcategories shown in Table 9.1.

Table 9.1   Payroll Expense Subcategories

Name	Description
Gross	Gross Wages
Comp FICA	Social Security
Comp MCARE	Medicare
Comp SUI	State Unemployment Ins.
Comp FUTA	Federal Unemployment Ins.

Work through the following steps, changing the Name and Description each time but leaving the rest of the information as specified:

1. Click **New** and create the new categories using the following details:

- **Name**   (Insert each of the names listed in Table 9.1.)
- **Description**   (Insert each of the descriptions listed in Table 9.1.)
- **Type**   Subcategory of: **Payroll**
- **Tax**   Tax-related

2. Click **OK** to save.

You should also create subcategories for any other tax-related deductions your company makes from each paycheck.

Creating the Payroll Accounts

The payroll liability accounts track the ongoing and accruing liability formed through the removal of withholding tax from your employee's gross pay, as well as the contributions your own business must make.

As with the payroll categories, the payroll liability accounts must follow a particular format for Quicken's payroll reports to do their job. In short, all payroll liability accounts must begin with **Payroll-**, as shown in Figure 9.2.

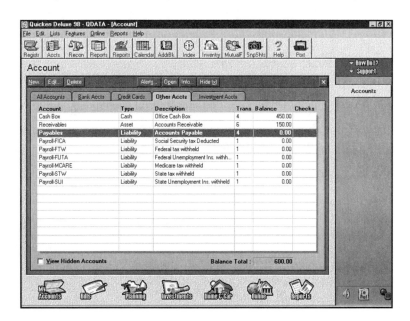

Figure 9.2   Payroll liability accounts track the ebb and flow of your payroll.

Follow these steps to set up the first liability account:

1. Select **Lists, Account** and click **New**.
2. Select **Liability** and click **Next**.
3. At this point, you can speed things up considerably by clicking the **Summary** tab at the top of the window. Fill in each field with the following details:

- **Account Name** Payroll-FWH
- **Description** Federal Tax withheld
- **Balance** $0.00
- **As of** (Ignore)
- **Optional Information** (Ignore)

4. Click **Done** to continue.

5. Click **No** to ignore the offer of setting up an amortized loan.

Now, repeat the previous steps for every entry in Table 9.2. Note, however, that you do not need to create liability accounts for gross or net pay because neither of these form an ongoing liability. Indeed, they are generated and paid as soon as you fill out the paycheck.

Table 9.2 Payroll Liability Accounts

Account Name	Description
Payroll-FTW	Federal tax withheld
Payroll-STW	State tax withheld
Payroll-FICA	Social Security tax withheld
Payroll-MCARE	Medicare tax withheld
Payroll-SUI	State Unemployment Ins. withheld
Payroll-FUTA	Federal Unemployment Ins. withheld

As with the payroll subcategories, you will need to create liability accounts for any other forms of tax that are withheld. Make sure the names of those accounts also begin with **Payroll-**.

 TIP **Jumping Between Register Tabs** Unfortunately, every new liability account you create plays its part in making an unavoidable mess of the register screen. While you can always **Hide (x)** the accounts in the Account List window, hiding them there doesn't affect their appearance as register tabs. To quickly jump from one register to the next, right-click any tab and select that tab from the list. Left-click and drag any tab to move it to a new position.

How Does the Payroll System Work?

The payroll expense subcategories and payroll liability accounts work together in what, at first, appears to be a needlessly complex mesh of interaction.

In brief, it goes like this:

1. Every paycheck is calculated on gross pay minus various withholdings and deductions.

2. The employee gets the net pay, and this amount is immediately withdrawn from your bank account (at least, from Quicken's point of view).

3. Meanwhile, the withholdings are shifted to the payroll liability accounts. Your business's contributions are indicated on the paycheck by a series of positive and negative but equal postings to the Payroll tax categories and liability accounts. As these transactions are balanced, they don't change the net pay. However, they do adjust your own accounts, logging a liability that comes from the contributions you are also obligated to pay.

4. The funds in the liability account act as money your business owes, so the balance sheet reports remain true. Furthermore, those funds have already been counted as a loss, even though you still have the money sitting in your bank account. They are counted as a loss because you have already "incurred" that debt.

5. When the time comes to pay that tax, you simply write a check or enter a transaction whose category entry transfers those funds from the liability account. This depletes your payroll tax liability by the amount of the transaction. It also depletes your bank account.

If you've never prepared payroll tax before, your head's probably spinning. However, you can break the entire procedure into several simple steps, and Quicken's capability to remember past transactions is about to prove enormously useful.

Creating Paychecks

The payroll check is probably the most complex form of check you will ever write. At first glance, it also seems to make very little sense, but not once it has been broken down into its component parts.

The split transaction side of a payroll check is made up of four parts. To help you understand how it all fits together, here's a sneak preview:

1. **Part 1: Compensation**   This is the total or gross compensation the employee earned. It should include wages, salary, bonuses, commissions, tips, and any other monetary items regarded as compensation by the IRS. Even though the paycheck won't show this compensation in total, it forms an important foundation for the calculations that follow.

2. **Part 2: Withholding**   The withholding covers all deductions from the paycheck. Enter these as negative amounts so that each line reduces the total paycheck. For example, if an employee earned gross pay of $1,109.53 and withheld amounts totaled $367.20, the net paycheck would equal $742.33. This is the net pay and is the total amount by which your bank account is depleted.

3. **Part 3: Buffer Lines**   These are blank lines that sit between the end of the withholding and the next section of the split beginning at line 17. There's a good reason for this buffer section: the voucher-style check is perfect for payroll purposes but only allows for up to sixteen printed lines of detailed information. The check cannot hold anything from line 17 and beyond, so Quicken doesn't even try to print it onto the check. This means that your employer contributions remain hidden.

4. **Part 4: Employer Contributions**   This final section is used to store your own mandatory contributions to the employee's tax burden. These are entered as a series of balanced negative and positive transactions so they don't actually alter the net pay. However, they do create a payroll tax liability along with an associated expense transaction.

To write a payroll check, follow these steps:

1. Select **Features, Paying Bills, Write Checks**.
2. Fill in the check using these details:
   - **Date**   Set the date for the end of the pay period.
   - **Pay to the Order of**   Enter your employee's name.
   - **$**   Leave this blank; it will be automatically filled in later.
   - **Address**   Type in your employee's postal address.
   - **Memo**   Paycheck.

- **Category** Click **Split** and enter the details described next (see Table 8.3 for a more detailed sample lines):

    Line 1: Type in the gross pay expense category (Payroll:Gross), a suitable memo (Gross Pay), and the amount as a positive number (1109.53).

    Lines 2-16: Enter the withholdings using the payroll withholding accounts (for example, [Payroll:FTW]), a memo (for example, Fed tax withheld), and the amount as a negative number (for example, -367.20). Do this for every type of withholding, as shown in Figure 9.3. When you finish, leave every line blank up to Line 17.

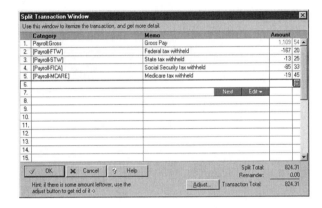

Figure 9.3 The upper part of a paycheck showing gross pay and pay withheld. This is the part the employee sees.

    Line 17 and on: Continue with a new line for every type of contribution you must make as part of your payroll tax liabilities. These should be entered in pairs with the first line acting as a positive contribution to its payroll expense account and the second acting as a negative contribution to that contribution's liability account, as shown in Figure 9.4.

    When you're done, click **Adjust->** and then **Finished** to store the split.

3. Click **Record Check** to store the check in the "to be printed" list.

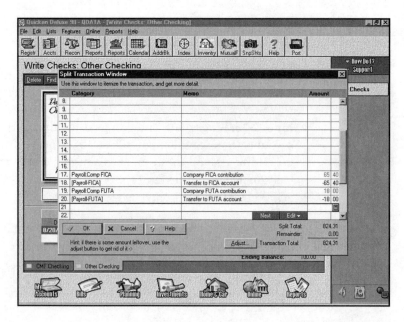

Figure 9.4 Your own payroll contributions should be entered starting at Line 17 and in matched pairs.

Table 9.3 Paycheck Splits Detail

Line	Category	Memo	Sign
1	Payroll:Gross	Gross Pay	+
2	[Payroll-FTW]	Fed tax withheld	-
3	[Payroll-STW]	State tax withheld	-
4	[Payroll-FICA]	Social Security tax withheld	-
5	[Payroll-FUTA]	Federal unemployment tax withheld	-
6	[Payroll-MCARE]	Medicare tax withheld	-
7	[Payroll-SUI)	State unemployment insurance withheld	
8-16	(Blank)		
17	Payroll:Comp FUTA	Company FUTA contribution	+
18	[Payroll-FUTA]	Transfer to FUTA account	-
19	Payroll:Comp FICA	Company FICA contribution	+
20	[Payroll-FICA]	Transfer to FICA account	-

Line	Category	Memo	Sign
21	Payroll:Comp MCARE	Company MCARE contribution	+
22	[Payroll-MCARE]	Transfer to MCARE account	-
23	Payroll:Comp SUI	Company SUI contribution	+
24	[Payroll-SUI]	Transfer to SUI account	-

If you refer to the example shown in Table 8.3, it is easy to see that the employee's voucher-style paycheck will show the gross pay plus any deductions taken directly from that amount. Summed together, these form the net pay. It is also easy to see that lines 17 to 24 are made up of balanced pairs and so make no adjustment to the net pay. Instead, your checking account decreases by the amount posted to the expense account but its balance is immediately restored by the equivalent amount transferred from the liability account. None of this takes place with real money, but it does create a debt, which you will eventually have to pay.

Creating Pay Notifications

If you write your own checks, you will need to enter the payroll transactions directly into the register.

Open the register by selecting **Features, Banking, Use Register**. Fill in the date, check number and payee and create the category split as previously detailed. When you're done, click **Finished**. Quicken will ask you to confirm if you would like the out of balance amount to be a payment or deposit. Select **Payment** and click **OK**. Create a new transaction for every employee.

 TIP   **Using Previous Transactions**   You can avoid retyping the detail of the transaction for every new employee by calling up a previous payroll transaction and editing the payee and payment amounts.

Grouping Payroll Transactions

While each individual payroll transaction may seem like a rather drawn-out business, there's one surefire way to speed up the process. By grouping the transactions together and dropping them into the transaction schedule, you can automatically log every payroll transaction at the end of each pay period.

Quicken's default behavior is to memorize every new transaction. These are stored in a list accessed by selecting **Lists, Memorized Transaction**.

You can also schedule memorized transactions to occur once in the future or repeatedly at certain time intervals. By grouping transactions, you can have Quicken automatically execute many at the one time. This is perfectly suited to the payroll.

To create a grouped payroll transaction, follow these steps:

1. Create every payroll check or transaction. To speed things up, recall the first and edit it for every new payee. While Quicken doesn't automatically memorize the edits to a previously used memorized transaction, it does so if the Payee changes. Note: If you really do want to memorize the edits to a transaction, right click the transaction and select **Memorize Transaction** from the drop-down list.

2. Open the scheduled transaction list by selecting **Lists, Scheduled Transaction**.

3. Click **New** to open the dialog box shown in Figure 9.5.

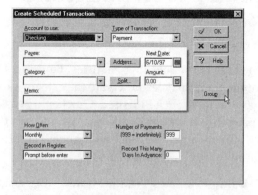

Figure 9.5   When creating a grouped transaction, ignore everything in this dialog box except the Account to Use list and the Group button.

4. Under **Account to Use**, select **Checking** (or your specific Payroll account, if you use one).

5. Ignore the rest of the dialog box, but click **Group** to open the dialog box shown in Figure 9.6.

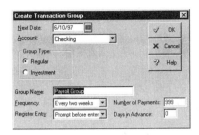

Figure 9.6   Use the frequency features of a payroll group to create a transaction that occur every payday.

6. Enter a **Group Name**, for example: Payroll.

7. Use **Frequency** to specify your pay period and click **OK**. Choose **Once Only** to manually specify when you want the payroll paid. Each payday you should re-open the Scheduled Transaction list, select the payroll group, click **Pay** and then **Record**.

8. Click in the **Grp** column of the next window (shown in Figure 9.7) to choose each of the previously created payroll transactions that should be included in this group. If you make a mistake, just click once more.

9. Click **Done** to save the group.

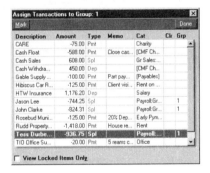

Figure 9.7   Transactions must be memorized before appearing in this group list.

In this lesson, you learned how to set up a payroll and create payroll transactions. In the next lesson, you will learn how Quicken can help you pay the payroll tax at the end of each tax period.

Paying the Payroll Tax

In this lesson, you learn how Quicken can help you calculate your tax liability and pay the payroll tax.

Paying the Payroll

Every payday, a little more payroll tax accrues in the payroll liability accounts. Some of this comes from direct deductions from the employee's paycheck while the rest is an extra expense that your business will have to pay.

Each form of tax accrues in a different liability account. Every second week, once a month, or every three months, you must pay that tax to an authorized collection body. As with personal tax, there are schedules that specify the type of tax that needs paying and when it should be paid. For more information on those schedules, consult the IRS's Publication 15.

The most common tax you'll pay covers income tax withheld and the employer and employee's Social Security and Medicare taxes. These must be submitted on Form 941, Employer's Quarterly Federal Tax Return.

When and how often you must pay these taxes is determined by the following rules:

- Once a month, most small businesses pay income tax withheld and the employer and employee's Social Security and Medicare taxes.
- If the total taxes over a specific three-month lookback period (see Publication 15) total $50,000, those taxes must be paid semiweekly.

The exceptions are known as the $500 Rule and the $100,000 One-Day Rule, however, these apply only to Federal tax. There are many other exceptions on a state, city, and county level:

- **$500 Rule** If the total taxes for the previous three months (as shown on Form 941) were less than $500, you can wait until such time as the total has grown beyond that. However, you must attach any unpaid taxes to Form 941. As this must be filed quarterly, it is impossible to file taxes any less regularly than that.

- **$100,000 One-Day Rule** If the total taxes incurred after any pay period totals more than $100,000, then those taxes must be paid on the next business day.

The Federal Unemployment (FUTA) tax is paid quarterly while the State taxes may vary. However, once you've worked out when you must pay, you need to calculate how much you should pay. This, as you might have guessed, is right up Quicken's alley.

Calculating the Tax Liability

There is a simple way to calculate the tax you owe. Follow these steps:

1. Select **Features, Banking, Use Register**.

2. Click the appropriate tax liability tab (for example, Payroll-FTW) and look at the balance shown in the lower right corner of the screen. This is the total of that particular tax accrued so far. This is also how much you will have to pay.

3. Do the same for any other taxes due.

4. Taxes are deposited by using different coupons. You must write out a check or create a transaction for the total due under any one coupon, but never pay two different coupons with the one check or transaction. If you are paying more than one type of tax on that single coupon (for instance, you will often have to pay Federal tax, Medicare, and Social Security, using the one coupon), use the splits window to organize transfers from the different payroll liability accounts, as shown in Figure 10.1. These amounts should all be positive amounts. Enter a memo that describes the coupon type. This will make it easy for you to track previous payments.

5. Jot down the figures where indicated on your tax coupons, total it up, write out a check (or organize it electronically through EFTPS), and lodge the payment.

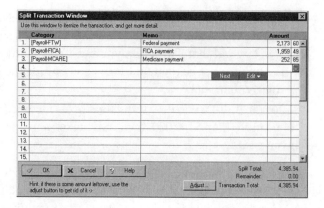

Figure 10.1 Use Splits to record transfers from multiple Payroll liability accounts.

  EFTPS The IRS is gradually moving all businesses to EFTPS (Electronic Funds Transfer Payment System). If you fall into the basket of businesses that must use EFTPS, you may be fined a penalty of up to 10% for not doing so. If you aren't one of those specified to use EFTPS, you can still take advantage of the convenience. Call the IRS at 1-800-045-8400 or 1-800-555-4477 for more information. These lines are for EFTPS information only.

Actually, paying the tax is easy enough. The trick comes in filling out the forms that go along with it. Fortunately, if you've been using Quicken's payroll expense categories and liability accounts, all the figures you need are already there.

Throughout the year, you will need to file four different types of employee tax-related forms (possibly more depending on your state or county). These are:

- Form 941   Employer's Quarterly Federal Tax Return
- Form W-2   Wage and Tax Statement
- Form W-3   Transmittal of Wage and Tax Statement
- Form 940   Employer's Annual FUTA Tax Return

Unlike a dedicated payroll package, Quicken does not neatly collate the information required for each. Indeed, quite the opposite.

TIP **QuickPay** For a program that collates all of the information required, consider investing in QuickPay. It will go a long way toward simplifying your payroll-associated tax requirements.

However, what it does do is print out all of the payroll information you can possibly want in the form of a single payroll report. You'll find the Payroll report by selecting **Reports, Business, Payroll**.

The Payroll report collates payroll information by employee. How does it know who your employees are? Easy. It creates a bunch of columns based on the payees that make up the transactions in every payroll-associated expense and liability account. Each column equals one employee.

The payroll report on its own is something of a mixed bag, but not once you start to hammer it into shape. Table 10.1 shows the parameters you will need to adjust to make the payroll report suitable for each particular form. Click **Customize** and use the **Report Dates** pull-down menu to select the last quarter or year. If that doesn't achieve the required result, enter the dates by hand in the two fields provided.

Table 10.1 Payroll Report Adjustments

Form	Date Adjustment
Form 941	Set to the previous quarter.
Form W-2	Set to the previous year.
Form W-3	Set to the previous year.
Form 940	Set to the previous year.

In this lesson, you learned how to summarize and pay the payroll tax. In the next part of this book, you will learn how to use Quicken to manage your investment portfolio.

Investing

What Is Personal Investment?

In this lesson, you learn some of the basic rules of personal investment. If you feel comfortable with these and the Personal Investment Road Map discussed in Lesson 2 of this part, you can go to Lesson 3 for more Quicken-specific information.

Understanding Personal Investment

Personal investment is about one very simple concept: making your money work for you. Instead of letting your savings languish in a bank where low interest rates, inflation, bank fees, and other charges gradually erode its capital, indulging in a little personal investment can easily double or triple its value. Figure 1.1 shows just one example of a successful technology stock.

Furthermore, you choose how your finances work. Whether you want your money to head down the gold mines, move into computers or communications technology, break new ground in agricultural or scientific research, it's entirely up to you. These days, you can even send your money into space!

There are many reasons why people get involved in personal investment. For some, it's about reaching otherwise unattainable goals, no matter their form. For others, it's about maximizing their retirement income. For still others, it's simply an opportunity to make their money grow at rates that can never be met by a bank.

Quicken will help you not only to manage your investments but also to find the best investments currently available. You will learn about these capabilities through the rest of this part.

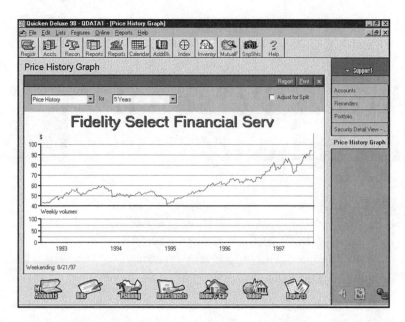

Figure 1.1 Gateway 2000, a leading manufacturer of personal computers, has excelled at steady growth over the previous two years, tripling the value of its shares.

While personal investment can be very exciting, you should follow some basic rules. Don't worry, they're all very easy, but they can also make the difference between a successful portfolio and a disastrous investment experience.

CAUTION

Important Disclaimer We strongly recommend you obtain professional investment advice before investing in any shares, funds, or other schemes. There is no substitute for research, and while the figures resulting from some of the investment scenarios discussed in this section of the book look very encouraging on paper, they are fictitious examples and may prove totally unattainable in the real world. If you can't tailor your own personal investment plan, speak to a professional. Do not rely on this book alone. It has been written to teach you how Quicken can help you manage your investments. What you invest in and how much you invest are entirely up to you.

The Rules of Investment

Personal investment is quite easy, but there are some things you should know before you begin. Apply these rules and you'll be well on your way to a powerfully productive portfolio.

Rule 1: Invest with Money You Can Afford to Lose

Never invest money you can't afford to lose. Set a budget and use Quicken's budgeting features to make sure you stick to it. First, take your after-tax income (including any upcoming estimated tax payments) and subtract whatever it takes to pay off your credit cards in full every month. Don't even think of investing until you can at least do that. Work out how much it costs to live, remove what it costs to meet the mortgage (or any other non-discretionary expenses), take out a little more so that you can still have fun, and work on whatever's left.

As you will soon see, it doesn't take a lot of money to build a large amount of money, and if you can afford to slice 10 percent or even 5 percent off the top of your income and put that into your investment accounts, you may end up doing very well.

CAUTION

What If I Want to Invest More than 10 Percent?   Good for you! There are no maximum limits except that which you can afford. However, don't place it all on the stock market. Make sure you develop an investment strategy and that you understand where your money is going.

Rule 2: Take the Long-Term View

There are many ways to approach personal investment. The worst, however, is to worry too much about it. To understand why, consider the stock market: If you have invested in shares and you have a broad portfolio, you may double your money every four to five years, no matter the size of those holdings simply by sticking to the indexed stocks.

TERM

Indexed Stocks   These are the stocks chosen to make up the S&P 500, the Dow Jones Index, and the many others listed alongside regular stocks. The stocks are chosen for their size and stability. Quicken can track index prices alongside regular stock prices.

The people who lost money during the crash of '87 were those who sold. The cool-headed investors simply bided their time until the descent started to slow; then they went on a buying spree. It didn't matter whether they were buying at the bottom of the crash, halfway down, or halfway up the other side. Today, the market is worth four and a half times what it was worth prior to the crash, and those who held on when others panicked did very well.

Look at the big picture—not just now but also in the future. Even Dell Computers, an extraordinary performer by anyone's measure, went through a backward period a couple of years after the company first listed. However, if you had invested $1,000 with them back then, it would be worth $16,000 at this writing. By the time you read this, the stock could easily have doubled once or twice more, making that original investment worth $32,000 or more!

Quicken is very good at helping you to track your investments on a daily basis, and that's fine, so long as you don't let a short-term dive worry you. Quicken's investment tracking system can tell you precisely how you're doing at that moment, but also how that moment compares to other moments. The comparisons are useful because you can easily ignore small downturns while waiting for the big gains. If you know that your investments are worth 160 percent more than they were three years ago, that will help you to ignore the fact that they might have lost 20 percent in the previous month.

Figure 1.2 shows Harley Davidson, Inc., spread over a five-year period. While many companies haven't performed as well (but others much more strongly), having a diverse investment portfolio and resisting the urge to constantly dabble with your stock levels generally breeds success.

The lesson is clear: There is only one way to minimize investment risk and that is to look at it over a much longer term.

Rule 3: Don't Let Investing Rule Your Life

Some of the most successful personal investors are successful precisely because they don't let their investing rule their life. Investing can be fun, satisfying, and very rewarding. It's a whole different world—and if you've never known it before, one which may prove very exciting and richly rewarding.

Rule 4: Understand Your Investments

What's understanding? Essentially, research before commitment. If someone tells you to buy x units in a fund and you don't know what that fund is about, how it pays its returns, past growth rates and so on, steer well clear. Of course, not understanding something is no reason to not invest in it. Just don't invest until you've done a little research.

Figure 1.2 The Harley Davidson five-year stock history just beats the NASDAQ line beneath to double in price over four years.

Today, it is possible for anyone to grab an amazing amount of information on any fund or publicly listed stock. The Internet is packed with Web sites offering financial data, evaluations, and critiques. This is, in fact, why a personal investor can match the performance of a professional fund manager. While most sites provide stock quotes delayed by 15 or 20 minutes, no personal investor should be working on that immediate a level.

If someone tells you of a "sure thing," take the time to examine it by using every weapon at your disposal. And don't worry: The coming chapters will equip you with quite an arsenal.

Rule 5: Believe in Compound Growth

Smart personal investment means that anyone can be wealthy. It doesn't happen overnight, but it does happen. By working the market, staying ahead of inflation, and utilizing compound growth, it is possible for anyone, anyone at all, to accumulate truly vast sums of money.

Consider this: An 18 year-old puts away $1,000 each year until he or she turns 65. With a growth rate of a modest 12 percent, in 47 years that investment would

355

total $1.9 million. David and Tom Gardner, creators of "The Motley Fool" investment guide and Web site (**http://www.fool.com**), believe that anyone using their "no-brainer" formula can earn an average of 22 percent per annum, and it only takes about 30 minutes of effort once a year. That would boost our 18-year old's lump sum to $65.5 million. Assuming 4 percent inflation, in today's money, that would be equal to a little over $10 million, making the forward-thinking kid a very wealthy retiree. No matter how you look at it, that's a huge return on a total investment of just $47,000. Imagine, then, if that $1,000 were boosted to 10 percent of her income. The numbers are enormous.

 TIP   **Calculating Compound Growth**   You'll learn about manual annuities calculation in Lesson 2. Still, if you are using any version of Quicken other than Quicken Basic and you can't wait to see how your nest egg will grow, open the Quicken Savings Calculator and start tapping away. You'll find it hidden under **Features, Planning, Financial Planners, Savings**. Unfortunately, its upper range is rather limited.

The message is clear: Leave your money sitting in the bank and the bulk of that money's growth will be siphoned off into the bank's coffers. However, send that money out to work and you will receive a far larger slice of that money's growth. Sow that back into the capital and your money will take off at an exponential rate. Incredible as it may seem, the longer you leave it, the faster it will grow.

Of course, very few 18-year-olds worry about such distant matters as retirement, lump sums, and so on, but you can start on the track to financial wealth and health at almost any age. It's the hands-on approach that makes all the difference, and that's what you'll be learning about in the following chapters.

Rule 6: Take Advantage of Tax Deferral

Planning for retirement is one of the most important tasks you will undertake. Even if your retirement seems like it's years and years away, you should be starting now. In fact, the sooner you start, the less you need to contribute overall and the more money you'll have in the end. It might seem illogical, but it's true.

The U.S. Government tries to encourage retirement planning through tax-deferred accounts. The tax deferral simply means that you do not pay tax on the income placed in those accounts until you use that money. The tradeoff is that you can't touch that money until you turn 59 and a half.

Through tax-deferral, you can use that tax-deferred amount to add to your compound growth. As you've already seen, small amounts compounded quickly become very large amounts, and that pretax income adds enormously to the whole.

When you do retire, you draw on that income and pay tax on what you draw. However, chances are you will be in a lower tax bracket than your high-income days, so you won't end up paying as much tax as you might have without tax-deferral. Tax shelters take many forms and the one you need depends on your employment status. For more information, read the lesson on Retirement Planning later in this part. You should also talk to your financial adviser.

In this lesson, you learned some of the basic rules of personal investment. In the next lesson, you'll learn how to create a personal investment road map.

A Personal Investment Road Map

In this lesson, you learn how to plan your journey to full financial security. If you feel you already have a strong plan, move to Lesson 3.

Popular Investments

The road to financial security is an exciting one, but you need to plan ahead. Not only will you need to decide how much you can afford to invest, but where it is best invested. As always, you should consult an investment professional. However, this lesson provides you with a useful introduction.

Look at these more popular investments:

- **Banks**   In effect, you loan your money to the bank by depositing it in your account. Of course, that money doesn't sit in the account; the bank immediately makes use of it, either on the short-term money market or through other forms of investment such as personal loans, leasing deals, or mortgage-lending. They might even loan it back to you, at a higher interest rate! While the standard interest rate is poor, you can obtain a higher rate by either depositing more money or leaving it in there for a longer fixed term. However, even then, this is not an effective investment. Banks charge for their services and that's how you should look at them—as service companies. Use their checkbook facilities, take advantage of their ATMs, and borrow their money, if you must. Just don't expect your investment to grow.

- **Managed funds**   Managed funds (also known as mutual funds or unit funds) pool your money with that of other investors. The fund manager determines the best investments to make according to that fund's guide-lines. You receive the benefit of a professional while the fund manager receives a cut of the proceeds.

Managed funds are a great way to make money from money. You can invest in some funds for as little as a few hundred dollars and make as much as 60 percent on that investment in a year. These funds also come in numerous flavors with some geared toward blue-chip stocks, others toword property portfolios, still others toword emerging companies, and yet more toword odd investments such as the royalties that may spring from an oil field. In general, the higher the fund flies in terms of percentage returns, the faster it can fall.

If you use any version of Quicken other than Quicken Basic, you can use the Mutual Fund Finder shown in Figure 2.1 to find funds that most suit your needs. You learn about the Mutual Fund Finder in Part 5, Lesson 9.

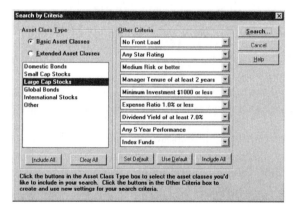

Figure 2.1 The Mutual Fund Finder will help track down the right fund for you.

- **Real estate** Real estate makes for a great long-term investment and can lead to some very useful tax breaks.

- **Stocks** From a short-term perspective, the stock market can appear frighteningly volatile with fortunes gained and lost in seconds on the trading floor. However, from a long-term point of view, the share market is the most powerful investment tool available, and there are some tried and trued strategies that will help you to minimize the risk.

- **Bonds** Bonds provide income and are far more stable than shares. By purchasing tax-exempt bonds, you can also earn and reinvest income.

359

These are just some of the many investment options available. However, before you consider getting involved in any, you should learn to ask and answer the following questions:

- What's your goal?
- Do you understand acceptable risk?
- Should you develop an investment strategy?
- Do you know the taxation ramifications?
- Do you need professional advice?

Identify Your Goals

The feeling of personal security stems as much from physical property as it is does from the state of mind. We all have different expectations for our futures. For some, those expectations will require a significant nest egg while for others, future happiness might rely on well-being first, looking after others second, and personal finances third. Whichever the case, self-sufficiency will always be a significant part of the equation.

You will find that for as little as $50 per week, you can guarantee your future peace of mind, but you need to set yourself attainable goals.

Even if you never state those goal(s) out loud, make sure you can readily identify them. Decide what you want, how much it will cost, and how you can realistically achieve it. If it helps, write it down and include it in your financial plan.

 TIP **Goal Setting with Quicken** You can use Quicken to set savings goals. This is useful for saving for small events such as a trip overseas, but not for longer term investment goals. However, create regular investment reports by selecting **Reports**, **Investment**, **Investment Performance**. These help you see precisely where you started and how far you still need to go.

Of course, goals can take almost any form, but the following includes some of the more common financial goals:

- **Retirement** This is the big one. To retire comfortably, you should aim to have set aside at least six times your annual salary. You can then invest that money and live off the income it generates, plowing a little back into the principal to shore it up against inflation. Quicken's retirement planner is an easy way to find out how much you'll need. You learn about this in the next lesson.

- **Children**   Supporting a child from the time it is born to the time it turns 18 can easily cost $500,000. While you wouldn't plan to save this money before having a child, keep in mind that any dependent will have a large impact on the financial plan. You can do this using the forecasting feature detailed in Part 1, Lesson 13.

- **College**   Unless your children earn full scholarships, a good education costs a lot of money. While you might not want to contribute 100 percent to that education, any amount is better than none at all. The college planner is the easiest way to work out how you can afford to pay for that education. See Lesson 3.

- **House**   Whether you are looking at buying a penthouse in New York or a run-down shack somewhere west of Hicksville, the family home is the single largest purchase most of us will ever make. While the loan planner will help you work out how much you'll need, don't forget to try the online Mortgage Center shown in Figure 2.2, for the best rates. Just select **Online, Quicken on the Web, Mortgage Center**.

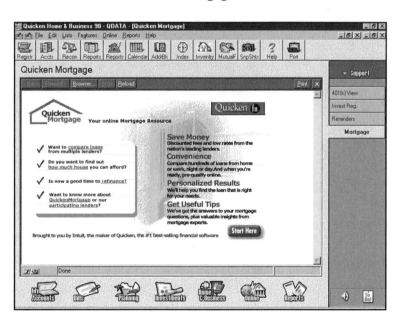

Figure 2.2   The Mortgage Center is an easy, online utility that will search out the best rates and more.

- **Car**   Again, it doesn't matter if you are buying a status symbol or a workhorse, the car will probably prove to be your second largest purchase after real estate. Quicken includes categories that will track your car expenses, telling you precisely how much your car costs not only to buy, but also to drive.

- **Rainy Days**   It's good to have some money set aside for that rainy day, no matter if the downpour is caused by job loss, sickness, or the sudden, unconquerable urge to spend six months in the south of France. If you don't seem to have any rainy day pay left aside after making ends meet, review your budgeting strategy. To learn how, see Part 1, Lesson 13.

- **Lifestyle**   There is nothing wrong with spending an extravagant amount of money on lifestyle items. Just be sure you can afford them.

Understanding Acceptable Risk

Personal investment is risky. But then again, all investment is risky. Banks can collapse, wars can start, inflation can go through the roof, or the share market can take that fall everyone's been expecting. There are hundreds of other potential disasters just waiting for the right moment to strike.

However, the thing about risk is that it can be managed. It is that management that makes the difference between the smart investor who knows how to make the most of his or her money, and the foolhardy investor who risks and loses the life savings on the "sure thing" that wasn't.

Risk isn't bad. In fact, it is the element of risk that makes it possible to make money. The important thing is to understand the level of that risk and to limit your exposure.

TIP   **Managing Your Risk with Quicken**   Quicken and its associated utilities such as Investor Insight and Mutual Fund Finder will help you to establish and then manage your investment risk. While some of these utilities are only bundled in the Deluxe version of Quicken, several are available free of charge from the Intuit World Wide Web site at **http://www.intuit.com**.

The world is made up of five types of investments (and investors):

- Conservative
- Moderately Conservative

- Balanced
- Moderately Aggressive
- Aggressive

The difference between each type of investment is simply the amount of risk associated with each and whether the return is growth-based, income-based, or a mixture of both.

For example, an aggressive investment is built around higher short-term risk in return for greater capital growth. The aggressive investment is made up of volatile markets or sleeper stocks likely to take off with a surge. If you want to indulge in aggressive investments, make very sure the money you play with isn't earmarked for anything else. You must be able to afford to and even be willing to lose that money in the interests of doubling your capital in just a few months.

The moderately aggressive investment is made up of performance stocks that favor strong growth over income yet aren't quite so volatile as an aggressive investment. The returns won't prove as great, but then again, there isn't quite so much risk. A balanced investment is one which provides equal amounts of income and growth. A moderately conservative investment provides an income and is moderately stable, although there is still room for growth. A conservative investment is geared toward income production with minimal risk of loss of capital.

Investors also categorize themselves (not just their investments) in terms of their conservativeness or aggressiveness. However, the best bet is to buy into a mix of aggressive and conservative investments, thus spreading the risk. Many investors start aggressively and then, as the years pass by, creep toward the conservative side. This means that their portfolio starts off growth-oriented (perfect for the early stages), and then slowly becomes income-oriented (ideal for the retirement years).

So, what's your acceptable risk? You need to decide what you want your money to do. If you want to see your capital grow, build a portfolio (see Lesson 4) that is more aggressive than conservative. If you require income, adjust the portfolio so that it swings the other way. (Naturally, the best balance will depend on your specific financial requirements. Speak to a financial planner first.)

Develop an Investment Strategy

Developing a strategy is the same as working out how you'll put together your investment vehicle. In other words, how are you going to fund those investments? There are three ways to do this:

1. Pay a lump sum through funds you have already saved.
2. Pay a little bit each time you receive a paycheck.
3. Borrow the money.

The lump sum is the easiest, obviously, because you already know how much you want to invest and can split the total as needed across a variety of investments.

However, it is also good to add to your investment with a predetermined amount taken from each paycheck. Some people invest as much as 15 percent of their income while others set aside just 10 percent or even 5 percent. The amount doesn't matter so much as putting that recurring investment into action. By investing just a small amount each week, or every time you receive a paycheck, you will make the most of the power of compound growth, effectively doubling the returns you would otherwise receive from, say, a once-yearly contribution. Just remember that every share market transaction attracts a brokerage fee, so running up multiple small purchases may negate any long-term gain. However, buying into mutual funds only attracts a percentage fee rather than a flat brokerage, so investing even very small amounts can work quite well.

 TIP **Automatic Account Transfers** Quicken will let you automatically transfer a predetermined amount from one account to the next by using memorized transactions. If you are set up for Online Banking, you can use this feature to automatically deplete one account and increase another account each specific period. However, you can also do the same by creating a recurring check made out to the investment account. Either way, Quicken will make it easy.

The third option is one that appears to go against the grain of the rule "Never invest money you don't have." That's true, but there are times when borrowing investment funds can work completely in your favor. Consider, for instance, a stock that is growing at around 100 percent per annum. That's obviously a very high-growth stock, far more than the market average. However, if you believe from your research that nothing is likely to slow that rate of growth, it might just pay enormous dividends to add to your own investment with funds borrowed at an interest rate of around 16 percent. Most stock brokers offer this service, offering up to half of the total purchase. (The other half is held in their account under your name as security.)

Borrowing funds gives you the leverage to convert a doubling investment into an investment that triples—minus any interest—over the same period. It is a powerful technique, but correspondingly risky. Just remember: don't borrow unless you can afford to not only lose your original investment but also to pay back those funds. It's a tough call, but one that can give your portfolio a very large boost. (Incidentally, most brokers insist you have sufficient equity in your holdings to repay all borrowed funds at notice. They reserve the right to sell your stock to ensure you retain positive equity.)

Understand the Tax Ramifications

If you invest well, those investments will either grow in size or generate income. Both of these events can attract tax. However, if you approach the problem with a little forethought and professional consultation, you will leave yourself plenty of time to reduce that tax liability. There are lots of ways to reduce your tax liability.

Some tax shelters rely on the good intentions of the government to encourage saving for the future, be it for education or retirement. Others encourage investment in highly speculative ventures such as oil and gas exploration. In recent times, Congress has called a halt to the proliferation of speculative tax shelters and they are fast becoming a dying breed. However, the benefit of tax-deferred savings such as those built into IRA, SEP, SIMPLE, Keogh, 401(k), and 403(k) plans won't disappear any time soon. The Government wants to encourage self-sufficiency throughout an individual's retirement, and that's one of the best ways of doing it.

Retirement plans are designed to defer your tax until you withdraw those funds at age 59 1/2 or later. However, there are other schemes that can give you the immediate benefit of tax-exempt income. The most popular include investments in your local and state governments and utilities through securities such as bonds.

For more information on tax shelters, speak to your taxation professional. To find out how Quicken can help you fulfill your tax requirements, see Part 2.

TIP **Tax Deduction Finder** The tax deduction finder (see Figure 2.3) is a useful product included with Quicken Deluxe 98 and Quicken Home and Business 98. Between the deduction finder and the many online tax-related books included in a product such as Intuit's TurboTax Deluxe, you might find all of the expert advice you need bundled up in two CD-ROMs.

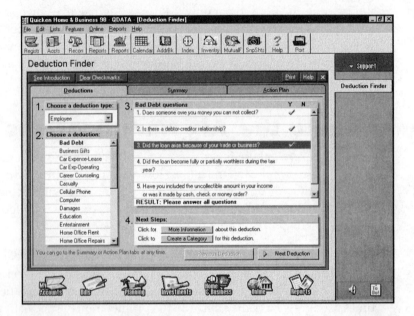

Figure 2.3 Use the Tax Deduction Finder to make sure your tax return makes the most of all available benefits.

Talk to a Professional

No matter how tortured your current financial situation, a financial planner (and financial plan) will almost certainly help you find a way out. Even if the mortgage has you over a barrel, the boss has just downsized you, and the IRS decided that it really would like that estimated tax after all, there is always a way out. What's more, like the example of compound growth given at the start of this lesson, it's all in the percentages.

A professional taxation advisor can help you to work out how much of your income can go here, how much there, and how much everywhere else, minimizing your tax and maximizing your investment income.

In this lesson, you learned how to plan your investments. In the next lesson, you will learn how to use Quicken's Financial Planners to work out how much money you need, and by when.

Financial Calculators

*In this lesson, you learn about the financial planners to be
found in Quicken Deluxe 98 and Quicken Home and Business
98. They will help you to determine how much money you will
need to retire, create a suitable college fund, and save to meet those goals.*

Financial Planning with Quicken Deluxe 98 and Quicken Home and Business 98

Quicken's financial planning tools are handy for not only establishing your existing financial position, but also calculating for the future. They are ideal for running through any number of "what if" scenarios. The Deluxe and Home and Business editions of Quicken provide the following planners (these are not included in Quicken Basic):

- **Loan**   Use this planner to calculate repayments on a loan or, given the repayments you can afford, how much you can borrow.

- **Refinance**   Should you consider refinancing your mortgage? This planner will give you the full story.

- **Savings**   Use this planner to find out how compound interest can make an investment.

- **College**   This planner will help you calculate how much you should set aside to send yourself or your dependents to college.

- **Retirement**   This is a great calculator for working out how much you should contribute to a fund to create an adequate retirement income.

These planners are very powerful tools when used to the extent of their capabilities. Let's take a look at each.

Calculating Affordable Loans

The Loan Planner shown in Figure 3.1 will tell you either how much money you must repay or how much money you can afford to borrow, limited by your maximum affordable repayments. You should use this planner for the following tasks:

- Calculating a mortgage based on the amount you currently pay in rent or the amount you can spare after all other expenses and investments have been taken into account. Remember, if you do borrow based on your current rental payments, you will be even further ahead because your interest payments are tax deductible.

- Figuring small personal loans. The planner will quickly show you how much that $20,000 you might like to borrow will cost each month. The loan planner would be even more useful if it also showed the total repayments over that time, but you will need to figure that yourself, or resort to a spreadsheet.

Using the Loan Planner window is easy. Follow these steps:

1. Select **Features, Planning, Financial Planners, Loan**. You will see the window shown in Figure 3.1.

2. Type in the **Loan Amount**. If you want to calculate the loan amount based on affordable repayments, click **Loan Amount** in the **Calculate For** group and leave this field blank.

3. Provide the **Annual Interest Rate** as a decimal percentage, for example: 8.5 percent.

4. Specify the term. In general, the quicker you can pay off a loan, the better. Otherwise, you will spend more time paying the interest bill than you will repaying the actual loan.

5. Use **Periods Per Year** to indicate how often you make repayments. Keep in mind that just as contributing to a compounding investment account weekly rather than annually can double your interest gained, so contributing weekly to a loan account can halve the interest bill. The more payments per year you can arrange, the better. Of course, this depends on the compounding period.

6. The **Compounding Period** determines how often the interest is recalculated (and so, compounded). You can choose between **Daily, Monthly,** or **Semi-Annually**.

7. If you are calculating the **Payment Per Period**, this field will show your repayments. Otherwise, type in the payment you can afford and look at **Loan Amount** to see how much you can borrow.

8. (Optional) Click **Calculate** if the Loan Planner doesn't automatically do so.

9. (Optional) To view and optionally print your repayment schedule, click **Schedule**. The schedule shows your payment, the reducing principal and interest, and the balance left over.

10. When you finish click **Done**.

Figure 3.1 Use the Loan Planner to calculate either maximum repayments or the amount of money you can afford to borrow.

 TIP **Forecasting Your Future** For more information on forecasting your finances, budgeting, or simply working out how much you can afford to put aside for a loan, see Part 1 of this book.

Refinancing Your Loans

As interest rates and other circumstances change, so do the terms that define an ideal mortgage. While many people consider a mortgage to be a pain they could do without, in reality, a mortgage can be considered a very useful tool.

There are several reasons that might cause you to consider refinancing or adjusting your mortgage:

- Your circumstances have changed and you want to either increase or decrease your monthly payments. If your mortgagors won't let you adjust your repayments, you may need to refinance that mortgage by paying out the existing loan with a lump sum borrowed against a new mortgage.

- You want to consolidate other loans. Personal loans tend to attract a higher interest rate than mortgages. If you have already repaid some of the principal making up your existing mortgage, or have sufficient equity in your home as is, you might consider extending your mortgage, paying out the existing personal loans through extra funds borrowed against your mortgage.

- You believe you can negotiate a better mortgage with a more competitive lender, either through reduced annual servicing fees or interest rates.

The refinancing planner is one of the most complex of the Quicken planners. It works by looking at your existing payments, the conditions relating to the new mortgage, and any penalties incurred for closing the previous mortgage and starting the new one. Quicken will tell you how much you can save each month and how long, given those savings, it will take you to break even on the new mortgage.

 TIP **Mortgage Savings** After you break even on your loan, all monthly savings equal money in your pocket. Quicken doesn't reveal the total saving, but that's something you can easily calculate. Take the number of months remaining in the loan and subtract the months it will take you to break even. Multiply the remainder by your monthly savings. That's how much you'll save. Of course, if you're really good, you'll take each month's saving and put it straight into an investment or retirement fund, as discussed in Lessons 1 and 2.

So, is your mortgage worth refinancing? To find out, follow these steps:

1. Select **Features, Planning, Financial Planners, Refinance**. You will see the window shown in Figure 3.2.

2. Type in your total **Current Payment**. This is the monthly principal and interest repayment. (If you pay semimonthly, just double that amount.) The amount should also include all associated fees—everything associated with repaying the mortgage.

3. The **Impound/Escrow Amount** will be deducted from your monthly principal repayments. The impound and escrow fees are independent of the mortgage and have to be paid no matter how you refinance, so these are ignored for the remainder of the refinance calculations.

4. Type the proposed mortgage amount into **Principal Amount**. This is the sum you intend to remortgage for. If you are transferring your mortgage to another mortgagor, this is the remaining principal on your current mortgage.

5. Type in the **Years** and annual **Interest Rate**.

6. Quicken will calculate the new mortgage and, in **Monthly Savings**, show you where you stand compared to the current mortgage. If this field shows a negative, your new mortgage will cost you more than your existing mortgage. If it shows a positive sum, you are already ahead, but the actual amount depends upon the costs of closing the existing mortgage and opening the new one.

7. To complete the refinancing calculation, fill in the Break Even Analysis. The **Closing Costs** are those fees charged by your current mortgagor. The **Mortgage Points** is a percentage calculation based on the amount of the new mortgage.

8. When you complete entering the required information, read the **Months to Break Even**. In Figure 3.2, it comes out to approximately 138 months, or 11.5 years. Over a 30-year mortgage, that leaves approximately 222 months after the break-even point, gaining the mortgagee about $7,878 in savings. Although this looks like a savings, if the $4,900 in upfront costs were properly invested, the mortgagee would be significantly further ahead than if he invested the small savings each month. So in this case, at least, it probably wouldn't be wise to proceed.

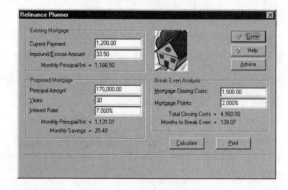

Figure 3.2 This mortgage refinancing exercise shows the homeowners will break even on their new loan within about 11.5 years.

Calculating Your Savings

The Quicken Savings Planner is a fun way to see what happens to principal amounts and ongoing contributions when compound interest is taken into account. To use the planner, follow these steps:

1. Select **Features, Planning, Financial Planners, Savings**. You will see the window shown in Figure 3.3.

2. Enter your **Opening Savings Balance** and type in the **Annual Yield** (or growth rate).

3. Select the compounding period—**Weeks**, **Months**, **Quarters** or **Years**—and the number of periods in the investment. (For example, 10 Years equals 520 Weeks.)

4. If you will be adding to the opening balance, type in the **Contribution** each period.

5. The planner will quickly calculate the balance of the savings by the end of the investment.

6. (Optional) Use the **Inflation** group to figure the balance according to an estimated inflation rate. Click **Inflate Contributions** to increase your periodic contributions in line with the inflation rate and **Ending Balance in Today's $** to calculate the final balance as an adjusted amount that works for today, after taking future inflation into account. To see how this works, just click it on and off, looking at the **Ending Savings Balance**. Click the **Schedule** button and then **Print** to create an inflated contribution report.

7. (Optional) Use the **Calculate For** group to change the pivot of the calculation from ending balance (**Ending Savings Balance**) to payments required to meet a savings goal (**Regular Contribution**) or opening balance required to meet that goal (**Opening Savings Balance**).

8. When you finish, either view and optionally print the **Schedule** or click **Done** to return to Quicken.

TIP **Faster Savings Growth** By contributing monthly rather than annually, it is possible for a retirement fund to more than double over a typical working life. In fact, if our 18-year-old from Lesson 1 contributed 47 annual payments of $520 at 22 percent return, the total equals a rather awesome $4,284,378.54. However, by contributing in monthly installments of $43.30, the payout more than doubles to $10,187,146.63! Not bad for the equivalent of $10 per week. In fact, pay weekly and the results are even better, although you'll find the numbers larger than the Financial Planner can calculate.

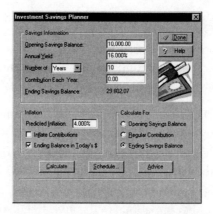

Figure 3.3 The Savings Planner is handy for those times when you're offered a good interest rate and want to quickly know how much it will net.

Saving for College

College is expensive, but a good education shouldn't be beyond anyone's reach. Working out just how much you need to save to send yourself or the kids to college is easy with Quicken's College Planner.

Quicken treats the cost of the college as a goal and the length of time as the number of years left before enrollment. The problem is solved to show either how much you need to contribute, the cost of the best college you can afford, or how much you should put away right now to meet the college costs with regular predetermined payments.

To use the College Planner, follow these steps:

1. Select **Features, Planning, Financial Planners, College** to open the window shown in Figure 3.4.

2. Select the type of calculation you want in the **Calculate For** group. **Annual College Costs** will tell you how much of a college you can afford. **Current College Savings** will tell you how much you should put away right now in order to meet the college savings goal, while **Annual Contribution** will tell you how much you should put away each year to go to the college of your choice.

3. (Optional) Change the **Predicted Inflation** and click **Inflate Contributions** to take the effects of inflation into account. Click the **Schedule** button and then **Print** to create an inflated contribution report.

4. When you finish, click **Done** to return to Quicken.

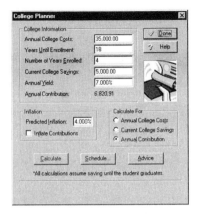

Figure 3.4 College is expensive, but not if you start saving right away.

Planning for Retirement

The Retirement Planner is by far the most comprehensive. This is a powerful tool that can tell you not only how your savings will progress in both taxed and tax-deferred accounts but will also show you how much income you will be able to budget for each year of your retirement. Of course, many more factors will come into play than can be included in this planner, but it is still an ideal tool for creating realistic and completely attainable goals.

If you've ever needed motivation to increase your contributions to a retirement plan, there should be almost no doubt in your mind that this is the planner to provide it. It is the ideal place to play around with a few figures and receive instant results. Follow these steps:

1. Select **Features, Planning, Financial Planners, Retirement** to open the window shown in Figure 3.5.

2. The planner has four main areas. Enter your financial information and plans into the **Retirement Information** group. The planner spreads the retirement income between your **Retirement Age** and your **Withdraw Until Age**. However, throughout your retirement, there will always be some investment capital waiting in the wings. The good news is that whether you draw your income over the default of twenty years, or are lucky enough to live until you are 105, your annual income adjusted for inflation will hardly budge.

3. (Optional) If your contributions are going to a nonsheltered investment, indicate this and the tax rate in the **Tax Information** group. This makes a huge difference to your retirement income, and the Government's message is loud and clear: Tax-deferred accounts are the only way to go.

4. (Optional) Use the **Inflation** group to boost your contributions according to inflation and to also read the retirement income in today's dollars, rather than the future's. (In Figure 3.5, the nonadjusted income is around $2.5 million, but it equals only about $500,000 in today's dollars.) Click the **Schedule** button and then **Print** to create an inflated contribution report.

5. (Optional) Change the basis of the retirement calculation in **Calculate For**. Click **Current Savings** to work out how much you must put away right now to meet your goals; click **Annual Contribution** to find out how much you should put away each year to meet a particular goal; and use the default, **Annual Retirement Income**, to work out your future income according to your current savings plan. Click the **Schedule** button and then **Print** to create an inflated contribution report.

6. When you finish, click **Done** to return to Quicken.

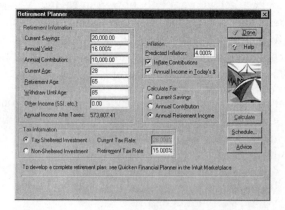

Figure 3.5 This is a very modest retirement based on a fairly low annual yield (most mutual funds return at least this), and small contributions. Still, look at that annual retirement income!

If Quicken's Financial Planners can provide one very salutary lesson, it is that planning is always in your best interest. The easiest way to meet your goals is to start thinking about them right now—no matter how far ahead they may seem.

And if you want to make the most of them, go and get yourself a decent annual yield. It's easy, and you'll find out how over the next few lessons.

In this lesson, you learned how to use Quicken's great financial planners. In the next lesson, you will learn how to create and maintain your investment portfolio.

Creating a Portfolio

In this lesson, you learn how to create your investment portfolio and enter your initial shares and bonds.

Managing Investments

Quicken's securities investment and portfolio management features are second to none. A superb interface, easy price tracking, online updates, great graphs, integration into net worth reports, and more mean that you can stay on top of your investments, not only day-by-day but hour-by-hour, if you need to. Of course, for reasons discussed in the previous lesson, that's not an ideal way to approach investing, but it's still fun to know where you stand.

Quicken's approach to investing is a very logical one: Just as your Quicken checkbook account perfectly follows the ebb and flow of the balance in the bank, so too, each of your investment accounts rise and fall in time with the value of the securities held and the available cash balance. There are three steps to using Quicken to manage your investments:

1. Create an investment account or register.
2. Create individual securities.
3. Enter transactions that buy, sell, and otherwise manage those securities.

For best results, you should create one investment account for every real world account you hold with a broker or trading house. By treating your actual accounts in this way, you can easily use Quicken to:

- Track the value of your investments on a historical and current basis.
- Maintain a full set of transaction records including buys, sells, dividends, and stock splits.
- Link to an online stockbroker.

- Know precisely how your managed funds are performing, both compared to each other and compared to those you are managing.

- Manage your 401(k) retirement account.

- Calculate your capital gains tax and taxable investment income.

- Keep tabs on the cash balance in your investment account, always knowing just how many shares of that hot new stock you can really afford to buy. If you don't have the funds, you can also use Quicken to purchase on margin or sell short.

- Set investment goals for particular securities such as a college fund or house purchase plan.

Quicken can track your investments through three forms of account. These are:

- **Asset accounts**   These accounts track the value of investments and should be used for large assets such as your house and other real estate, vehicles and vessels, and your household (and/or business) inventory. These accounts are also ideal for securities investments where you don't track individual share or unit transactions but simply update the balance according to monthly statements provided by your broker or fund manager. You can also use asset accounts to track the appreciation and depreciation of other assets.

- **Investment accounts**   These accounts track the value and performance of other types of assets. Investment accounts are best suited at targeting securities with fluctuating prices. They support activities such as buying and selling shares, reinvesting income, tracking growth and price histories, and so on. If your account includes or can include a cash balance (for instance, almost any share trading account), you should track it as an investment account.

- **401(k) accounts**   The 401(k) run by your employer forms a valuable part of your net worth. Quicken Deluxe and Quicken Home and Business both support a special 401(k) account type which will help you track the value of one or more 401(k) plans.

Even though these accounts come out on the asset side of a balance sheet (investment and 401(k) accounts are just special forms of asset account), you should carefully consider which side of the divide certain investments fall.

TIP **A Real World Example** Mary owns Treasury Bonds, has a 401(k) retirement plan with a fund manager, and also dabbles on the market. Her 401(k) is
reported as a basic end of month balance so this joins her Treasury Bonds in a
standard Quicken asset account. However, she tracks her own stock market
investments through a Quicken investment account, enabling her to keep a
much tighter tab on those investments for which she is directly responsible.

You learned how to set up an asset account in Part 1, Lesson 6.

Quicken Deluxe and Quicken Home & Business support the special 401(k)
account type, but if you use Quicken Basic, you can still track the value of one
or more 401(k) accounts using the standard investment account. You will learn
about this next.

Creating an Investment Account

Using Quicken, you can easily set up and maintain one or more investment
accounts or registers. Each register may contain one or more securities, and all
of the registers combined form your investment portfolio.

Diversification is good for any portfolio and it is also good for Quicken. By
arranging your brokerage and other funds in separate Quicken investment
registers, you will be in a better position to keep track of each.

To create a Quicken investment register, just follow these steps:

1. Select **Lists, Account** and click **New** in the upper left corner.

2. Choose an **Investment** type of account and click **Next**.

3. Click the **Summary** tab to bypass the EasyStep questions and jump to the
dialog box shown in Figure 4.1. Fill in the Account group as follows:

> **Account Name** Provide an account name such as Investments or
> My Investments.

> **Description** (Optional) The description is used on some reports.

> **Account Contains a Single Mutual Fund** Select this if the account
> will only be used for tracking a single fund. Single fund accounts will
> still appear in your investment register but are simpler to manage.
> Instead of tracking a cash balance, Quicken only concerns itself with
> the share balance, and the Easy Actions menu is correspondingly
> simplified. You can convert a single fund account to a multiple fund
> account, but you cannot covert a multiple fund account to a single
> fund account.

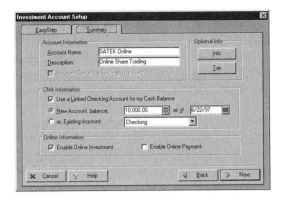

Figure 4.1 This account has been set up for online brokering, including check-writing facilities rather than online payments and showing the initial investment deposit.

4. (Optional) If this investment account provides a check-writing facility, select **Use a Linked Checking Account for my Cash Balance**. You may either create a **New Account**, entering the starting balance and date as shown on your last statement, or link it to an **Existing Account**. Do not link this account to your standard checking account unless that account is your investment account.

5. (Optional) Click the **Info** button to enter any additional information. Quicken does not process this information; it is merely for your own convenience.

6. (Optional) If this is a tax-deferred account (for example, an IRA, 401(k), Municipal Bonds, and so on), click **Tax** and select **Tax-Deferred Account**. Don't forget to also select **W-2 Salary** under **Transfers In**. This means that any money used to fund this account (for example, by transferring $10,000 from your checking account) will decrease your taxable income. Do not select **W-2 Salary** if this account is not tax-deferred. Click **OK** to save the changes made to this dialog box.

TIP **Quicken Deluxe and Quicken Home & Business Users** If you need to track a 401(k), use the special 401(k) account type described next, rather than setting up a standard investment account as tax-deferred.

7. (Optional) Click **Enable Online Investment** to link this account to an online financial institution. Online investment accounts must contain more than a single mutual fund. Click **Done** and you will have the additional step of setting up the financial institution. This is described in Part 3.

8. (Optional) Click **Enable Online Payment** to tie this account to the Quicken bill-paying system. Online payment accounts must be linked to a check-writing facility. As with the previous option, you will need to set up a financial institution once you click **Done**. For more information, see Part 3.

9. When you finish, review the information and then click **Done** to create the investment account and, if you selected a new linked checking account, the new checking account. Quicken will continue the EasyStep Interview with Security Setup, described next.

TIP   **Changing the Linked Account's Name**   By default, Quicken names the new linked checking account as your investment account followed by **-Cash**. For example, the linked checking account for an investment account called **Five Star Funds** would become **Five Star Funds-Cash**. You can change its name by editing it. Select **Lists, Account**. Quicken will maintain the checking account link, even though its name has changed.

As soon as you have completed setting up your investment account, you will move into an interview that will help you add various securities. This is described next. Quicken's investment accounts can store any type of security, but the Security Setup interview only supports three: Stocks (or Shares), Mutual Funds, and Bonds.

TIP   **Deleting a Linked Checking Account**   If you do create a linked checking account and decide that was the wrong thing to do, don't try to delete it, as you will also delete the investment account. Instead, edit the investment account by selecting **Lists, Account**, highlighting the Investment account, then clicking the **Edit** button and deselecting the **Linked Checking Account** option. Then select the checking account, click **Delete** and type in **yes** to confirm. Quicken will delete the checking account but retain your investment account.

Recording Stocks or Mutual Funds

To record a stock or fund, follow these steps:

1. Type in the stock or fund's name and optional ticker symbol. The ticker will help you to update the price of a stock using Intuit's free Internet service. If you won't be doing this, you can leave the ticker blank, but you

will need the ticker to look up the value of this stock in any published share lists. If you don't know the ticker, you can use Quicken to look it up at a later date.

CAUTION

I've Left the Original Setup Routine. How Do I Get Back? If you aren't at the Security Setup window, select **Features**, **Investments**, **Create New Investment**. Select the first option: **I want to set up a new security in an existing account** and click **Next**. Click **Next** once more and select the investment account that you want to add this security to. Click **Next** a final time and you'll be right back on track.

2. Select **Stock** or **Mutual Fund** and click **Next**.

3. (Optional) Choose an **Investment Goal** from the pull-down list. These goals will help you to track how well your stock is doing. For instance, say you decide to invest in some high-growth stocks on the bet that they will develop quickly enough for you to buy a new home. Specify **Growth** from the pull-down list when entering any growth stocks. This will let you sort and subtotal those stocks in certain investment reports and graphs, helping you to see how close you are to meeting that particular goal.

4. (Optional) The **Asset Class** works similarly to the Investment Goal, allowing you to sort and subtotal your stocks by their asset class. In this way, you can quickly see how your small-cap (often volatile) stocks have performed as compared to your large-cap (typically blue-chip) stocks.

TERM

Blue Chip These are stocks heralding from big, stable companies such as IBM, AT&T, General Motors and the larger utilities. With enormous market capitalizations, their stock prices counteract the wild price fluctuations seen in smaller stocks. It is for this reason that blue chip stocks are used to calculate market indices.

5. Click **Next** to continue.

6. In the next dialog box, you need to choose how you want to track this stock:

   - **Today** This is the quickest method, but you need to manually calculate any capital gains for taxation purposes, and you won't be able to view the stock's growth since the date of purchase.

383

- **The end of last year** This option will help you to prepare your taxation for the current financial year, but you will need to enter some historical data including the price of the stock at the end of the last financial year and any transactions or splits that have occurred along the way.

- **The date you purchased this stock** For most people, this option makes the most sense because it allows you to see how your stock and your net worth have changed over time. The date field uses today's date as the default. Adjust this to the date from which you want to track this stock. That date does not have to be the day you actually purchased it. If you are an Investor Insight user (see Lesson 8), you can use Quicken's Price History feature to automatically load stock prices for the previous five years.

7. Click **Next** to move on and enter the number of shares of the stock or units in the fund that you owned at the date shown in the heading. Also enter their purchase cost and any associated fees or commissions. The date is calculated according to the choice you made in the previous window. If your stock has split, don't enter the split number or halve the cost; you should enter the split transaction later.

8. Click **Next** once more and either choose **Yes** and **Next** to run through the sequence once more, or **No** and **Next** to move to the summary window.

9. Use the summary window shown in Figure 4.2 to confirm your security's details (click **Edit** to adjust any security, as shown in Figure 4.3) and click **Done** when you finish.

Figure 4.2 Quicken displays a summary of all newly created securities.

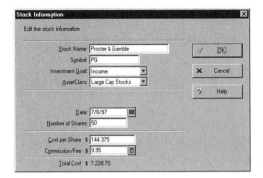

Figure 4.3 Click Edit in the Summary window to open this special dialog box.

Recording Bonds

Bonds are a great way to diversify your investments because they tend to follow a different rise and fall to the share and property markets. They also tend to be less volatile than stocks, can provide you with a tax-free income, and almost always earn more than can be earned through leaving those funds sitting in the bank.

 TIP **Finding the Right Bond** If you own Quicken Deluxe or Quicken Home & Business, you can use the Mutual Fund Finder to search for the right bond by volatility, yield, and several other factors. You will learn about this useful tool in Lesson 9.

Bonds are rather different to funds or stocks because they mature at a certain date. Furthermore, some bonds mature and realize an intrinsic value while other bonds expire, whereupon they are deemed worthless.

This makes managing your bonds a complex affair; Quicken can't offer a great deal of assistance because there are just too many factors and possibilities. However, the software is not completely helpless. In fact, you will probably find some of its features rather handy.

Here, then, is the least you need to know to successfully set up a bond in your investment register. Simply follow these steps:

1. Type in a name and optional ticker symbol. Don't worry if you don't know the ticker.
2. Select **Bond** and click **Next**.

3. (Optional) Choose an **Investment Goal** from the pull-down list.

4. (Optional) Select an **Asset Class**.

5. Click **Next** to continue.

6. In the next dialog box, enter the **Purchase Date** and **Maturity Date** for this bond and click **Next**.

7. (Optional) Enter the **Annual Yield** as a percentage amount.

8. (Optional) Enter the **Face Value**. This is the amount shown on the front of each bond.

9. (Optional) The **Accrued Interest** is the amount of unpaid interest already earned by the bonds.

10. Click **Next** to continue.

11. Enter the **Number of Bonds** of this type that you currently own. Quicken will multiply this amount by 10 to account for the way prices are quoted in newspapers.

12. Enter the **Price per bond**. Quicken will divide this amount by 10, for the same reason as the previous step.

CAUTION

Entering Other Bonds   Not all bonds are based on a factor of 10. For instance, Ginnie Maes and many other types of bonds work on factors of 100. You should enter these manually, calculating the price per share on the total cost of the transaction minus any accrued interest divided by 100.

13. Click **Next** once more and either choose **Yes** and **Next** to run through the sequence once more, or **No** and **Next** to move to the summary window.

14. Use the summary window to confirm your security's details (click **Edit** to adjust any security) and click **Done** when you finish.

Creating a 401(k) Account

If you use Quicken Deluxe or Quicken Home & Business, you have access to a further type of account designed especially to help you track one or more 401(k) investments.

Setting up your 401(k) takes just a few minutes, but you should make sure you have your last 401(k) statement handy before you do. When you're ready, follow these steps:

1. Select **Lists, Account** and click **New** in the upper-left corner.

2. Choose a **401(k)** type of account and click **Next**.

3. Skip past the introductory screen by clicking **Next** once more. (Unlike the investment accounts, you must proceed through the interview step by step. Quicken will not allow you to jump to the summary.)

4. Provide an account name and optional description. Click **Next**.

5. Record the date shown on your 401(k) statement. This will help the Quicken 401(k) and your real 401(k) stay in step. Also indicate how many funds you hold in that 401(k), then click **Next**.

6. If your statement tells you how many shares you hold in each fund, indicate so here. Otherwise, don't worry; so long as you know the total investment in each fund, Quicken will still be able to give you a lot of help. Click **Next**.

7. For each fund you hold, provide the name, number of shares held (if known), and the fund's ending balance. Click **Next** after each.

8. You should now be in front of the Contributions dialog box. Answer both questions and click **Next**.

9. Use the Summary screen shown in Figure 4.4 to review the 401(k) information. When you click **Done**, Quicken creates the 401(k) account and places you immediately in the 401(k) view. You can see a sample of this in Figure 4.5. To learn about updating 401(k) accounts, turn to Lesson 5.

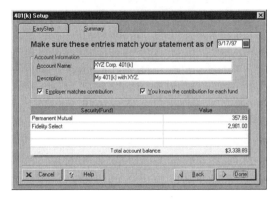

Figure 4.4 Check your 401(k) details in this summary screen.

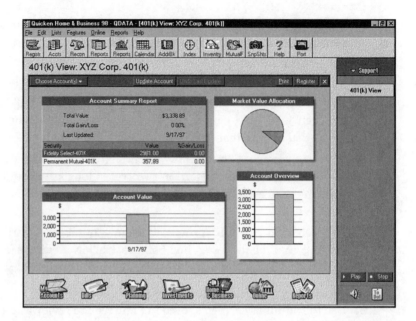

Figure 4.5 The 401(k) view provides a summary of your 401(k)'s most pertinent data.

In this lesson, you learned how to set up your portfolio. In the next lesson, you will learn how to enter the most common portfolio transactions.

Buying, Selling, and Other Transactions

In this lesson, you learn how to record the basic transaction needed to manage an investment portfolio, including buying and selling securities, transferring funds, performing stock splits, updating your 401(k), and more.

Understanding Your Investment Register

Your investment register is central to your investment transactions. From here, you can buy and sell shares, record investment income, reinvest dividends, split stocks, and more. All of these events are stored under the Easy Actions pull-down menu. In this lesson, you use the Easy Actions menu for almost every task relating to your investment accounts. These include:

- Buying and selling shares
- Transferring funds between your checking and investment accounts
- Recording and reinvesting stock dividends
- Recording and reinvesting interest earned
- Recording stock splits
- Recording margin interest

While you can directly type many of these transactions into the investment register, the Easy Actions menu opens up a series of well-prompted, easy-to-use dialog boxes that will step you through the recording of various securities transactions.

Make sure you have opened your investment register or specific security. To open your register, select **Investments, Use My Investment Register** from the Activity Bar at the bottom of your screen.

TIP   **Opening the Register Without an Activity Bar**   If you prefer to use Quicken with your Activity Bar turned off, you can access the investment register by selecting **Features, Investments, Portfolio View (Ctrl+U)**. Then click Register at the top of the portfolio display.

Buying and Selling Shares

To buy or add shares or mutual fund units to your portfolio, select **Easy Actions, Buy/Add Shares**. Click the **Summary** tab to skip past the EasyStep process and complete the dialog box shown in Figure 5.1.

To sell or remove shares or mutual fund units, select **Easy Actions, Sell/Remove Shares**, click the **Summary** tab and also follow Figure 5.1.

To add shares to your portfolio without buying them, select No, deposit shares only. Why would you need to do this? It's ideal when you first set up your investment register. By depositing shares without an associated monetary transfer, you can add them to your portfolio without affecting your finances.

While you purchase shares in lots, Quicken assumes that any selling activity simply runs through the lots in numerical order from oldest to most recent. If you need to specify which shares out of each lump purchased should be sold (or purchased if you have previously sold short), you can override this by clicking the **Lots** button in the Sell/Remove Shares dialog box.

TIP   **Selling Short**   When you sell short, you sell stocks that are borrowed, not owned. If the price of those stocks goes down, you can repurchase the same number of stocks for less and return them to their owner. You get to keep the difference between the original sale price and the subsequent re-purchase cost. Of course, if the stocks go up, you still have to purchase the same number of shares, but this time for more than they were sold.

The Lots window is shown in Figure 5.2. The upper scrolling list shows each lot or group of shares purchased, their purchase date, and their price. It also shows how many are available out of each lot and how many have been assigned to the current transaction.

Use the seven buttons below to specify how to divide the current transaction. You can use these to maximize or minimize your capital gain. Each button will change the adjustments as follows:

> **Use All** Click to include all of the shares available in the current lot.
>
> **Use Part** Click to specify the quantity of shares from the current lot that will be included.
>
> **Clear** Clear the figure specified in the current lot.
>
> **First Shares In** Sell shares from the oldest lot moving forward.
>
> **Last Shares In** Sell shares from the most recently purchased moving backward.
>
> **Maximum Gain** Sell the shares that will achieve the maximum capital gain. In other words, sell the shares with the lowest purchase price.
>
> **Minimum Gain** Minimize your capital gain, selling the shares with the highest purchase price.

Click **OK** when you finish to return to the Sell/Remove dialog.

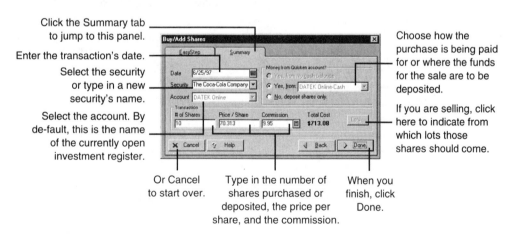

Figure 5.1 The Easy Actions Buy/Add Shares facility simplifies adding shares to your portfolio.

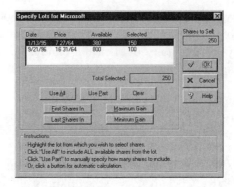

Figure 5.2 The Lots window helps you to sell particular shares out of your holdings.

Transferring Funds Between Accounts

Quicken handles the cash in your investment account in two ways. If your account has a linked checking account, no matter if it takes the form of a checkbook or online banking facility, Quicken assumes the funds in that account will be used for all of your purchases and to receive the proceeds from all of your sales.

However, if you set up your investment account without a linked checking account, Quicken assumes you will be using the cash balance in that account for all debits and credits.

If you created your investment account with an opening balance or linked checking account, you probably already have a credit balance that you can use to purchase more securities. However, from time to time, you will need to either add more funds to your accounts to pay for another purchase or remove funds after a sale.

You cannot transfer funds into or out of a linked checking account using the Easy Actions menu. Instead, you should ignore the investment register altogether, using the check-writing facilities of your standard and brokerage checking accounts. Just follow these steps to transfer funds in either direction:

1. Open the account from which you will transfer the funds. If you are making the transfer by traditional check, open your checkbook register and then select **Features, Paying Bills, Write Checks** to open Quicken's check-writing facility. If the check has been handwritten, open your checking account register instead and create a new transaction. If you are transferring funds from your brokerage check-writing account back to your everyday bank account, open the brokerage check-writing account first and then open Quicken's check-writing facility. To pay the bill online, see Part 3, "Online Services."

2. Fill out the check or transaction as you have already learned. However, instead of applying the payment to one of your Quicken categories, make it a transfer to the brokerage cash account. For example, if you have an investment account called **DATEK Online**, which provides check-writing facilities, the transfer should be made to the DATEK check-writing account instead of the investment register. If you haven't changed Quicken's default account naming system, that would be entered as **[DATEK Online-Cash]**. (An incorrect transfer direct to the register would be entered as [DATEK Online]). If you are transferring funds from your brokerage check writing facility, simply make the transfer to your checking account. For example: **[checking]**.

To transfer funds into your investment account, make sure your investment register is open, select **Easy Actions, Transfer Cash into Account,** and fill out the Transfer Cash In dialog box shown in Figure 5.3. (If you don't see this menu item then your account has been set up with a linked checking account and you should follow the previous steps.)

To transfer funds out of your investment account, open your investment register and select **Easy Actions, Transfer Cash from Account**.

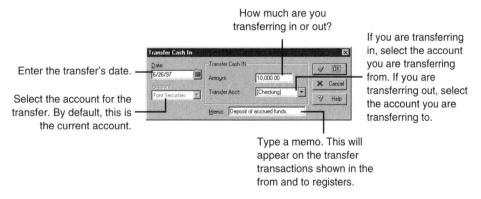

Figure 5.3   Use this dialog to transfer funds into or out of your investment accounts.

Recording and Reinvesting Securities Dividends

If you have invested for income rather than growth, you will almost certainly need to deal with regular dividends from various funds and stocks. And even if you have invested in growth stocks, you may still need to record dividends from time to time.

There are two ways you can treat a recorded dividend or other income event. The first is to take that income and deposit it in your bank account. This leaves you free to spend that income on whatever you want, be it to support your lifestyle or place in some other form of investment.

 TIP   **Dividend**   A dividend is a distribution made by a company to its stock holders. Not all shares attract dividends, preferring to reinvest those funds in further growth. This means that non-dividend shares are good for fast growth while dividend shares are good for income generation. Make sure you know what type of shares you are buying before you invest.

The second is to compound your investment by using that income to purchase more units in that fund or shares in that stock. This can be enormously advantageous if you don't require that income to maintain your standard of living. By reinvesting in that security, the next income event will generate even more money, giving you more to invest, and thus generate an even greater sum the next time around, sitting you squarely on that ride up the exponential curve.

For owners of stock that is steadily improving in value, this is an almost surefire way to attain all of your financial goals, at least over time. Of course, if that stock starts to go backward, you could also lose a lot of accrued wealth rather quickly, but that's just another reason to keep at least half an eye on your investments.

Quicken supports both methods using two different forms. If you use an online financial institution, you may be able to automatically download these events. You can learn about this in Part 3. Otherwise, you will need to record the details as follows.

Recording an Income Event

If you don't want to reinvest that income but would prefer to drop it into your account's cash balance, follow these steps:

1. Open your investment register and select **Easy Actions, Record an Income Event** to open the Record Income dialog shown in Figure 5.4.

2. Enter the **Date**, select the **Account,** and select the **Security** to which this income event applies.

3. Under Distribution, apply the income as follows:

Dividend: Use this field to record dividends received. Most stock dividends are tax free because the tax has already been paid by the corporation. However, if you are not sure whether the dividends you have received are taxable or not, contact the Investor Relations department of the company involved, or speak to your tax professional.

Interest: Interest is generated through money market investments, bonds, and certain mutual funds. Most interest income is taxable. If you have received tax-free interest, record it under **Miscellaneous**.

Capital Gain Dist Short: This is not a capital gain on your own property. Rather, it is any distribution made by a fund (and received by you) based on their own short-term capital gain. Short-term is anything held for one year or less.

Capital Gain Dist Long: Use this field to record distributions made and received on the basis of long-term capital gain. Long-term is anything held for over one year.

Miscellaneous: Consider miscellaneous income for everything else. If you enter an amount here, you can choose the target income category under **Category for Miscellaneous**. If this is tax-free income, make sure it is recorded with a tax-free category so that your Tax Summary and Tax Schedule reports accurately reflect your true taxable income.

 TIP **Reporting Investment Income** You may receive regular notifications regarding dividends and interest income on a monthly statement or through an online investment account. In that case, you can ignore recording dividends as they occur. Rather, wait until you receive that notification. This will help you to match your accounts to your broker's accounts and also match your reported information to that passed on to the IRS.

Long- and short-term capital gain should be reported on your annual return using Schedule D. The IRS will match your information with that recorded on their own copies of the Form 1099s.

4. Select a **Transfer Account**. This is the account into which you will deposit this income. It may be your investment account, a linked investment checking account, an IRA fund that you are maintaining through Quicken, or just your plain, everyday savings/checking account.

5. When you finish, type in a **Memo** and click **OK**.

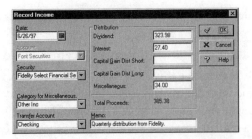

Figure 5.4 Use this dialog to record a variety of investment income. The quickest way is to enter the details straight from a Form 1099-DIV or Form 1099-INC.

Reinvesting Your Income

Reinvesting is a powerful way to boost your investment. Some securities don't allow the reinvestment of income but most of them do.

If you want to purchase more shares, units, or discrete chunks of any other investment, you should use Quicken's Reinvest Income Easy Action. Note that this dialog box assumes all of the income entered will be converted to shares. For this reason, it also supports the notion of fractional shares for those times (the majority) when the share price does not neatly divide into the income received. If you prefer not to deal in fractional shares, calculate the reinvested income and record it here. Then go back and record whatever is left over as an income event, as described previously. To reinvest your income, follow these steps:

1. Open your investment register and select **Easy Actions, Reinvest Income** to open the Reinvest Income dialog box shown in Figure 5.5.

2. Enter the **Date**, select the **Account,** and select the **Security** to which this income event applies.

3. Under **Distribution**, apply the income to each form of distribution as described for the "Record an Income Event" Easy Action. Beside each, enter the number of shares you are purchasing out of each distribution's income. If you are concerned with retaining your shares as whole numbers rather than fractions, use the current share price to calculate the maximum shares you can purchase given the total of each form of distribution. Enter that total price in whole shares and the number of shares beside it. Quicken will display the share price in **Price per Share**. If this matches the actual

share price, you've carried out your calculations correctly. Take any funds remaining and enter them using **Easy Actions, Record an Income Event**.

4. When you finish, type in a **Memo** and click **OK**.

Note that you shouldn't record stock splits as reinvestments. Stock splits are tax-free because while your shares have increased, their total value remains the same. If you are in any doubt about how to record certain dividends, bonus stocks, or income received, speak to a professional tax consultant.

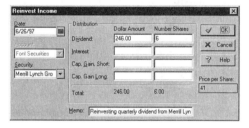

Figure 5.5 Reinvesting income is easy, but you should pre-calculate the reinvested totals to avoid ending up with fractional shares.

Recording Stock Splits

Stock splits occur when the share price climbs higher or falls lower than the corporation's vision of the ideal share price. Stocks may also split to increase the number of shares still held by the company. These are often used as employee or customer incentives to promote loyalty in employment and trade.

When a stock splits, the value of your holdings doesn't necessarily increase, although news of a split is often greeted with increased trading activity. Instead, you will receive a certain number of shares for every share you currently hold. The price of the shares is correspondingly adjusted.

The most common split is a 2 for 1. This means that for every old share you currently hold, you will receive one more share, leaving you with two shares in total. The share price is halved so that everything else remains equal. However, shares aren't always split 2 for 1. You might receive 1.5 for one, giving you 50 percent more shares than you previously held. In a situation such as this, if you own an odd number of shares, you will receive a divestment equal to the value of the odd share out, ending up with 1.5 times your current holdings minus one.

To record a split, just follow these steps:

1. Open your investment register and select **Easy Actions, Stock Split** to open the Stock Split dialog box shown in Figure 5.6.

2. Type in the **Date**, select the investment **Account,** and select a **Security**.

3. Use the Split Ratio group to record the ratio of old shares to new. For example, if the split was a 2-for-1, enter **2** into New Shares and **1** into Old Shares. Alternatively, just record your old and new shareholding. For example, if you had 300 shares and now own 450 shares (a 1.5-for-1 split) just type **450** into new shares and **300** into old shares.

4. Quicken doesn't calculate the new share price according to the ratio provided here. Instead, you should enter the new price in **Price after Split** or update your portfolio's prices as soon as possible.

5. Type in a **Memo** and click **OK** to record the transaction.

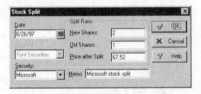

Figure 5.6 Recording stock splits is easy using Quicken's Stock Split Easy Action.

Recording Margin Interest

There are two ways to make money on the stock market without owning any seed capital. These are, if you like, about as close as you'll get to free money.

The first is to trade short. The second is to purchase on margin.

Margin Trading When you purchase on margin, you do so with money borrowed from your broker or another margin lender. Brokers and lenders offer up to 50% on most stocks, 75% on some, and 100% on very few. By borrowing the purchase price, you increase the amount you can lose if the price falls, but also increase the amount you can make if the price rises.

If you trade on margin, you will need to record monthly marginal interest expenses. This is the easy part. Just follow these steps:

1. Open your investment register and select **Easy Actions, Advanced, Margin Interest Expense** to open the Margin Interest Expense dialog box shown in Figure 5.7.

2. Type in the **Date**, and enter the margin interest into **Amount**.

3. Select the **Transfer Account**. This is the account from which the margin interest expense will be paid. If your stockbroker has deducted this automatically, select the account that stores your investment account's cash balance, whether it is the investment account itself or a linked checking account.

4. Enter a **Memo** and click **OK**.

In most cases, margin interest expenses are tax deductible. Even though there doesn't appear to be any entry made in a tax-deductible expense account, Quicken will remember the margin interest transaction and record it as an investment interest expense, ready to be dropped onto Form 4952 when tax time comes.

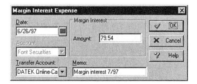

Figure 5.7 Be sure to record your margin interest expenses to prove your tax deduction.

TIP **Margin Liability Accounts** If you often buy on margin, consider setting up a margin liability account. You learn about this in Lesson 7.

Manual Updating

While Easy Actions are a great way for inexperienced Quicken users to manage their investments, you can also enter transactions directly into the register. The precise steps will change according to the action selected, as will the headers used in the transaction register. For instance, a StkSplit changes the columns to Old Shares and New Shares, while a Buy or Sell uses Shares and Price.

To record a buy or sell transaction, follow these steps:

1. Open the appropriate investment register.
2. Select a Date.
3. Type in an action according to the third column in Table 5.1, or select it from the pull-down list.
4. Type in or select a security.
5. Enter the price per share or unit and, in the next column, enter the number of shares or units affected by this transaction.
6. (Optional) Adjust the total and assign that adjustment to the share price, number of shares, or commission.
7. (Optional) Type in a memo.
8. Type in the commission.
9. Click **Enter** to record the transaction.

With time, you will become very experienced at entering transactions directly, but don't try to do so immediately. Why? Unless you really know how Quicken's Actions relate to the real world, you'll find it a lot easier just to rely on Easy Actions and let Quicken handle the transactions for you. Many of the Easy Actions dialog boxes create multipart transactions, and this reflects the complex nature of the securities industry.

Table 5.1 shows the actions stored on the Easy Actions menu and how they relate to those available under the Action field. Any Actions shown with an **X** on the end are a special case.

There are two forms of most actions, but you will only see those with an **X** if you do not have a cash balance in your investment account. This means that if you use a linked checking account, you will only see **X** actions. However, if you use a cash investment account and you have transferred money into that account or indicated that it contains a starting balance, you will see both the **X** forms and the non-**X** forms.

The first form is used for cash investment accounts, for example, the action called **Buy**. These actions are kept entirely local to the current investment account. However, if you see the same action with an **X** tacked on the end, it means the transaction involves a transfer of funds to or from another account. As linked checking accounts are still separate accounts, any investment account linked to a checking account will only be able to record actions with an **X**.

Where's My X? If you are using a cash investment account and can't find any of the **X** actions, make sure you have cash in your investment account. Use the **Easy Actions** menu to select **Transfer Cash into Account** if you don't already have cash in the investment account.

Use Table 5.1 as a guide to recording investment transactions. The table shows both the Easy Action and the related register transaction, if applicable. Those Easy Actions that create multiple register transactions have no directly equivalent register transaction.

Table 5.1 Supported Transactions

To Do This	Select This Under Easy Actions	Or Type This Action
Buy securities	Buy/Add Shares	Buy, BuyX
Sell securities	Sell/Remove Shares	Sell, SellX
Add securities without purchasing	Buy/Add Shares	ShrsIn
Remove securities without selling	Sell/Remove Shares	ShrsOut
Record interest earned	Record an Income Event	IntInc, IntIncX
Record a dividend	Record an Income Event	Div, DivX
Record a short capital gain	Record an Income Event	CGShort, CGShortX
Record a long capital gain	Record an Income Event	CGLong, CGLongX
Record miscellaneous income	Record an Income Event	MiscInc, MiscIncX
Record a miscellaneous expense	Miscellaneous Expense	MiscExp, MiscExpX
Reinvest dividends	Reinvest Income	ReinvDiv
Reinvest interest	Reinvest Income	ReinvInt
Reinvest short capital gain	Reinvest Income	ReinvSh
Reinvest long capital gain	Reinvest Income	ReinvLg
Transfer cash in	Transfer Cash into Account	XIn

continues

Table 5.1 Continued

To Do This	Select This Under Easy Actions	Or Type This Action
Transfer cash out	Transfer Cash from Account	XOut
Record a stock split	Stock Split	StkSplit
Record a return of capital RtrnCapX	Return of Capital	RtrnCap,
Record your margin interest MargIntX	Margin Interest Expense	MargInt,
Transfer to another account Between Accounts	Advanced:Transfer Shares	ShrsOut
Transfer from another account Between Accounts	Advanced:Transfer Shares	ShrsIn
Change a security's name Change	Advanced:Corporate Name equivalent)	(No
Record a change to a security's structure	Advanced:Corporate Securities Spin-Off	(No equivalent)
Record a corporate takeover	Advanced:Corporate Acquisition (stock for stock)	(No equivalent)
Record a stock dividend	Advanced:Stock Dividend (non-cash dividend)	StkSplit
Set a reminder in Quicken's calendar	Advanced:Reminder Transaction	Reminder

Updating 401(k) Accounts

The 401(k) is a special type of account. While it is possible to open the 401(k) register as you would any investment register and record the full range of transactions described through the rest of this lesson, that isn't the best way to go about it. (Of course, if you are managing your 401(k) through a standard investment account, that's the only way you can do it.)

Instead, if you use Quicken Deluxe or Quicken Home and Business and have set up an account of the special 401(k) type, you can update it whenever you receive your 401(k) statement by following these steps:

1. Select Features, Investments, Track 401(k).

2. Select the middle option option from the Track My 401(k) dialog box. That's "**I want to update an existing account.**" Click **OK** to continue.

3. Select the 401(k) account form the next dialog and click **OK**.

4. Type in the date shown on the statement most recently received and click **Next**.

5. You should now see a dialog that display your current holdings. (See Figure 5.8.) If any of these holdings have been sold, remove the checkmark. If any funds have been added, click **Add New Fund** and type in the name of the new fund. Click **Next**.

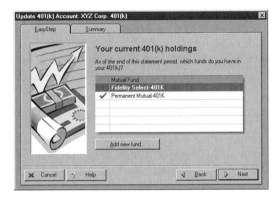

Figure 5.8 Indicate which holdings or funds are included in the 401(k) update.

6. For the period detailed by your statement, record your and your employer's total contributions to the fund, dividends or interest earned and the fund's current total market value. Click **Next** to repeat these question for all of the funds including in your account.

7. When you arrive at the Transfers dialog, click **Yes** if there have been any transfers between funds. If so, provide the number of transfers and click **Next**. For every transfer indicate the fund transferred from, the fund transferred to, and the amount actually transferred. Click **Next** to move to the next transfer.

8. Once you have completed the transfers you will be shown an Update Summary similar to Figure 5.9. Check the amounts carefully. If any require editing, simply click on them once and insert the new amounts as required. (You can also use the Calculator icon that appears next to each field to help you with your calculations.) When you finish, click **Done** to record the changes to your 401(k).

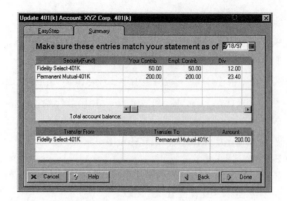

Figure 5.9 The 401(k) updating system provides a fully-editable summary.

In this lesson, you learned how to buy and sell securities, record a range of other Easy Actions and investment register transactions, and to update your 401(k) account. In the next lesson, you will learn how to track the worth of your investments.

Tracking Your Investments

In this lesson, you will learn to use Quicken's price-updating and portfolio-viewing features to track the value of your investments and update your 401(k).

Using Quicken's Investment Tracking Features

Quicken's investment tracking features will help you to judge when you should buy more of one stock, sell more of the other, or hang on to what you already own. Tracking will also help you to work out your return on investment, an important part of fine-tuning any portfolio. Whether you consider your investments individually or as a whole, learn to use Quicken's investment tracking features and you will almost certainly come out ahead.

Investment tracking works best if you following these four steps:

1. Ensure you enter your investment transactions as soon as they have been made in the real world.

2. Update your portfolio's pricing on a regular basis, either by using Quicken's Internet connectivity or by manually typing in the updates.

3. Study your portfolio's return on investment and how that would compare to the potential rate of return if those funds were invested elsewhere.

4. Adjust your portfolio to maximize your opportunity for gain, but also know when you should leave an investment where it is, either to ride out a down-turn in the market or to simply be best positioned for those unforeseen price surges that tend to lift all stocks, no matter their intrinsic value.

Your learned about maintaining your portfolio in the previous lesson. Now look at updating.

Using the Portfolio View

The Portfolio view provides an integrated and highly customizable system for viewing all of your securities, accounts, goals, and investment types. To open the Portfolio view, select **Features, Investments, Portfolio View**. The main list is a collapsible hierarchy. Click the folder icons to shrink the listing underneath each folder down to a single summary that totals across all columns. Use the **Group by:** pull-down list to select the view. Figure 6.1 provides an easy guide to the rest of the Portfolio view's features.

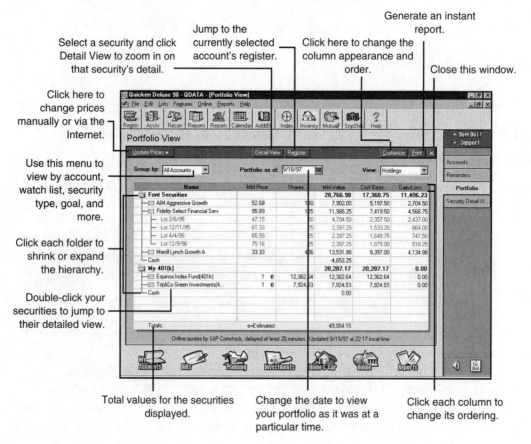

Generate an instant report.

Jump to the currently selected account's register.

Select a security and click Detail View to zoom in on that security's detail.

Click here to change the column appearance and order.

Close this window.

Click here to change prices manually or via the Internet.

Use this menu to view by account, watch list, security type, goal, and more.

Click each folder to shrink or expand the hierarchy.

Double-click your securities to jump to their detailed view.

Total values for the securities displayed.

Change the date to view your portfolio as it was at a particular time.

Click each column to change its ordering.

Figure 6.1 The Portfolio view provides a useful summary of each of your investments.

Using the Detail View

The Detail view is useful for two reasons: Viewing those transactions that relate to a particular security, and studying that security's price history in a graphical format. To open the Detail view, either select a security in the Portfolio view and click the **Detail View** button at the top of the window, or simply double-click that security.

Figure 6.2 provides an easy guide to this window.

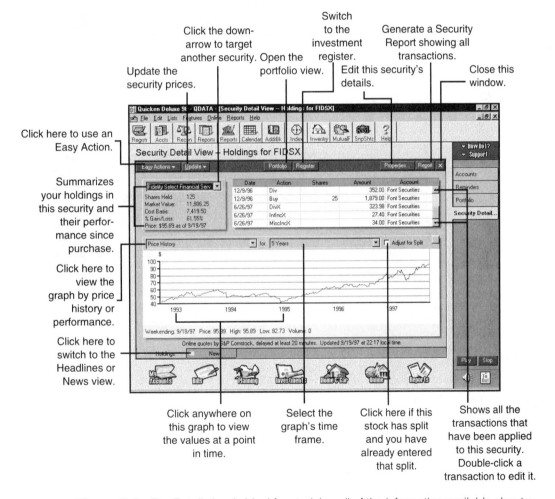

Figure 6.2 The Detail view is ideal for studying all of the information available about a particular security.

To view news about the security, click **Headlines**. This will take you to the window shown in Figure 6.3. Click the underlined items in the News window to launch the built-in Web browser and load that item. The standard browser bundled with Quicken is Microsoft Internet Explorer 3.02. This runs in a window from within Quicken. You must be online to read the news. If not, Quicken will start your Internet connection for you.

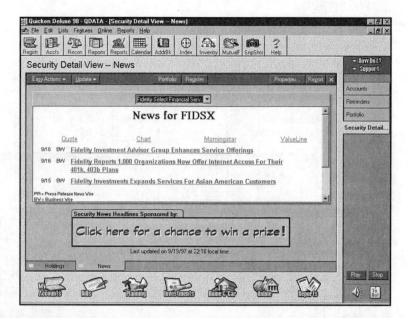

Figure 6.3   Not all news is good news, but with this Quicken feature, you'll receive it all the same.

Updating Your Portfolio

Updating your portfolio can be as easy as clicking a button. If you have access to the Internet, Quicken will look after your stocks, updating the price of each on demand. Through a Quicken Alert, it will even let you know when that stock reaches a specified high or low price.

Updating across the Internet only takes seconds and is cheaper, easier, and more current than looking those prices up in the share listings of a newspaper. However, if you don't have an Internet connection, you will need to resort to manual updates. These are described first.

Watching List Stocks

You have already seen how Quicken stores securities in investment registers, but what about those that you haven't yet purchased but still want to keep a close eye on? Just store them in a Watch List.

To create a Watch List, follow these steps:

1. Select **Lists, Investment, Security**.
2. Click **New** to create a new security and fill in the details. Before you save that security, click **Other Info** and select **Add to Watch List**. Click **OK** twice to save the security.
3. To view your Watch List, go to the Portfolio view by selecting **Features, Investments, Portfolio View**. Use the **Group by:** pull-down list to select **Watch List**.

Watching Market Indices

You are not limited to only watching securities; you can also follow the most popular market indices.

What is a market index? You have probably heard reported on numerous occasions the latest movements of the Dow Jones Industrial Average, NASDAQ Composite, or S&P 500. The indices are created by watching the prices of carefully selected stocks and then feeding those values to a formula. The end result is (hopefully) a highly representative value of the stock market overall or a facet of the stock market such as capitalization size, industry type, and so on.

Quicken is able to track the following indices, comparing them to your own portfolios:

- Dow Jones Industrial Average
- S&P 500 Stock Index
- NASDAQ Composite Index
- AMEX Composite Index
- Dow Jones Transportation Average
- Dow Jones Utilities Average
- PSE High Technology Index
- Wilshire Small Cap Index
- PHLX Gold & Silver Index

To use this feature, follow these steps:

1. Select **Features, Investments, Setup Online Quotes and News**.
2. Click the **Market Indexes** tab.
3. Use the left column to mark those indices you want to track. Use the right column to select the investment accounts you want to compare to those indices.
4. Click **OK** to save the changes or **Update Now** to save the changes, go online immediately and download the latest information.

TIP   **Creating Your Own Index**   If you want to create your own marke index, set up a new security type such as **Top 10 High-Tech Stocks**, and store each security you want to include in the calculation. Deposit a single share in each security using a dummy investment account (remembering to exclude these shares from your Net Worth and other reports by using the report's **Customize, Include** function), and change the portfolio view as described next to show the percent gained or lost.

Updating Securities Manually

To update your security prices manually, follow these steps:

1. Select **Features, Investment, Portfolio View**.
2. From the **Group by:** pull-down menu, select **All Accounts**. This will display all your working securities grouped by their investment account. After you complete these steps, repeat them for any securities in your watch list by selecting **Watch List** from the **Group by:** menu.
3. Check that the Price column is displayed. If not, click **Customize**, select the entry labeled **Mkt Price** in the left-hand list and click **Add>>** to copy it to the right-hand list. Click **OK** to add that column to the Portfolio view.
4. Check that the date shown is the same as the date applicable to this pricing data. If not, type in a new date or select the new date by clicking the Calendar icon.
5. Select the security you need to change, click within **Mkt Price**, and enter the new price using fractions or decimals. By default, Quicken copies the updated price to all security entries holding the same ticker symbol.

Updating Securities Automatically

Automatic updates are much easier than manual updates. However, before you can take advantage of them, you will require a working Internet connection. Assuming you have this up and running (if not, see Part 3 of this book), you can update your prices simply by doing the following:

1. Select **Features, Investment, Portfolio View**.

2. Pull down the **Update Prices** menu and select **Get Online Quotes and News**. This opens a window similar to that shown in Figure 6.4. If this is the first time you have used a Quicken Internet feature, you will need to skip past an introductory screen first. If you want to bypass this download confirmation screen from now on, click **Skip this screen in the future**.

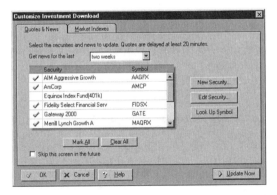

Figure 6.4 Use this dialog box to change the way Quicken updates securities online.

3. Quicken's default behavior assumes you will want to update every security. If that isn't the case, click the security to remove its check mark.

4. Click **Get news for the last** and enter the number of days to download any headlines that have been stored over that time.

5. When you finish adjusting the list, click **Update Now**. Quicken displays an update summary. You can ignore this window and continue working in Quicken. If you are already online, Quicken will connect using your existing connection. Otherwise, it will dial your Internet provider and continue from there.

> TIP   **Security Price Alerts**   To receive an alert when a security rises above or
> falls below two specified levels, you should create a price alert by selecting
> **Features, Reminders, Alerts**. Set the price using the alert area called Stock
> Price Limits. The full procedure is described in Part 1.

If you are a subscriber to *Investor Insight*, you can update up to five years of
historical stock prices by selecting the new **Update Prices** menu item **Get
Investor Insight Prices**. While it might seem tempting to grab five years' worth
of daily data, that pricing information will tend to clog up Quicken's investment
reports. For best results, restrict Quotes Frequency to **BiMonthly** or **Monthly**.

Valuing Your Investments

After entering all those securities and transactions and updating the prices, you
probably can't wait to see how much your investments are actually worth.
Quicken provides several methods through which you can view and calculate
the market value and performance of your investments. These are:

- Via the total market value field in the Portfolio view.
- Through a Portfolio Value report.
- With an Asset Allocation pie chart.
- Using an Investment Performance graph. Just click the on-screen buttons
  to switch between all accounts, some accounts, investment goals, or asset
  classes.
- By creating a Net Worth report or graph.

Viewing Through the Portfolio View

To open the Portfolio view, select **Features, Investments, Porfolio View**, or click
the Activity Bar icon **Investments** and select **View My Portfolio**.

Ensure **Group by:** is set to **Accounts** and **Prices as of** is set to today's date.

The **Totals:** field in the Mkt Value column shows the value of your investments
across all your investment accounts. This includes any cash stored in those
accounts. The exception to the rule is cash excluded because it is held in a linked
checking account.

To see your accounts ordered by their percentage gain, follow these steps:

1. Click **Customize**, select **% Gain/Loss** in the left-hand list, and click **Add >>**.
2. (Optional) Select an entry in the right-hand list, and click **Move Up** or **Move Down** to change its position in the Portfolio view.
3. Click **OK** to add that column to the Portfolio view. You may need to use the horizontal scrolling bar to see the column in full.

Creating a Portfolio Value Report

To create a Portfolio Value report, from the **Reports** menu, select **Investments, Portfolio Value**. Click **Create** to generate the report.

At first glance, the Portfolio Value report shown in Figure 6.5 looks like a printable version of the Portfolio view. Both offer cost basis, current price, gain or loss, and the balance. However, the Portfolio Value report improves on the Portfolio view because it also offers subtotaling by investment goal, asset class, or security type.

Click **Customize** and click the pull-down item **Subtotal By:**. Choose between **Account, Security Type, Investment Goal,** or **Asset Class**. Click **Create** to generate the new report.

TIP **A Real World Example** John and Joan are building up an investment goal to open the first of what they hope will become a chain of fast-food eateries. They are also trying to get the funds together to put the twins through college. They've decided the best way to do both is to build their assets through aggressive play on the stock market. With this in mind, they have created two investment goals: one for college and the other for the restaurant. By subtotaling the portfolio value reports by investment goal, they can quickly and easily see how close they are to attaining each, even while keeping tabs on the progress of the portfolio as a whole.

CAUTION

Where Are My Remaining Accounts? Even though Customize seems to let you subtotal by account, the standard report may not include all of your accounts. If you don't think you're seeing the full picture, click the **Customize** button at the top of the report window, click the **Accounts** tab, and choose from the investment accounts that you want included in this report. Click **Create** when you're done. Note that whatever you select, Quicken only includes accounts marked as **Invest**.

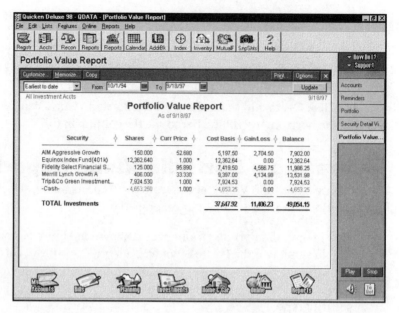

Figure 6.5   The Portfolio Value report provides a clear picture of the figures underlying your investment performance.

Creating an Asset Allocation Chart

Asset Allocation charts (see Figure 6.6) are useful because they show you at a glance how your investments are divided.

To create this chart, select **Reports, Graphs, Investment Asset Allocation**. Click **Create**.

This graph shows all securities that have had their Asset Class specified either when they were created or later. To change a security's asset class, open the Portfolio view by selecting **Features, Investments, Portfolio View**. Use the right mouse button to click the security and select **Properties** from the pull-down menu. Change the **Asset Class** as required and click **OK**.

The first level of the graph shows a breakdown by all asset classes. However, Quicken's standard QuickZoom feature will help you to zoom in until you can target individual investments.

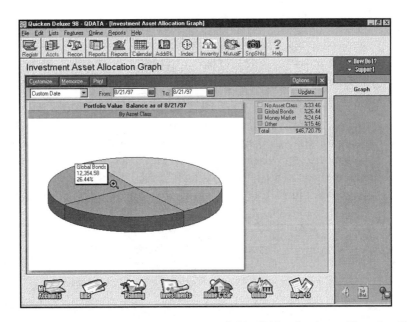

Figure 6.6 Want to see how your assets are divided? Use the Asset Allocation Chart to see this information at a glance.

Click once anywhere. You see Quicken's Magnifying Glass icon replace your mouse cursor to view a numeric readout showing the figures behind that section of the graph. Double-click to jump from the pie chart showing your total investment broken down by asset class to a pie chart that shows all of the investments within that asset class. Double-click once more to jump to a further level where you can view a bar chart showing that investment's growth. To jump back out, click the Close (**X**) box in the upper-right corner of each graph's window.

Creating an Investment Performance Graph

To create this type of graph, select **Reports, Graphs, Investment Performance**. The Investment Performance graph shown in Figure 6.7 is made up of two windows. The uppermost graph shows your portfolio's dollar value either for all securities or just those that have been selected using the **Customize** function.

Try clicking the buttons labeled **Type**, **Goal**, **Security**, **Account**, **Asset Class** that run across the top of the graphing window. You can use these to compare the

415

performance of accounts held with different stockbrokers or mutual fund managers, or set up a race comparing one investment goal to another. If you want to exclude certain accounts or securities from the graph, return to **Customize** and deselect them from the appropriate list.

This graph is enormously useful for seeing how your investments have performed, not only on their own but also as compared to the rest of your investments. As with all Quicken graphs, double-click with the **QuickZoom** icon to see a more detailed view of the makeup of each column. The lower graph indicates your portfolio's Average Annual Total Return. This is shown as a heavy black horizontal line that runs in front of each column.

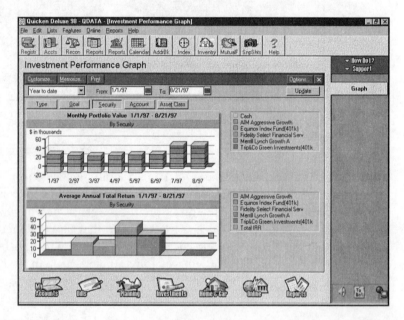

Figure 6.7 To see how your investments are performing, try creating an Investment Performance graph.

Also known as the Internal Rate of Return (IRR), this is an important indicator of your portfolio's performance because it shows in percentage terms just how well your investments are doing. In the example shown in Figure 6.7, the IRR is equal to about 27 percent. You can find out the exact percentage by pausing your mouse over either of the boxes that define each end of the horizontal line.

An IRR of 27 percent means that those investments have earned or grown (both factors are taken into account) at a rate equal to them being deposited in a bank account that happens to earn interest at 27 percent. This is a lot to expect, but it is not uncommon to see IRRs in highly aggressive accounts of 50 to 80 percent, although the shrinkage on some years may turn out to be equally severe.

CAUTION

How Does the IRR Compare to Other Growth Rates? The IRR is different to the growth rate figures you have already seen on other investment reports because it takes historical activity, compounding, and the investment period into account.

In doing so, the IRR formula looks at when the investments were purchased and when they were sold, considering dividends, market value, reinvestments, and other factors.

The IRR provides a convenient way for you to compare your investment to the published growth rates of other investments such as term deposits, mutual funds, investment trusts, bonds, and so on. Get into the habit of comparing your IRR to a typical bank account, and you'll see just how far ahead you really are.

Each column in the lower graph shows the IRR of the individual accounts, investments, goals, asset classes, or investment types, according to the button selected at the top of the graph. By comparing these to the annual average line, you can easily see which investments are not performing up to the market average and which are pulling more than their own weight.

The ability to adjust the timeline and the components that contribute to the graph makes it almost infinitely adaptable. For example, to see how your investment goals stack up since their inception, click **Goal**. This shows your investment performance over the current year. To change the date, click **Customize** and in the Graph Dates pull-down list, select the first item: **Include all dates**.

TIP **Improved Graphing Accuracy** While Quicken's 3-D column graphs look wonderfully aesthetic, they're not as accurate as 2-D graphs because their 3-D depiction makes it more difficult to compare the top edge of one column to another. You can fix this by switching to 2-D graphs. Click **Options** in the upper-right corner of the graph window and select **Draw in 2D (faster)**. This also does wonders for estimating the comparative size of different segments of a pie chart.

Net Worth Reports and Graphs

Your net worth is the value of your assets minus your liabilities. In other words, your equity. From an investment point of view, it is a very convenient means of seeing how your investments stack up. For example, if you buy stocks on margin, a slightly doctored Net Worth report or graph will help you to view your changing assets, liabilities, and what you would be worth if your investment assets were immediately liquidated and your investment liabilities immediately satisfied with the proceeds.

To create a net worth graph targeted purely at your investment assets and liabilities, follow these steps:

1. Select **Reports, Graphs, Net Worth**.

2. The standard Net Worth graph includes all of your assets and liabilities. For our means, that's a little over the top. Instead, click **Customize** to open the Customize Graph dialog box.

3. Make sure the **Accounts** tab is selected. You will see a long list of ticks beside every type of Quicken account. Remove the ticks beside every account with the exception of your investment and linked checking and margin accounts.

4. Click **Create** to produce the graph.

The Net Worth report provides the same information as the graph, except that it provides that information as a series of figures instead of a single graph. Also, you may choose a time interval and period; for instance, weekly, monthly, quarterly. This will show your changing net worth over that time at that interval.

 TIP **Net Worth Reports for Non-investors** To create a net worth report based on everything but your investment accounts, follow the steps below but deselect your investment account. Reselect all your other accounts. You can learn more about net worth reports and financial snapshots in Part 1, Lessons 11 and 12.

To create this report, follow these steps.

1. Select **Reports, Home, Net Worth**.

2. Click **Customize** and change the Display tab's **Interval** setting from **none** (which provides an "as of now" report) to the desired interval.

3. Adjust the date at the top of the **Display** tab and then click the **Accounts** tab.

4. Deselect all those accounts not concerned with or linked to your investments, and click **Create**.

Once you have customized the report and graph, you can generate a hard copy by clicking **Print** at the top of each window.

In this lesson, you learned to use the portfolio view, work with your security detail windows, update your security prices, and create a variety of investment graphs and reports. In the next lesson, you will learn several useful investment techniques and strategies to apply through Quicken.

Useful Investment Strategies

In this lesson, you learn several useful investment strategies that may help you make the most of your investments.

Fund Management for Everyone

The world has seen the birth of almost as many investment strategies as get-rich-quick schemes. Some work but require constant supervision. Others work but require access to information not available to the part-time investor.

So what can a keen amateur do? It's easy. Professional fund managers have a tough time of it because their funds are so large. More often than not, their prospectus states they can't get involved in the small-cap but high-growth stocks, so they have to try to make their money on billion-dollar companies that dominate their markets, leaving little opportunity for fast growth. Witness slowing share prices for some industry giants, despite the fact that their profit levels might be better than ever.

While professional fund managers and stockbrokers spend their time sifting through enormous amounts of information, trying to pick the investments that will give their multibillion dollar portfolios a swift injection of growth or return, the individual investor has a much easier and far less stressed time of it.

There are lots of places you can turn to get the information you need. These include the numerous investment sites on the World Wide Web, not to mention Quicken's own Financial Network shown in Figure 7.1 and available through **Online, Quicken on the Web, Quicken.com**. However, information isn't all you need. After all, the professional fund managers have more than enough information.

What you also need is a method of leveraging your investment, such as buying on margin to make the most of a small upturn. These methods help you make the most of downturns, and serve as a means of spreading your risk not just across the entire portfolio but also across each security. These are discussed here.

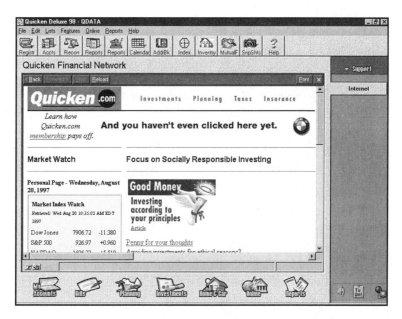

Figure 7.1 The Quicken Financial Network is a great place to start your investment research.

Understanding Dollar Cost Averaging

Dollar cost averaging works on the basis that you can never know when a stock will hit its lowest ebb (the right time to buy), or its highest peak (the right time to sell).

TIP **High, Low, and Close** While there is no certainty in predicting the peaks or lows of a stock, see "Using the High, Low, and Close Prices" section later in this chapter for a method that can help.

By averaging the cost of a security over a period of time, dollar cost averaging ensures that any small dip in the price of that security will become an advantage once the market recovers. The method is quite easy to use and it works very

421

well, bringing even particularly aggressive stocks back to a less risky level. By regularly investing a set sum in a security, no matter the price of that security, you can buy more when the prices are low and less when the prices are high.

Dollar cost averaging is like a regular investment plan that protects you from making emotionally charged decisions. Certainly, if you believe that a particular stock is about to do astonishingly well, do your homework, consult with a investment professional, and then go for it. However, set yourself a plan to invest a certain amount over a certain time, rather than all at once. A good way to start is to look at investing the total sum of $10,000 over 10 months.

Let's say you believe the stock of XYZ Corporation is very undervalued. With a disillusioned market keeping the lid on prices, it's definitely a good time to invest. What you don't know is if the stock is at its lowest ebb. Maybe it is, but maybe it isn't. You decide to invest $1,000 each month over a period of 10 months, as shown in Table 7.1. You will lose some money in brokerage fees, but discount brokers offer their services for as little as $9.95 per trade.

The average share price works out to be $27.75. If you had invested $10,000 in the first month alone, you would be further ahead than through dollar cost averaging; however, you wouldn't have the protection dollar cost averaging affords: When the share price was $12.50, the rules of dollar cost averaging ensured you would have picked up 80 shares; when the price climbed, you would have purchased fewer shares.

Table 7.1 A Sample Investment Plan

Month	Investment	Share Price	Shares Purchased	Total Shares Owned
1	$1,000	$25	40	40
2	$1,000	$20	50	90
3	$1,000	$12.5	80	170
4	$1,000	$20	50	220
5	$1,000	$25	40	260
6	$1,000	$20	50	310
7	$1,000	$25	40	350
8	$1,000	$40	25	375
9	$1,000	$50	20	395
10	$1,000	$40	25	420

You can use Quicken to manage your dollar cost averaging. Its investment tracking features are great for working out your average buying price and how well the total investment has done, but that's not all. By creating a scheduled transaction that transfers funds from your checking account to your Investment account, you can automatically remind yourself to buy those shares as part of a regular investment plan.

Quicken can write the check or perform an online payment and automatically deposit those funds into your investment account when and as they are needed. You will, however, still need to organize the purchase of those shares if you do not use a Quicken-savvy online broker, and enter that transaction into your investment register.

Buying on Margin

Buying on margin is a great way to leverage your buying power—although at some risk.

When you buy on margin, you purchase some shares and borrow the funds to purchase more from your stockbroker. Most stockbrokers allow margins of up to 50 percent on any stock, 75 percent on some, and 100 percent on relatively few.

Margin borrowing works like this: Say you've managed to target a stock whose price looks like it will go through the roof. You believe you can make a veritable killing and figure you would like to risk $10,000 on the gamble that you'll almost certainly double your money within 12 months. The only problem is, you only have about $7,000 in your cash balance, and you would prefer to avoid liquidating your other investments unless it proved absolutely necessary.

No problem. Just call your broker and convert your cash trading account to a margin trading account. This will give you the ability to borrow up to 50 percent of the value of any stock purchase at around 8 percent interest. So, you now have your original $7,000 plus an extra $3,500. Your new buying power equals $10,500. Now, say the stock does what you expected and doubles in value over the next 12 months. If you had invested only $7,000, your stock would be worth $14,000. However, by investing $10,500, that stock is now worth $21,000!

You repay the broker, selling $3,790.50 of stock to repay the principal plus compounded interest, leaving you with a balance of $17,209.50. Your investment is now worth approximately 250 percent of the seed capital, instead of just 200 percent.

From Quicken's point of view, buying on margin has no effect on your net worth. The problem is that after you've entered the share transaction and recorded the total purchase price, the cash balance in your account will appear lower than it actually is (if not sitting in the red). This happens because Quicken thinks those funds have all come from the cash balance rather than being partially supported through the margin facility of your stockbroker.

Your assets and liability are still in balance, of course, because while the value of the shares has increased your assets, your account balance has been decreased by a similar amount. However, what should have really happened is that your assets should have increased to show the value of the funds you've borrowed and your liabilities should have increased by the amount of that loan. In both situations, your equity or net worth stays the same, but only the second can be said to be truly accurate.

So, how should you organize your Quicken books when you buy on margin? The answer is to create a margins liability account. This will provide you with many advantages, not least of which is knowing precisely where your cash balance stands. To create a margin liability account, follow these steps (see Figure 7.2):

1. Select **Lists, Account** and click **New**.

2. Select **Liability** and click **Next**.

3. Click the **Summary** tab to skip the interview process and enter the following details:

    Account Name   Margins

    Description   Margin Investments

    Balance   (Optional) If you have an existing margin liability, enter it here according to the information shown on your last broker's statement. Don't forget to specify the statement's date. Otherwise, leave it at zero.

4. (Optional)   Click **Info** to take note of any other information such as the margin interest rate.

5. Click **Done** to save the new account and answer **No** to the offer to set up an amortized loan.

When you record a margin share purchase, you should do so normally, decreasing either the cash balance in that account or the balance of the linked checking account.

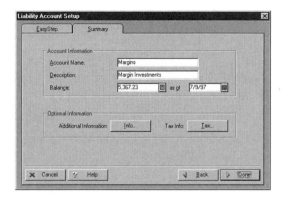

Figure 7.2 Margin liability accounts are the ideal way to track margin investments.

However, as soon as you have done so, you need to assign the value of the borrowed or margin amount to the margins liability account. Depending on whether you are using a straight cash account or a linked checking account, do one of the following:

- If you don't have a linked checking account, open the investment register used to record the share purchase, pull down the **Easy Actions** menu and select **Transfer Cash into Account**. Type in the **Amount** of the margin—this will probably be a percentage of your stock purchase—and use **Transfer Acct:** to select the Margin account from the pull-down list. Type in a **Memo** such as **23 shares of XYZ purchased on margin** and click **OK**, as shown in Figure 7.3.

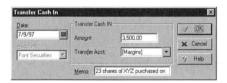

Figure 7.3 To balance shares purchased on margin, you should transfer funds into your investment account from the margin liability account.

- If you do have a linked checking account, you need to transfer the funds straight to the checking account rather than the investment account, which doesn't support a cash transfer facility. Open the checking account instead of the investment register, fill out a new transaction using these details, and click **Enter** when you're done:

- **Date**   Enter the date of the transfer.

- **Num**   (Ignore.)

- **Payee**   This isn't a real transaction with a real payee. However, you might like to create a Payee such as **Margin Payments** for future reference.

- **Payment**   Enter the margin amount, not the total purchase price.

- **Category**   Enter a transfer to the Margins liability account, for example: **[Margins]**.

- **Memo**   Type in a memo such as **23 shares of XYZ purchased on margin**.

Both of these methods boost your cash balance but also record a liability in the margins account.

When you pay back the margin, you can reduce that liability in one of two ways. One option would be to transfer funds back into the liability account from your checkbook (paying off the debt using external funds). Another option would be to sell some of the shares you have borrowed against, arranging the transfer from your investment account's cash balance or the linked checking account's balance.

Managing your margins this way has one more excellent advantage. Every transaction in the Margins liability account provides a continuing record of your margin borrowings. Simply clear each margin transaction as it is paid off and you can see at any stage through Quicken's Payables report just how much you owe on each stock. If you do a lot of margin borrowing, this is by far the easiest way to keep track of precisely where you stand.

Creating Short Sales

First, let's get two definitions out of the way:

Long Position   One in which you own the stocks you are trading.

Short Position   One in which you don't own the stocks you are trading.

When you trade long, you follow that ancient maxim of the securities industry: Buy low, sell high. In long trading, you try to make money out of an upturn in the market.

Do I Own Shares Purchased on Margin? You certainly do. If you buy shares on margin, you still own the shares, you are still trading long, and you are still hoping for an upturn in the market in order to pay back the margin

CAUTION amount.

When you sell short, you "borrow" a quantity of shares and immediately dispose of them on the market. After a while, you return the original quantity of shares to the broker by purchasing the same number of new shares at what is hopefully a lower price.

By selling short, you try to make money out of a downturn in the market. Your gamble is that the price of those stocks will go down. This lets you pocket the difference between the original selling price and the later buying price. Of course, if the stocks rise in price, then you'll end up repurchasing them at a price greater than they were originally sold. That's the risk.

Selling Short

Quicken supports short sales quite simply. To create a short sale, follow these steps:

1. Open your investment register and select **EasyActions, Sell/Remove Shares**.
2. Fill out the dialog box the same way you would for selling any group of shares, completing the fields for date, security, sale price, destination for proceeds, and any commission associated with the transaction.
3. Click **Done** to finish. When Quicken asks you to confirm that you are recording a short transaction, click **OK**. This approves the sale of shares that you don't have. Click **Cancel** if you don't want to sell short after all.

Returning the Borrowed Shares

To return a short sale, you need to buy back the original shares—hopefully at a lower price. The procedure is easy; just follow these steps:

1. Open your investment register and select **EasyActions, Buy/Add Shares**.
2. Fill out the dialog box the same as you would do for purchasing any group of shares but with the following exception.
3. Click **Lots** and select the parcel of shares previously sold short. Click **Use All** to assign all of the purchased shares to that lot and click **OK**.
4. Back at the Summary screen, click **Done** to complete the transaction.

Selling short may very well have led to the expression "to be caught short." If you are left holding a short position with the market on the rise, your position will continue to deteriorate. At some stage, your broker may decide to start liquidating your other holdings in order to shore up your equity (and negate the broker's risk). Short selling is therefore quite a gamble. However, if you approach it with what you believe to be relatively certain knowledge, it's possible to make as much money out of the downturns in the market as you do on the upturns.

There are certain limits to holding a short position. For example, you cannot sell short on an IPO (Initial Public Offering). For more information, consult your stockbroker or an online share trading guide, such as the Invest FAQ at **http://invest-faq.com/articles/stock-shorting.html**.

IPO (Initial Public Offering)   When a company lists its shares on the stock market, it does so through an IPO. The IPO is always accompanied by a prospectus detailing the company's history (financial and otherwise) as well as its future prospects. Never buy shares on a newly listed company without reading the prospectus first and, preferably, seeking a professional opinion.

What Is the P/E Ratio?

The P/E Ratio is one of the most useful indicators of a company's potential. Put simply, it compares the company's share price to its per-share earnings. A company's earnings are its after-tax profit. This shouldn't be confused with dividends, which are discussed in the "What Is the Yield?" section next.

The per-share earnings are calculated on the earnings divided by the number of outstanding (that is, publicly held) shares. A company that earned $10 million last year with two million shares outstanding has per-share earnings of $2. If that company's shares trade at $20, then the company's P/E Ratio is 20/2, or 10.

You can discover a company's P/E Ratio in Investor Insight and the Quicken MarketWatch. You learn about Investor Insight in Lesson 8. To access the MarketWatch, select **Online, Quicken on the Web, Quicken.com**. To see the P/E Ratio, just request a price quote on that stock.

The P/E Ratio provides a good indicator of how expensive a stock is. For instance, no matter the share price, a stock with a P/E Ratio of 50 is ten times more expensive than one with a P/E Ratio of 5, even if the share price for both is identical. However, the higher the P/E, the more confidence the market has that the stock will grow.

The P/E is useful but also prone to deflection in one direction or another, depending on the industry sector. Never compare the P/E of computer stocks, for instance, to the P/E of stocks within, say, the fruit industry. That would be comparing apples with oranges.

What Is the Yield?

A stock's yield is calculated by dividing the annual dividend by its share price. For example, if a company pays an annual dividend that totals $0.50 per share and the shares are trading at $5.00, then that stock enjoys a 10 percent yield.

The yield is just one way of calculating your return on investment, but it's a good one, especially if you are interested in generating an income.

However, do keep in mind that not all stocks pay dividends. Often the company's management will decide that money that would otherwise be paid in dividends should be placed back into the company to stimulate further growth. Very few fast-growing companies rarely pay any dividends at all, but because their share price is constantly increasing in value, you will realize a bulk yield as soon as you cash in your shares.

Book-to-Bill Ratio

The book-to-bill ratio compares orders received ("booked" business) with orders satisfied (goods or services shipped and so "billed"). Typically, the book-to-bill ratio is applied to a three-month period and announced along with the quarterly results.

A company with a book-to-bill of 1.0 is running steady, satisfying its incoming orders with a steady stream of goods or services provided. A company with a book-to-bill of higher than 1.0 (say 1.1 or even 1.5) has more incoming business than it can immediately satisfy. A book-to-bill of less than 1.0 shows a company temporarily or permanently in decline.

The book-to-bill ratio is an interesting indicator because it shows how well a company is doing at the present. A constantly high ratio shows steady growth while a constantly low ratio shows a steady decline. However, bear in mind that seasonal downturns can play havoc with the book-to-bill.

Like all investment indicators, this one should be considered historically across as great a period of time as possible.

Walking the Dogs of the Dow

The Dogs of the Dow is a well-known investment system that has historically outperformed most mutual funds. The strategy is easy to implement: Just place an equal amount of money into the 10 highest-yielding Dow stocks. Hold them for one year. On the anniversary of that first investment, work out the new list of highest-yielding stocks and replace those that have fallen off. To really make the investment grow, reinvest all dividends.

The Dogs of the Dow works because it deals with companies that have already been through the Dow Jones filtering process. These are large and stable companies.

However, keep in mind at all times that the Dogs is a long-term strategy. The Dogs approach has returned 16.85 percent for 25 years, but in some years it did quite poorly while in others it performed brilliantly. The only sure-fire approach is to invest your money and leave it invested. Even if the Dogs takes a nosedive, it should eventually pick up.

Quicken is great for managing a Dogs portfolio. Not only can it update your share prices automatically, it also can compare your Dogs portfolio to the market indices discussed earlier in this part.

There are several variations on the Dogs given fanciful names such as The Puppies of the Dow and so on. One of the most common is to take the ten highest-yielding stocks but invest only in the lower five. This approach returns about four percent more than the standard Dogs, soundly thrashing most mutual funds.

TIP   **Going to the Dogs**   For more information on the Dogs of the Dow and alternative approaches, visit the Motley Fool HQ at **http://www.fool.com/ DDow/DDExplained.htm**. If an average return on investment of 22.23 percent sounds tasty, you're in luck. Otherwise, visit the Dogs of the Dow page at **http:// www.dogsofthedow.com/**. Each site contains a lot of information on this investment approach.

Using the High, Low, and Close Prices

One final investment technique doesn't take any special effort. It relies on the high, low, and close prices of a stock. When a stock is in decline or on the rise, it won't necessarily move in a consistent manner. Indeed, it will probably wander up and down day by day. However, looked at over a period of weeks or even months, there is, in retrospect, a fairly clear trend.

The trick comes in picking whether a stock has turned the corner—that is, it has moved from a decline to a climb or vice versa—or if it is still wandering at apparent random. While there is no hard and fast rule, the closing price of the stock can form a useful indicator.

As you most likely know, the high, low, and close lines show the stock's highest-priced trade and lowest-priced trade during the day. The close line shows at what position that stock closed. By definition, the close must sit somewhere between or on top of the high point and the low point.

You can view these lines if you have regularly updated the prices online by using the security Detail view. Open your Portfolio view and double-click the security you want to inspect. Change the date range to bring it back to a week or month, and click the upward-facing arrow in the top-right corner of the graph window to blow the graph up to full-screen size. By looking at how close the close line lies to the high or low lines, you can obtain a very good idea as to whether that stock has closed on a negative or positive note.

 High, Low and Close Pricing You can see the prices behind the high, low, and close lines by choosing **Update, Edit Price History**. This window also shows the volume of stock traded on any day.

For example, a stock that closes closer to the low could well be in a continuing decline. However, a stock that has been declining but closed close to the high, could well have turned the corner and is now on the up-and-up.

There is nothing certain about this indicator and it will often prove totally misleading, but often it proves correct. Besides, playing the stock market is a game of chance, so anything that can shorten your odds should be a welcome addition to your investment toolbox.

In this lesson, you learned several useful investment strategies, as well as how to interpret key financial data such as the P/E ratio, dividend yield, and book-to-bill ratio. In the next lesson, you will learn how to use the powerful Investor Insight.

431

Using Investor Insight

In this lesson, you learn how to obtain and use Investor Insight, a researching, graphing, and securities news-reading tool.

Introducing Investor Insight

Investor Insight is a powerful online data-mining tool that will help you to manage your investments in stocks and mutual funds. It works hand-in-hand with Quicken to give you access to securities news, historical prices, and more.

Investor Insight adds several key capabilities to your investment toolbox. These include:

- Historical data downloads of up to five years for any stock or mutual fund listed on NYSE, AMEX, or NASDAQ, as well as access to historical information on thousands of unlisted funds.

- Access to a wide range of newsworthy information including press releases and articles. Clippings originate with Dow Jones News Service, PR NewsWire, and Business Wire.

- Two-way communications capability with Quicken that will let you mirror your portfolio in both programs.

- Powerful analysis capabilities that chart and compare particular stocks, funds, and downloadable stockmarket indices.

- The ability to create your own indices to track particular segments of the market.

- Automatic personal reports that combine price data and news in a user-friendly, printed format.

- For a small extra fee, access to in-depth company reports.

Of course, all of this functionality comes at a cost. At this writing, an Investor Insight online account costs $9.95 per month, but that is subject to change.

Investor Insight is easy to use, but it is also somewhat limited. For instance, while it will display the current P/E Ratio and Yield for any stock, there is no way to use that information in reports. You cannot, for instance, generate a query that shows the top 200 stocks with the highest yield; perfect for people looking for high-income stocks. Nor can you query for the stocks with the strongest P/E ratio; which means you miss out on a handy indicator for strong future growth.

This makes Investor Insight an excellent portfolio management system, but not the best research tool available. It should be used alongside Quicken's other researching capabilities, not as a replacement.

TIP **Researching Investments** Intuit provides a service across the Internet that will help you to research stocks according to highest yield and many other factors. Select **Online, Quicken on the Web, Quicken.com** and click **Investments** in the Web browser window. Once the new page loads, click **Research** to sift through up to 12,000 stocks.

With Investor Insight, you can:

- Copy your portfolio from Quicken.
- Add securities to the watch list.
- Create graphs.
- Record transactions.
- Update your data across the Internet.
- Read your security news.
- Create your own personal investment report.

Obtaining and Installing Investor Insight

To download Investor Insight, load your Web browser, go to **http:// www.intuit.com/investorinsight/** and follow the on-screen instructions. Once Investor Insight has been installed, it will appear in its own program group and the Windows Start menu.

Copying Your Portfolio from Quicken

If you have already set up a Quicken portfolio, you can quickly and easily copy that data to Investor Insight. Investor Insight supports four types of portfolio. Only one of these can be used for your Quicken data. The four types are:

Simple Maintains a list of stocks, the shares held in each, and the price paid for those shares. Simple portfolios do not support transactions such as buying, selling, and reinvestment. They are, in every sense, simple portfolios.

Advanced Supports all of the usual transactions, with the notable exception of short sales. If you use Investor Insight to manage your portfolio rather than doing so through Quicken, the Advanced portfolio will provide you with a good array of features.

Quicken Based on the data contained in your Quicken investment accounts. While you cannot enter transactions into a Quicken portfolio through Investor Insight, you can open that portfolio from within Investor Insight, view the holdings and performance, and quickly update the portfolio with any new transactions entered into Quicken.

Net Worth A super-portfolio that doesn't hold investments of its own. Instead, it can combine the holdings of every other portfolio accessible through Investor Insight. Just indicate those portfolios that you want to contribute to the big picture, and it will do the rest.

You can create all but the Quicken portfolio by selecting **List, Portfolio List**. Click **New** in the Portfolio window to open the dialog box shown in Figure 8.1, type in a name for the Portfolio, select its type, and click **OK**.

If you create a portfolio of the Simple type, you can immediately start adding shares. See "Recording Transactions in Simple Portfolios" later in this chapter.

If you create a portfolio of the Advanced type, you will need to provide the portfolio's starting date and its cash balance.

Why would you want to track a portfolio in Investor Insight that isn't also mirrored in Quicken? In short, it's a great way to look after portfolios when you don't want those portfolios to make any contribution to your finances.

Figure 8.1 Investor Insight supports four types of portfolios. If you want to maintain a portfolio external to your Quicken data, select one of the three types shown here.

To create a Quicken portfolio, you must connect Investor Insight to Quicken. Follow these steps:

1. Launch Investor Insight using the Windows Start menu. The first time you run this program, you need to navigate past a splash page announcing Investor Insight's features. Just click to move on.

2. Select **File, Get Quicken Investments**.

3. Use the window shown in Figure 8.2 to select the portfolios that you want to import into Investor Insight.

4. Click **Get Data** when you finish. Investor Insight will import each of the portfolios you selected, turning each into an Investor Insight portfolio of the Quicken type.

CAUTION

Importing Stocks Without Tickers If any of your Quicken stocks lack ticker symbols, they will be imported into Investor Insight as cash equal to the value of the stock held in Quicken. Fortunately, you can use Investor Insight's ticker searcher described below to match those stocks to actual symbols.

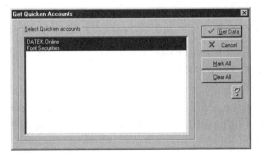

Figure 8.2 Investor Insight can work with all, some, or none of your Quicken portfolios; select them here and click **OK**.

Adding Securities to the Watch List

The Investor Insight Watch List shown in Figure 8.3 is the window you'll use most often. You can use the Watch List to track stocks, funds, and market indices. Unlike Quicken's Watch List, which is separate to other securities, you can only add stocks or funds to your Investor Insight portfolios that are included in this global Watch List. However, if that stock or fund is listed in Quicken and you import a Quicken portfolio, Investor Insight will automatically add it to the Watch List. However, as mentioned in the earlier caution, it must have a ticker symbol to appear as stock, rather than cash.

Figure 8.3 The Watch List maintains a list of all your selected securities and market indices.

To add your own securities to the Watch List, follow these steps:

1. If the Watch List window isn't open, select **List, Watch List**.

2. Click **Add** to open the Add Securities window shown in Figure 8.4.

3. To find a security by its ticker symbol, select **Symbol** in the **Find By** group. Enter the symbol in the text box provided.

4. To find a security by its corporate or fund name, select **Name** in the Find By group. Enter the name in the text box provided. Don't worry if you don't know all of the names; Investor Insight can search on just the first letter or two.

5. Click **Search** to find that security. Investor Insight will display up to 50 matching securities in the list box.

6. Select the security and click **Add**. Otherwise, refine the search still further and go again.

TIP **Show All Securities** To save disk space, Investor Insight works with a hidden list of securities. If you'd rather view all the stored securities in the list box every time you start a search, click **Show All Securities.** It will take a minute or two to build the index, but it only has to do that once. The next time you open this window, you will see every security available.

7. Once a security has been added, click **Close** to close the window or type in another search to add another. Investor Insight can track a total of 500 securities and indices at once, although downloading the quotes for each may slow down your online sessions.

8. If you want to update the new security prices after closing the Add Securities window, click **Update Now** to download the latest quotes, news, and e-mail. If you haven't used Investor Insight's Internet features before, you will need to answer **No** to the question that you already have a name and password. Fill out the application form as discussed in the "Updating Across the Internet" section later in this lesson.

Figure 8.4 Investor Insight includes every stock or fund listed on the major U.S. exchanges.

Once a security has been added to the watch list, you can either read **News** about that security, view its **Chart**, make and read your own **Notes**, or **Remove** it from the list. To record transactions that will change your holdings in that security, go across to the Portfolio List by selecting **List, Portfolio List**.

Creating Graphs

One of Investor Insight's most impressive features is one that far exceeds Quicken's own capabilities. This is the graphing feature shown in Figure 8.5. To create a graph, follow these steps:

1. If it isn't already open, pull up the Watch list by selecting List, **Watch List**.

2. Select the security and click the **Chart** button in the Watch List window.

3. Use the buttons below the graph to change the security or the period of time over which the graph is drawn.

4. Click **Options** to superimpose market indices, draw a moving average, display the hot spots, and specify high and low reference lines.

5. View the high, low, and close on any day, by clicking anywhere in the graph with the left mouse button and dragging the vertical bar left or right. To set that date precisely, change it using the date field in the upper left corner of the graph window.

To view graphs of every security included in your Watch List, select **Chart, Price-Volume Overview**. Double-click any box to zoom to a detailed chart. To view the relative performance of your investments, select **Chart, Comparative Charts**.

Figure 8.5   This graph shows a mutual fund, a 50-day moving average, and performance in comparison to the S&P 500 market index.

Recording Transactions

If you will only use Investor Insight with your Quicken data, you should record all of your portfolio transactions using the Quicken investment management capabilities. However, if you do want to use Investor Insights features to manage portfolios separate from Quicken, you need to decide first whether you need a simple or advanced portfolio.

Recording Transactions in Simple Portfolios

The simple portfolio is limited to tracking the number of shares you own in a certain stock, as well as a single per share purchase price. This is ideal if you don't do a lot of trading but is also rather limiting.

If you haven't just created this portfolio, check that it is open by selecting if from the Portfolio List and clicking **Open**. Select the stock or fund from the dialog box shown in Figure 8.6. Click **Add** to copy that security into the portfolio. Enter the number of shares purchased and the purchase price.

Click **OK** to record the transaction.

CAUTION

How Do I Add Shares Purchased at Several Different Prices?
Because the Simple portfolio doesn't support more than one transaction for any share type, you should calculate the average share price and use that instead. Just calculate the total amount paid for each bundle of shares. Sum the totals and divide that by the total shares purchased. For example, if you had purchased 10 shares at $25 and 5 shares at $40, you would record 15 as the total shares owned and $30 (10x25 + 5x40 / 15) as the average purchase price.

If you sell all of your holdings in a particular stock or fund, delete that security from your portfolio. Investor Insight doesn't track the cash balance of this type of portfolio so there is no need to indicate the sale price.

If you sell part of your holdings, don't subtract the sale price from the total and deduct the shares sold as that will skew your market gain. Instead, you should edit that security to reflect the number of shares left and their average purchase price.

If you have purchased more than one bundle of shares, you can choose which bundle you sell by the FIFO (first in, first out)—or LIFO (last in, first out) methods. FIFO will bring you the highest immediate capital gain. LIFO defers that capital gain, but if you should sell all of your holdings, the gain will be correspondingly larger. Alternatively, switch to an advanced portfolio.

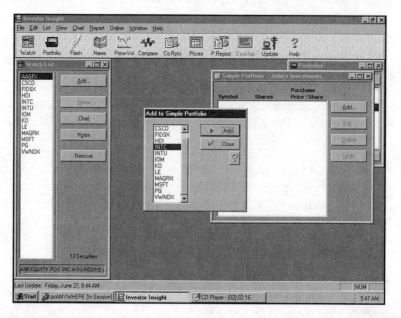

Figure 8.6   To add shares to a Simple portfolio, select your security from the list. This list is limited to securities tracked using the Watch List.

Recording Transactions in Advanced Portfolios

An Investor Insight Advanced portfolio is almost as comprehensive as Quicken's Investment Register. If your Advanced portfolio isn't already open, select it from the Portfolio List and click **Open**. You will see the window shown in Figure 8.7.

Advanced portfolios use an investment register approach, maintaining an account balance and recording the transactions that affect various shareholdings.

The middle of the window contains a scrolling list of transactions. Around the left and lower sides of the window are the various transaction buttons. Use them to perform the following functions:

Buy   Purchase a parcel of shares or funds. You may only purchase securities included in the Watch List.

Sell   Sell a parcel of shares or funds. You may choose the lot that should be applied to each sale. Investor Insight does not support short sales.

Contrib.   Add funds to the account.

Withdr.   Withdraw funds from the account.

Income   Record dividends received, long- and short-term capital gains, and interest income.

Split   Record a stock split.

Adj. Cash   Reconcile the account. The adjustment may be recorded using the same categories as the Income function.

Edit   Edit the selected transaction. As a shortcut, double-click any transaction to open the Edit window.

Delete   Delete the selected transaction.

Undo   Undo the last command.

While this transaction window approaches the power of Quicken's Investment register, it isn't quite so comprehensive.

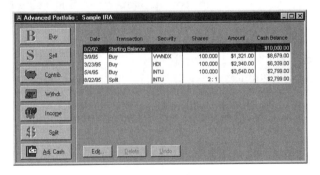

Figure 8.7 Advanced Portfolios work similar to the Quicken Investment register. Notice the Starting Balance transaction in this sample portfolio.

Updating Across the Internet

Previous releases of Investor Insight relied on the user manually entering daily, weekly, or monthly price movements. Version 2.0 and later are all Internet-aware.

Through a standard dial-up or permanent connection, you can automatically update the share prices and download the latest e-mail news from Intuit. Intuit's news offerings usually consist of announcements regarding updated versions of the Insight software or special offers, as well as news releases that pertain to any stocks included in the current Watch List.

Before Investor Insight can access the Internet, you need to sign up for an account. Follow these steps to sign up and complete the connection:

1. To go to the License Agreement window, select **Online, Update**.

2. If you have previously signed up for Investor Insight, answer **Yes** to the next window, type in your previously assigned name and password, and skip the rest of these steps.

3. If you aren't a current user, answer **No**, read the Investor Insight Subscription Agreement and, if you agree, click **Accept**.

4. Fill in the user registration, type in an account name, and select a password.

5. Click **Register Now**. If Investor Insight already has a user by your account name, it will adjust the account name by adding a single digit to the end. The software uses the RSA encryption system to ensure that your credit card details are protected in transit.

6. Once you finish, Investor Insight will connect, update your quotes, grab the latest company news, collect any waiting e-mail, and disconnect.

You can use the Online menu to change your connection settings as required.

Reading the News

Have you read your security news today? If not, Investor Insight's Internet updating service will fill you in. By matching the stocks and funds included in the Watch List with press releases, reports, and other news put out by companies, fund managers, and news services, Investor Insight delivers timely news about your investments not just to your door but straight to your computer.

Investor Insight's approach matches the news to a stock or fund's price history graph. Every time a piece of news comes in, Investor Insight adds a small red dot to the graph. Just look at your graph, click the dot, and read the news. This system acts as a handy timeline that not only shows when there is news to be read, but also what effect that news had on the security's price! This is fun, but not very useful for day-to-day management. After all, by the time you've read the stock and watched the price move, you might have missed the boat.

Still, maybe not. A single piece of news can turn a stock around, sending it on a long trip up the charts. Consider, for instance, the chart shown in Figure 8.8. An analyst announced that he expected Harley Davidson to better its earnings over the next two years and pegged it with a long-term buy rating. The stock immediately responded and two months later was still climbing.

If you had been watching this stock and started purchasing after that announcement, selling shortly after the downturn at the top, you would have made a fast 41 percent. Of course, this is only a short term gain, and it is achieved through the wonders of hindsight, but it does demonstrate how Investor Insight broadens your information base. While you won't get to hear the whispers on the trading floor, you may receive important financial news before it filters through to the financial press.

While the linked charts and news is a useful utility, you'll probably find yourself turning to the broader news facility for most of your information browsing.

To use the news facility, follow these steps:

1. If it isn't already open, go to the Watch list by selecting **List, Watch List**.
2. Select the security and click the **News** button in the Watch List window. This will open the window shown in Figure 8.9.
3. You can filter the news by each security or click **All** to view the news for every security.
4. Select the news item in the right-hand list box, and either scroll through the item in the lower window or click the **Scan** button to jump to the next mention of the security's name in the text.

5. Click **Chart** to jump to that security's chart or **Next** to move to the next news item. The news is arranged from most recent to oldest, so **Next** actually moves you back in time. Curiously, to move forward, you must click **Back**.

6. When you finish, click the **Close (x)** box to exit the window.

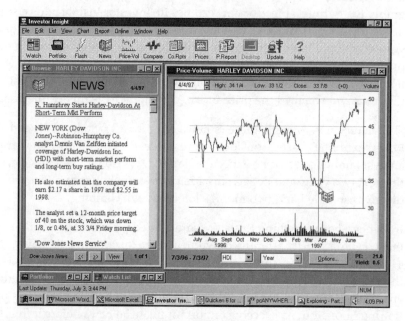

Figure 8.8   A market analyst announced high expectations for Harley Davidson as shown in the left hand window. The "newspaper" mouse pointer highlights the news on the price history chart.

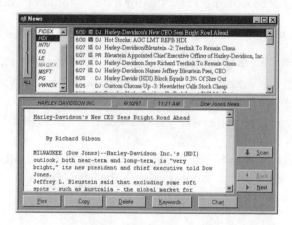

Figure 8.9   The News browser is a great way to quickly gain a summary of recent events.

Creating Your Own Personal Report

Undoubtedly one of Quicken's best features, the Personal report combines graphs and news to provide you with the complete picture. If you want to stay on top of your investments, print out one of these once a week; you'll catch up on the latest news. Investor Insight is smart enough to generate a front page that summarizes movements over the period chosen for the report. It will highlight the gainers and losers and show you how each investment has compared to other investments. The news relating to each security includes a great little index that will help you to find the stories you're most interested in. To create a Personal report, just do the following:

1. Select **Report, Personal Report**. You will see a window similar to that shown in Figure 8.10.

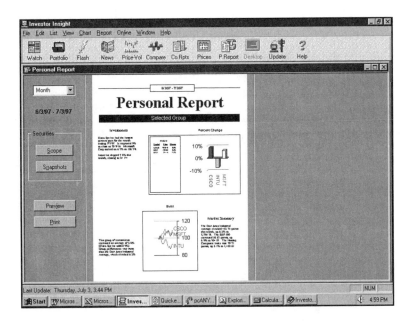

Figure 8.10 Print out a weekly or monthly Personal report to stay on top of your investments.

2. Take the time to customize this report. Investor Insight sets a limit of 50 pages for any Personal report, but it's easy to exceed that. You can customize the report with the **Scope** button. Select the securities from the list or choose a particular portfolio or custom index. If you select all of your securities, the Personal report will only include the top 16 with the greatest price movements. You can also change the company **Snapshots;** EACH snapshot includes a chart and news overview.

3. Click the **Preview** button to see the report on-screen, or **Print** to generate a hard copy.

Other Features

Investor Insight is a powerful product and has features too numerous to include in what is, after all, a book about Quicken. This lesson has given you an introduction and will help you to start, but don't think the procedures described here are the limit to Investor Insight's prowess. There are many other reports and charts that will throw new light on your portfolios.

Whether you are a small- or big-time investor, this product can provide some of the most beneficial insights you are likely to see. Even better, it's cheaper than a full-service brokerage house and will probably provide you with better and more timely information. Used alongside Quicken, the two make a particularly powerful pair.

In this lesson, you learned how to use Investor Insight. In the next lesson, you will learn about the Mutual Fund Finder.

The Mutual Fund Finder

In this lesson, you learn to use the Mutual Fund Finder. This is supplied with Quicken Deluxe and Quicken Home and Business.

Understanding Mutual Funds

There are quite literally hundreds of thousands of mutual funds spread around the world, some of them with investments totaling tens of billions of dollars.

Mutual funds offer their investors several advantages including professional management, the ability to cost-effectively invest in a highly diverse portfolio, and the opportunity to have your share of potentially quite lucrative investments that you wouldn't otherwise be able to afford. One example of this is a mutual fund that includes investments in commercial real estate.

They also have their disadvantages. If you are a very hands-on investor, you might regret not being able to determine how your money is invested, at least within the broader limits of that mutual fund's published investment guidelines. For example, you might invest in a mutual fund that does specialize in commercial real estate, only to discover that they seem to be pouring your funds into an area you believe is headed for an extended property slump.

Some of the advantages to be had from investing in a mutual fund include:

- Access to a greater range of investments
- Your investments are looked after by full-time professional fund managers
- A broad selection of flavors of fund, from small but aggressive through to big and safe

- It's easy to divest yourself of a fund, quickly converting your investment to cash
- Utilities such as Mutual Fund Finder and Intuit's online Fund Finding service make it easy to track down the fund that's perfect for you

Some of the disadvantages include:

- Losing a percentage of the return to management fees
- Possible entry and exit fees
- Poor market performance by the larger funds, which are too big to be nimble
- You have no say in the management of a professional fund
- You may feel out of touch with your investment

There are mutual funds to suit almost any taste. Many smaller funds offer aggressive portfolios targeted at emerging companies, and occasionally these funds will boast enormous yields.

However, as always, the more aggressive the fund, the riskier your investment. In some years they may prove very big winners, while others prove to be significant losers.

For every aggressive fund there are any number of conservative funds offering steady, stable and long-term investments in a range of big, solid corporations and property.

The Mutual Fund Finder is packed with information on over 4,000 top-performing funds. This utility will help you to find the fund that's right for you. It offers the following capabilities:

- Find the highest yielding or fastest growing funds.
- Find funds that are currently underperforming so that you can invest at the bottom of their growth cycle.
- Filter funds by a variety of criteria including how long the fund manager has been on the job, the fund's rating, minimum investment amount, ongoing fees and more.
- Target the funds in a particular asset class. The classes include aggressive growth, corporate bonds, foreign stock and certain industry sectors such as technology, financial, health, utilities and many more.
- View extensive performance data on any fund.

The D.I.Y. Mutual Fund What if you've looked around, researched the Net until your fingers are ready to drop off at the knuckles, and still can't find a fund that offers you what you need? Perhaps you don't like the thought of paying management fees, yet you still want some of the benefits of mutual funds such as the pooling of resources and the sharing of costs.

In that case, why not create your own mutual fund? After all, a mutual fund is by definition just a pool of funds contributed to by more than one person.

Consider starting an investment club. You can't advertise the fund, but there's nothing stopping you from getting your colleagues, neighbors and friends involved. When the fund purchases a block of shares, the cost of that purchase is distributed across all units, just the way it occurs in a commercial fund. Start by investing in liquid assets so that anyone who wants to pull-out can have their funds returned almost immediately. Use Quicken and Investor Insight to track the fund's daily or weekly value. This will give you a working NAV (Net Asset Value), so that you can price the fund's shares accordingly. After a while, the fund may grow large enough to invest at least part of its capital into less liquid assets such as residential or commercial real estate.

However, remember that above all else a friendly fund such as this must stay friendly. Like all personal investing, it can be fun and very rewarding, but approached the wrong way it can cause resentment, stress and the splitting up of good friendships.

Starting the Mutual Fund Finder

You can access the Mutual Fund Finder in two ways:

- From within Quicken, select the menu **Features**, **Investments**, **Mutual Fund Finder**.
- From Windows 95, select the Windows **Start** button and choose **Programs**, **Quicken**, **Mutual Fund Finder**.

The Mutual Fund Finder opens into the EasyStep interview. This interview will take you through the following steps:

1. To move into the full EasyStep process, select **Search by Criteria**, click **Next** and move to the next step. Otherwise, select **Search by Name**, click **Next**, type in the name or ticker symbol and click **Done**.

2. Select the category of asset classes that should be included in the search. The **Basic Asset Classes** are determined by Callan Associates, a fund ratings company. These are a great way to target funds within several large

groups. The **Extended Asset Classes** are determined by Morningstar and let you target much finer classes of funds. You can select classes from each group and search on them simultaneously. To select more than one asset class, just use the mouse to click on each while holding down the Ctrl key. Click **Next** after this and every following step.

3. Select the maximum front load allowed. The front load is a percentage amount charged on all funds deposited with that fund. You can choose between any front load, no front load or those funds up to a range of maximum percentage amounts.

4. Morningstar gives funds a star rating. A 5-star fund provides excellent return and low risk. Select **Star Rating of at least 5 stars** when only the best will do.

5. Risky or aggressive funds may generate higher returns, but they also run the risk of dropping sharply in value. These ratings are provided by Morningstar. The most stable funds are rated as low risk. Even if you have specified a star rating, you should use this selection to weed out the riskiest funds.

6. How long has the manager been on the job? A top-performing fund with a long-term manager is more likely to continue doing well than a fund with an untested manager. This is another risk decision that only you can make, but don't automatically dismiss a fund because the manager hasn't been on the job for the equivalent of a presidential term. What if the manager was head-hunted away from another top-performing fund? It happens.

7. Some funds limit the minimum initial investment as a way to cut down on internal paperwork and, presumably, management fees. The limit can vary widely, ranging from just one or two hundred dollars up to $25,000 and beyond.

8. The expense ratio is the annual amount charged by a fund in management fees. Aggressive funds tend to be more expensive (they do more work, after all) but also provide greater potential return. Use this window to choose the maximum allowable expense ratio.

9. If you intend to invest in mutual funds that provide an income, use the Dividend Yield selection to choose those funds with various minimum dividends up to at least 10 percent. If you are investing strictly for growth, specify a very low dividend yield.

10. How has this fund performed in the past? The performance is based on dividends and growth. Use this selection to exclude all funds below a minimum level of growth.

11. This final step lets you further filter the funds to those that have been screened and recommended by Callan Associates or are indexed funds.

 Indexed Funds Indexed funds follow the market. If the market goes up, their value goes up. If the market does down, their value goes down.

12. Review your choices in the Summary Screen shown in Figure 9.1 and click **Done**. The Mutual Fund Finder will quickly draw up a list of all of those funds that satisfy your criteria.

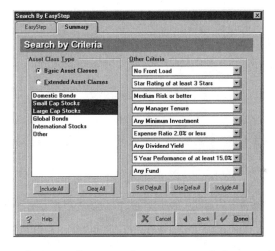

Figure 9.1 Use the Summary Screen to fine-tune your choices made so far. The parameters in this example aim for high-growth, low-cost funds.

Researching Funds

Once you have created the list, it's time to decide which funds really fit the bill. Use this as a guide to working with the fund list window.

Once you have found one that piques your interest, double-click it or select it and click **Fund Details** to open up a veritable wealth of information.

Click here to change
the selection criteria
for the current list of
funds.

Click here to search
for a fund by name
of ticker symbol.

Click here to
redo the
EasyStep
interview.

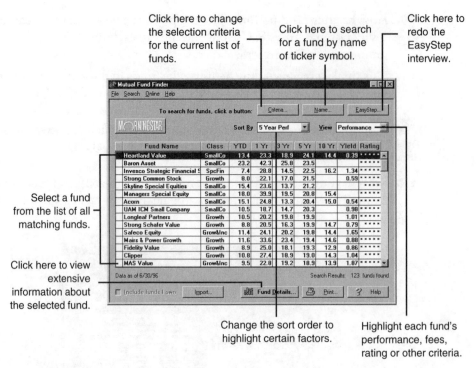

Select a fund
from the list of all
matching funds.

Click here to view
extensive
information about
the selected fund.

Change the sort order to
highlight certain factors.

Highlight each fund's
performance, fees,
rating or other criteria.

Figure 9.2 The Mutual Fund Finder browser list is great for quickly comparing different funds.

TIP **Strategy-Based Funds** Not all funds invest in certain areas or markets. Some operate on an investment stratagem, applying principles such as the Dogs of the Dow (see Lesson 7) to all their purchases. Investing in these funds will save you the cost of the annual share purchases and sales involved in following your own Dogs approach. However, you should balance the amount the fund costs you to invest against the fees charged by discount brokers.

Understanding the Fund Summary

The Fund Summary window provides the following groups of information:

Header Fund ticker symbol, name and contact telephone number.

Asset Categorizations under the Basic and Extended Asset Classes developed by Callan Associates and Morningstar. This group also shows the yield, net assets (equal to the market capitalization) and the current

NAV (net asset value). The NAV is calculated on the market capitalization and the number of share outstanding. A growth fund's NAV should climb while an income generating fund sacrifices NAV for yield.

Total Returns   This group shows the yield and growth for this fund averaged over certain time periods. The returns are compared to two indices, showing you how well this fund matched the market. Click **Load Adjusted** to take into account initial share purchase costs.

General Info   This group is useful because it shows not just the contact information but also how many years the manager has been on the job, when the fund was formed and the minimum initial purchase and additional purchase values.

Rating & Risk   The Morningstar ratings and risk were discussed above, but you may not have heard of the Beta and R2 indicators. Beta measures the volatility of a fund. The market is rated as Beta 1.0. A fund with a Beta of 1.2 is expected to perform 20 percent better than the market on a rise, but perform 20 percent worse than the rest of the market on a fall. In other words, its rises and falls tend to be 20 percent greater than the rest of the market. A fund with a Beta of 0.8 will perform 20 percent worse than the market on a rise, but perform 20 percent better than the rest of the market on a fall. This fund tends to rise and fall 20 percent less than the rest of the market.

The R2 (really R-squared) indicator is a percentage measure that shows how this fund's price movements match those of the market. An R2 of 100 means that this fund's price movements match the market 100 percent of the time. (Not in size, but in direction and relative strength.) An R2 of 50 percent means that only half of the rises and falls can be attributed to general market forces. The higher the R2, the more reliance you can place on the Beta value.

Fees & Expenses   The Maximum Front Load covers sales and marketing costs. It does not gain you, the investor, any benefit, so nil load funds are best. The Expense Ratio shows all ongoing fees as a percentage of the fund's asset base. The example fund shown in Figure 9.3 spends around $19,640,250 every year on promotional and management activities. This is money that should otherwise be coming to you. The Redemption is an exit fee charged when you cash in your stocks. The 12 b-1 is a percentage-based annual fee charged for distribution and marketing.

Style   The style grid is created by Morningstar and shows their interpretation of the fund's investment philosophy. The size indicators (Small,

Medium, and Large) show the capitalization of the stocks in which this fund invests. The return indicators (Value, Blend, and Growth) show whether the fund invests in stocks the manager believes to be underperforming but on the verge of taking off (this is a Value portfolio), increasing in value at a rate faster than the rest of the market (this is a Growth portfolio), or some mix of the two (this is a Blend portfolio). This grid gives you a quick overview of the type of investments this fund typically makes. For instance, the example fund obviously invests in small company stocks that it hopes will turn into high growth stocks.

TIP   **Printing the Summary**   Just click the **Print** button down the bottom of the summary window to print a handy report. This is especially useful if you are weighing up the differences between several funds.

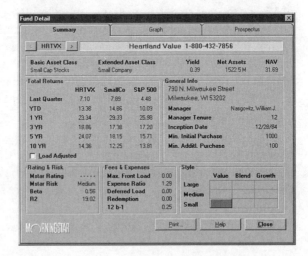

Figure 9.3 The Fund Detail's Summary tab is packed with information on a fund's performance, size, rating, and more.

Reading the Fund's Graph

Click the **Graph** tab of the Fund Detail dialog to open the window shown in Figure 9.4.

There are three main sections to this window. Use the uppermost to switch between **Yearly Return** and **Cumulative** graphs, and also to choose the period for the graph. To see how well a fund performed over time relative to the market indices, switch to the Cumulative graph. However, to get a good feel for a fund's volatility, look at it through the Yearly Return graph. While considering all funds according to their 10-year performance might seem the safest way to go, comparing graphics on a 5-year basis will highlight those funds which have either changed managers or strategy and significantly boosted their returns.

The middle section is, of course, the graph itself. Mutual Fund Finder compares the funds to its chosen market indices. This graph is a great way to see the Beta and R2 indicators in action, and how they can, on occasion, prove rather misleading. For example, the fund shown in Figure 9.4 is built around small company stocks. The S&P 500 measures the 500 largest stocks. Obviously this fund doesn't move in step with the S&P 500. In fact, the R2 indicator shows the it only moves in step less than 20 percent of the time. However, as you can see from the graph, on most years when the S&P 500 grew, so too did the fund. There are only two years in which it bucked the trend. Incidentally, the Beta indicator of .56 shows that the fund should perform on the whole only 50 percent as well and only 50 percent as poorly as the S&P 500. However, in the graph you can see that the relative performance is truly all over the place. A low R2 suggests an inaccurate Beta, and this part, at least, is clearly the case.

TIP   **Printing the Graph**   To print a copy of this graph, click the **Print** button. The Mutual Fund Finder will arrange the graph in a portrait (vertical) format. This accentuates the differences between each column.

The lower section shows how this fund has performed when compared to other funds in the same Extended Asset Class developed by Morningstar. This is useful because it compares peers with peers. If your fund has managed to spend over 25 percent of its time in the top 25 percent, or 50 percent of it's time in the top 50 percent, it is, on the whole, doing better than the rest. The sample fund shown in has spent 60 percent of its time in the top 25 percent, most of that recently. You could probably look upon such a fund very favorably.

Ordering a Prospectus

Before a mutual fund can be recognized as such, it must lodge a prospectus with the SEC (Securities and Exchange Commission).

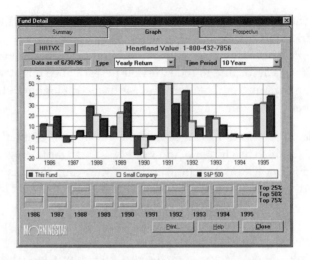

Figure 9.4 The graph provides an instant overview of a fund's performance.

 Prospectus A prospectus defines the parameters under which that fund will operate. It specifies the type of investments that fund will participate in and describes in precise detail the fund's objectives, fee structure, strategy and management.

The Mutual Fund Finder can use the Internet to link to the Quicken Financial Network. If information on the fund or its fund family is available across the Internet, you will be able to click the Fund Family button to obtain more information.

If the prospectus is available across the Internet, just click the Prospectus button to read it online.

If the Fund Family and Prospectus buttons are grayed out, that means the information you require isn't available online. Instead, follow the instructions displayed on the Prospectus tab to receive that information through the regular mail.

 TIP **How does Mutual Fund Finder know what's available and what's not?** Every time you update Mutual Fund Finder you also update the list of Fund Family and Prospectus information available across the Internet.

Updating Mutual Fund Finder

The information contained in the Mutual Fund Finder doesn't automatically update. However, it can be updated across the Internet—at a cost. Intuit sells updates to Mutual Fund Finder for $4.95. These are released once every quarter.

To update your copy of Mutual Fund Finder, select the menu **Online**, **Update Mutual Fund Data**. Mutual Fund Finder will provide the date of your most recent update. To update the data, click **Continue**. This will take you online, load your default Web Browser, and point you at the Financial Planner Home Page. Find the link **Mutual Fund Data Update**, click once and then follow the instructions on your screen. You will need to provide your credit card information, but the connection is secure, so your details should remain safe during transit.

In this lesson, you learned to use the Mutual Fund Finder supplied with Quicken Deluxe. In Part 6, you will learn about some advanced tips and tricks that will make Quicken more customized, productive and useful than ever before.

Advanced Tips
& Tricks

Customizing Quicken's Color Schemes

In this lesson, you learn about Quicken's color scheme, color palettes, and the color initialization file.

Changing Quicken's Colors

Why would you want to change Quicken's colors? The answer is easy: because it's fun! Forget all that hard-hitting investment advice, the brain-bending income tax guide, and the small-business accounting contortions. Despite its power, Quicken really is a fun product to use—by design. Otherwise, why would Intuit have thrown in those interesting menu sounds or that ka-ching! of the cash register every time you enter a new transaction?

The color scheme you choose will almost certainly change the way you view your figures, subconsciously or not. Fortunately, Quicken doesn't actually change the color of the figures. If your checking account's in the black, it will stay in the black; if it's in the red, you can't escape that slash of bleeding ink.

While it is impossible to show you the color schemes in a book with black and white screen shots, we can do the next best thing: show you how to find them for yourself. There are two ways to change Quicken's colors. The first is to use the menus, which is long and tedious, while the second is to use the right mouse button, which is fast and fun.

Right-Clicking to Change the Color Scheme

To change the color scheme using the right mouse button, right-click anywhere on the screen except within the icon bar or the working area of an open window (for instance, the register lines in a register).

Select **Color Schemes** from the shortcut menu. Select the target scheme from the pop-up menu, as shown in Figure 1.1, and click the left or right mouse button to select it. Quicken will instantly apply the new scheme.

Figure 1.1 The quickest way to change the Quicken color scheme is to use the context-sensitive shortcut menu.

Suggested Schemes

Unlike many other programs, Quicken doesn't allow you to individually customize each scheme. In other words, no do-it-yourself interior design. However, you will find many professional designs in the Color Schemes list.

The list changes depending on whether you use a 256-color, or greater, palette or a 16-color palette. If you use a 16-color palette, you may be able to increase this to 256 colors, but you should consult your Windows 95 documentation or the documentation that came with your computer.

Table 1.1 shows every Quicken color scheme, along with the minimum color palette required to use it.

Table 1.1 Color Schemes

Name	16-Color	256-Color
Aqua Screen	x	
Arabian Nights		x
The Blues		x
Black and Blue	x	
Blue Frenzy	x	
Club Room 1		x
Club Room 2		x
Default 16-color	x	
Default 256-color		x
Earth Tones		x
Fresh Spring		x
Gray Haze	x	
Gray and Yellow	x	
Gray and Blue Dots	x	
Gray and Pink Dots	x	
Parchment 1		x
Parchment 2		x
Quicken 5		x
Red Frenzy	x	
'Round Midnight		x
Shades of Gray		x
Shocking Purple		x
Southwest Mesa		x
Tranquility		x

Quicken also provides a very limited color customizer that you can use to change the default colors attached to every register. You'll find the color customizer by selecting **Edit, Options, Register**.

Click the **Colors** button to change the color assigned to every register. You can use this to change the default shade used in your checking register to match the color of your checkbook, or whatever you want. Click the **Fonts** button to change the type and size of the text that appears therein. For more information on fonts and the options menu, see Lesson 2.

Manual Customization

First, a warning. This is for experienced Windows 95 users who don't mind adjusting initialization files.

While Quicken doesn't provide a complete color customization utility, you will find the specifications for every color listed in a file in your Quicken folder called qwcolor.ini.

The default location for the Quicken folder is at c:\quickenw.

The three sets of numbers after each line are built around the Windows RGB (Red/Green/Blue) standard color definition format and should be familiar to anyone with a little programming experience.

While you shouldn't play around with this file without making a backup first (drag a copy to a suitable backup folder created in your Quicken folder), you can use it to change the Quicken color scheme. As an example, look at the background colors that make up every register.

The first line in any pair of register lines is painted in the standard color used by every color scheme. The second line changes depending on the type of register currently open. For example, the color of every second line in an asset register is different to that used in a liability register. In fact, this is what gives each register its personality.

You can change the color of the second line using the Options menu already described; however, it takes a different approach to adjust the color of the first line. Open the qwcolor.ini file using any editor and scroll to the very end of the file. The final entries in the file are as follows:

[Register]

RegChecking=225 228 190

RegCash=250 243 194

RegAsset=152 222 171

RegCredit=206 236 240

RegOthLiab=247 206 202

RegPort=212 226 217

Each entry and series of three numbers defines the color that will be used by the second line in each register. If you don't like the pinks used for liability accounts or the baby blue used for credit card accounts, you can change them here as an alternative to the Options menu.

The numbers are arranged Red Green Blue and run from 0 to 255. 0 equals the highest color saturation while 255 equals the lowest. Therefore, 0 0 0 shows up as black and 255 255 255 as white. 128 128 128 is a 50% shade. You can turn up one color and turn down the others to break away from the black, white, and gray. For example, 128 0 128 is equivalent to a deep purple while 0 128 128 provides the background color used by the standard Windows desktop.

The easiest way to find the right color, however, is to use the Windows 95-color palette. Click the **Start** button in the Windows task bar and choose **Settings, Control Panel**. Double-click the **Display** icon, click the **Appearance** tab, click the **Color** pull-down menu, and select **Other** to open the window shown in Figure 1.2.

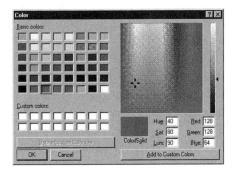

Figure 1.2   The Windows color palette makes it easy to see which RGB color numbers match which color.

Use the color palette to browse the color choices. Once you find the one you want, copy the numbers in the boxes labeled **Red**, **Green**, and **Blue** to the appropriate lines in qwcolor.ini.

CAUTION

How Do I Experiment with the New Colors Without Wiping Out the Old Ones?   Copy the old line and paste it below the one you'll edit. Precede it with an apostrophe ('). For example, the second line in the list previously given would read **'RegChecking=255 228 190**. Quicken and Windows 95 ignore any lines beginning with an apostrophe, treating them as comments.

Save the file and reselect the color scheme using the right mouse button procedure described earlier. There is no need to shut down Quicken; Quicken will load the new settings automatically.

As long as you know how to restore your backup of the original qwcolor.ini file, feel free to explore and adjust the rest of the entries in this file. You can use this system to change most parts of Quicken. However, there are some features over which you have no control. These include the color of the text used in each register (therefore, avoiding dark background colors will help you to see the figures written therein) and also the textures that make up the QuickTabs and Frame patterns. However, if you're not happy with the style included with one scheme, you can always change it to another.

If you've made your Quicken screen totally unreadable and you can't find (or don't know how to copy across) the backed up copy of qwcolor.ini, just delete that file from your Quicken folder and reinstall Quicken. You won't lose any data, but you will receive a fresh copy of the original Quicken color schema.

In this lesson, you learned how to select between different color schemes and also to manually adjust Quicken's color settings. In the next lesson, you will learn about Quicken's numerous optional settings.

Setting Quicken's Preferences

In this lesson, you will learn to change the way Quicken looks and works.

Locating the Options Dialog Box

Quicken's preferences provide limited, but useful, control over many aspects of the program's operation.

To open the list of preferences dialogs, select **Edit, Options**. The small submenu provides access to each major preferences area. You learn about these in this lesson.

Quicken Program Options

Select **Options, Quicken Program** to open the General Options dialog box shown in Figure 2.1.

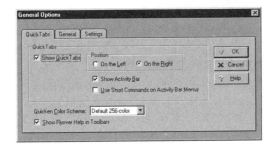

Figure 2.1 The three tabs cover a variety of settings.

Changing Screen Layout

QuickTabs are the small tabs that appear to the right of every Quicken window, under the menus **How Do I?** and **Support**, and above the Speaker and To Do icons. By clicking a QuickTab, you select that window. Use the **QuickTabs** tab in the General Options dialog box to set the following options:

- **Show QuickTabs**   Turn the tabs on or off.
- **Position**   Select your QuickTabs location: **right** or **left**.
- **Show Activity Bar**   This is the row of icons along the lower edge of the screen, which provides quick access to common activities such as paying bills, using a register, updating stock quotes, and so on. Just pause the mouse pointer on any icon to cause its associated menu to fly open.
- **Use Short Commands on Activity Bar Menus**   While the Activity Bar menus were designed to provide lengthier plain-English descriptions of common tasks, use this option to switch to succinct replicas of the standard command menus.
- **Quicken Color Scheme**   Use this dialog box to select an alternate color scheme for your registers and window borders.

 TIP   **Color Scheme Quick Picks**   To quickly pick an alternate color scheme without going through the Options menu, right-click anywhere in the QuickTabs area that extends down the right side of the Quicken window. Select **Color Schemes** from the menu and choose your scheme from the list. Quicken immediately updates the display.

- **Show Flyover Help in Toolbar**   This method of help applies only to the iconbar. With Flyover Help turned on, pause your mouse over any iconbar entry to display a quick tool tip. The terms iconbar and toolbar are inter-changeable. If you don't see an iconbar, you need to turn it on. To find out how, read the "Iconbar Options" section this lesson.

Backups, Tax Categories, and Memorized Transactions

The **General** tab shown in Figure 2.2 provides the following options:

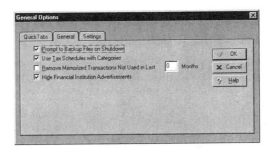

Figure 2.2 The General Options dialog box lets you set several interesting appearance preferences.

- **Prompt to Backup Files on Shutdown** Clear option to also turn off the backup reminder dialog box that appears every time you exit—or shut down—the program. By backing up, you make a copy of your current Quicken files for safekeeping on another computer or floppy disk. You learn about this in Part 1, Lesson 2.

CAUTION

Backing Up Quicken prompts to back up your files only if those files have changed during that Quicken session. To force a backup of your current data, select **File, Backup** (Ctrl+B).

- **Use Tax Schedules with Categories** Leave this option checked if you want to assign specific Tax Form Line Items to your categories. This is especially important if you use Quicken to help prepare your tax return. For more information on categories, turn to Part 1, Lesson 8.

- **Remove Memorized Transactions** Every time you record a new transaction, Quicken adds it to its list of memorized transactions. You can recall that transaction in the future with just a few keystrokes.

  The list is limited to 2,000 entries. When the software reaches that limit, Quicken turns off automatic memorizing. After that point, you must manually delete memorized transactions and switch the memorizing on once more using the **QuickFill** tab. If you want to automatically retire transactions that haven't been repeated within x months, type in the number of months here and check the check box. Quicken will clear the memory banks every time you start the program.

- **Hide Financial Institution Advertisements** You see advertisements from financial institutions anywhere Quicken displays information downloaded using the Internet from an online source. Clear this setting to hide those advertisements.

Keyboard Mappings and the Fiscal Year

Use the **Settings** tab to change the following:

- **Keyboard Mappings** In almost every Windows program, Ctrl+Z stands for Undo Last Command, Ctrl+X stands for Cut, Ctrl+C stands for Copy, and Ctrl+V stands for Paste. Not in Quicken.

  In Quicken, Ctrl+Z will activate QuickZoom, Ctrl+X will take you to the other half of a selected transfer, Ctrl+C will take you to the Category & Transfer List, and Ctrl+V will void a transaction.

  To use standard Windows 95 keyboard commands, check **Undo/Cut/Copy/ Paste**. You then can easily locate and use QuickZoom, Category & Transfer Lists, or move through a transaction using the Quicken menus, keyboard, or mouse commands.

- **Working Calendar** This group has important financial ramifications. Anyone working in a standard U.S. financial year (from January 1 to December 31) doesn't need to worry about this, but if you work a non-standard year (many companies choose to work from July 1 to June 30), you should select **Fiscal Year** and specify the **Starting Month**.

 TIP **Changing Your Financial Year** If you have filed returns using one financial year and want to change your financial year on future returns, you must first lodge an application with the IRS, pay an application fee, and await approval. Contact your local IRS office for more information or visit their site on the Web at http://irs.ustreas.gov.

When you finish adjusting your General options, click **OK** to save those changes or **Cancel** to discard them.

Register Options

You'll find the register options on the options submenu. Select **Edit, Options, Register**.

These options are great for customizing Quicken's registers. Registers are used for recording transactions, so making them work the way you want them to work will also help you get the most out of Quicken.

Changing the Register's Appearance

Use the first tab, **Display**, to change the look of each transaction entry. The options are as follows:

- **Register Fields**   There are three entries in this group. **Show Date in First Column** swaps the Date field with the Num field. **Show Memo before Category** switches the Memo field with the Category field. Try them one way, then the other. It's a matter of personal preference, nothing more. **Show Buttons on QuickFill Fields** turns off the small Calendar button that appears in the Date field, the down arrow that opens up the list of memorized transactions (even though you can still see the list), and the small Calculator icon that appears beside any amount field. This simplifies the data entry screen at the expense of some functionality. To learn more about how the register works and what these fields mean, see Part 1, Lesson 7.

- **Register Appearance**   **Use Color Shading** enables or disables the appearance of color on the Quicken screen. If you use a low-contrast laptop or notebook computer, you might like to select this to substitute Quicken's colorful color schemes with an all-white transaction window. **Show Transaction Toolbar** controls the group of three buttons that appear at the end of every transaction in progress. Feel free to clear them if you prefer to use the keyboard shortcuts, instead. **Use One Check Register window** controls the appearance of Quicken's QuickTabs. With it enabled, all registers will show through a single Register QuickTab. Clear this option and each register you open will add its own QuickTab to the list. Finally, click the **Color** and **Font** buttons to change the shading and typeface used for the transaction window. You can choose your own background shading for each type of register and change the size and style of typeface used throughout Quicken's registers.

 TIP   **A Sight for Sore Eyes**   The **Font** button under the **Register Appearance** tab is especially useful for boosting the size of Quicken's fonts for people with poor eyesight. You can set almost any sized typeface using the Font dialog box.

Automatic Notifications

The next tab, **Miscellaneous**, is shown in Figure 2.3.

Use the **Notify** group to turn off all of those pesky requests for confirmation that appear every time you edit a transaction, record a backdated transaction, and so on. If you also find that the cash register's ka-ching sound gets on your nerves, just turn it off with **Beep When Recording and Memorizing**.

Check **When Recording Out of Date Transactions** to warn you when you try to record a backdated transaction, that is, one dated before the current date.

Check **Before Changing Existing Transactions** to warn when you try to edit previously recorded transactions.

Check **When Recording Uncategorized Transactions** to warn when you try to record a transaction without specifying a category or transfer to another account. If you are recording an invoice by using Quicken Home and Business 98, you can also record transactions in the Invoices/Receivables register that are categorized as Form.

Changing Quicken's Sounds

If your computer and Windows 95 installation are set up for multimedia, you don't have to put up with Quicken's bleeps and squawks. Open the Windows Explorer and find your Quicken folder. For most people, that's c:\quickenw. Drag and drop the Sounds folder onto the Backup folder to silence Quicken's incidental sounds forever—or at least until you drag the folder back again. Audio Cues and Video Help will continue to function.

You can also change those sounds by using the Windows Recorder available under **Start, Programs, Accessories, Multimedia**. For instance, Quicken's title sound is called Qopen.wav. Feel free to personalize the opening sequence with your own sound. With a microphone attached to your sound card, you can record a reminder such as "Remember, always set a category." Or with a CD-ROM, you might like to record the opening five seconds of your favorite music by using a cable to connect the **line out** to the **line in** sockets on your sound card. As long as that sound card is full duplex (all the recent ones are), you can use the Windows Recorder to grab a sound sample.

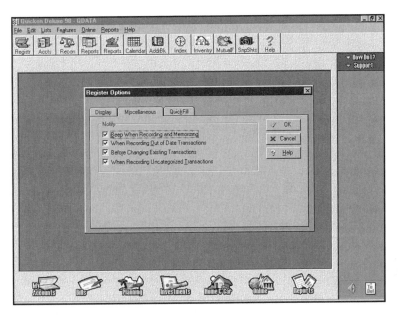

Figure 2.3 If you're tired of Quicken interrupting you with confirmation requests, turn off the Notify options shown here to silence the software.

Changing the QuickFill Feature

The **QuickFill** tab provides two sets of options:

- **Data Entry** This first group of options is handy for changing the way you enter your transaction data. The first line, **Use Enter Key to Move Between Fields**, changes the behavior of the return key from completing and saving a new transaction to behaving like the Tab key, jumping from one field to the next.

- **Complete Fields Using Previous Entries** turns Quicken's auto-completion on or off. Auto-completion helpfully finishes a field based on the characters you have typed so far. It is a useful tool that is best left on.

- **Recall Memorized Transactions (requires auto-completion)** extends auto-completion to automatically insert the contents of the memorized transaction associated with that auto-completion. This is useful if you regularly record transactions with the same payee. However, if you often record

473

transactions to the same payee whose amounts may, for example, increase or decrease your accounts receivable, you should keep a close eye on the transactions Quicken recalls from the memorized list. You may find you have automatically recorded an increase rather than a decrease. In other words, always check recalled transactions.

- **Drop Down Lists on Field Entry** controls Quicken's drop-down lists such as those that appear whenever you start to enter something into the Num, Payee, or Category fields. If you turn this off, make sure **Show Buttons on QuickFill Fields** is turned on under the **Display** tab. Otherwise, you will not be able to access the memorized transactions and other pull-down menus available in each register window.

- **Auto-Capitalize Payee & Categories**, as its title suggests, determines whether or not Quicken converts a lowercase starting letter in the payee and category fields to an uppercase letter.

- **Automatic List Updating**   This group of options changes the action Quicken takes after you record each transaction. **Auto Memorize New Transactions** turns on the memorizing feature. If you don't want memorized transactions added to the calendar's drag-and-drop list, clear **Auto Memorize to the Calendar List**. You can learn more about this in Part 1, Lesson 10. If you use any version of Quicken other than Quicken Basic 98, you can also add items recorded in the Financial Address Book to the QuickFill list by checking **Add Financial Address Book Items to QuickFill List**. You learn about the Financial Address Book in Lesson 5.

When you finish adjusting your Register options, click **OK** to save those changes or **Cancel** to discard them.

Check Options

The Check options appear on the third submenu. Select **Edit, Options, Write Checks** to open the dialog box shown in Figure 2.4.

While the Miscellaneous and QuickFill tabs are almost identical to those under Register Options, there are some important differences as well as a completely new tab.

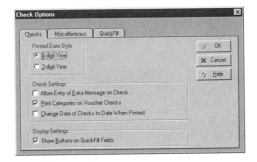

Figure 2.4 Check options allow you to add extra messages, change the date checks are recorded, and adjust the automatic memorizing feature.

Changing Dates and Check Options

The Checks tab adjusts the following settings:

- **Printed Date Style**   Select between 2- and 4-digit years. This is just a matter of personal style and has no bearing on the dates actually recorded by Quicken, even through the year 2000.

- **Check Settings**   Check **Allow Entry of Extra Message on Check** to include an extra message on your checks. The message prints below the address, out of sight of Quicken's window envelopes. This is useful if you want to include confidential information on the check such as an account number or other matter.

- Use **Print Categories on Voucher Checks** to specify whether your income and expense categories should appear on the detailed listing printed below the check. Hide these by clearing this option if those categories are for your own records only. You can learn about the different styles of checks in Part 1, Lesson 9.

- Check **Change Date of Checks to Date When Printe**d to adjust the date of the transactions recorded in your register. If you record a transaction but don't print it until several days later, checking this option will update that transaction to the date the check was actually printed.

- **Display Settings**   Check **Show Button on QuickFill Fields** to display Quicken's calculator, date, and pull-down menu buttons in the check-writing window.

Miscellaneous and QuickFill Tabs

The remaining tabs are identical to those described for Register Options except that you can, by using the Miscellaneous tab, set an automatic warning should you try to use an already used check number (check **Warn if a Check Number is Re-used**). Of course, this can't happen if you make a habit of selecting **Next Check Num** when filling out a checking account transaction, but it's a good way to pick up typos. This option also is useful if you handwrite your checks.

All of the options under the QuickFill tab are identical to those under Register Options previously listed.

When you finish adjusting your Write Checks options, click **OK** to save those changes or **Cancel** to discard them.

Report Options

You can set your report options as shown in Figure 2.5 by selecting **Edit, Options, Reports**.

Take a look at the options:

- **Account Display**   You can choose to have your accounts listed by their **Name** (for instance, Payables), their **Description** (Accounts Payable), or **Both**.

- **Category Display**   The same applies to your categories. However, in this case, it may be more useful. If you refer to your clients by a coded numbering system rather than their name, you can speed up the entry of data. Choosing to print the reports by code and description (by selecting **Both**) will make it much easier to make sense of those reports later.

- **Default Report Date Range**   Quicken's default report dates can be set to almost anything you prefer, from the last year to the last quarter to any specific interval. If you like to concentrate on the big picture, you might set reports to cover a year, but if you prefer the microcosmic approach, you might like to try a quarter or even a month. Note that the **Include all Dates** selection in the pull-down list will force the report to extend from the time you first started using Quicken to the present day.

- **Default Comparison Report Date Range**   Comparison reports show the amount of change in a category or account over two time periods. For example, if you want to compare your accounts of this quarter this year with those of this quarter last year, set the default comparison to the earlier date and the **Default Report Date Range** to the more recent period. Figures from both will be compared on-screen.

Use the remaining options as follows:

- **Skip Create Report Prompt** Check this to create reports without stopping at the Create Report dialog box first.

- **Use Color in Report** Check this to display negative amounts and report titles in color.

- **QuickZoom to Investment Forms** This option takes you from a transaction you have double-clicked in an investment report to the form used to record that transaction. With this option cleared, you will be taken to that transaction in your investment register instead.

- **Show the Customize Bar** Controls the display of the Customize Report bar in all report windows. The Customize bar is useful for changing the information used to create that report in an interactive manner.

- **Decimal Digits of the Price and Shares** How many numbers do you want displayed after the decimal point? Two or three is usual.

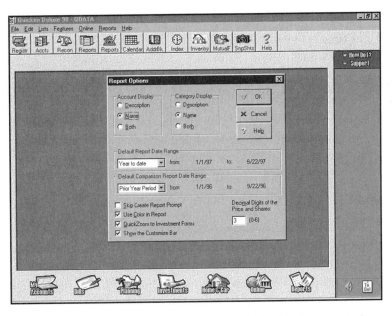

Figure 2.5 Use reporting options to change the defaults that form most of your reports.

When you finish adjusting your Report options, click **OK** to save those changes or **Cancel** to discard them.

Graphing Options

The graph options are easy. Select **Edit**, **Options**, **Graphs** to open the Options dialog box. You have the following choices:

- **Use Patterns Instead of Colors**   Check this if you prefer to use patterns instead of colors to draw your graphs. This is an issue for anyone using a monochrome display.

- **Create all Graphs in Separate Windows**   Check this if you want to create each new graph in a separate window, rather than using one graph window for all of your graphs.

- **Draw in 2D (faster)**   Check this to view your graphs as 2-D oblongs rather than 3-D columns.

- **Show the Customize Bar**   This option controls the display of the Customize Bar. With this option checked, you quickly can change the data that contributes to each graph.

When you finish adjusting your Graph options, click **OK** to save those changes or **Cancel** to discard them.

Reminder and Billminder Options

Select **Edit, Options, Reminders** to open the Reminder Options dialog box shown in Figure 2.6. These options control the settings for the reminder window (available by selecting **Features, Reminders, Reminders**) and the Billminder utility that flags upcoming transactions every time you launch Windows.

The Reminders Options dialog box is divided into two main parts. Use the Reminders tab to set the following options:

- **Show Reminders when starting Quicken**   Check this option to cause the reminders pane to open every time you start Quicken.

- **Show Reminders from Other Files**   Check this if you would also like to see reminders from other Quicken files Quicken finds on your hard disk drive. This is handy if you maintain separate files for home and business, and so on.

- **Days in Advance**   Indicate how many days in advance you want a reminder to appear before it falls due.
- **Show notes For**   Choose what period you would like to display calendar notes in the reminders pane.

The Billminder tab provides the following options:

- **Show Billminder When Starting Windows**   Clear this option if you don't want to view the Billminder utility when you start Windows. You can learn about Billminder in Part 1, Lesson 10.
- **Show Details for:**   Check those types of reminders you want Quicken to generate in the Billminder window. For example, you may want to see Scheduled Transactions, Investment Reminders, and Calendar Notes, but not Checks To Print or Online Payments.

Figure 2.6   Quicken's Billminder does a great job of replacing the knot around your finger.

When you finish adjusting your Reminder options, click **OK** to save those changes or **Cancel** to discard them.

Desktop Options

Usually, Quicken keeps track of whichever windows were open when you last exited the program. The next time you start, it reopens all of those windows. Chances are, this isn't ideal. During a Quicken session, you will probably open numerous windows and forget to close a good deal of them. While this won't make you lose any data, it will mean that the next time you start the program, it opens with a particularly cluttered set of QuickTabs.

The alternative is to create the perfect set of windows. This might include the Register, Snapshot, Portfolio, Write Checks, and Reminders windows.

479

Open the windows and arrange them as you require (drag the QuickTabs up and down the list); then open Desktop Options (**Edit, Options, Desktop**), select **Save Current Desktop,** and click **OK**. When you check **Save Current Desktop**, Quicken will save your current window setup and restore it every time you restart the software.

Iconbar Options

The Quicken iconbar appears beneath the menu bar and provides fast access to often-used commands and features. If you can't see your iconbar, you can turn it on by using one of the options described next.

The iconbar provides quick access to certain commands and features. A lot of its functionality is replicated in the Activity Bar, and all of it through Quicken's other menus, but if you often need to jump between two sections of the program—for example, between a particular report and your registers—you will find the iconbar useful.

Selecting **Edit, Options, Iconbar** opens the Customize Iconbar window shown in Figure 2.7.

While the standard Quicken Iconbar is something of a lackluster affair, it doesn't have to be. In fact, you can drop in icons for all of your favorite commands and even assign speed keys.

TERM   **Speed Keys**   Quicken also refers to these as Shortcut Keys, Quick Keys, and Accelerator Keys. You're probably quite used to seeing Quicken's built-in shortcut keys. For example, beside the menu item **Features, Bills, Write Checks** is the shortcut key Ctrl+W. Quicken also supports user-defined shortcut keys, although for some reason prefers to call them Speed Keys. You can find a complete list of speed keys in Quicken's Help.

Figure 2.7 The Quicken Iconbar will take you to the features that count...fast!

The Iconbar Options window is a little deceptive with multiple levels hidden; however, it's easy enough to use.

Customizing the Iconbar

The first window shows your current iconbar. Use the arrows to scroll back and forth if you can't see them all.

The two check boxes **Show Icons** and **Show Text** control the display of the buttons making up the iconbar. If these aren't checked, you can turn on your icons by selecting one or both of them. (My personal preference is for text only. After all, the icons aren't the greatest, the text is far more self-explanatory, and it doesn't take up as much screen space, leaving more room for registers, graphs, and reports: all the useful stuff.)

Incidentally, Quicken correctly calls the graphic elements used for the iconbar buttons "Icons." However, even if you choose to display only text buttons, it will still refer to the row of buttons as an iconbar.

The four buttons under the scrolling row of icons control the commands that will appear in the iconbar:

- **New**   Adds a command, icon, and optionally a Speed Key to the end of the iconbar. Select the command in the Add Action to Iconbar dialog box and then click **Change** to specify a graphic, label, and Speed Key. Click **OK** to save the new icon or cancel to discard. This procedure is described in more detail next.

- **Edit**   Changes the currently selected icon. You can edit the command or action associated with that icon as described for **New**, the icon graphic, and the text label. This procedure is described in more detail next.

TIP   **Changing the Icon Order**   You can't change the order of icons from within the Iconbar options window. However, you can drag the buttons around *on* the iconbar. Click **Done** to close the customization window and save your changes. From the iconbar, click and hold any icon. Drag it onto the icon you want to replace. The button you are dragging slides in front of the button you drop it onto.

- **Delete**   Remove the selected icon from the iconbar.
- **Reset**   Go back to the default Quicken iconbar. This will discard all of your edits.

481

Creating or Editing an Iconbar Button

To create or edit an iconbar button, you need to work through three possible stages:

1. **Select a Command:** If you need to create a new button, click **New** to open the window shown in Figure 2.8. If you are editing an existing button, select the button from the horizontal row of buttons and click **Edit**. Choose the icon's command from the **Icon Action** list. The **Description** to its right will briefly describe that command and the **Graphic** will let you preview that icon.

2. (Optional) **Change the Graphic:** Click **Change** to open the Change Iconbar Item dialog box and select the button's icon from the list. You may also record a label of up to seven letters and specify a Speed Key by using the letters A–Z. Click **OK** to record the changes.

3. Click **OK** to save the changes to the iconbar.

4. (Optional) **Select a Target for the Icon's Action:** Some actions prompt a third dialog box in which you must specify the target for that icon's action. Just work through the options and click **OK**.

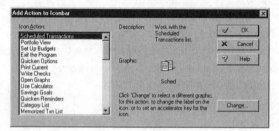

Figure 2.8 The Iconbar is at your command...literally. Take your pick from the list.

In this lesson, you learned how to adjust the more subtle aspects of Quicken's operation. In the next lesson, you will learn how to integrate Quicken with other software.

Importing and Exporting Data

In this lesson, you learn how to move your data between Quicken files, the Clipboard, and other software.

The Well-Connected Computer

Today, it is a rare event that a software program can't exchange data and information with another program, and Quicken is no exception. Using Quicken's export and import functions, you can work with other Quicken files, merging data or splitting off sections of your own accounts. You can also export your reports to other software for further manipulation.

Importing and exporting takes place through the following methods:

- **QIF Format** The QIF (Quicken Interchange Format) is built around an ASCII file and is used for exporting or importing raw Quicken data. ASCII text is compatible with any text editor including your word processor, the Windows notepad, or any DOS-based editor. However, there's no guarantee it will make much sense as the structure of the data making up the file is not exactly self-explanatory.

  The QIF standard means that almost any other software package can access your Quicken data. In fact, if you are a programmer, you will find a full explanation of the QIF format in Quicken's Help system, along with an example file and a description of each line. However, where QIF comes in handy is when copying data from one Quicken file to the next.

- **DDE** Dynamic Data Exchange is a communications standard built into Windows that is used to transfer data between one application and another. DDE is fast and seamless. It is also used between most of the software developed by Intuit, but the specifications of the DDE interface have never been made available to other software publishers, so while Quicken can talk to TurboTax and Investor Insight, there isn't any other software that can take advantage of this to also exchange data with and, perhaps, add to Quicken's features.

- **Windows Clipboard** Although this is the most basic exchange mechanism, it's also the one you'll probably use the most. Many Quicken data objects can't be copied to the Clipboard. Or if they can, then they can't be understood by any other software; however, some data objects can be copied, including the text that makes up any report.

- **Printing To Disk** Quicken can not only print reports to your printer but also to a disk file. Just click the **Print** button that appears at the top of any report window and take your pick from the list. An ASCII disk file is the simplest format, but a tab-delimited report is useful for importing that report into other programs for further massaging.

Exporting Reports

Quicken can export data through the Clipboard by printing reports to a disk file and via a QIF file. The system you use will depend on your purpose. For example, QIF files are great for working directly with Quicken's files, but they won't help you much when you need to work with information that has already been extracted by Quicken from those files.

Exported reports are used for the following purposes:

- Importing into a word processing or DTP (desktop publishing) package ready to be turned it into a slick, professionally presented report or table.

- Importing into a spreadsheet program such as Microsoft Excel or Lotus 1-2-3 where they can be further analyzed or used with that software's more extensive graphing tools.

- Imported into a database, ready for further analysis or long-term storage.

- Electronically transmitted across the Internet.

TIP **A Real World Example** Block & Tackle Shipping suffers more than its fair share of bad debtors. In the interests of a healthy bank balance and a shorter Receivables register, they have taken on the services of a professional debt collector. Each month they create an A/R report, export it to a file, and then send it across the Internet to Knobble & Son Debt Collection. Now their outstanding accounts are down by 50% and their bank balance has never looked better.

The only way to extract this preprocessed information is either by using the Clipboard or by printing it to disk.

Exporting to the Clipboard

There is only one way to copy report data to the Windows Clipboard: Open that report and click the **Copy** button near the top of the report window. This copies the complete report; there is no way to copy a section of a report. Open the document into which you need to copy the report and select **Edit, Paste**.

At first sight, you will almost certainly be disappointed by the results. The report, at least when pasted into a word processor or desktop publishing (DTP) software, looks less like neat columns of figures and more like a mish-mash of scrambled digits. However, copy and paste this data into a spreadsheet, and it will probably turn out just about perfect.

Here, then, are some quick tips for making the most of your copied reports:

1. Everything relies on tabs. Tabs are used to align the columns in reports, as shown in Figure 3.1. If anyone suggests you can do the same by repeatedly tapping the Spacebar, don't listen to them. The spaces in the nonproportional typefaces, such as Arial or Times, have a different width to the characters and it is next to impossible to arrange them so that they fall into neat, vertical columns. However, this isn't true if you use a proportional typeface, such as Courier.

As Quicken doesn't send the tab and font settings to the Clipboard along with the text, pasting a Quicken report into your word processor or DTP package will initially yield unattractive results.

Fortunately, the fix is easy. Quicken assigns a tab to every column in the report—with one exception. All you have to do is either insert those tabs or shift their position until everything aligns. The exception is the area leading up to the first column. Any lines indented within that column are indented using spaces rather than tabs.

485

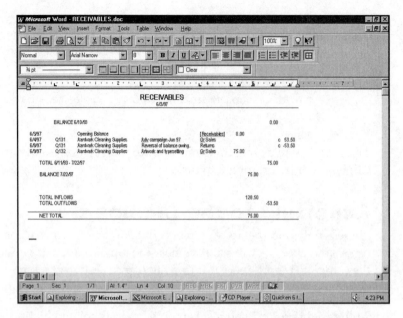

Figure 3.1 Tabs are one of the easiest ways to align the columns in exported Quicken reports.

2. Use decimal tabs for any column that deals with a monetary amount. Decimal tabs align columns of numbers according to the position of the decimal point, rather than an arbitrary setting such as the left or right edge of the text. This creates a precisely aligned column of decimal points.

3. Quicken doesn't export a report title or column headings so you will need to create your own. To export a report with these features, read the "Exporting to a Disk File" section.

4. Use a thin font. Quicken truncates any text that spills into the next column, replacing the truncated letters with an ellipsis (...). A report copied to the Clipboard contains the full text from every column. To make the columns fit, you can either take the virtual scissors to them as per the Quicken method, or set them in a tighter typeface such as Helvetica Narrow or Futura Condensed. Experiment with your font list until you find one that works. In general, serif typefaces such as Times (or Times New Roman) squeeze more text onto the page (or within a column) than sans serif typefaces such as Arial. However, condensed versions of sans serif typefaces work better than serif typefaces, hence the availability of Helvetica and Future in their compressed forms. If you can't find a thin font, try using a smaller typesize. While most computers use 12-point type as a matter of course, certain sans serif typefaces down to about 7 points in size should remain quite readable when printed on a 600-dpi laser printer.

CAUTION

Serif/Sans Serif   Serifs are the small curlicues (or spikey bits, to be less precise) and other artifices that adorn the letters of many fonts, including the text used for the paragraph preceding this one. The serif style originally was developed to hold the ink within the recessed letter-image on the face of a printing block. Sans serif (or, "without serif") is a typeface with clean sides: for example, the font used for the headings within this book. Because of their clarity, these are more readable on a computer screen and, for the same reason, are more readable than serif typefaces when reproduced at a smaller size on the printed page.

5. Set your page to landscape. Turning a page on its side is, of course, ideal for printing reports with loads of columns extending across the page. You should be able to do this from nearly any word processing or DTP package by selecting **File, Page Setup**, although you may also need to change your printer setup. If you still experience trouble squeezing the columns onto a single page, try decreasing your margins and then the point size of the desired font.

Exporting to a Disk File

If you don't want to work with the report data immediately, need to send the report to someone else, or simply need to store it somewhere for archival purposes, you should print the report to a disk file.

Quicken supports several disk file formats. These are:

- **ASCII Disk File**   Unlike a copied report, the ASCII format writes the report to disk exactly as it would appear on your printer, complete with a report title and column headings. The ASCII format also replaces tabs with spaces. This means that you don't need to worry about setting tabs to make sense of the columns. In fact, you should be able to drop this report into any word processing or DTP package, set it in a nonproportional typeface such as Courier, and it will come out right.

TIP   **Nonproportional**   A nonproportional typeface is one whose letter and space characters take the same amount of horizontal room; an "I" requires the same space as an "O," even though the first is much narrower. In a proportional typeface such as the one used in this book, "II" takes far less room than "OO." The space between characters (the kerning) also changes in a proportional typeface from one pair of characters to the next.

These reports also have the distinct advantage of being perfectly DOS-compatible. The horizontal width is limited to 80 characters, and choosing **Portrait** or **Landscape** within the Print window will make no difference to the end result. You can look at these reports by using any DOS text-editing package. You can also view them by using the Windows Notepad accessory (**Start, Accessories, Notepad**), but these reports won't make much sense when viewed in a word processor unless you select the text and set it in a nonproportional typeface such as Courier. Quicken also truncates text spilling over the preset column limit.

- **Tab-Delimited Disk File**   The Tab-delimited format is similar to the Copy to Clipboard function except that it saves the column headings with the report body. This format won't make much sense when viewed through a DOS editor or the Windows Notepad, but it does work if you reset it using tabs in a word processing or DTP package. Whether you use a proportional or nonproportional typeface is up to you, but you'll find the former looks better.

  The tab-delimited format is ideal for importing the report into some spreadsheets, but not all. Because Quicken saves the report by using the full text contained in every column (in other words, without truncation), and because Quicken also saves the text with tabs and column headers, most spreadsheets have everything they require to import and recognize the report. Some, however, will fail to pick up the difference between the report's text and numerical elements.

- **123 (.PRN) Disk File**   The final format was designed for Lotus 1-2-3 spreadsheets but will work with any program that can read comma-delimited text. As this is as common a format as tab-delimited, chances are compatible products include your own spreadsheet software.

  The comma-delimited format swaps tabs for commas. In addition, it surrounds the text with quotation marks but leaves the numbers as is. This is a universally recognized system, so don't let the "123" demarcation put you off. All three of the major spreadsheets understand this format, as well as many others. Figure 3.2 shows a 123 (.PRN) file imported and formatted using Microsoft Excel.

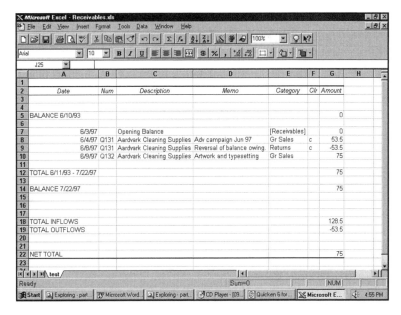

Figure 3.2 The 123 (.PRN) format works best with almost any spreadsheet.

Understanding QIF

Quicken's QIF format is ideal for shifting data between two or more Quicken files. However, for the reasons mentioned at the start of this lesson, it isn't much good at shifting data between Quicken and other software. QIF is very flexible. You can use it to export not only existing transactions, but also account names, category names, and memorized transactions.

This will prove very useful in all sorts of situations. Here are just a few examples:

- **Combining business and personal records**   Let's say you have always kept your business and personal records separate, storing your business books and the computer at work and your personal transactions on the computer at home. Assuming you are self-employed, you will need to combine both books to provide an overall picture at tax time. Fortunately, that's easy. Just export each of your business's accounts with full transactions and category names. Save the files on a disk, take them home and import them into your personal accounts. That's all it takes.

- **Combining records after marriage**   What do two Quicken users do after they get married? Forget the honeymoon, forget the house, and forget the kids. For a commitment that counts, it's hard to beat merging both Quicken files. The QIF system makes this a cinch, although you will need to decide which categories you keep and those that you discard.

- **Creating an ideal set of accounts and categories**   This is a great tip for service-oriented accounting practices. Quicken's default categories are rather limited, more for simplicity's sake than any other. To give your Quicken users even better service, create a standard set of accounts and categories and supply them to new clients on a 3.5-inch disk. Have your users import these rather than create their own in an ad-hoc manner. You can even customize the list for each client. At tax time, knowing your clients have been working to a certain Quicken standard will make everyone's job easier.

- **Correct a bookkeeping error**   The ability to shift transactions between one account and the next makes it possible to correct a range of bookkeeping errors. For instance, say you created an account of the wrong type and have been using it steadily for a week, month, or even the entire year. The fix is easy: Just export the transactions from that account and import them into the correct account. Then go back and delete the original transactions (or even the entire original account).

Knowing how to use the QIF export system is an important part of mastering Quicken. It will help you in many ways.

Exporting with QIF

To open the QIF exporter, select **File, File Operations, Export**. You will see the QIF Export dialog box shown in Figure 3.3.

Using the exporter is easy. Just follow these steps:

1. **QIF File to Export To**   Either type in a file name or click **Find File** to select an existing file. If you are exporting to a new file, open the destination folder using **Find File**, type in the file name, and click **OK**. Note that Quicken understands the long file format of Windows 95, so you can get away with a file name such as **My Exported Quicken Data**.

2. **Quicken Account to Export**   Select your account from the pull-down list. Quicken can export only one account's content at a time, so while you might export your Checking account and your Credit Card account to separate files, you can't export them both to the one file.

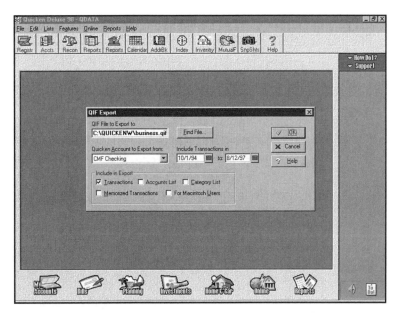

Figure 3.3 QIF exports from one account at a time but can include the full list of accounts and categories.

3. **Include Transactions In** You can choose to export only those transactions between the dates you specify here. The default date covers the earliest transaction date to the latest transaction date.

TIP **Quicken and the Year 2000** Dates for 2000 or later are recorded starting at 00. While the rest of the world may suffer millennium problems, Quicken will not consider these as dates targeting the 1900s. Indeed, 51 is recorded as 1951 and 50 as 1950, but then a date of 49 is assumed to be 2049; 48 is 2048; and so forth.

4. **Include in Export** You can check one or all of these options. Obviously, if you just want to export a list of category names, you should check only **Category List**. However, if you want to also include transactions, make sure you check **Transactions**. The option **For Macintosh Users** is an interesting one. Quicken doesn't include historical stock prices in any of the standard exports. In fact, there is no way to shift historical stock prices from one Windows Quicken file to another. However, they can be exported to the Macintosh version. Unfortunately, it doesn't work to export to the Macintosh and then import that file into the Windows version. The stock history will not follow through.

5. Click **OK** to save the file.

491

Importing with QIF

The Quicken QIF importing screen is very similar to the exporting screen, but with some important operational differences.

Select **File, File Operations, Import** to open the QIF Import dialog box shown in Figure 3.4.

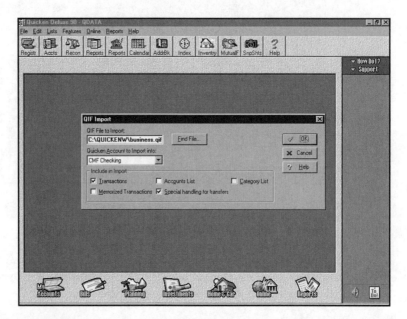

Figure 3.4 The QIF system can import to only one account at a time, but it can still match account transfers across subsequent imports.

Then follow these steps:

1. **QIF File to Import** Select the file you want to import either by typing its name or browsing for it through **Find File**.

2. **Quicken Account to Import Into** Quicken can export and import only one account at a time. Choose the target account from the pull-down list. Even if the exported file includes account and category names, you must still have at least one account in your existing file. This makes it impossible to import a QIF file if you don't already have at least one register in place. However, you can create a dummy account and select that from the pull-down list. The imported file can then create all the stored categories, accounts, and transactions (but do read Step 3). Delete the dummy account at your leisure.

3. **Include in Import**   Choose the parts of the file you want to import. If you will be importing from several QIF files in order to re-create part or all of a set of books, you should also select **Special handling for Transfers**. This will match up and link paired transactions that shift money between two accounts.

4. Click **OK** to complete the import.

In this lesson, you learned how to import and export data through the Clipboard, QIF files, and reports. In the next lesson, you will learn how to use Quicken Home Inventory at home and in business.

Quicken Home Inventory

*In this lesson, you learn how to use Quicken Home Inventory
to manage your assets at home and your stock in business.
This feature is included in Quicken Deluxe and Quicken
Home and Business.*

The Quicken Home Inventory is part of Quicken Deluxe and Quicken Home &
Business. This is a useful addition for two reasons. First, it integrates with
Quicken. This means that the value of the items entered into the inventory will
be reflected in a special Quicken asset account. Unfortunately, transactions
entered into Quicken do not reflect back the other way.

Second, the Home Inventory is the perfect place to store details that might be
needed for insurance claims and other matters. Just make sure you make a
backup of your data and keep it somewhere safe; preferably off the premises
where, if your house is destroyed by fire or flood, you'll still have the information you need to make that claim.

TIP   **InsureMarket**   If you are connected to the Internet, you can grab quick
quotes and other insurance information for your home, car, and other be-
longings from InsureMarket. To go there, open the menu **Online, Quicken on
the Web, InsureMarket**.

Starting the Inventory

There are several ways to start your inventory management session:

- From the Windows taskbar by selecting **Start, Programs, Quicken, Quicken Home Inventory**.
- Clicking the **Home Inventory** icon in the Quicken iconbar.
- From the menu bar by selecting **Features, Planning, Quicken Home Inventory**.
- By pointing to the **Home & Car** button in the Activity Bar and choosing **Record My Home Inventory**.

Whichever you choose, the first time you start the inventory software (or create a new inventory file), you should click **Continue** to move past the introductory screen and to open the window shown in Figure 4.1.

The buttons that make up the iconbar provide quick access to Quicken Home Inventory's most useful features. Table 4.1 lists the iconbar buttons and their functions.

Table 4.1 Iconbar buttons for Quicken Home Inventory

Button	Name	Function
Locations	Locations	Opens the list of locations. These are the areas of your home where your belongings are located.
Categories	Categories	Opens the list of categories. Each item is grouped by category. Typical categories include Appliances, Clothing, and Electronics.
Policies	Policies	Opens the list of policies. The Home Inventory can track multiple insurance policies.
Claims	Claims	Creates or edits an insurance claim.
Find	Find	Finds an item by description or notes.
Move Item	Move Item	Moves an item to another location.

continues

495

Table 4.1   Continued

Button	Name	Function
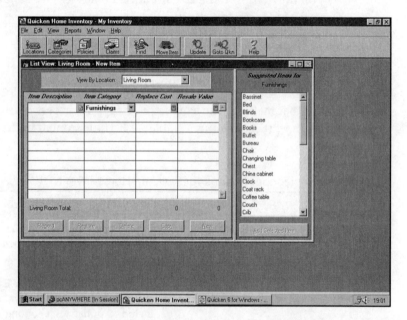 Update	Update	Updates the balance of Quicken's Home Inventory account.
Goto Qkn	Goto Qkn	Launches Quicken.
Help	Help	Gets Online Help.

Figure 4.1   The Home Inventory opens with a window into which you can immediately begin typing your assets.

The inventory is made up of items, categories, and locations. As this suggests, items are assigned to categories which group your possessions by type. Items also are grouped by the location in which they are stored. Just how you choose to use those categories and locations can lend the Home Inventory a great deal of flexibility.

Creating Your Inventory

The inventory provides two views: List and Detail. The List view is the default view, showing all items in a certain location. It displays those items in a table view and includes the item's name (referred to in the List View as Description), its category, its replacement cost, and its resale value. You learn about these next.

You can access the Detail view from the List view by clicking the small "Detail View" icon beside any item description. You use the Detail View to provide more specific information about that item such as the date and place of purchase, which insurance policy applies to that item, the location of receipts and other records, and more.

The default inventory includes numerous items and locations. This will save you from a lot of tedious typing. In fact, creating an inventory is as easy as following these steps:

1. From the List View window, click the **View by Location** drop-down button to select the place this item is located.
2. In the second column of the first blank line of the List View, select a category from the Item Category drop-down list.

CAUTION

Items that Don't Suit Locations If you have an item that doesn't suit a location—for example, a portable CD-player that tends to move from room to room—simply specify it as **Unassigned**. While an Unassigned location is stored as a location and so instantly becomes a paradoxical loop, this doesn't worry Home Inventory, and it will treat Unassigned items like any other in your reports and claims.

3. Locate the item you want to add to your list from the Suggested Item list, then either double-click the item name or select it and click **Add Selected Item**.
4. Under **Replace Cost**, enter a replacement cost calculated on what it would cost to replace that item with a new, equivalent, item.
5. The **Resale Value** is set to 50% of the **Replace Cost**, but you may edit this as required.
6. Move on to the next item, repeating these steps.

Just creating a list of items is not enough to establish an insurance claim. While Quicken Home Inventory doesn't replace the need for physical documentation such as purchase or credit card receipts—check your insurance policy so that you know exactly what might be required—it does provide a useful and, perhaps, key backup.

You can associate extensive background information with every item entered into the List View. Just select that item and select **View, Detail View** to open the dialog box shown in Figure 4.2. Of course, unlike the figure shown, the first time you open the Detail View for any icon, you will see mostly blank fields.

 Alternatively, click the small **Detail View** icon beside the item in the List View's item **Description** column.

Fill in as many of the fields as you can, especially those items against which you may need to claim. You need the purchase price at least, and, depending on your policy, either replacement cost or resale value. Link each item to its relevant insurance policy. When you need to make a claim, Quicken Home Inventory can automatically produce a summary or detail report.

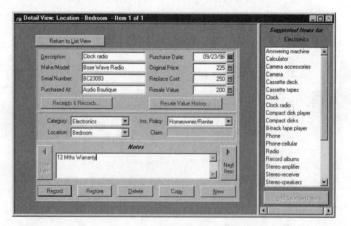

Figure 4.2 Use the Detail view to provide more information about each of the items selected for the List view.

(Optional) Click **Receipts & Records** to indicate which records you have to support your claim of ownership, as shown in Figure 4.3. The value of most items change over time, so use **Resale Value History** to record those changes. While the changes won't automatically appear in a Quicken depreciation account (and if that is a tax issue, you will need to manually ensure that they do), every little bit helps.

Finally, use the **Notes** text box to store additional information such as warranty information or anything else that may prove useful.

Click **Return to List View** when you're done, or use the large scrolling arrows on either side of the **Notes** text box to move back and forth through the list of items already stored for that location.

The buttons running along the lower edge of the window are used to manage the items in the list. They perform the following functions:

- **Record**   Saves any updates made to an existing item.
- **Restore**   Discards any changes made while editing this item.
- **Delete**   Deletes this item. (The item remains on the Suggested Items list, but any additional information you have recorded is deleted from your inventory.)
- **Copy**   Copies this item's details to a new item.
- **New**   Creates a new item.

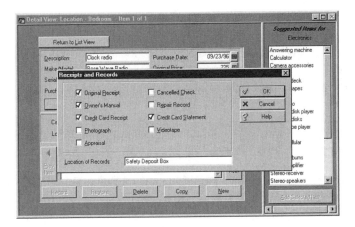

Figure 4.3   Establishing Proof of Ownership is an important part of any insurance claim.

When you finish entering your household items, click **Update** in the iconbar. This will take the total resale value of your assets entered to date and place that value into a read-only Household Quicken asset account. From now on, those items will accurately reflect their value in your Net Worth reports.

499

Editing the Category and Location Lists

The category and location lists are useful not just because of the way they interact with items. Open either list and Quicken Home Inventory can show you at a glance how many items have been used from each category or placed within each location. The list also shows the total replacement cost or resale value of all the items assigned to or used from each category or location, as shown in Figure 4.4.

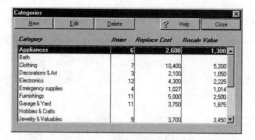

Figure 4.4 The Category Lists shows not only the categories but the value of those items that have been assigned and used.

Click **New** to add a new category or location. To change the name of a category or location (without changing the list of assigned items), click **Edit**. To delete a category, click **Delete**. When you finish, click **OK** to return to the Category or Location list, then **Close** to return to the previous window.

Editing Your Insurance Policies

To open the insurance policy list, select **View, Policy List**, or click the **Policies** button in the iconbar. You will see the Policies window shown in Figure 4.5.

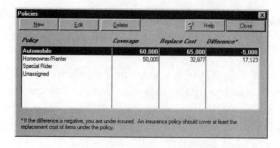

Figure 4.5 Use the Insurance Policy list to check if your assigned items have hit your policies' limits.

This window lists Quicken Home Inventory's default policies. Edit these as needed by selecting the appropriate policy and clicking the **Edit** button. As a minimum, you should open the automotive and household policies and adjust the **Coverage** amount so that it equals the maximum claim possible according to your own policy.

As you continue to add items to the inventory, their total value will show in the policy list. This is a handy way of quickly finding out if you are over- or under-insured.

Making a Claim

After you finish updating your inventory and adjusting the insurance policies, there is one final step to complete before you should consider your inventory truly complete.

If the worst happens and you need to make a claim, you will need as much supporting evidence as you can lay your hands upon. Besides the receipts, warranties, credit-card statements, and other items that will help you to establish your proof of ownership, you should print a detailed report that summarizes all of the information you have entered into the inventory package.

Quicken Home Inventory can print six different reports. These are shown in Table 4.2 and are available under the **Reports** menu on the menu bar.

Table 4.2 Home Inventory Reports

Name	Purpose
Inventory Value Summary	Totals items by category, location, or insurance policy.
Inventory Detail	Shows detailed information on each item, sorted by category, location, or insurance policy.
Insurance Coverage Summary	Displays items sorted by policy including their replacement cost, resale value, purchase date, and purchase price. Includes totals and policy contact information.
Insurance Coverage Detail	Shows detailed information on each item sorted by insurance policy. Includes policy contact information but no totals.

In general, print the Inventory Value Summary report sorted by location. Then generate another copy sorted by category. Finally, create and print Insurance Coverage Detail. This will provide you with information based on the type of goods (handy when you need to break down the claim by electrical, clothing, and so on), by location (especially useful if faced with a localized fire or flood), as well as all of the information entered into each item's detail window. This will all help support your claim.

Store these reports and a backup of the inventory file in a safe location, preferably away from the premises they refer to.

To prepare a claim, follow these steps:

1. Select **View, Claims List** or click the **Claims** button in the iconbar.

2. Click **New** and, once you have optionally read the New Claim Instructions, **OK** to move forward.

3. Type a brief description for the claim, select or type the date for the claim and the date the event prompting the claim occurred. Select the appropriate policy from the Policy Name drop-down list, and then type in a claim number. If you don't have a claim number, contact your insurance company. Figure 4.6 shows a sample claim form.

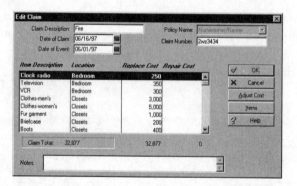

Figure 4.6   The New Claims form will help you to submit and manage your insurance claims.

4. Click **Items** to open the Select Items for Insurance Claim dialog box. Click each item to be added to the claim, and click **OK** when you're done.

5. Click **Adjust Cost** to determine the price basis for that item. The options are replacement cost or repair cost. Obviously, if an item is beyond help, you should base the claim on replacement cost. Otherwise, use the repair cost based on the requirements in your insurance policy. Click **OK** to continue.

6. Enter additional notes and click **OK** to save the claim.

7. Quicken Home Inventory will offer to create the report immediately. Click **Yes** to go ahead or **No** to go back to the main window; you can always create the report later by selecting **Reports, Insurance Claim Detail**.

When your insurance claim has been paid, return to the Claims List by selecting **View, Claims List** and click **Paid**. This opens the Claim Paid dialog box. Type in the date the claim was paid and the amount paid, and click **OK** to return to the Insurance Claims dialog box. Quicken again prompts you to create a claim report. Click **Yes** to create the report, or **No** to manually create the report at a later time. Quicken then returns you to the main Quicken Home Inventory window. Meanwhile, the software returns any items to the inventory that have been marked on the original claim as using a repaired price basis. It will delete any items paid on a replacement basis. It is up to you to purchase the replacements, if wanted, and create a new inventory item.

Using the Inventory for Business

Can you use the Home Inventory for business purposes? Yes, but with some reservations. There is little advantage in using the inventory system over an Inventory Asset account unless you want to store more than the usual level of detail allowed in a Quicken transaction's memo. The Home Inventory links to Quicken through a read-only asset account. That account is only used to represent the total of Home Inventory's stock for Net Worth reports and can't be worked with directly.

In fact, there is no way to send purchase transactions, sales transactions, or automatic updates to the expense and gross income categories. Still, Quicken Home Inventory does work as a basic business inventory database.

The following general steps show how a manager might use the software to manage a used car lot's stock. Of course, you will need to make appropriate changes for your own business:

1. The manager of "Prestige Auto" creates a new Quicken Home Inventory file called **Business**.

2. He replaces every entry in the Location list with vehicle types, for example: Car, Light Utility, and Van.

3. He then deletes every category, replacing them with specific makes and models of automobile.

4. He uses **Edit, Options, General** to change the default Quicken inventory account from Home Inventory to Inventory.

5. He then selects **Edit, Options, Suggested Item List** to convert the automatic resale value calculation to 100% of the buy price.

6. Finally, he creates a record for every existing vehicle. With the change made in the previous step, the resale value will equal the buy price. This is done in case Prestige Auto needs to make its own insurance claim. It has nothing to do with a vehicle's eventual sale price.

7. Once complete, he updates Quicken by selecting **File, Update Quicken**.

8. Any finance received to purchase stock is stored in Quicken through a Finance liability account. Finance transactions are entered directly into the liability account, using a Cost Of Goods Sold expense category to note the total funds borrowed. (Important: This assumes there aren't previously created transactions already storing the wholesale purchase price of each vehicle.)

9. From time to time, he can view the value of his holdings using Quicken's Net Worth report. The value of the business' stock on hand appears in the Inventory asset account.

Every time the car lot purchases a new vehicle, he carries out the following steps:

1. He records the amount paid for each car by cash or check in the appropriate account, assigning the transaction to Cost Of Goods Sold.

2. The component of the sum borrowed is recorded in the Finance liability account. This sum is also assigned to Cost of Goods Sold. Thus, the total sum assigned to Cost of Goods Sold represents the total cost of that vehicle.

3. He uses Quicken Home Inventory to create a record for the car, including the purchase price, serial numbers, and other relevant information. The resale price reflects the actual cost of the vehicle, not the list price.

4. After selecting **File, Update Quicken**, Quicken's inventory account is shown as updated inventory value.

When a car is sold, here's what happens:

1. He records the money received in the checking account and assigns the transaction to Gross Sales.
2. If he owes any amount on that car, it is paid off by writing a check to the finance company. The funds are transferred from the liability account.
3. He then wipes the value of the vehicle from Home Inventory. He does this by reducing the resale value to zero, also editing the record to show the name and address of the purchaser, Social Security Number, the date of purchase, and any other prudent information.

Of course, using Home Inventory to manage a business inventory isn't ideal. With no real flow of transactions between Quicken and Quicken Home Inventory except for that designed to update the total in the Quicken Inventory asset account, this is hardly an integrated solution, no matter how you choose to look at it. However, the Location and Category lists are a great way to quickly sum up the stock, and if you ever need to make an insurance claim, could you ask for an easier solution?

In this lesson, you learned how to use Quicken Deluxe and Quicken Home and Business's Home Inventory add-on to manage your home inventory, insurance claims, and business stock. In the next lesson, you will learn how to use Quicken Deluxe's Financial Address Book.

Managing the Financial Address Book

In this lesson, you will learn how to use the Financial Address Book to maintain your personal and business contact details, print mailing labels, and more. The Financial Address Book is included with Quicken Deluxe and Quicken Home & Business.

Introducing the Financial Address Book

The Quicken Financial Address Book included with Quicken Deluxe and Quicken Home & Business will help you to manage your personal and business contacts.

While it is a separate utility, it conveniently coordinates itself with your existing Quicken data. Therefore, any changes you make in Quicken to your memorized and scheduled transaction lists and online payees also appear in the Financial Address Book.

The Financial Address Book manages this coordination by scanning your current Quicken file for new or changed entries.

If it finds a new entry, it copies the details to a new record within the address book. If it finds a changed entry, it updates its existing record. Under certain conditions, Quicken can also update its own records according to the data held in the Financial Address Book. However, for this to work, you must adhere to the following restrictions:

- When recording that address within Quicken, do not record an address longer than five lines.

- The last line of the address must contain the ZIP Code, postal code, or one of the following: U.S., U.S.A., United States of America, United States, or America.
- Don't use the Financial Address Book to record the address for the first time. Make sure you do it in Quicken.
- You cannot use the Financial Address Book to update the name, organization, primary address, or phone number of an online payee. This must be done from within Quicken.

Starting the Financial Address Book

You can start the Financial Address Book from Quicken or through the Windows Start menu. Quicken does not need to be running for the Financial Address Book to open.

 From within Quicken, select **Lists, Track Important Addresses**. Alternatively, if you have your iconbar turned on, click the **AddrBk** icon.

If you use another program instead of Quicken, you can open the Financial Address Book by selecting from Windows **Start, Programs, Quicken, Financial Address Book**.

Whichever method you use, you will see a window similar to that shown in Figure 5.1. Use this figure as a guide to the Financial Address Book's major functions.

CAUTION

Working with More Than One Quicken File   Each address book is stored alongside the current Quicken file. If you use more than one Quicken file, the addresses and other contact information recorded in one will not be accessible through any other. This means that if you intend to build up a mailing list or other database, make sure you always do so from the same file.

The Financial Address Book always opens the most recent file used, but you can also select another by selecting **File, Open Address Book File**.

Once you start the Financial Address Book, there are several tasks you will probably want to perform. These include:

- Recording new and editing existing contacts.
- Searching for contacts that meet certain criteria.
- Grouping your contacts to make them easier to manage.
- Printing lists of addresses and mailing labels.

Let's look at each.

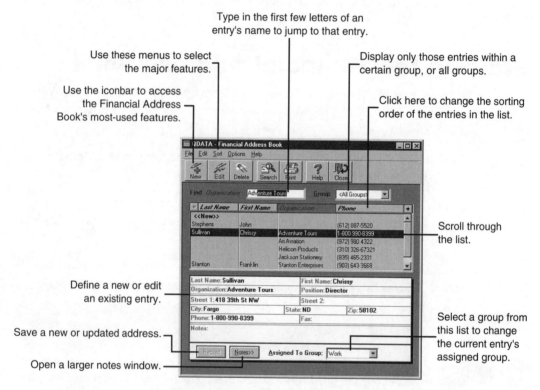

Figure 5.1 This figure shows the Financial Address Book.

Recording and Editing Contacts

When you start the Financial Address Book, it automatically opens on a new entry. To record a new entry, simply fill in the fields in the lower half of the window.

To edit an entry, click any existing field and type over its current contents. If a field belonging to an online payee cannot be changed, the address book will let you know.

When you finish, click **Record**.

To delete an entry, select it from the list and choose the menu **Edit, Delete,** or click the Delete icon on the toolbar at the top of the window.

 TIP **Quicken Imports** When Quicken stores a personal payee in the Address Book, it does so treating the person's first and last names as an organization. It does this because Quicken doesn't provide separate support for organizations and personal names—they're both stored as the payer or payee. Fortunately, the Financial Address Book has a handy feature that will fix just that. Simply select the new entry and choose **Edit, Move Organization into Names**.

Searching for a Contact

To quickly find any contact, use the **Find Organization** field to enter the first few letters of the contact's name. As soon as the Financial Address Book recognizes a unique entry, it fills in the rest.

As **Find Organization** suggests, this feature works only on the organization field. To search by other fields, select **Edit, Search**. Figure 5.2 shows one such search in progress. Any matches are turned into a special temporary group. For example, searching on Sullivan will create a new group in the main Address Book window for all contacts with a first or last name of "Sullivan." This is useful for quickly targeting one contact out of many. Alternatively, a search on TX in the Zip code field would build a new group whose contacts all had a Texas address. After you have performed and viewed or printed the results of the search, you can return to the complete contact list using the **Group** pull-down list.

To construct your own search, follow these steps:

1. Select **Edit, Search** (Ctrl+S) or click the Search icon in the iconbar. Record part or all of the search term in **Find**.

2. (Optional) Select **Find Words That Sound LIKE this Word** to search for words that sound like the current search term, for example, **plow** and

plough. This is handy function if you are unsure of the spelling of the search term.

3. (Optional) Use the **Field to be Searched** list to search for matches in all fields or those you select within the list. (Hold down the Ctrl key to select more than one field.)

4. (Optional) Use **Groups to be Searched** in the same way.

5. Click **OK** to perform the search. You will return to the Financial Address Book where you can view and work with the new group created out of all the items that search managed to match.

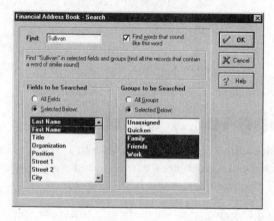

Figure 5.2 The Financial Address Book has a powerful search facility.

Grouping Your Contacts

By grouping your Financial Address Book records, you can more easily manage related sets of contacts. Grouping helps you to filter the list by one type of contact or another. This is handy for such tasks as printing mailing labels for one set of contacts or another. For example, throughout the year, you might regularly print mailing labels for your business contacts, but at Christmas time, you may instead only print mailing labels for everyone on your Christmas card list.

The Financial Address Book has five groups predefined. These are: Quicken, Family, Friends, Word, and Unassigned. The Quicken group is reserved for addresses that have originated through Quicken. The rest can be used as required.

To change the assigned group of any one contact, select that contact from the list and choose the new group from the **Assigned to Group** pull-down list. (You will find it sitting just about the lower edge of the Address Book window.)

To revert back to no group, select the group **Unassigned**. By default, the Financial Address Book displays contacts from all of your groups at once. However, you can change that to display just those from any one group. Just select the group using the **Group:** pull-down menu. Use **Options, Set Up Groups** to add new groups to the list. You can also use the Options menu to change the order in which columns appear and to turn particular fields on or off.

Printing Addresses and Mailing Labels

The Financial Address Book makes it easy to create a list of commonly called clients, carry out that marketing campaign, or just speed up your annual Christmas Card mailing frenzy.

When you print an address or mailing label, you can either print the currently selected entry or the currently displayed list. If you have just performed a search or selected a group, this means you will only print addresses or mailing labels for those contacts. Any not included in the search or group are ignored. You can choose to print your address book data as any of the following:

- An address book showing complete addresses for every entry.
- A telephone list showing the name and phone number for each entry.
- Mailing labels that show names, organizations, and addresses.
- Rolodex cards.
- Envelopes.

To preview your addresses or labels on screen, select **File, Print Preview**. Use the **Print** list to choose the format and **On** to choose the paper stock. You may choose between standard paper or several Avery label formats.

 TIP **Changing Fonts** If you aren't happy with the default Arial font, it's easy to change it to one that is, perhaps, a little more festive, more in keeping with your business, or just right for that special occasion. Click the **Change** button in the Font panel and make you selection of type and size from the list. And here's another quick hint: always remember that the plainer and more readable the font, the better chance it has of zipping through the postal service's automated sorting machines.

When you finish, click **OK**. Use the preview window's buttons to zoom in and out and jump between pages. Click **Close** to return to the Financial Address Book.

If you are satisfied with how it looks and are ready to print on paper, envelopes, or labels, select **File, Print**. Choose the same options and click **OK**.

In this lesson, you learned how to use the Financial Address Book. In the next lesson, you will discover the magic of the Paycheck Wizard.

The Paycheck Wizard

In this lesson, you learn how to use the Paycheck Wizard to record one or more regular paychecks. This will help you to track employer deductions and, at tax time, print useful tax reports and use tax-preparation software.

How the Paycheck Wizard Will Help

The Paycheck Wizard simplifies tracking your paycheck income and deductions by helping you to specify, in advance, for what purpose portions of your gross pay were deducted. From then on, your paychecks and a large amount of your taxation worries are automatically handled.

Recording this information now and throughout the rest of the financial year will help you use your Quicken data to create tax reports or use tax-preparation software, such as the Quicken Tax Planner or Intuit TurboTax.

Even with the assistance of the Paycheck Wizard, it will still take you between five and 15 minutes to work through all of the steps. However, unless the details in your paycheck radically change, you need do this only once.

You will find it easiest to complete this lesson if you have your most recent paycheck handy. If this doesn't list the breakdown of your income and deductions, turn to your most recent Form W-2.

Setting Up the Paycheck Wizard

When ready, follow these steps:

1. Select **Features, Banking, Set Up Paycheck**. You will see the dialog box shown in Figure 6.1.

CAUTION

I Don't See the Paycheck Wizard Dialog Box! If you have set up previous paychecks, you will see the Manage Paychecks dialog box first. Click **New** to move to the Paycheck Wizard.

2. Click **Next** to continue. Assume you should do this after each of the remaining steps.

3. Quicken can track a wide variety of deductions, including your standard tax deductions for Federal Income Tax, State Income Tax, Social Security (FICA), Federal Medicare, and State Disability Insurance. You can record these deductions later in the Paycheck Wizard. However, if you make any other deductions, indicate their nature here. Other deductions include amounts paid into a retirement fund, automated mortgage reduction payments, long-term savings accounts, and more. These may, but not necessarily, reduce your taxation liability as deductions can be made to other than tax-deferred accounts. Each box that you check relates directly to a later window. For instance, by selecting **Deposits to Other Bank Accounts**, you can record transfers to other Quicken accounts in a later dialog box. Don't worry if you are not sure about selecting something; you can always ignore that deduction's dialog box later on.

TERM

Deductions These are the amounts removed from your gross pay by your employer before that pay ends up in your own pocket. The deductions form the difference between your gross and your net pay and should be listed on every paycheck and summarized on the Form W-2.

CAUTION

Deduction Frequency Quicken assumes any specified deductions occur at the same frequency as you receive your paycheck. This is correct if those deductions are made direct from your paycheck, but may not always be most advantageous to you. For example, you may earn a monthly salary with a deduction that goes straight from your paycheck into a mortgage repayment. However, you may be able to cut years off your mortgage by making the payment once every second week rather than once each month. In that case, you should cancel the direct deduction. Instead, set up a biweekly transfer from your savings account, recording it in Quicken as a scheduled transaction.

Figure 6.1 Starting the Paycheck Wizard.

4. Use the next dialog box to name your paycheck and also to indicate how often you are paid. You can set up any number of paychecks—handy if you work two or more jobs—so providing a unique name for each will help you differentiate each register transaction.

5. Record the date shown on your most recent paycheck and the Quicken account into which it was deposited. If this paycheck is paid into more than one account, record the principal deposit account. Then go back to Step 2 and select **Deposits to Other Bank Accounts**. This will let you specify the other transfers later.

TIP **Forward Dating Your First Paycheck** As soon as you finish this wizard, Quicken will record your first paycheck transaction at the date entered here. Therefore, you should enter only the date shown on your last paycheck if you haven't already recorded that paycheck manually. If you have already recorded that paycheck, set the date as the date you will receive your next paycheck. Quicken still records the transaction, but forward dates it so it won't take effect until you receive your next check.

6. In the next dialog box, shown in Figure 6.2, the default category is Salary. If you are recording your spouse's paycheck, you should edit this to read Salary Spouse. Fortunately, you can create categories or subcategories whenever you want. Simply type in the new name, press **Tab,** and click **Yes** to approve creating the new category. However, you must set up Salary-related categories as tax-related. If you want to use the Tax Planner or TurboTax to prepare your return, assign these to the Tax Form Line item Form W-2, salary. The other two fields are used to record the gross pay and the net pay. You should take this information from the last paycheck, assuming it was representative of the ordinary pay.

Figure 6.2 The difference between your gross and net pay is made up of deductions. You will record these in a moment.

7. The next dialog box will help you to record the standard deductions. Again, this information should be shown on your paycheck stub. The categories are already set up, so just run down the list, recording the amounts for each.

8. If there are any other taxes, click **Yes** and record them next. Quicken uses the category Tax:Other, but you may need to be more specific. If you don't have any other taxes, just leave it at **No**. Once you leave this dialog box, you will move into a series of dialog boxes relating to each option selected in Step 2. These are shown here as optional steps because you may or may not need to perform them.

9. (Optional) Enter your 401(k) or other Retirement Plan deductions: Select the account and the amount. If you contribute to more than one plan, you should manually edit the scheduled transaction once you complete this wizard. If you haven't already set up this account, select **Create New Account** from the pull-down menu and set up the account. You can do this in any of the dialog boxes that request you to specify a Quicken account.

10. (Optional) Enter your Employee Stock Purchase Plan (ESPP) deduction: Again, select the account and the amount.

11. (Optional) Enter your Flexible Spending Deduction: If you contribute to a flexible spending account, specify the account and the amount contributed.

12. Are there any other deductions listed on your paycheck? If so, click **Yes**, and then specify the category and the deduction amount. Don't worry if you don't already have the appropriate deductions category set up—just type in the new name and click **Yes** to save the category.

13. (Optional) Enter name and amount of other accounts that you deposit money into: Specify the account and the amount.

14. (Optional) Enter your 401(k) loan deduction: Select the appropriate liability account and specify the amount.

15. The final step in the EasyStep interview asks if you would like Quicken to automatically remind you if it should enter your paycheck on the next pay period. Click **Yes** to create a permanently scheduled transaction. Click **No** if you would rather create a memorized transaction. You can easily call this up and record it each payday.

16. The summary screen shown in Figure 6.3 shows the paycheck transaction as it will be recorded in your register. The top line shows the gross amount with various deductions along the way. The Net Amount obviously displays the net amount. If it all adds up, click **Done** to finish. Otherwise, go back and check over the figures.

17. If you set up Quicken to automatically remind you when your paychecks are due, a final dialog box tells you when the first scheduled transaction will appear.

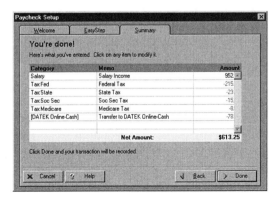

Figure 6.3 If your paycheck gross, net, and deductions balance, you will see the Click Done message shown here.

You can record any number of paychecks through the Paycheck Wizard and edit them anytime thereafter. Once you have recorded the first paycheck, selecting **Features, Banking, Set Up Paycheck** opens the Manage Paychecks dialog box.

From here, you can edit or delete your paychecks. If you receive a paycheck that is more or less than it would normally be or contains a special once-only deduction, don't edit the memorized paycheck. Instead, change it in the register by using the Splits window. This will save you from again editing the scheduled or memorized transaction once your pay reverts to normal.

In this lesson, you learned how to run the Paycheck Wizard. In the next lesson, you will learn about the Emergency Records Organizer.

Using the Emergency Records Organizer

In this lesson, you will learn about Quicken's Emergency Records Organizer.

Start Using the Emergency Records Organizer

The Emergency Records Organizer is a convenient place to store critical information about you and your family's most important personal contact details. It is the ideal place to record your medical history, attorney information, insurance agent information, as well as the location of documents such as your will, your desired funeral arrangements, passports, and more.

There are two times when the Emergency Records Organizer can prove vitally important. The first is if tragedy strikes. If something should happen to you, your family members are obviously going to have enough on their minds without having to immediately search through your papers for the documents necessary to comply with or even discover your wishes.

The second is in the middle of an emergency which could prove tragic if you can't find the information you need very, very quickly. Maintaining a list of allergies, important medical contacts, and other known medical conditions for all the members of your family is obviously an important task.

The Emergency Records Organizer gathers this and other important information around a central point, making it easy to find and use. However, before you begin recording your vital facts and statistics, keep the following points in mind:

- It is okay to store this information in Quicken, but don't forget you should also maintain paper copies, preferably somewhere other than your house, be that with a public trustee, your attorney, or in a safe-deposit box. Print the Detail Report as described in this lesson so that your relatives don't need to work through Quicken in order to discover this information. As always, you should also keep current backups of all your Quicken data, storing the disks well away from the computer. For more information on backing up your data, see Part 1, Lesson 2.

- If you have password-protected your Quicken data with a code known only to you, your family will have some difficulty accessing those records. Again, it's hard to beat the printed report.

- Don't assume that just because you specify your funeral arrangements here, they must be legally adhered to. You must create a legally acceptable will, duly signed and witnessed.

Of course, the organizer can be used for far more than this worst-case scenario. You can use it as a central store perfect for recording everything from your children's school contact details and daily schedules to the phone numbers and addresses of physicians, contact details, and account numbers for your bank and investment accounts, and more. Think of it as a handy database.

Creating a New Information Store

To open the Emergency Records Organizer, select **Features, Planning, Emergency Records Organizer**. You will see the screen shown in Figure 7.1.

To start working with your database, click the tab **Create/Update Records**. There's no need to create a new file as Quicken automatically sets up the information store, recording it with the rest of your financial data.

The screen consists of three window panes:

1. **Select an area**   Choose a broad category of information you want to store. You cannot add to this list, but it is made up of a wide variety of categories.

2. **Select a topic**   This list changes according to the category selected in the first area. If you have recorded any information against a topic, a check mark appears to its left.

3. **Enter**   Record the information. Each field is fully self-explanatory. Once you complete a record, click Save to save those details, Delete to delete the current record, or Cancel to discard your changes. You do not need to click Save because Quicken automatically saves any changes.

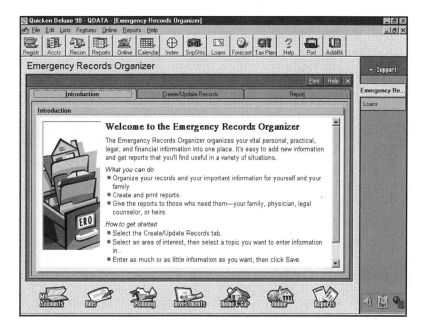

Figure 7.1 The Emergency Records Organizer features a simple tab-based interface.

Each topic can contain multiple records. Use the small down-arrow to the right of the first field in area 3 to move between the records stored under that topic, as shown in Figure 7.2.

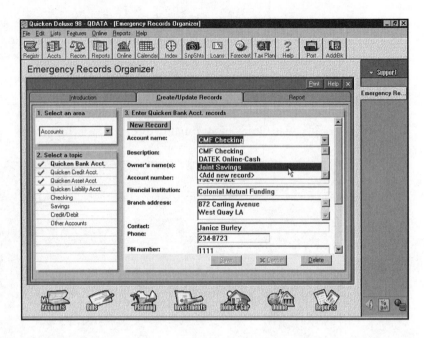

Figure 7.2   Browse through your records by using the pull-down list attached to the first field in every record.

Printing Emergency Reports

Once you finish entering the records, it's time to consider printing a report. As mentioned at the start of this lesson, you should try to keep this report in a safe place. If your house has a fireproof safe or room, that's a fairly good place. Otherwise, keep it with your attorney or place it in a safe-deposit box. Obviously, the necessity of this will depend on the type of records you have entered, but if it is anything your family or other loved ones may one day require, consider its storage very carefully, and don't forget to tell them where these records are stored.

Printing emergency record reports is easy. Simply click the final tab, **Report**.

Select the report type at the top of the window. Click **Display Blank Topics** to include those for which you have not yet recorded any information. The report will appear in the lower window. Preview it on screen as shown in Figure 7.3 and then click **Print** to produce the hard copy.

That's it! Use the Emergency Records Organizer diligently and you will make everyone's life easier in a crisis, but also keep in mind that it can help you day-to-day with your most important phone numbers and contact addresses.

As always, you should always obtain professional advice when planning your estate, constructing a will, or planning for the future of your loved ones.

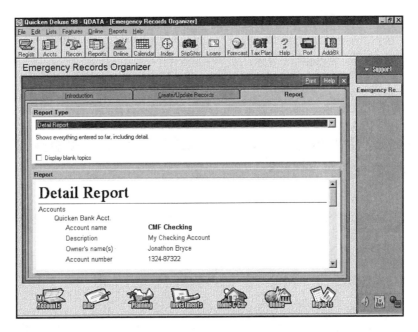

Figure 7.3 Preview your emergency records to make sure you haven't left out any vital information.

In this lesson, you learned how to use the Emergency Records Organizer. In the next lesson, you will learn how to set up loans.

Managing Loans

8

In this lesson, you learn how to use Quicken's loan management features. This will help you to track existing loans and also to plan for the future.

Use Quicken to Track Borrowed and Loaned Funds

Quicken has an extensive armory of features designed to help you plan, track, and complete loans. What's more, Quicken can keep track of money you have borrowed as well as money you have loaned someone else.

Creating a New Loan

All of your loan management takes place in Quicken when you select **Features, Bills, Loans**. The first time you open this menu, you will see the window shown in Figure 8.1.

 TIP **Can You Afford That Loan?** Perhaps the easiest way to tell is to first stop by the Loan calculator. Select **Features, Planning, Financial Planners, Loan**. You can read about this and the other financial planners in Part 5, Lesson 3.

To create a new loan, follow these steps:

1. Click **New** at the top of the window. This will lead you into an EasyStep Interview.

2. Quicken asks: **Are you borrowing or lending these funds?** Provide your answer and click **Next**.

3. Quicken tracks loans in liability accounts and moneys you are owed in asset accounts. Each loan needs to be tracked in a separate account. To create a new one, type in an appropriate name in the **New Account** field. Otherwise, select an **Existing Account** using the pull-down list. Click **Next**.

4. If you have already made payments, click **Yes**. You do not need to have recorded these payments in Quicken; the software can calculate the remaining balance for you. Otherwise, click **No**. Click **Next**.

5. Enter the initial loan information including the date it was opened and the original balance. If you have already made payments, do not record the current balance. Click **Next**.

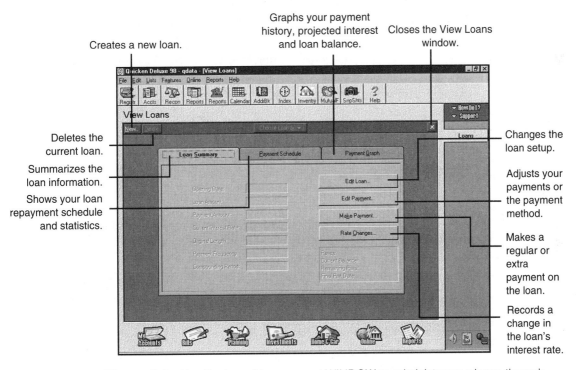

Figure 8.1 Use the Loan Management WINDOW to administer your loans through Quicken.

6. A balloon payment is a final payment that is larger than the regular payments. Often it can equal as much as 40 percent of the loan. If your loan has a balloon, enter it here. Click **Next**.

7. Record the original length of the loan in years, months, weeks, or payments. Click **Next**.

8. Specify the payment period in either fixed calendar terms (monthly, biweekly and so on), or as a certain number of payments per year. Click **Next**.

9. The compounding period is important for calculating the interest accrued through the course of the loan. For large sums across long periods, the compounding period can have an enormous impact. You must specify the correct compounding period for Quicken's own calculations to be accurate. Click **Next**.

10. The date of the first payment is really the date the next payment is due. If you have already made payments, do not use this to indicate the first payment you made. Rather, it is the date of the next payment you need to make. Click **Next**.

11. Do you know the amount of the first payment? If you do, you can record the total interest, principal, and any extra payments in the next window. If not, click **No** and Quicken will calculate the repayments for you using the information you have recorded so far. Click **Next**.

12. Type in the interest rate. If this is an adjustable or variable rate loan, use the most recent rate known. You can record changes in the interest rate later. Click **Next**.

13. By now you should have reached the Summary screens. Check the entries in each screen and adjust them as necessary. If you didn't specify the payment amounts earlier, Quicken will calculate it for you as soon as you try to move past the final summary screen. The calculated payment is shown in the field **Payment Amount (P+I):**.

Making Payments

As soon as you have completed the EasyStep Interview, you need to set up your regular or scheduled payments. Quicken takes you there automatically, but you can open the Set Up Loan Payment window at any time by clicking the **Edit Payment** button in the View Loans window.

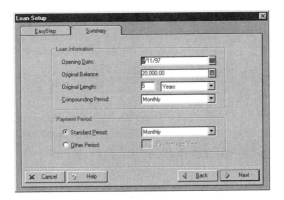

Figure 8.2 Use the Summary screens to check the loan information

The window is shown in Figure 8.3. As you can see, you can adjust the payments and interest rate. More importantly, you can also edit the payment to include other amounts in each payment unrelated to the principal and interest. These might include some form of state tax, a borrowing fee, or any amount you wish to add to pay out the loan more quickly. You can also make an additional payment at any time. For instructions, see "Managing Your Loan" next.

Click **Edit** and record these payments using the Splits window provided. You may also need to assign them to an appropriate expense category if you are making the payments, or an income category if you are receiving those extra payments.

In the transaction area, first choose the type of payment. If you will hand-write the checks, select **Payment**. For Quicken to add the checks to your print list, select **Print Check**. Use the **Payment Method** dialog box to choose between Scheduled, Memorized, Repeating Online Payments or CheckFree Fixed Payments. You see Repeating Online Payments if you have set up your Online Center. To learn more about this, turn to Part 3. You see CheckFree Fixed Payment if you have not yet defined any form of online payment. This option is grayed out until you either set up your CheckFree account or, preferably, set up your checking account with online capabilities.

A scheduled payment occurs automatically (with or without prompting, as you specify in the Payment Method dialog box). A memorized transaction is stored in your memorized transaction list, but you will be responsible for looking after the payment when it falls due. Repeating Online Payments are similar to scheduled payments but occur electronically. After you have created it here, you will find it in your Repeating Online tab in the Scheduled Transactions list.

Next, record the Payee, a memo to be written into your register on each payment (and possibly also sent to the Online Payee), the next payment due date, and an interest category. If you are making the payments, the interest category is an expense item such as Interest Exp. However, if you are receiving these payments, it is an income item such as Interest Inc.

Finally, if you will be printing your checks and dropping them into a window envelope. click **Address**. Use the message line in the address box to specify your loan account number. If you send in your payments with slips from a payments book, you can ignore this line.

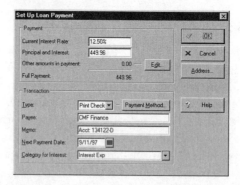

Figure 8.3   Use this dialog box to set up the payments.

Managing Your Loan

Now you're almost there. The loan is set up and Quicken understands its parameters and how you intend to satisfy the payments—or receive them, if you're the one doing the lending.

Use the **Payment Schedule** (see Figure 8.4) and **Payment Graph** tabs to view more information about your loan. If you will be making extra payments, click the **Make Payment** button, click **Extra,** and record the amount. You can use this to record lump sum payments. As Quicken maintains your loan in a regular Quicken account, it can easily follow the balance and curtail your payment schedule should you finalize the loan early. Select **File, Print Loan** to produce a hard copy of the schedule.

TIP **Running Totals** Want to know how much interest you will end up paying through the course of your loan? Click the **Payment Schedule** tab and select **Show Running Totals**. Scroll to the end of the schedule and read off the final figure in the Interest column. Add this to the amount shown for the Principal to calculate the total amount repaid.

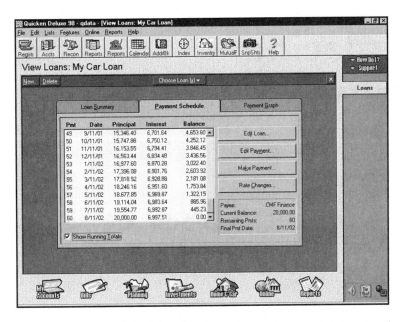

Figure 8.4 The Payment Schedule will help you to see how much interest and principal is still owed.

When you have completed the loan, Quicken will automatically tidy it up. However, if you cancel the loan, just select it using **Choose Loan (x)** and click **Delete**. All previous payments are retained but future payments deleted.

That's it! Loan management in a nutshell. When combined with Quicken's budgeting, forecasting, savings goals, and tax planning features, it represents a superb final part to Quicken's comprehensive financial management tools.

In this lesson, you learned how to create and manage loans. In the final lesson, you will learn how to use Quicken's Search and Replace tool to quickly recategorize, rename, or otherwise adjust transactions already recorded.

Searching and Replacing Transactions

In this final lesson, you learn how to use Quicken's Find and Replace tool.

When to Find, Replace, Or Recategorize

Quicken has a range of great searching facilities. These will help you to not only find transactions linked by some common feature, but also to quickly replace that information.

Open up any register and take a look under **Edit, Find & Replace**.

You will see the following entries:

- **Find**   This is Quicken's quickest Search tool. It will quickly take you to the nearest match in the current register. You can learn about it under the heading "Searching for Transactions" next.

- **Find/Replace**   Generates a list of transactions that match a certain criteria. You can also use it to replace data contained in those transactions with any other that you specify. You can learn about this tool under the heading "Finding and Replacing."

- **Recategorize**   Helps you to replace the categories in your transactions with another category. You can learn about this tool in Part 1.

Searching for Transactions

The Find tool is a powerful method for searching through any register for data based on several conditions. If you are familiar with spreadsheets or databases, you will recognize this tool as a true database query system. Admittedly, it doesn't have as many options as your typical SQL engine, but it is powerful nonetheless.

1. Open the register you want to search. Then select **Edit, Find & Replace, Find**. Figure 9.1 shows the Find dialog box.

Figure 9.1 The Find tool provides quick access to searches on any field for any data.

2. Define your search using each of the following fields:

- **Find:** Type in part or all of a name, account, amount, memo, or whatever. To access the Calculator or Calendar icons, first select a date or amount field using **Search**.

- **Search:** Select the field you need to search or **All Fields** to search every field at once.

- **Match if:** This pull-down list defines how the search is conducted. For example, does the field **Contain** the **Find** data, or does it **Start With** or **End With** that data? If you are searching on a date or amount, you might choose **Equals**, **Greater or Equal**, **Less or Equal**, or **Less**.

TIP **A Real World Example** Pat receives a call from a creditor saying that his account is overdue. Pat is sure he has paid this bill so, while the creditor is on the telephone, he does a quick search. The account totaled $789. He types this into **Find:** as 789, selects **Amount** under **Search:** and chooses **Equals** under **Match if:**. He clicks **Find** and Quicken immediately targets the transaction.

3. To find one instance of that criteria, click **Find**. Click again to find another. Quicken usually searches backward because you are placed, by default, at the end of the register. To search forward, click **Search Backwards** to remove the check mark.

4. To find all instances of that criteria, click **Find All**. Quicken opens the Quicken Find window shown in Figure 9.2. Double-click any transaction to jump to its entry in the register. Click the **Find** tab in the QuickTabs list when you finish to inspect another.

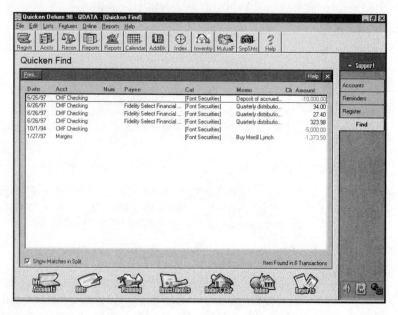

Figure 9.2 The Find All summary shows all transactions matching the search criteria.

Finding and Replacing

Finding and Replacing is a very handy tool. For example, if you have recorded a series of checks to the wrong payee, you can easily fix the error. Just find every transaction belonging to the old payee, mark those you want to fix, and replace them with the new payee. Or perhaps you entered a series of transactions using an incorrect date. Just target those transactions by date, and you can instantly update them with the correct information.

TIP

Moving Transactions Between Accounts The Find and Replace tool cannot move transactions between accounts. To do that, you must select each transaction and select **Edit, Transaction, Move**. Select the new account from the list provided.

CAUTION

Global Searching Quicken cannot search across all registers at once. The Find and Find and Replace tools will only work with the current register. To repeat that function with your other accounts, you must go to each and duplicate the search.

Remember that you can search on one criteria and replace with another. For example, you can search on date, but rather than correcting the date, you can recategorize each of those transactions or perhaps mark them down as payable to some other payee. Unlike the Search and Replace capability of many word processors, the information you use to perform the search is not replaced once the search is complete. The searching is, in fact, a totally separate process to the replacing, and it is up to you whether you replace that search data or instead replace some other aspect of the found transactions.

Follow these steps to sophisticated searches and effortless replacing:

1. Open the register you want to search. Then select the Find and Replace tool using **Edit, Find & Replace, Find/Replace**. Figure 9.3 shows a find and replace in action.

2. Use the fields in the following way:
   - **Find:** Type in part or all of the search text. To access the Calculator or Calendar icons, first select a date or amount field using **Search:**.
   - **Search:** Select the field you need to search, or **All Fields** to search every field at once.
   - **Match if:** Choose the match criteria as described for the Find tool.
   - **Replace:** Which field do you want to replace? This does not need to be the search field. For example, you may have searched on Date but can choose to replace on Category.
   - **With:** What do you want to record in the replacement field? If you have selected a date or amount under **Replace:**, you will have access to the Calendar and Calculator icons.

3. (Optional) Select **Show Matches in Split** to also search the split fields of your transactions. This is most useful if you need to search by category.

533

4. Click **Find All** to find all transactions matching the search criteria. Quicken will let you know if it can't find any matching transactions. However, if it does, you will see them flow into the list box filling the lower part of the Find and Replace dialog box.

5. Click in the left-hand column of each transaction you are replacing. The check marks indicate they will be replaced. Otherwise, click **Mark All** to mark every transaction or **Clear All** to remove those marks.

6. When you finish, click **Replace** to perform the replacement on every marked transaction. Quicken displays one final dialog box asking you to confirm the procedure. Click **OK** to go ahead or **Cancel** to return to Find and Replace.

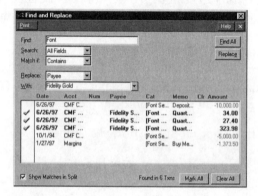

Figure 9.3 This is the quick way to search for and replace Quicken data.

The Find and Replace tool is an excellent addition to Quicken's arsenal, but use it with caution. It is all too easy to wipe out hours of good work with one swipe of that **OK** button. And remember, it only applies to one register at a time.

In this lesson, you learned how to find and replace your existing data. Now you're on your own. Enjoy, keep learning, and tell your friends. Quicken is a fantastic tool—one that should bring you fun, prosperity, and lots and lots of financial peace of mind.

Installing Quicken 98

In this lesson, you learn how to install and set up Quicken 98 for Windows.

Why Should I Install?

When you buy a new application such as Quicken, you usually purchase the software on a CD-ROM or series of disks. Before you can use that application, its files must be copied to your hard disk. A Setup or Install program usually is supplied to perform this task.

Installing from the Internet If you purchased and downloaded your copy of Quicken or any other software from the Intuit Software site on the Internet, you still need to install that software, even though it has already been copied to your hard disk. Use Windows Explorer to locate the Setup program and follow the instructions provided as follows starting at Step 4.

Installing Quicken 98

To install Quicken 98 on your PC, follow these steps:

1. Close all open applications.
2. If you are installing from CD-ROM, insert the Quicken 98 CD in your CD-ROM drive. The Quicken Install program should automatically start and ask you if you would like to install the program on your hard drive.

CAUTION

Automatic Install Doesn't!   If the Quicken Install program doesn't start on its own, your computer may not be set up for Autorun CDs. Just open your **My Computer** icon and double-click the CD drive's icon. Locate and double-click the **Install** icon.

3. If you are installing from disk, insert the first Quicken 98 disk into your floppy drive. Open the **My Computer** window and double-click the floppy drive's icon. Locate and double-click the **Setup** icon.

4. Click **Yes** to continue.

5. At the Welcome dialog box, click **Next**.

6. In the Type of Installation dialog box (see Figure A.1), choose between Express or Custom installation. **Express** Installation installs Quicken 98 and various add-on features. However, the precise set depends on whether you purchase the Deluxe or Standard versions. **Express** is the recommended option. Use **Custom** installation if you would like to choose which software is installed and where it should be placed.

7. If you are a Canadian user, make sure you also select **Canadian Version**.

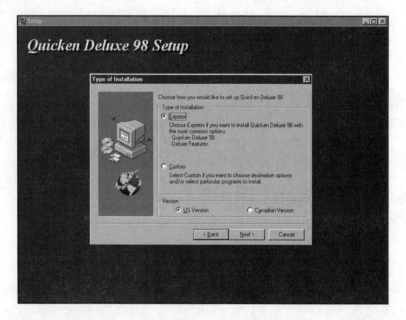

Figure A.1   If you are new to PCs, Windows, or Quicken, it is recommended you leave Express as the selected installation option.

TIP **Internet Explorer 3.0 and Your Home Page** If you already use
Microsoft Internet Explorer 3.0, installing the version bundled with Quicken 98
points your home page to the Intuit site on the Web. If you already use Internet
Explorer 3.0 or later, you do not need to reinstall this browser unless you want
to update your installation to version 3.02. The Web browser is installed by
default in the Express installation so you must chose a Custom installation if you
would like to bypass the installation. Alternatively, you can always install
Internet Explorer and reset your home page by selecting the Explorer menu
View, Options, Navigation. Type your home page address into the Address
field and click **OK**.

8. If you chose an Express installation, click **Next** to move to the Check Settings
dialog box shown and review your choices. If all are present and correct,
click **Next** to install Quicken 98. Otherwise, click **Back** to review your
choices.

If you chose a Custom installation, verify the folder into which Quicken will
be installed, or change it by clicking **Browse,** and click **Next**. If that folder
doesn't exist, you also need to click **Yes** to confirm Setup should create the
folder, then click **Next**. Use the Select Installation Components dialog box to
check those parts of the program that should be installed. Finally, confirm or
rename the Program Folder and click **Next** (see Figure A.2) .

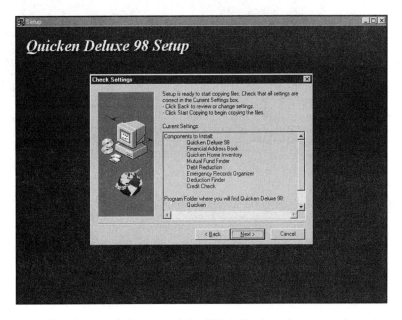

Figure A.2 Check your choices carefully. This is the last chance you have to make
any changes to the installation.

9. Click **Start Copying** for Quicken Setup to install the files needed to run the software. As soon as it has finished, it will scan your hard drive for a compatible World Wide Web browser such as Microsoft Internet Explorer or Netscape Navigator. If you are connected to the Internet, you will need one of these to access Quicken's many Web-based online features. You may need to click OK to launch Internet Explorer setup. If so, read the End-User License Agreement and click **Yes** if you agree. After Internet Explorer has been installed, click **No** at the request to restart your computer; you'll have the opportunity to do this in a moment.

10. When the installation has finished, you will see the Setup Complete dialog box shown in Figure A.3. If you have other applications open, click **No, I will restart my computer later** to exit the Quicken Setup program. Save any files open in those applications. (While the restart procedure should prompt you to do this before discarding your work, it's best to play it safe.) Then restart your computer from the **Start** button, selecting **Shutdown** from the dialog box. If you don't have any other applications open, click **Yes, I want to restart my computer now.** Click **Finish** for Quicken to finalize its settings and restart your PC.

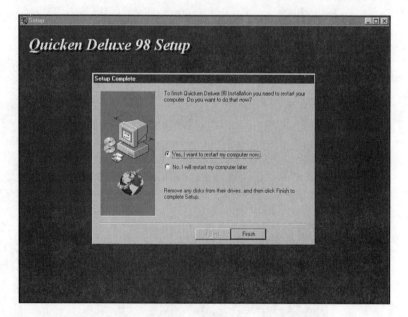

Figure A.3   Bravo! You've just completed your Quicken installation.

TIP **Upgrading Quicken** Quicken 98 for Windows is compatible with almost all previous versions of Quicken for Windows, DOS, and Macinosh. To upgrade your data, simply open the file using the latest version. Quicken automatically converts the file to the latest format.

In this lesson, you learned how to install Quicken and, optionally, a Web browser onto your computer. Now it's time to begin using it! Turn back to Part 1...and good luck!

Index

MACMILLAN COMPUTER PUBLISHING USA

A VIACOM COMPANY

Technical ---- **Support:**

If you need assistance with the information in this book or with a CD/Disk
accompanying the book, please access the Knowledge Base on our Web
site at **http://www.superlibrary.com/general/support**. Our most
Frequently Asked Questions are answered there. If you do not find the
answer to your questions on our Web site, you may contact Macmillan
Technical Support **(317) 581-3833** or e-mail us at **support@mcp.com**.